CRITICAL THINKING
FOR COLLEGE STUDENTS

CRITICAL THINKING FOR COLLEGE STUDENTS

JON STRATTON

An Ardsley House Book

ROWMAN & LITTLEFIELD PUBLISHERS, INC.
Lanham • Boulder • New York • Oxford

ROWMAN & LITTLEFIELD PUBLISHERS, INC.

Published in the United States of America
by Rowman & Littlefield Publishers, Inc.
4720 Boston Way, Lanham, Maryland 20706

12 Hid's Copse Road
Cumnor Hill, Oxford OX2 9JJ, England

British Library Cataloguing in Publication Information Available

Library of Congress Cataloging-in-Publication Data

Stratton, Jon.
    Critical thinking for college students / Jon Stratton.
      p.   cm.
    Includes bibliographical references (p.) and index.
    ISBN 0–8476-9602–2 (paper : alk. paper). — ISBN 0–8476-9603–0
(manual : alk. paper)
    1. Critical thinking—Study and teaching (Higher) I. Title.
LB2395.35.S77 2000
160—dc21   99-37194
                                                CIP

Printed in the United States of America

♾™The paper used in this publication meets the minimum requirements of
American National Standard for Information Sciences—Permanence of Paper for
Printed Library Materials, ANSI/NISO Z39.48–1992.

CONTENTS

VERBAL AND LOGICAL THINKING

VERBAL, LOGICAL, AND INTUITIVE THINKING

INTRODUCTION

The purpose of this book is to provide an environment for the understanding and practice of critical thinking: the type of thinking that reviews, evaluates, and revises thought in order to improve it. That environment includes a description of the primary elements of critical thinking: proper definition, summarizing, paraphrasing, reconstruction, empathy, analysis of arguments, evaluation of reasoning, evaluation of evidence, brainstorming, imagination, and problem solving. In addition to discussing these primary elements, the book discusses the reasons why each of these elements is believed to be important to critical thinking, justifying its claims by referring to evidence from cognitive psychology, semantics, linguistics, and logic. It also clarifies the two major studies of critical thinking, that of Benjamin S. Bloom (1956) and the more recent *Delphi Report* (1990), a study on critical thinking conducted under the auspices of the American Philosophical Association. It would be insulting to the college student to merely present the primary standards of critical thinking as if there were no reasons, theoretical concerns, or criticisms behind them. To do so would be to ask the student to accept the standards of critical thinking in a noncritical, nonthoughtful way.

It is important to recognize that critical thinking is not a completed body of knowledge. Thinking is much too human a subject to ever be regarded as completely described by mere "data." We know something about thinking, of course, and about critical thinking, but critical thinking is not simply a list of skills. Rather, it is a holistic human activity that involves attitudes and emotions as well as linguistic and logical proficiency.

This book assumes that its readers already know how to think. It is written for college students, people who have already made some important decisions in life, and who realize, to some extent, the value of thought. Just how deeply the appreciation for thought goes, however, is at issue. Our society does not provide much overt praise for thinking, and in fact seems to encourage all of us—students, professors, and everyone else—to passively accept whatever ideas and beliefs currently appeal to us, for whatever reason. Nevertheless, the

conversation concerning the difference between adequate and inadequate thinking that has been going on for centuries is still taking place. College students are
capable of joining in, benefiting from it, and contributing to it.

Several individuals have contributed a great deal to the conversation that
is in process. While the term "critical thinking" is quite new, philosophers have
been discussing the topic for hundreds of years. In 350 B.C.E., Aristotle wrote in
the first few lines of his *Metaphysics* that all human beings have a deep need to
know and to understand the world. We have this need not only because it is useful to us to know things but also because we love to know simply for the sake
of knowing. Ever since Aristotle pointed this out, philosophers have distinguished two types of thinking. Thinking that is involved with exploring timeless questions, with meditating on the eternal truths (assuming there are such
truths), and meeting our innermost need for thought is often referred to as
"theoretical," "abstract," or "philosophical" thinking. On the other hand, thinking that is useful, which seeks to effect a practical result in the world either
presently or at some future date, is usually called "practical," "concrete," or
more recently, "critical" thinking. Aristotle had a high opinion of critical thinking; in his *Ethics* he made it quite clear that happiness, goodness, and success in
life are due to practical, critical thinking.

Much of the foundation for our current conversation about critical thinking today goes back to Aristotle. Aristotle tells us how important it is to understand that critical thinking always begins with a healthy body. A body that has
difficulty perceiving the world for what it really is will not provide sound material to the mind. He also points out that we need to be careful with our use of
language. Aristotle points out that critical thinking is always done in words, and
that a careless use of words leads to poor thinking. He tells us that we cannot
hope to think well unless we first gain a respect for language, especially for the
clarity language can provide to thought. Our happiness, success, and health cannot be ensured unless we ingrain in ourselves the habit of thinking clearly.

Although a great deal of time has passed since Aristotle first began the
conversation about critical thinking, even today there is the same conviction on
the part of critical thinking theorists about the necessity of clear perceptions and
careful use of language in our lives. How will we ever achieve personal and fa-
milial happiness, success in our careers and personal growth, harmony in our
communities, and peace in the world if we are not thinking about our problems
in a practical way? Truly, our world can become a better place if we can resolve
specific problems in a clear and reasonable way.

Some will disagree. There have always been individuals who claim that our
lives are not in our control, who believe that it is fate, and not ourselves, which
has the final say in our lives. These people—and there have been philosophers,
religious leaders, poets, and artists among them—do not believe that we ever
really solve problems by thinking critically. They see human life as incapable of
improving itself. This view, known as "fatalism," is contrary to the assumption
inherent in the ongoing discussion about critical thinking. Fatalism maintains
that the cures for diseases, reclamation of the environment, and achievement
of world peace are not in our hands. Fatalism claims that personal happiness,

success in the world, and the possibility of a better life are merely a matter of chance. There is nothing we can do about our sorry situation.

Even in the face of fatalism, the conversation that seeks to nurture critical thinking continues enthusiastically. After all, to what do we owe the good qualities of our lives, if not to critical thinking? Our advances in science, medicine, education, and international understanding are the result of practical, careful thought about our problems. Our present social ills, institutional breakdowns, as well as our personal difficulties are, for the most part, due to a *lack* of critical thinking.

The value of critical thinking is clear. Understanding and acquiring it can only benefit us.

The purpose of this book is to provide the opportunity for the understanding and acquisition of critical thinking.

Chapter One discusses the relationship of cognition to perception and sensation. Thinking is a brain activity that is essentially related to language.

Chapter Two examines the descriptions of critical thinking presented by Bloom's *Taxonomy* and the *Delphi Report*. The studies provide the basis of the Seven Standards of Critical Thinking, which are continuously referred to throughout the text. Chapter Three examines in detail the flexibility, richness of expression, and adaptability of language, as well as the first four standards derived from Bloom's *Taxonomy* and the *Delphi Report*. Language is a conventional system that can either enrich or impoverish thinking, depending upon the way it is used. The four ability standards—clarity, accuracy, specificity, and significance—when properly applied, strengthen verbal thinking, especially definitions, summaries, and paraphrases. Chapter Four continues the discussion of standards, focusing on the three attitudinal principles—sincerity in seeking truth, respect for the thoughts of others, and commitment to consensus. Empathy is introduced as essential for effective implementation of these standards because effective communication depends upon empathetic linguistic interaction.

Chapter Five introduces logical thinking. A thorough discussion of the nature of implication is followed by an introduction to the elements of arguments: premises, hidden premises, and conclusions. A method of organizing arguments is introduced, and the distinction between formal and practical (informal) logic is explained. Chapter Six examines practical logic's evaluation of reasoning. Vagueness and ambiguity are explained, along with the fallacies of inappropriate authority, appeal to force, attacking the person, and oversimplification. Chapter Seven continues the discussion of fallacies with the fallacy of shifting the burden of proof, the straw man fallacy, and the fallacies of mindless conformity, irrelevant emotion, and overgeneralization. The chapter concludes with an Eight Step Method of argument evaluation, which is modeled by an appropriate application to an argument.

Chapter Eight discusses evidence by explaining that there are four general types of evidence—experimental, observational, anecdotal, and observational. Each type of evidence has varying degrees of emotional, theoretical, and factual components. For example, experimental evidence has a very low emotional component, while anecdotal evidence has a very high emotional component. Methods for determining the strength and weakness of evidence for a given claim are examined. Chapter Nine introduces "The Format," an organized summary that includes every standard of evaluation discussed in the text. The Format is modeled with a step-by-step, detailed evaluation application to a five hundred-word opinion piece. Each step is thoroughly explained and references to previous chapters are provided so that students have the opportunity to review material. A "Mini-Format," a less-detailed version, is also provided. Chapter Ten explains that critical thinking is not limited to written pieces. Problem solving, which includes oral discussion and brainstorming as well as written work, is explained in citing the importance of intuition and imagination for effective problem solving. The chapter concludes with "An Interview with a Critical Thinker," which is a discussion of the personal values that critical thinking implies.

An appendix is included that contains four opinion pieces for student analysis.

Each chapter contains dozens of exercises strategically placed to capitalize on student comprehension of the material. They are meant to encourage large and small group discussion, written work in and out of the classroom, and thoughtful reflection. Examples throughout the text as well as those used in the exercises are timely, relevant, and interesting to today's college students.

Critical thinking—the review, evaluation, and revision of thinking—improves thinking. However, critical thinking is something we *do*, and not something we merely study and forget. The value of this text consists only in how well it nurtures the *actual* critical thinking of those who use it.

CHAPTER ONE

THINKING, THE BODY, THE BRAIN, AND LANGUAGE

VERBAL THINKING

Thinking is the activity of understanding, processing, and communicating information for the purposes of solving problems, understanding experiences, and producing ideas. Thinking is one of the most common activities performed by human beings. When we are joking, laughing, and chatting with friends, we understand, we process, and we communicate in words. When we are putting together a term paper, composing a poem, or writing a letter, we are understanding, processing, and communicating verbally. The type of thinking involved in talking with others, or in writing academic assignments, poetry, or letters makes use of language. This type of thinking is called verbal thinking. Much of the thinking done in formal education is verbal. In fact, verbal thinking is the predominant sort of thinking in our culture.

AFTER STUDYING CHAPTER 1

You should be able to explain each of the seven types of thinking, and provide a detailed description of critical thinking as the review, evaluation, and revision of thinking. You should be able to discuss and write an essay on how sensation, perception, and the three different parts of the brain work together to provide a meaningful world for human beings. Finally, you should recognize that the way we use language has great influence on how and what we think.

Western culture is a culture of words.[1] From the early Greeks to the present, Western culture has placed immense value on the understanding, processing, and communicating of words. There are some very good reasons for this attention to words. The early Greeks were seafaring traders who had to barter with others to earn their living. This life of trading was one in which those who were able to speak and write well were more financially successful than those who had not learned to understand, process, and communicate as clearly and accurately with words. The economic prosperity of the early Greeks depended upon their ability to trade successfully with other people. The Greek traders had to be clear, specific, and accurate in explaining the value of their goods. They had to listen well to other traders' descriptions of their own goods. If the Greeks were to "make good deals" with the other traders, they had to keep an open mind with regard to what they were being told.

Obviously, a trader who could listen well, who could process verbal information clearly and accurately, and who could communicate significant, specific details during negotiations would be more successful than one who could not. Thus, verbal thinking came to be prized highly by the ancient Greek business community. However, respect for language went far beyond this group. An individual's ability to use words well became the chief mark of respect in ancient Greek society. Young men paid large amounts of tuition to teachers (called Sophists) in order to learn how to use words effectively in social life and in politics. The Greeks regarded verbal thinking so highly that they included drama and poetry in their Olympic games. Prizes for the best plays, best poems, and most well constructed essays were as valued as those for athletic championships. Greek philosophers even claimed that because women and children could not use verbal thinking as well as men, men were more "loved by the gods" than were women and children! (Of course, the Greek men denied women the right to take part in their philosophical conversations, so they didn't have to listen to what the women had to say about this biased belief!)

Our Western culture has its origin in the culture of the ancient Greeks. For us, as for the ancient Greeks, verbal thinking is extremely important. Our business world relies on verbal thinking for financial success, our legal establishment is completely absorbed in verbal thinking, our educational institutions center their attention upon verbal thinking, and our writers, poets, and television talk show hosts use verbal thinking to explore and communicate ideas.

Verbal thinking relies upon the successful understanding, processing, and communication of words in an ordinary, day-to-day "natural language," the term which describes the languages that are used by people around the world in their daily lives for ordinary, common purposes. Every natural language,

---

1. "Western culture" is a sociological, not a geographical term; it refers to a way of living, not to a particular place. Western culture, which is characterized by logical, verbal, mathematical, and scientific thinking, can be found in Asia and Africa as well as in Europe, and in the United States. At the same time there are many people living in these places who do not share Western culture. It is also important to realize that verbal thinking is important for—even central to—all cultures, not merely Western culture.

whether Spanish, Vietnamese, or English, has a unique "grammar" and a "syntax." The grammar of a natural language consists of the customs governing the various functions, meanings, and pronunciations of words used by speakers of the particular language. The syntax of a natural language refers to the customary patterns that speakers follow when putting words in proper order to create meaningful sentences and paragraphs. Learning a natural language consists of learning its grammar and its syntax. Verbal thinking is the understanding, processing, and communication of information that follows the grammatical and syntactical customs of a particular natural language. Verbal thinking is highly flexible, rich in meeting any human need, and amazing in its adaptability for different uses. Verbal thinking can be specific or general, detailed or broad, sophisticated or vulgar. It is used with equal success in the living room, the boardroom, or the locker room. It is used successfully for description, expression, understanding, and communication of the innumerable purposes that crop up in our daily lives, for the infinite variety of social and legal activities we have in our communities around the world, and for expressing and inspiring creative, thoughtful, and beautiful works of literature. Western culture has developed a deep respect as well as a cultural dependency on verbal thinking. Without it, we would be different creatures than we are. From the ancient Greek businessman to the contemporary student struggling to express her ideas in a college term paper, we all owe our variety of successes in life to our ability to think verbally. However, we are mistaken if we equate verbal thinking with thinking itself. The fact that verbal thinking is extremely important to us and that it is predominate in our culture does not mean that verbal thinking is the *only* sort of thinking.

SCIENTIFIC THINKING, MATHEMATICAL THINKING, AND LOGICAL THINKING

When we are performing a scientific experiment in a biology laboratory, or when we are seeking to explain the mysteries of time, energy, and space in a physics class, we are thinking scientifically. Scientific thinking does not process ideas by relying on the grammar and syntax of a natural language so much as it relies on the abstract formulas used in that science. For example, in chemistry, the expression H_2O is an abstract formula that describes the chemical compound from hydrogen and oxygen. "H_2O" is not a word in a natural language; it is a scientific formula that is used by scientists all over the world to describe what in English we mean when we say the word "water." Scientific thinking is much more exact, much more rigid, and much more rigorous than verbal thinking. For example, when we are thinking scientifically, specifically within the science of chemistry, the difference between "H_2O" and "H_2O_2 " is immense. For verbal thinking the difference between the two may seem insignificant until we realize that verbally "H_2O" is "water" and "H_2O_2" is "hydrogen peroxide," a bleach that in concentrated forms is contained in rocket fuel! For verbal thinking, the difference between O and O_2 can, and often will, appear to be unimportant. Verbal thinking understands, processes, and communicates information between people who use words in informal ways. Small differences of expression are often unimportant. Verbal thinking can be successful whenever the people using it understand one another well enough to achieve their purposes.[2] This inherent flexibility is one of the strengths of verbal thinking. However, scientific thinking *always* requires us to pay close attention to the details of its formulas. For scientific thinking, it is not enough that communication takes place; there are other considerations. Exactness of expression, a rigid adherence to proper methodology, and a rigorous search for true descriptions of reality, of facts; these are all characteristics—and strengths—of scientific thinking that distinguish it from verbal thinking.

Mathematical thinking rarely uses words. It is a way of thinking about quantities that largely makes use of numbers and special symbols that signify relationships between numbers. Mathematical thinking is more similar to scientific thinking than to verbal thinking. It possesses a high level of exactness, rigidity, and rigorousness about quantity that verbal thinking cannot achieve. We use words such as "quite a few" or "some" or "a couple" to designate quantities, but mathematical thinking, of course, is much more exact. Imagine a second grader who, when asked the sum of ninety-five and eighty-four, responds "a large amount!" This young student would be using verbal thinking in a situation in which mathematical thinking is more appropriate. Unlike scientific thinking, mathematical thinking is not concerned with describing the truth about facts. Mathematics is only concerned with providing exact, rigorous understanding, processing, and communication of quantities.

Logical thinking does not make use of the grammar and syntax of any natural language, and it is not concerned with facts. Logical thinking does not use numbers. Logical thinking, however, is more similar to scientific and mathematical thinking than to verbal thinking because it shares the exactitude, rigidity, and rigor of the scientific, mathematical way of thinking in three ways. First, logical thinking is the sort of thinking that closely and carefully examines how well we support our beliefs with evidence. Second, logical thinking is concerned with whether or not our beliefs can be proven to be true. Third, unlike verbal thinking, which relies on a natural language's grammar and syntax in order to "make sense," logical thinking relies on "rules of reason" by which it evaluates the quality of thought. These laws, similar to many scientific and mathematical rules, were first discovered by the ancient Greeks, and are being refined and supplemented up to the present day. The most important of these rules is the "law of contradiction," which states that a sentence that describes a fact cannot be both true and false at the same time. For example, "The planet Earth rotates around the planet Saturn" cannot be true and false at the same time. We know that the sentence is false. Therefore, according to the law of contradiction, it cannot also be true. Logical thinking is "either-or" thinking. Beliefs are either true or false; there are no "gray areas."

Logical thinking seeks and identifies "fallacies," specific errors that signal violations of the rules of reason. An example is the "attacking the person" fallacy, which occurs when someone ignores the evidence that a person presents

---

2. Of course, *successful* communication often requires more clarity, accuracy, specificity, and significance from verbal thinking than we may initially provide.

for a belief and focuses on an aspect of his or her personality instead: "I disagree with Ms. Martinez's view of taxation because she is an obnoxious person." Logical thinking requires us to pay attention to the support Ms. Martinez has for her beliefs about taxation. Whether we find her to be "obnoxious" or not is irrelevant. The only question logical thinking asks about this example is, "Can Ms. Martinez prove that her view on taxes is true?"

Verbal thinking, although not the same as scientific, mathematical, or logical thinking, is still present within these thought processes. After all, science, mathematics, and logic all use words in several ways. They are learned by the use of verbal thinking. Furthermore, each of them uses verbal thinking to communicate its ideas; scientific thinking describes its experiments and findings by means of verbal thinking in journals, books, and presentations. Mathematics uses verbal thinking to communicate its discoveries and methods of operation. Logical thinking uses verbal thinking to explain its laws. All three—scientific, mathematical, and logical—are more exact, more rigid, and more rigorous than verbal thinking. However, verbal thinking, because of its flexibility, is nevertheless necessary for these sorts of thinking to communicate their ideas.

SPATIAL THINKING, KINESTHETIC THINKING, AND INTUITIVE THINKING

Some types of thinking do not involve verbal thinking at all in understanding, processing, or communicating ideas. Spatial thinking, for example, is the type of thinking we do in understanding a map or in processing how we are going to manage our various stops when going on errands. These tasks are usually done nonverbally. When we think spatially, we remember the previous position of objects, notice their current position, and make proper adjustments in the objects or in our own location. Spatial thinking is the practical understanding, processing, and communication of distances between places or objects. Another example of spatial thinking is the process we go through in finding our location by referring to familiar landmarks. Imagine that you have stepped off the city bus at the wrong stop. You look at the buildings, perhaps the skyline, eventually find something familiar, and then know where you are. We use spatial thinking for more than finding our way when we are lost. We use it in engineering, in architecture, and in design. The role of spatial thinking in the development of technology is very important. Spatial thinking also takes place in artistic work, such as sculpture and painting. As with all types of thinking, spatial thinking is involved with solving problems and understanding, processing, and communicating ideas.

It is important to recognize that spatial thinking involves communication. When an artist creates a painting, he finds himself processing the possible locations of lines and shadows to create the best picture possible. Spatial thinking involved in dance, sculpture, architecture, engineering, and design is a nonverbal communication that we sometimes overlook.

Perhaps the single, most fascinating illustration of spatial thinking is the production of films. When we see a film that "made us think," it is often difficult to put into words just what the film made us think *about*. That may be because the film "made us think" spatially, not verbally. Every scene in a film is purposively constructed by placing objects and actors in particular places. This "place-ment" is referred to in the film industry by the French term *"mise-en-scène,"* The *mise-en-scène* communicates the mood and theme of the film as effectively as the spoken dialogue or the music. The relative positioning of actors communi-cates to the audience the underlying feelings of the characters they depict as well as the relationships of power, emotion, and significance between them. The objects that appear in scenes communicate the setting of the film as well as the more significant values and feelings the film is attempting to convey. As mem-bers of the audience we are understanding, processing, and communicating—thinking—in a spatial way when we view the *mise-en-scène*.

Kinesthetic thinking is a way of thinking involved with physical movement that is used in athletics and other activities in which we understand, process, and communicate by controlling our bodies. The term "kinesthetic" refers to the sen-sation we have of the position and movement of parts of our bodies. For exam-ple, whenever we are riding a bicycle, hitting a golf ball, or swimming a lap in the pool, we are aware of our bodies in a rather obvious way. Verbal thinking is normally not helpful in developing the sorts of activities involved with kines-thetic thinking; it just "gets in the way." Kinesthetic thinking is involved when we learn how to do something by observing someone else do it, practicing it, and gradually understanding how to do it ourselves. Athletes often describe a good performance as "feeling right," or as "balance." If their activity is not kinestheti-cally balanced, they practice it over and over again, seeking that "right feeling."

Intuitive thinking is the immediate separation of important aspects of ex-perience from the unimportant. When we put together a jigsaw puzzle, for example, we sometimes are quickly able to select the proper pieces from the pile, while ignoring the improper ones. When listening to a friend describe his diffi-culties in a personal relationship, we may be able to notice some clues to his own behavior even though he hardly mentions them verbally at all. The inflec-tions of his voice, or the ways his eyes glance to the side when he alludes to his behavior allow us to recognize "sore spots" in his relationship immediately. Another illustration of intuitive thinking is the experience a person returning to a burglarized apartment has of something "not being right" upon opening the door. Intuitive thinking is not logical, not verbal, and certainly not scientific thinking. Yet it can be involved to some degree with all three. No one could deny that poets often develop intuitions verbally. And most people have expe-rienced an intuition that they tried to "put into words" in order to communicate more clearly their insight to others. Logicians and scientists sometimes point out that their problem solving began with an intuition or hunch. Of course, they were not satisfied to continue with intuition. They shifted to logical or scientific thinking in order to use a more rigorous way of processing information.

CRITICAL THINKING

Critical thinking is correctly defined as *the review, evaluation, and revision* of pre-vious thinking. Imagine that a Greek trader and his crew of sailors are returning from a trading voyage to Persia. Let's further imagine that on the return voyage, a storm tosses the little trading vessel about in the terrifying swells of the Mediterranean for several days. When the waters become calm and the threatening clouds leave the sky, the trading party *reviews,* or *carefully examines,* the stars. The sailors discover that they are lost. They *evaluate* how far they are off course for home, and *revise* their position. Ancient sailors, as we know, made a practice of watching and thinking about the stars in the night sky. The position of the stars, when related to their known position at sea, provided a means of spatial location. Our Greek sailors remembered the positions of the stars from previous journeys that concluded successfully at homeport. When lost, as they were now, they routinely repositioned their vessels so that the stars were in the same position as on those previous, happier voyages. With all the "glowing objects" in their proper place, the vessel was no longer lost. When our sailors *reviewed, evaluated, and revised* their original spatial position, they were thinking critically. Their thinking was not necessarily verbal or logical; most likely, it was predominately spatial thinking. They must have had only a short time for a discussion of their location, and most likely, they could not evaluate all of their spatial knowledge by means of logical laws, anyway.

Once the merchant is safely at home and recovers from the storm-tossed voyage, he examines his merchandise to find the Persian carpets he had traded for Greek silver to be less colorful than he had thought when he negotiated for them. He immediately engages in *a review* of his verbal and intuitive thinking at the time of the trade.

> "What was I thinking about?" he might say to himself or to an associate. "I should have recognized that when the Persian merchant said that the colors in these carpets were as brilliant as I have learned to expect in fine Persian goods, he was either lying or was ignorant. That is very odd, though, since my experience with him has been extensive, and in the past he has always been honest and very knowledgeable. It is difficult to believe he could change so quickly into a dishonest or ignorant man! The colors are really quite dull. I should have thought more carefully about what he said, and I should have examined the carpets more closely, instead of being so anxious to close the deal at a good price. Perhaps he told me they were not as bright, but I didn't listen well. I should have taken a closer look at these carpets. Oh well, it is too late to take them back to Persia. What can I do now?"

The merchant is thinking critically. He is *reviewing* and *evaluating thinking that he has already done, as well as trying to find a way to revise, or change what he did for the better.* Since the merchant was primarily thinking verbally in making the original business agreement, the critical thinking that he subsequently found himself doing was a *review* of what he said, of what he heard, and an *evaluation* of how well he had used (and listened to) words. He also reviewed and evaluated his intuitive thinking about the Persian's moral and intellectual character. Critical thinking is *rethinking:* a review, an evaluation, and a revision of thinking that has already taken place.

A further illustration of critical thinking can be made if we imagine the merchant taking the poor-quality carpets to a local craftsperson. He discusses his lack of satisfaction with them, and explains that it is not economically feasible to return them to Persia. Can the craftsperson help him by making changes in the carpets? She examines the carpets carefully, seeking the flaws. Her spatial and intuitive thinking require all her concentration. She notices that the colorful patterns and shapes are well-proportioned and that the intricate weaves of the carpet are intact, with no loose threads. However, there is a very thin oily film on the carpets. She examines the film more closely. She contrasts the surface of the dull carpets with other Persian carpets supplied by the merchant that are bright and clear. These, her examinations reveal, have no oily film. The crafts-person makes an *evaluation;* the oily substance is interfering with the brightness of the carpets' colors. Her rethinking is an assessment, an evaluation of what lays behind the poor quality of the dull carpets. She is thinking critically.

Finally, she consults with some experts who have more experience with soiled carpets. One of them suggests that during the storm a small amount of olive oil stored in casks in the ship's hold may have leaked out and eventually seeped into the rolled carpets. Our critically thinking craftsperson seeks other authorities: those with good reputations in cleaning fine carpets without dam-aging the sorts of dyes the Persians use. She experiments with the cleaners they suggest and finds one that removes the oil and restores the bright colors. She has *revised* the carpets, changed them for the better.

Critical thinking reviews, evaluates, and revises. It solves problems. It col-laborates with others and seeks expertise. It is persistent. It seeks to change things for the better. Sometimes we need to think critically about things because, as with the lost sailors, circumstances have forced us to do so. At other times we need to think critically about our own ways of thinking. The merchant had to do that. And very often, like the craftsperson, we need to review, evaluate, and revise the ideas, plans, or projects of other people.

Aspects of Critical Thinking.   Critical thinking reviews and assesses thinking that has already been done. While critical thinking need not always be verbal and logical, nevertheless verbalization and logical thinking are usually involved in any review, no matter what sort of thinking has been previously done. The Greek sailors in the extended example probably discussed with one another briefly their position at sea when they realized that they were lost, and it makes sense to suppose that they made use of some basic logical laws, such as avoid-ing contradictions, in assessing their position with respect to the stars. The mer-chant most likely used verbal thinking when he reviewed the meaning of the Persian trader's words, and used logical thinking when he decided that it was very unlikely that this man, who had been honest in the past, had suddenly changed into a cheater. The merchant used intuitive thinking in deciding that the Persian had been sincere and honest, even though the carpets were not what he had said they were. In explaining the problem to the craftsperson, the merchant, of course, engaged in verbal and logical thinking. The craftsperson used verbal and logical thinking in evaluating the possible causes of the poor color quality, and engaged in scientific thinking by experimenting with different cleansers.

It is sometimes the case that intuitive thinking is at the heart of critical thinking. In our extended example, intuitive thinking took place when the sailors noticed that they were lost, and when the merchant assumed that the Persian was sincere and honest at the time of the purchase of the carpets. The craftsperson, too, used intuitive thinking in evaluating possible causes of the dullness in the colors.

Critical thinking, however, is usually verbal thinking because reviews or examinations as well as evaluations and revisions involve listening and speaking with other people. In the same way critical thinking requires logical thinking because when we contradict ourselves or violate other logical laws, we simply don't make any sense. As has been said, Western culture is a culture of words. However, even more than that, our whole world is one of words because it is a world of people trying to solve their problems and improve their lives by communicating and thinking in words. Verbal thinking's flexibility, its richness and power to describe, and its adaptability can hardly be overstated.

Critical thinking is a particular type of thinking that makes use of other types of thinking to review, evaluate, and revise the way ideas have been understood, processed, and communicated. Critical thinking is the type of thinking we do when we need to correct mistakes, whether they are our own or those of others. (Making mistakes is an unavoidable part of life; the only way to never make a mistake is to stop living!) Critical thinking is the sort of thinking we do when we need to improve the way things are being done and solve problems. Usually, it is verbal thinking and logical thinking that most successfully accomplishes these improvements.

EXERCISES

▲ MOST INTRIGUING ISSUE

Write a one-paragraph description of the most interesting idea, topic, or process described in the chapter so far. Be prepared to explain what you find interesting in class discussion.

▲ THE MUDDIEST POINT

Write a sentence or, if possible, a paragraph that describes the idea, topic, expression, term, or process in the chapter so far that you find most difficult to understand.

▲ CARTOONS AND DIAGRAMS

Cartoons are drawings that characterize or symbolize ideas, processes, or expressions in imaginative ways. Diagrams are drawings, tables, or charts that show how specific details of an idea, process, or expression are interrelated.

1. Provide a cartoon that shows a coach using verbal thinking and an athlete using kinesthetic thinking in order to improve the athlete's performance.
2. Provide a cartoon that shows a child lost in the forest using spatial thinking and intuitive thinking.

3. Provide a cartoon that shows the differences in degree of exactitude, rigidity, and rigor between verbal and mathematical thinking.
4. Provide a cartoon that shows the differences in the degree of flexibility, richness, and adaptability between verbal and scientific thinking.
5. Provide a cartoon that shows the three primary characteristics of critical thinking: review, evaluation, and revision.

▲ DEFINITIONS OF KEY TERMS

Provide a definition for each of the following terms as they are used in this chapter. Most of the terms are not defined in the chapter, although their meanings are described by the context in which they appear. You need to review the material to create the definition yourself.

Adaptability	Communicating	Exactness of expression
Flexibility	Processing	Richness
Rigidity	Rigor	Understanding

▲ SHORT ESSAY QUESTIONS

Provide a written response of approximately two hundred words for each topic. Your responses should be well organized, grammatically correct, and neatly produced.

1. Select a college course (other than this one) that you are currently taking, or a course you have taken in the past. Describe the types of thinking the course requires. Provide examples to help explain your description.
2. Explain why critical thinking usually makes use of verbal and logical thinking.
3. Describe the three primary characteristics of critical thinking for a person who has not read this chapter.
4. Explain the three characteristics of verbal thinking: adaptability, richness, and flexibility. Provide an example of your own for each characteristic.
5. Explain the difference between critical thinking and logical thinking.

▲ QUESTIONS FOR DISCUSSION

Provide an essay of three to five hundred words that responds to each of the following questions which ask for your opinion. You should respond by stating it, and by providing thoughts, examples, and insights that support it. You should be willing to revise your response; you may change your opinion during or after a class discussion.

1. The chapter discusses six types of thinking in addition to critical thinking. Can you think of any type of thinking not mentioned? If you can, describe it and explain how it relates to at least two of the types discussed. If you cannot, explain why you feel that the chapter has covered every possible way of thinking.
2. The chapter explains that critical thinking usually involves verbal and logical thinking, but that this need not be so. A movie director, for example, may change the *mise-en-scène* of a scene after thinking about it critically, spatially, and intuitively,

but neither verbally nor logically. Explain how the director would do this. Do you think movie directors often think critically this way? Why or why not?

3. The chapter provides an extended example of critical thinking. Create your own extended example, indicating each element of critical thinking as well as the various other types of thinking involved.

4. Do you feel that critical thinking is a common practice among political leaders in our society? How about religious leaders? Educational leaders? Do you find yourself generally thinking critically?

▲ QUOTATION TO PONDER

"I think and think, for months, for years, ninety-nine times the conclusion is false. The hundredth time I am right."

Albert Einstein

▲ JOURNAL TOPIC

Describe, in some detail, two specific instances in which you engaged in critical thinking within the last two weeks.

Each journal topic asks you to provide your own relevant examples and thoughtful reflections about the practical applications of specific concepts presented in the chapter. The entries should be from two to four hundred words in length. They should be kept in a notebook (or section of a notebook) solely used for that purpose. The journal should be kept for the duration of the course. When you have completed the course, you may review your journal. It will be an excellent collection of your practical applications of critical thinking.

▲ PORTFOLIO PAPER

The quality of people's verbal thinking depends upon their facility in using a natural language. The more comfortable they are with the syntax, grammar, and vocabulary of the language, the better their verbal thinking should be. How can people improve their facility in using their natural language?

A portfolio paper is a four to eight hundred word essay that describes your own thoughts and feelings about theoretical issues related to critical thinking. Most portfolio assignments ask you to write about ideas from several different chapters and to relate them to concepts from other courses or to your general knowledge. There are ten assignments. Four of them ask you to review, evaluate, and revise previous portfolio papers. You should keep all of your portfolio papers (including those you revise) in a folder. When you have completed the course, your portfolio will be an excellent source of ideas for a term paper on the theoretical aspects of critical thinking. Your portfolio will also be a record of your personal development as a critical thinker.

THE ROLE OF THE BODY IN THINKING

Thinking, no matter of what kind, is an activity of the whole person. Of course, thinking involves the nervous system and the brain, but it is important to recognize that thinking cannot be reduced merely to what the brain and nervous system do when we think. We know that running a marathon, for example, involves the feet, legs, lungs, and so forth. However, we cannot reduce running a marathon to the activities of the organs directly related to it. Running is something a *person* does, and although the activities of the feet, legs, and lungs are essential to the marathon, there are other important elements we should not overlook. Certainly, the heart, skin, and other bodily organs are involved. However, the emotional attitude of the runner, the social and physical environment of the marathon, and intangible personal values of running the marathon are also important in understanding the whole picture. We would not have a good understanding of running a marathon if we limited our attention to the bodily organs involved, although we need to recognize the important role those organs play in the process. It is much the same with understanding thinking. All thinking involves the body, including the brain and nervous system, but there are other elements equally important to an understanding of thinking.

All thinking is "about" something; that is, there is always a content to our thinking. We never simply think; whenever we think, we think about something. The content of our thought comes to us through the psychological processes of sensation and perception.

SENSATION

Sensation is the activity of detecting information from the world by the body's receptors: the eyes, ears, nose, skin, and tongue. We do not, strictly speaking, *sense* objects. We sense what psychologists and philosophers refer to as "stimuli" or "sense-data." We live in an environment of electro-chemical activity, a vast "sea of energy" that swirls about us in ways of which we are not at all aware. Radio and X-rays, ultraviolet and infrared light, very high and very low frequency sound waves abound in the environment, but we are not aware of them at all. We cannot hear the frequency of the whistle to which any dog easily responds, and yet we see colors that no dog has ever, and never will, experience. The sense-data our receptors detect provide the information our nervous system and brain process into what we call "objects" and "experiences."

The eyes detect a narrow range of electromagnetic energy and convert this energy into neural messages that we perceive as color. The skin receives sense-data and transforms them into what we perceive as pressure, warmth, coldness, or pain. The ears react to jostling molecules of air—sound waves—that we perceive as sounds of particular pitch and intensity. Our noses have clusters of millions of receptor cells that detect chemicals in the air and transform that sense-data into neural messages that we perceive as odors. The tongue's taste buds detect what are perceived as sweet, sour, salty, and bitter molecules as flavors. The "experience" of the sights, sounds, and smells of a barefoot walk in the park while eating an ice cream cone is, on the level of sensation, not an experience at all, but a complex reception and transference of electro-chemical sense-data into neural messages. The vivid colors and delightful odors of the flowers, the joyful sounds of the bird's singing, and the delicious flavor of the ice cream, as well as the sensation of cool wet grass between the toes, are nothing but received stimulation of the sense organs.

In the same way, when we read a book, listen to a conversation, or gain information from television or the Internet, we must receive the available sense-data before we can begin to perceive meaningful information. Everything we think about has to first come to our attention by means of sensation. The body, then, is essentially involved with thinking because it is the body that provides the content for thought. The health of the body plays an important role in the quality of the detection and transformation of sense-data into neural messages. The receptor cells and auditory nerves of the ear, for example, are damaged by prolonged exposure to intense sound over eighty decibels. A subway train at a distance of twenty feet produces about one hundred decibels. Amplified music can produce one hundred forty decibels at close range. Exposure to damaging sound for long periods of time can result in actual destruction of auditory nerves, which may result in deafness.

When the body is healthy and the receptors are allowed to function in a normal fashion, we can be confident that we are sensing the world as well as possible. Mistreating the body can result in poor sensation, and this, in turn, can lead to poor thinking. If the content of thinking is distorted at the level of sensation, then there is little chance that thinking will be successful in solving problems. The need for physical health becomes even more obvious when considering the role perception plays in forming the content of thinking.

PERCEPTION

Sense-data are not understood directly. The brain and nervous system refine sensory information in the activity known as *perception.* Perception is the process of selection, organization, and interpretation of sense-data into mental representations that can be used by the brain and nervous system to provide content for thought.

We do not perceive everything we sense. The brain and nervous system focus on some aspects of sensation rather than others. For example, if we are watching a movie in a theater, we perceive the movie on the screen, but not the various objects and events in the theater itself. The chairs, the aisles, the exit signs, even the other people watching the movie with us are all sensed by our receptors. We smell the popcorn, we hear the air conditioning unit, and we see the back of the head of the person sitting in front of us. However, under normal conditions, we do not perceive any of these. It is only when the person sitting next to us offers us popcorn, or when the person sitting in front of us makes an unusual movement that they, and not the movie, become objects of our perception. This refers to "selective attention." Everything we perceive has gone through the process of sensation, but we do not perceive everything we have sensed. We perceive what strikes our nervous system as unusual, i.e., as different than what it would expect. The activity of focusing on the unusual and of more or less ignoring the usual is called *selection.* In the movie theater, the dark environment, the chairs, the aisles, the exit signs, and so on, provide usual and expected sense-data. The movie itself, which consists of a constant and rapid flux of light wave received by the eyes, is noticed exclusively. The movie provides a constant barrage of unfamiliar and unusual sense-data. The unusual sense-data (in this example, the movie) are selected as the primary focus, or the "figure" of our perception. The more familiar and usual sense-data (the theater environment) are regarded as the background, or "ground," of the perception. If our nose detects the odor of smoke while we are watching the movie, of course, immediately the sense-data perceived as the movie becomes the ground and the odor (fire?) becomes the figure. The activity of selection always arranges sense-data in the figure-ground configuration. The brain probably recognizes the usual or the habitually sensed data as nonthreatening, whereas anything that is unusual or new is focused upon as a possible threat to our safety.

The second way the brain and nervous system process sense data is by *organization.* We do not need to sense all the sense-data provided to the receptors in order to perceive an object or to have an idea. We organize sense-data into complete wholes, referred to by psychologists by the German term *gestalt.* A gestalt is a unified perception. In reading, for example, we do not need to receive the entire sense-data provided by the light reflecting off the print on the page. It is enough to receive some of the sense-data because our brain, being familiar with the printed word, readily completes the partial information into the complete sentence that it expects to read, based on previous experiences. That is the reason that small typographical errors do not impede our reading. Even though the sentence "Bob ate three pieces of pi" does not make any sense, our brain more or less completes the meaning that the sentence fails to provide by adding the letter "e" to the end of the last word. Here is a diagram that illustrates this completion process.

Even though the diagram is not a complete rectangle, we nevertheless perceive it as one. The tendency to unify perceptions into gestalts is called closure. Closure fills in the gaps in our perceptions of shapes. The example of reading the sentence "Bob ate three pieces of pi" illustrates the principle of *constancy* in perceptual organization. Constancy is the principle that explains how we tend to organize our perceptions according to how we have successfully done so in the past. We are much more familiar with people eating three pieces of pie than we are of people eating three pieces of "pi" and so we perceive the sentence as having the more familiar meaning.

Consider this example:

THEDOGATEMEAT

Clearly, the most familiar perception here is

THE DOG ATE MEAT

It could, but does not, mean

THE DO GATE ME AT

It is important to realize that we perceptually organize everything we sense. In terms of understanding thinking, and especially critical thinking, we must further realize that we perceptually organize everything we read and listen to into gestalts that may be more influenced by what we are familiar with than by what the author or speaker is attempting to get across to us. We can especially misunderstand subtle references or insightful allusions because our brain leaps to organize perception in ways that are familiar. We need to be aware that our body, in this case the nervous system and the brain, is not always going to provide the attention to detail that critical thinking requires.

The third element of perception, *interpretation*, plays a very important role in reading and listening. Interpretation is perceptual judgment: it is the process of finding meaning in sense-data. Interpretation allows us to gain meaning from reading and listening. When we read, the print on the page is mere sense-data. A good way to recognize this fact is to read a sentence in a language with which we are not familiar. For example

SE O QUE ESCREVO TEM VALOR, NAO SOU EU QUE O TENHO O VALOR ESTA' ALI, NOS MEUS VERSOS.

is a sentence in Portuguese, a language few in our society understand. It is an example of how the written word is always first mere sense-data, requiring the selection, organization, and interpretation of the nervous system to have any meaning. The meaning of the Portuguese sentence, then, is not a simple event! The sentence has meaning only in the very complex process of the perception of a human being. If we have some familiarity with Spanish, the sentence has more meaning for us than if we do not. That, of course, is due in part to the slight similarity of the two languages. However, more than that, the meaning of the sentence is directly dependent upon the reader's ability to *interpret* the sentence, and a reader who has some familiarity with Spanish will have a more valuable linguistic background for interpreting the sentence than one who does not.

Interpretation is based on several factors, but early life experience, expectation, and cultural influence seem to be the most important ones.

Early Childhood Development. Our early childhood development has an enormous influence on how we interpret meaning, especially the meaning of language. For an American, the tune "Jingle Bells" calls forth thoughts of Christmas because most of us connect this little song with our earliest memories of that holiday. As children, we are able to learn our native language rather easily. We can interact with others, make known our needs, and hold conversations. These early-life experiences with language use establish the foundation for our eventual perceptions of meaning in our native language. The important role that early childhood development plays in the process of finding meaning in language can hardly be overestimated. A child who takes part in conversations, who is read to, and who is encouraged to express ideas and feelings in language at an early age is going to have a more solid base from which to interpret meaning in the native language as an adult.

Children who suffer from lack of conversation, who spend hours in front of television sets taking in sound bites instead of sentences, and who are not encouraged to develop images along with the words they hear while being read to, are not going to be able to interpret their native language with the depth, subtlety, and understanding that will be possible for children with a more rich, linguistic background. It is also important to recognize how important it is for children to become familiar with languages other than their native language. What if we had all been familiar with Portuguese as children? Our linguistic world would be much richer! In fact, we would perhaps recognize this line from one of Portugal's most celebrated poets, Fernando Pessoa:

> If what I write is good, the worth is not mine:
> the value lies there, in my poetry.

Expectation.   Early childhood experience is not the only factor in interpretation of meaning. Expectation also plays an important role. Expectation is sometimes referred to as our perceptual set or mental predisposition. Expectations frequently influence interpretation of meaning. Campers sitting around a fire listening to ghost stories may very well experience some ghastly sounds coming from the forest later that night! If they spend the evening discussing the probable presence of "Bigfoot" or aliens from outer space, they are much more liable to interpret the unusual sounds as the clumsy running of the gigantic Bigfoot himself, or the rustling sounds as tiny aliens from another galaxy. Sense-data do not have meaning unless they are interpreted, of course, and if we hear unusual sounds or see unusual things such as strange lights in the sky, we can often interpret what they mean on the basis of what we expect or want them to mean.

If we bring with us ideas and assumptions that are false, or that are based on false, one-sided views, we are inclined to interpret sense-data in a biased manner. One of the most common examples of bias is racism, a perceptual set that interprets the characteristics of a person on the basis of physical characteristics, especially skin tone. In an interesting experiment on the nature of racism in the mid-1970s, white college students were shown a staged photograph of a white man shoving a black man. The white students claimed that the white man in the photo was only "horsing around." However, when the same students were shown another staged photograph, this time with a black man shoving a white man, they more often saw the event as "violent." The students interpreted the meaning of the photographs on the basis of their expectations. Those who perceived violence in the picture of the black man shoving the white man while interpreting the white man shoving the black man as mere fun had a perceptual set that included expectations of violence in relation to black men. Clearly, their perceptual set, based on false and one-sided beliefs, was biased.

Expectation also plays a role in the interpretation of what we read and hear. Our perceptual set is the attitude we bring with us to a conversation or to the printed page. The perceptual set may not be biased; that is, it may be based on accurate, well-founded beliefs. If, for example, we have studied and enjoyed the opinions expressed in the editorials of our local newspaper as expressions of sound thinking, we will tend to read further editorials with an accepting and open attitude. It may be that we find ourselves in disagreement with an editorial from time to time, but we will most likely be more inclined to review our own ideas in light of what we have read. On the other hand, if we find ourselves in constant disagreement with the local newspaper's editorials because they appear to be instances of poor reasoning and bias, it may be difficult for us to recognize the good sense that may appear there from time to time.

Cultural Influences.   Finally, the perception of meaning or interpretation is very much influenced by cultural influences. Our culture has a great deal of influence on how we interpret meaning. Culture consists of the language, beliefs, values, norms, and behaviors that are passed from one generation to another. Sociologists, who study culture scientifically, point out the presence of subcultures, the members of whom maintain language habits, values, behavior patterns, and so on that distinguish its members from those of the main, or dominant, culture. There are also countercultures—groups of people who join in identifying themselves by their opposition to the values of the dominant culture. Whether we identify with the dominant culture, a subculture, or a counterculture, it is important to recognize the influence the elements of culture have on our interpretation of meaning. Many of our values, for example, are simply shared with us by others. We may persist in honoring the value even though we do not understand why we do so. For example, a teenage girl noticed that her mother always sliced an inch or so off the end of a piece of meat before placing it in the oven to be roasted. When she asked her mother why she did that, her mother replied that she didn't really know, but her own mother had done this and she had simply accepted the act as meaningful. The teenager, driven by curiosity, called her grandmother and asked about the practice. The grandmother responded that when she was a young woman she had only a small pan in which to cook her roasts, and so she used to cut the end off so it would fit in the pan. As the years went on and she obtained larger pans, she had simply cut off the end by habit.

One aspect of cultural influence that we need to be aware of is culturally centric belief, the attitude that whatever our individual culture, subculture, or counterculture affirms is more appropriate than any other group's cultural beliefs, simply because these beliefs are our own. Culturally centric belief is sometimes referred to as "mine is better" thinking.

EXERCISES

▲ MOST INTRIGUING ISSUE

Write a one-paragraph description of the most interesting idea, topic, or process described in pages 17–21. Be prepared to explain what you find interesting in class discussion.

▲ THE MUDDIEST POINT

Write a sentence or, if possible, a paragraph that describes the idea, topic, expression, term, or process in pages 17–21 that you find most difficult to understand.

▲ CARTOONS AND DIAGRAMS

Diagrams are drawings, charts, or tables that show how specific details of an idea, process, or expression are interrelated.

1. Provide a diagram or cartoon that shows the relationship of sense-data and perception.
2. Provide a cartoon that illustrates a child's perception of his or her pet kitten sleeping on a chair.
3. Draw a cartoon that shows the ways different cultural influences, early childhood experiences, and expectations influence two individual's different interpretations of the meaning of a movie they are watching.
4. Draw a diagram or cartoon that shows how sensation, selection, organization, and the three factors of interpretation influence the meaning a person finds in reading a textbook about critical thinking.

▲ DEFINITIONS OF KEY TERMS

Provide a definition for each of the following terms as they are used in this chapter. Most of the terms are not defined in the chapter, although their meanings are described by the context in which they appear. You need to review the material to create the definition yourself.

Interpretation	Organization
Perception	Receptors
Selection	Sense-data

▲ SHORT ESSAY QUESTIONS

Provide a written response of approximately 200 words for each topic. Your responses should be well organized, grammatically correct, and neatly produced.

1. Explain to someone who has not read the chapter what is meant by saying that thinking is always about perceptions, not sensations.
2. Describe how the receptors are involved with the sensation of a rose garden in a public park.

3. Provide and explain your own example of organization, including closure and constancy.
4. Provide and explain your own example of selection.
5. Explain why it is important for children to become familiar with languages other than their native language, as claimed on p. 20.

▲ QUESTIONS FOR DISCUSSION

Provide an essay of 300–500 words that responds to each of the following questions which ask for your opinion. You should respond by stating it, and by providing thoughts, examples, and insights that support it. You should be willing to revise your response; you may change your opinion during or after a class discussion.

1. Understanding the nature of perception should encourage us to be more tolerant of people with whom we disagree about social, political, and religious values. Why?
2. Some scholars believe that it is impossible to translate the meaning of a novel or short story from one natural language to another. Why do you suppose that they feel this way? Explain why you agree or disagree with them.
3. Foreign films are often shown with subtitles, at other times "dubbing" is used. Obviously, the film would be less meaningful to an audience unfamiliar with the film's language if neither subtitles nor dubbing were used. However, foreign film buffs disagree about which is better. Explain both points of view, and then explain your own.
4. Some people feel that travel to a foreign country for an extended period is a better way to achieve an education than to attend a college in their hometown. Discuss this idea in relation to what you have read in the chapter and explain why you feel it is true or false.

▲ QUOTATION TO PONDER

Paraphrase this quotation in a way that explains its relevance to the main ideas in the chapter.

"The brain does not seek or respond to information in the world—the brain imposes meaningfulness on the world. It is an active, experience-seeking, reality-creating organ. . . . We would not have reality without fantasy; reality is a fantasy that works."

Frank Smith, *To Think*

▲ JOURNAL TOPIC

Artworks can be found in museums and galleries as well as in public buildings. There may be opportunities to view art on your own campus or in your community. Your library probably has artworks on display; it certainly has some books in which you can find examples of art. The Internet has several good sites sponsored by art museums.

The chapter points out that meaning is an interpretation of selected and organized sense-data. Many artists paint pictures, create sculptures, or take photographs with this in mind. After examining a work of art, explain how its meaning is "in the eye of the beholder."

THE BRAIN

Strictly speaking, *cognition* is an activity of the brain that collects, stores, collates, and processes perceptual data. Our brain is made up of literally billions of neurons, each connected with thousands of others in a "neural network" that allows perceptual data to be stored, classified, compared, contrasted, extrapolated, and so on. We still know very little about the brain; however, in recent years research into the way the brain operates has produced important advances in understanding cognition.

A MODEL OF THE BRAIN

The brain is so complex that it is simply foolish to pretend that we understand it completely. Nevertheless, we can attain a basic familiarity with it by construction of a "model" of how it appears to operate. A *model* is an image or metaphor that serves as a simple representation of a complex event. We are familiar with globes, which are models of the planet Earth. A globe, no matter how detailed and rich, is still a mere simplistic image of the actual planet it represents. Still, a globe gives us a pretty good idea of the planet Earth.

We can think of the brain as a house with three family members living together under the same roof.[3] The oldest member, the grandfather, is in charge of daily maintenance chores. He provides food, disposes of waste, and takes care of safety and comfort needs. He is very resistant to changing the way he does things, since he has been so successful over the years. He does his chores without really thinking about them, and does not speak at all.

The second family member, the mother, handles feeling and emotion. She also takes care of storing new information and organizing family activities. When grandfather alerts her to danger, she makes the decision whether to stand and fight or to run away. She plays peacemaker in the family by keeping grandfather from totally dominating everyone, and by softening the always creative, but often insensitive ideas of the young child.

The child, the third member of the family, is creative and intelligent. The child uses language, composes music, engages in mathematics and logic, plans for the future, and enjoys change.

The family is very functional; each member supports the others even though there are times of conflict. The child is usually unaware of danger, and the grandfather and mother are quite protective. However, the child often comes up with new and imaginative plans that mother assesses for appropriateness and grandfather grudgingly agrees with, so long as no threats are viewed on the horizon.

The model of the brain as a family is meant to show that although the brain is divided into three regions with separate tasks, it works as a unit. The grandfather is the oldest part of the brain in terms of phylogeny, or evolutionary development. It is called the "reptilian complex" because we share this part of the brain with the most primitive organisms, such as lizards and snakes. The

---

3. Renate Nummela Caine, and Geoffrey Caine, *Teaching and the Human Brain* (1991), pp. 52–58.

reptilian complex manages the survival and maintenance of the body: digestion, reproduction, circulation, breathing, and stress responses. Activities of this part of the brain are automatic, driven by biological needs. It is imitative, adheres to routine, and is primarily concerned with survival and safety.

The mother of the family, the second part to evolve, is the emotion center, or limbic system. It is involved with self-awareness and with how we feel about ourselves. The desire for food and sex, our needs for bonding, and for expressing ourselves are located in the limbic system. In addition, the memory is located here, which means that memory and emotion are strongly related. This may be why it is much easier to remember the lyrics of popular songs we have listened to with friends than to memorize lines of poetry assigned in a literature course. When we feel intensely that something is personally important, the brain is much more capable of remembering it.

The child, known as the neocortex, was the last part of the brain to evolve. It is by far the largest part of the brain, making up five-sixths of its size. The neocortex is the language center of the brain, as well as the center of perceptual processing. It is the neocortex that selects, organizes, and interprets sense-data.

Just as a family functions best when all the members are allowed to "be themselves" and live their lives in a healthy, relaxed, cooperative way, the brain thinks well when all three aspects are functioning normally. That is, the reptilian complex needs to feel safe, protected, and secure. The limbic system needs a satisfying self-concept and sense of belonging. The neocortex requires meaningful sense-data and competence in language. The brain, in other words, needs to be in a state of health in order to think well. If it is afraid, insecure, lonely, lacking in stimulation, or damaged by injuries, drugs, or psychological factors, it cannot carry out its functions well.

THE BRAIN VS. THE WHOLE PERSON

If we were interested in preparing to run a marathon, it would be a good idea to learn something about the muscles of the body, the respiratory and circulatory systems, and other organs involved with running. However, it would be unwise, once we had discussed these things, to believe that we now knew all that we needed in order to actually run a marathon. In the same way reviewing some interesting and important information about the body and the brain in relation to thinking is certainly worthwhile. We can understand thinking more clearly if we remind ourselves that there is an organ involved, just as we would be wiser runners if we understood more about our bodies. On the other hand, the whole person runs a marathon, not just the muscles and other organs involved with running. We understand very little about the complexities of sensation, perception, and cognition. We have merely touched the surface with regard to understanding the functions of the brain. However, even when cognitive science has developed a large and coherent body of knowledge about the brain, we will still need to remember that it is not the brain that thinks—it is the whole person. Our legs and feet, heart and lungs, do not run the marathon; we run. The brain does not think critically; we do.

LANGUAGE

Not all thinking is verbal; but most critical thinking makes use of words in order to review the ideas, plans, beliefs, actions, creations, and so on that are the work of the different types of thinking. Language is the primary way the brain processes sense-data into meaningful ideas or concepts. Language is the system of symbols that "names" perceptions and links them with other "names" to provide a meaningful world of experience. A baby, first learning what it is to be a member of the human community, wants names for everything encountered. The baby, because of its humanity, needs the names, words, sentences, grammar, organization, and meaning that language provides. One way of understanding the need for language is to refer to our discussion of the brain. If the neocortex is not allowed to use language, it is helpless in the complex world of meaning in which human life takes place. Certainly, a child born with damage to the neo-cortex can sense danger, feel deep love for others, and have a genuine sense of self. However, that child, if unable to process language, will not be able to take part in the complex, technological world in which we live. It will also be, it seems, very difficult, if not impossible, for the child to think critically. For, as has been mentioned above, critical thinking is a review of previous thinking with an eye to improving the ideas, plans, and beliefs that resulted from it. This review takes place, for the most part, in language.

CONNOTATIVE AND DENOTATIVE MEANING

Language provides meaning in two general ways. It "names" perceptions by linking their name to other words, and by designating the perceptions as indi-viduals. Take, for example, the word "automobile." The word has meaning in two senses. In the first sense, the *denotative* sense, "automobile" means the Fords, Hondas, Oldsmobiles, and all other similar vehicles. If someone asks what "automobile" means, we can give the denotative meaning of the word by point-ing to one of the vehicles. The denotation of a word is the perception it names. There is no verbal equivalent of the denotative meaning of a word; the meaning is the perception itself. The second sense of the meaning of the word "automo-bile" is its *connotative* meaning. Every word has a connotative meaning, which is the meaning of the word as it is described by other words. A definition, since it is in words, always provides the connotative meaning. "Automobile" is a com-bination of two words, "auto" and "mobile." "Auto" means "self." "Mobile" means "movement." An "automobile" means "something that moves itself." When automobiles were first invented, they did not have a name; one had to be created. By combining two words already in use, "Automobile" was created. Not all words, of course, were created by combining words. The denotative meaning of the English word "cat" and the Spanish word "gato" is the same perception. If you ask the question, "What is a cat?" and a woman responds by pointing her finger at a cat, she is relying on you to sense, select, organize, and interpret sense-data in a way similar to her own perception with regard to the cat. She has provided you the denotative meaning of the word. If you asked the question a second time, she might respond with the connotative meaning of the term in English. "A cat is a small or large lithe, furry carnivore, many of which have been domesticated since ancient times."

Denotative meaning is *perceptual* meaning. Connotative meaning is *verbal* meaning. Perceptual and verbal meaning are essential to the function of language; language is dependent upon both. That is, language is *other-referential* and at the same time *self-referential*. What this means, simply, is that language always says something about a perception and at the same time does so within a grammatical system.

LANGUAGE AND PERCEPTION

Language does not merely assign meaning to perceptions; it also plays an essential role in the nature of perception itself. The neocortex selects, organizes, and interprets sense-data largely on the basis of language. As a matter of fact, the depth of our experience in many ways depends upon the richness of our understanding of language. One reason poetry enriches our lives is because it helps us to perceive more deeply, with more feeling and understanding. When we are familiar with the vocabulary and language of a specific discipline, for example, botany, we perceive with more detail and depth. A casual conversation about the flowers along a path in the park is not as rewarding as one that takes place while thinking about the first verse of Robert Frost's "Rose Pogonias."[4]

> A saturated meadow,
> Sun-shaped and jewel-small,
> A circle scarcely wider
> Than the trees around were tall;
> Where winds were quite excluded,
> And air was stifling sweet
> With the breath of many flowers—
> A temple of the heat

The words of the poem not only describe the flowers of Frost's own perceptions but also exert an influence on our own perceptions. Language provides a world of meaning for us; it does not merely describe sense-data. Language need not be poetic in order to shape perceptions. Scientific language is a precise, logical categorization and calculation of perceptions that allows for detailed, exact understanding. Two botanists walking along the park path would have different perceptions from the poet, but they would be no less, and no more, meaningful. They would be different. The botanists would perceive stamens, pistils, pedicels, and nodes. Understanding the language of botany would enrich and add detail to their perceptions.

Language as connotative allows the poet and the scientist, as well as the rest of us, to classify, systematize, compare, contrast, and combine perceptions

---

4. Robert Frost, *The Poetry of Robert Frost* (1967).

by use of symbols, words, and sentences. As denotative, language "points out" aspects of sense-data that are important, interesting, and attractive.

As the primary means of establishing meaning, language is especially important for critical thinking. By use of language, we recall, categorize, and in general *think about* our ideas. Language provides the meaning in our lives. Language directs our attention, expresses and calls forth our emotions, and allows us to relate to each other in communication. We use language to define, summarize, paraphrase, reconstruct, imagine, discuss, and evaluate ideas. Critical thinking makes use of all of these linguistic activities: They are tools of critical thinking.

A PHILOSOPHICAL CONUNDRUM: THE TWO-WORLD ASSUMPTION

We cannot think about something we do not know, and it is ideas, or perceptions, not things, that we know. So, we do not think about things, we think about perceptions, or ideas. Critical thinking is a review of thinking that has already taken place; it is an attempt to improve that previous way of thinking. However, philosophers have often posed the question, "How do we know if our thinking has actually improved? If all we can think about are perceptions, how do we ever know if we have the truth about things? How can we know if the idea or perception we have is true of the way things really are?"

Philosophers have puzzled over this issue for centuries. It even has a name: The "two-world assumption." This is how the conundrum is usually stated. There is, we assume, an objective world of things "out there" in which we all really live. There is a real world. However, since the only world we can *know* for sure is the one that each of us perceives, we can only assume that there is a real world of things "out there." As we have seen, perceptions are not simple copies of the objective world. Perceptions are complex brain events that shape sense-data into meaningful ideas. Language symbolizes sense-data, allowing us to remember it, process it, retrieve it, and so on. However, do we ever get in touch with that real, objective world of things?

It seems silly to claim that we do not. After all, the world we experience in perception seems real to us. We can tell the difference between our dreams and the real world, at least most of the time. Some philosophers have pointed out that it is a lot easier to know we have been dreaming once we wake up than to know we are dreaming while we are asleep! Who is to say whether we are all dreaming right now?

Most people don't take the philosophers very seriously when they ask questions such as the one in the last paragraph. Philosophers seem to thrive on unanswerable questions, and most of us have other, more practical thoughts on our minds. However, we can join the philosophers for just a moment and explore the issue of the two-world assumption. We may learn something.

Most people would say that they could certainly tell the difference between a real apple and an imaginary one. On the other hand, perhaps most people need to do some critical thinking about their previous ideas about the real world. Perhaps, in light of what we have learned about the body, the brain, and language, we should reflect on what the word "real" *means*.

According to the "two-world assumption," the real apple on the table is *different* from the apple we perceive to be on the table. One apple is actually "out there" on the table, and the other apple is only "in here" in our brain. The apple out there is real, objective. The apple in here is imaginary, subjective. We know the truth about the apple, according to the two-world assumption, only if the apple in our brain is an exact copy of the apple on the table.

However, it is *impossible to know* if we have in our brain an exact copy of the apple on the table. In fact, it is impossible to know if we have any kind of copy at all! The only way we can *know* is to use our brain, and so anything we know will automatically be a perception, an idea, and "in here." The rather unsettling conclusion the philosophers point out we must come to is that there is no way at all of determining if we actually know the truth about the objective, "real" apple on the table.

Does this mean that we cannot know the truth about anything real? Are we limited to our own little subjective "in here" world? If so, why should we bother to do any thinking, and why any critical thinking? How will we know if we have improved our thinking if the only way we have to evaluate whether it is improved or not is by use of our own little "subjective" world?

The philosophers offer us some help here. Clearly, they say, objective and subjective cannot be regarded as opposites. We know that sense-data come to us from "out there," and are objective. We do not create sense-data; if we did, the real world would be similar to our dreams. It isn't. And so, they say, let's recognize that the apple on the table is not actually an apple at all. It is an electro-chemical "event" that provides, among other things, sense-data. There is, however, an objective apple. However, it isn't all that different from the subjective apple. *The objective apple is the denotative meaning of the perception of the apple we describe in language.* And the subjective apple? *The subjective apple is the connotative meaning of the perception of the apple we describe in language.*

We *know* the complete truth about the apple on the table when we understand every possible aspect of the electro-chemical "event" that created the apple. For us to understand the "event" completely, we must consider its relationships with its environment. That includes the table, the room, and *us*. It is important to realize that our own sensation and perception of the apple are part of what we know of it. To say we "know" the apple is to say that we "perceive" it. There is no possible way to know the truth about the apple—or anything else—without recognizing the role we play in that knowing.

The two-world assumption, like many seemingly useless philosophical puzzles, has a very practical message. It shows us how important it is to recognize that no one has a "direct line" to reality. People must be content to accept that their ideas, beliefs, and values are actually based upon their perceptions, and not on "reality." No one has the absolute truth about reality. We have only our perception of it.

CONCLUSION

The "two-world assumption" is a profound philosophical conundrum, a timeless issue that will not be resolved by our brief discussion. However, it is an important issue for critical thinking. From it, we learn that no matter how much we review our thinking process, there is always a need for further review. Critical thinking is successful when problems are solved more successfully than they were previously, and when knowledge is more accurate than it was before. Critical thinking need not, in fact, cannot, achieve absolute certainty, absolute proof, about the absolute truth of our ideas and perceptions. We must recognize that all knowledge, based as it is on sensation, perception, and cognition, is limited, personal, and always in need of revision. Critical thinking needs to be aware of these limits of knowledge. In revising ideas, whether they are our own or someone else's, we need to pay close attention to how well we are thinking and to recognize that no one's thinking is ever perfect. We can always revise and improve.

We have focused our attention on the brain in this chapter, but we do not want to lose sight of the fact that it is *people* who think, not brains. People are not omniscient; our thinking is limited to the very limited number of perceptions we are capable of understanding. Indeed, that is why critical thinking is so important. We need to revise our thinking . . . because we are only human.

EXERCISES

▲ Most Intriguing Issue

Write a one-paragraph description of the most interesting idea, topic, or process described in the chapter. Be prepared to explain what you find interesting in class discussion.

▲ The Muddiest Point

Write a sentence or, if possible, a paragraph, that describes the idea, topic, expression, term, or process in the chapter that you find most difficult to understand.

▲ Cartoons and Diagrams

1. Draw a cartoon of the "brain family."
2. Provide a diagram that shows the differences between the connotative and denotative meanings of the words "book," "shoe," and "thinking."
3. Draw a cartoon that contrasts the differences in the perceptions of an amusement park roller coaster by two different twelve-year-olds. One has been on a roller coaster five times before and loved it each time. The other has never been on a roller coaster, but saw a movie the week before in which a terrible roller coaster tragedy took place.
4. Draw a cartoon that illustrates the "two-world assumption."

▲ DEFINITIONS OF KEY TERMS

Provide a definition for each of the following terms as they are used in this chapter. Most of the terms are not defined in the chapter, although their meanings are described by the context in which they appear. You need to review the material to create the definition yourself.

Connotative meaning	Denotative meaning
Language	Limbic system
Neocortex	Reptilian complex

▲ SHORT ESSAY QUESTIONS

Provide a written response of approximately 200 words for each topic. Your responses should be well organized, grammatically correct, and neatly produced.

1. Describe how all three areas of the brain are involved in the decision to eat a waffle for breakfast.
2. Explain why critical thinking is usually verbal.
3. Explain what this sentence means: "Language does not merely assign meaning to perceptions; it also plays an essential role in the nature of perception itself."
4. Describe a model for the three areas of the brain other than the "family model" provided by the chapter.

▲ QUESTIONS FOR DISCUSSION

Provide an essay of 300–500 words that responds to each of the following questions which ask for your opinion. You should respond by stating it, and by providing thoughts, examples, and insights that support it. You should be willing to revise your response; you may change your opinion during or after a class discussion.

1. Watching a movie is a very complex perceptual event. We realize that the sights and sounds are artificially produced in the theater, and yet we can become so involved in the movie that we are able to forget that it is not "real." Explain how the three elements of perception work together to make the movie "seem real" to us.

2. Some philosophers believe that without language, no one would be able to communicate with anyone else, and as a result, we would never be able to leave our own little perceptual worlds. These philosophers claim that without language, in fact, there would be no reality. Discuss what you think they are trying to say about language and reality, and explain why you agree or disagree with them.

3. In Hamlet, Shakespeare writes: "Nothing is good or bad, but thinking makes it so." Explain what this quotation means in relation to the chapter. Do you agree with the quotation? Why or why not?

4. A witness to an automobile accident that resulted in a trial was asked by a lawyer for the prosecution, "How fast were the cars going when they *smashed* into each other?" The witness responded that the cars were going about forty-five miles

per hour. When another witnesses was asked by the defense lawyer, "How fast were the cars going when they *bumped* into each other?" she replied, "About twenty-five miles per hour." Explain this discrepancy in testimony by referring to what you have learned about language and perception in this chapter.

▲ QUOTATION TO PONDER

"Although the brain weighs only about three pounds it is made up of roughly one million, million cells. By way of illustration, that is roughly all the stars in all the galaxies of the universe. The total length of 'wiring' between the neurons is roughly about sixty-five thousand miles."

John Abbott, *The 21st Century Learning Initiative*

▲ JOURNAL TOPIC

The chapter points out that language does not merely assign meaning to perceptions, but that it also influences them. Describe a book, movie, or a conversation that has seriously influenced your own perception of the value of a college education.

▲ PORTFOLIO PAPER

Language and perception are intermingled; they influence one another in very complex ways. Feminists point out that when we use the terms "him," "he," and "man" when we are referring to both men and women, we are establishing the man as the standard gender—the real person—and the woman as a subsidiary gender—a less real, secondary person. Feminists recommend that we avoid using masculine terms when we refer to human beings, and suggest we use more universal terms instead, such as "person," "him or her," "she or he," and "humanity." Some critics claim that such changes are unimportant and clumsy. What do you think? Why?

CHAPTER TWO

A CLOSER LOOK AT CRITICAL THINKING

In the first chapter, critical thinking was defined as a particular type of thinking that makes use of other types of thinking to review, evaluate, and revise the way ideas have been understood, processed, and communicated. We use critical thinking when we need to improve the way things are being done, when we need to correct mistakes, and when we need to solve problems. We also noted that critical thinking makes use of verbal and logical thinking, as well as intuitive thinking.

If we were to classify the different types of thinking, we could simply list each one in descending alphabetical order:

Types of Thinking

- Verbal Thinking
- Spatial Thinking
- Scientific Thinking
- Mathematical Thinking
- Logical Thinking
- Kinesthetic Thinking
- Intuitive Thinking
- Critical Thinking

AFTER STUDYING CHAPTER 2

You should be able to describe the similarities and differences between the two major studies of critical thinking—Bloom's *Taxonomy* and the *Delphi Report*. You should be able to write a detailed essay describing the distinction between skills and attitudes made by both reports. Finally, you should be able to prepare an essay to describe each of the Seven Ideal Standards derived from the reports.

However, we would have a more informative classification if we categorized the types of thinking in relation to common characteristics. For example, they can be listed according to those types that require the use of words or symbols and those that do not:

Types of Thinking

Use Words and Symbols

- Logical Thinking
- Mathematical Thinking
- Scientific Thinking
- Verbal Thinking
- Critical Thinking

Do Not Use Words and Symbols

- Intuitive Thinking
- Kinesthetic Thinking
- Spatial Thinking
- Critical Thinking

This way of listing the types of thinking is more interesting and more informative than a simple reverse alphabetical list because it distinguishes the types of thinking into two meaningful categories, those that do and those that do not require words and symbols. This categorization has also revealed something quite important about critical thinking. Critical thinking is the *only* type of thinking that belongs in *both* categories. This leads us to wonder if there may be further differences between critical thinking and the others that are as informative and interesting as this one.

It is interesting to note that scientific thinking, mathematical thinking, and logical thinking are characterized by exactness of expression, rigid adherence to proper methodology, and a rigorous search for true descriptions of reality. Verbal thinking is highly flexible, rich in meeting human needs, and is adaptable to a variety of uses. Critical thinking, however, can be as exact, rigid, and rigorous as logical thinking, and yet be as adaptable, rich, and flexible as verbal thinking. Intuitive thinking is a direct, almost instantaneous, often subtle recognition of differences and similarities. Critical thinking also can be direct and subtle. Slight differences in shades of meaning are often intuitively grasped, for example, during a review or evaluation of a piece of writing. An author's attitude, however subtly hidden in the text, can be intuitively detected in a written piece.

We can diagram these relationships (see next page). As the diagram shows, critical thinking shares important characteristics with other types of thinking. Of course, this is not to say that the other types of thinking do not share characteristics with each other. As discussed in Chapter 1, scientific and mathematical thinking make use of natural languages (verbal thinking). Verbal thinking, since it is so rich, can be as subtle as intuition and as rigorous as science.[1] Yet, critical thinking alone engages in review, evaluation, and revision. This means that it is a special type of thinking, one that stands apart from the others. Unlike the other

---

1. Spatial thinking and kinesthetic thinking have been left out of the discussion because neither shares obvious characteristics with the other types of thinking to the degree that would be instructive. However, both spatial and kinesthetic thinking are related to the other types in important ways. Howard Gardener's book, *Multiple Intelligences*, provides a very interesting discussion of this topic, which cannot be developed here.

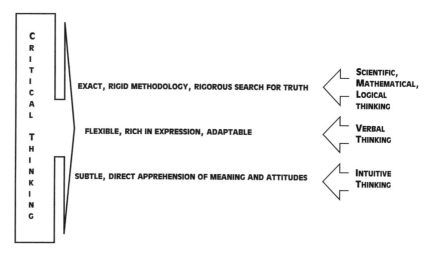

types of thinking, which can be said to *have* ideas, critical thinking *manages* ideas. Its primary function is not to generate ideas but to review, evaluate, and revise what is understood, processed, and communicated by the other types of thinking.

We can understand the special role critical thinking plays by considering an analogy with the data processing system used by libraries. The library is full of ideas—in books, journals, videotapes, and so on—all organized by the data processing system of the library's computer. The computer doesn't have any ideas of its own, but organizes and "manages" the ideas contained in the books, journals, and videotapes. Similarly, critical thinking manages the ideas of the other types of thinking by reviewing, evaluating, and revising them.

There are two major studies of critical thinking. The *Taxonomy of Educational Objectives* was published in 1956 that we will call "Bloom's *Taxonomy*."[2] The more recent 1990 study, *Critical Thinking: A Statement of Expert Consensus for Purposes of Educational Assessment and Instruction*,[3] is called "the *Delphi Report*." Both studies conclude that critical thinking involves the management, or conscious control, of ideas. We will discuss each of the studies in some detail, starting with Bloom's *Taxonomy*.

BLOOM'S *TAXONOMY*

Benjamin S. Bloom was the chairperson of a committee of college professors who, in the early 1950s, set out to describe the proper goals of education in the United States, including details on the sort of thinking skills that should be emphasized in American education. The result of the study was a "taxonomy," a system of classification borrowed from biology. Bloom's *Taxonomy* classified critical thinking into two major categories: "the cognitive domain" and "the affective domain."

---

2. Benjamin S. Bloom ed., *Taxonomy of Educational Objectives* (1956).
3. Peter Facione, *Critical Thinking: A Statement of Expert Consensus for Purposes of Educational Assessment and Instruction.* Executive Summary, the *Delphi Report* (1990).

Particular skills are included in the first domain, or classification. The affective domain consists of "attitudes" that are believed to be worthwhile in developing and maintaining the skills described in the first domain.

THE COGNITIVE DOMAIN

Bloom's *Taxonomy* provides a classification of "lower" and "higher" elements of thinking. As with all taxonomies, it is hierarchical: that is, it has a format in which elements are organized in terms of complexity. Bloom's *Taxonomy* organizes the elements of thinking in descending order, with the simplest element of thinking (knowledge) listed first and the more complex sorts of thinking listed below. In the cognitive domain, summarized on the following page, knowledge and all the other primary elements of thinking are themselves divided into subelements, which are also arranged in a hierarchical order, with "specifics" at the top of the hierarchy (least complex knowledge) and "theories and structures" on the bottom. Thus, the least complex level of thinking, knowledge, is sequenced from knowledge of specifics to terminology, or giving names to specific experiences, then to facts or knowing the meaning of the terminology, then to conventions, rules by which facts are related in a discipline, then to trends, categories, principles, and finally to theories and structures. According to the taxonomy, we "think" in different levels of complexity. Thus, if we only memorize a name for a specific experience, we are engaged in a lower level of thinking than if we know what the name means. We go up a step in our thinking when we organize specifics in a pattern. Finally, we have the highest degree of knowledge possible when we understand the theories that form the basis of the patterns of organization. The taxonomy of knowledge is a way of describing the transitions involved from the simplest sort of thinking (specific experience) to the most complex (theories and structures).

The taxonomy of knowledge is helpful in examining details about thinking. Certainly, it is true that we are involved in a more complex sort of thinking if we are gathering knowledge about theories than if we are gathering knowledge about terms. For example, we are thinking in a more complex way when we discuss the *theories* involved with how the brain operates in perceiving sense data than we are when we are simply memorizing the terms "selection," "organization," and "interpretation." The taxonomy of knowledge is also useful to us in that it describes the ways we can judge the depth of our knowledge. That is, we should not be satisfied with simply knowing how ideas are classified; we should try to understand the principles and generalizations (the theories) by which those classifications are created.

Bloom's *Taxonomy* gives us a list of the simplest ways of knowing to the most complex ways. The list begins with twelve sorts of knowledge that can be memorized, and continues with comprehension, application, analysis, synthesis, and evaluation, all of which require progressively more effort and provide more depth of understanding.

Bloom's *Taxonomy*
The Cognitive Domain

   I. Knowledge

       1 Knowledge of Specifics

    2 Knowledge of Terminology

    3 Knowledge of Specific Facts

    4 Knowledge of Ways and Means of Dealing with Specifics

    5 Knowledge of Conventions

    6 Knowledge of Trends and Sequences

    7 Knowledge of Classifications and Categories

    8 Knowledge of Criteria

    9 Knowledge of Methodology

    10 Knowledge of the Universals and Abstractions in a Field

    11 Knowledge of Principles and Generalizations

    12 Knowledge of Theories and Structures

II. Comprehension

    1 Translation

    2 Interpretation

    3 Extrapolation

III. Application of Abstractions, in Particular and Concrete Situations

    1 Abstractions may be in the form of general ideas, rules of procedures, or generalized methods.

    2 Abstractions that are technological principles, ideas, and theories that must be remembered and applied.

IV. Analysis

    1 Analysis of Elements

    2 Analysis of Relationships

    3 Analysis of Organizational Principles

V. Synthesis

    1 Production of a Unique Communication

    2 Production of a Plan, or Proposed Set of Operations

    3 Derivation of a Set of Abstract Relations

VI. Evaluation

    1 Judgments in Terms of Internal Evidence

    2 Judgments in Terms of External Criteria

By the general term *knowledge,* Bloom's *Taxonomy* refers to the sort of thinking involved with memorization. The taxonomy refers to knowledge as "lower-order" thinking to distinguish it from the "higher-order" thinking that involves analysis, synthesis, and evaluation. Comprehension and application are also classified as "lower-order" thinking skills. We comprehend when we can recite material we have memorized with the help of mnemonic devices. We can go beyond what we have memorized and interpret it in simple ways. *Comprehension* is a step up the hierarchy from mere memory; when we comprehend we grasp all the details of what we remember in a whole. Comprehension is a gestalt of what we have memorized.

Application, too, is regarded as a lower thinking skill by the taxonomy. Application is the use of abstract ideas in concrete situations. In mathematics, for example, we apply the formula for the area of a rectangle (Area = Length × Width) when we solve a given problem (Find the area of a rectangular lot having length 90 meters and width 50 meters) by use of the formula (4500 square meters = 90 meters × 50 meters). Since application involves using memorized ideas, such as mathematical formulas, it is not, according to *Bloom's Taxonomy*, higher-order thinking.

Higher-order thinking has come to be thought of as critical thinking by many people. According to Bloom's *Taxonomy*, higher-order thinking involves analysis, synthesis, and evaluation. The primary distinction between higher- and lower-order thinking is that whereas lower-order thinking involves memorization, simple understanding, and use of passively accepted information, higher-order thinking involves a more active, more creative processing of information into relatively original ideas.

Analysis clarifies ideas, summaries, and explanations by dividing them into their most important parts or most simple elements. Analysis is the sort of thinking that breaks down ideas into their important elements, relationships, and organizational principles. Bloom's *Taxonomy* regards analysis as the first, least complex, step in critical or higher-order thinking.

Certainly, analysis is essential in reviewing our own and others' thinking. We need to divide the ideas under review into their constituent parts so that we can assess each part for accuracy and coherence. For example, whenever we review a "first draft" of a written assignment, we break up the essay into paragraphs and sentences. We even analyze what we have written into individual terms, which we will proceed to check for appropriate usage and correct spelling. When we analyze a cartoon we have created, we divide it into its various components. Analysis is an essential aspect of *review of thinking*, and as such it is a constituent part of critical thinking.

The next step in the taxonomy's hierarchy of higher-order thinking is synthesis. *Syntheses* are defined by the taxonomy as "productions of unique communications." A synthesis is a combination of parts that form a creative whole. Synthesis has an element of creativity; it requires the generation of a new idea out of two or more old ones. According to Bloom's *Taxonomy*, whenever we *revise* a piece of writing, we synthesize because we make use of ideas from another source to improve the original.

Evaluation, the most exalted of higher-order thinking, consists of making judgments about quality. All judgments of quality are evaluations of whether something is good, bad, better, worse, best, or worst. In order to make such a judgment, we need to have standards. Standards are ideals, rules, or principles used to establish quality. According to the taxonomy, standards are either internal evidence—principles or rules established by the discipline itself—or external criteria, principles borrowed from another discipline. For example, a history professor could evaluate an essay describing the major causes of the Great Depression by judging the accuracy of the essay in relation to accepted authoritative historical studies of the event. This would be an evaluation based on internal evidence because the standard of evaluation used to determine the essay's accuracy comes from within the discipline. The professor would be using the higher-order thinking skill of evaluation in correcting the paper's historical accuracy. However, when the professor corrects the paper for its quality of composition, she would be evaluating it in terms of external criteria. Grammarians, not historians, establish the standards of good composition. She would be using criteria—standards of quality—from outside her discipline to evaluate the essay.

Since it is a hierarchy, Bloom's *Taxonomy* stresses that before we can reach the higher-order levels of analysis, synthesis, and evaluation, we need to first establish the skills of knowledge, comprehension, and application. The taxonomy emphasizes that higher-order thinking can be accomplished only *after* the lower order skills are put to use.

THE AFFECTIVE DOMAIN

Five "attitudinal dispositions" about critical thinking are listed in the taxonomy's "affective domain" of higher-order thinking. They can be summarized as follows.

1. Deliberate examination of controversial issues with a view to forming opinions about them.
2. Faith in the use of reasonable discussion of tentative beliefs.
3. Evaluation of public policies on the standard of what is good for the whole of society rather than on the basis of narrow and specialized interests.
4. Willingness to revise judgments and change behaviors in the light of evidence.
5. Judgment of problems and issues in terms of the situations, issues, and consequences involved rather than in terms of rigid rules or wishful thinking.

The disposition of higher-order thinking that Bloom's *Taxonomy* describes is a list of the attitudes the committee believed to be important in carrying out analysis, synthesis, and evaluation. Attitudes about thinking are tendencies, motivations, and ways people have of approaching particular ideas. Critical thinking, or in the terminology of Bloom's *Taxonomy*, higher-order thinking, involves the *whole person*. The attitudes involved with critical thinking are at least as important as the skills involved with it. Bloom's *Taxonomy*, one of the earliest statements on critical thinking, makes it clear that critical thinking is not a mechanical, robotic activity, but a human endeavor. Attitude, an emotional component, is essential to critical thinking. However, it must be pointed out that Bloom's *Taxonomy* does not provide an extended analysis of the affective domain. It simply lists the elements, and provides a brief, rather superficial description of each element.

CRITIQUES OF BLOOM'S *TAXONOMY*

Several critical thinking theorists have criticized Bloom's *Taxonomy* in recent years. Richard Paul claims that the taxonomy is too linear and too rigid. Paul points out that it is easy to be misled by the seemingly cut-and-dried listing of skills in the cognitive domain. In reality, there is a mix of understanding and evaluation in critical thinking. We need to be more aware of the subtleties involved with critical thinking, Paul says, and understand that "no neat set of recipes can foster critical thinking."[4] Frank Smith believes that Bloom's *Taxonomy* is not accurate in separating the different ways of knowing while knowledge and comprehension almost always take place at the same time. His chief criticism is that the taxonomy is too hierarchical; thinking does not operate in isolated stages. He also maintains that the taxonomy is too simple and rigid to provide a complete and accurate description.[5] Both theorists, however, believe that the taxonomy has been of great use in identifying the characteristics of critical thinking skills and dispositions.

Criticisms aside, Bloom's *Taxonomy* stands as a reliable general description of some major cognitive and dispositional elements of critical thinking. Paul, while criticizing Bloom's *Taxonomy*, nevertheless points out that the taxonomy is "a remarkable tour de force, a ground-breaking work filled with seminal insights into cognitive processes and their interrelations."[6] Indeed, Bloom's *Taxonomy* is the basis of most, if not all, theoretical approaches to critical thinking because of the stress it places on the necessity of *process* in critical, higher-order thinking, as opposed to mere memorization and factual comprehension.

EXERCISES

▲ Most Intriguing Issue

Write a one-paragraph description of the most interesting idea, topic, or process described in the section on Bloom's *Taxonomy*. Be prepared to explain what you find interesting in class discussion.

▲ The Muddiest Point

Write a sentence or, if possible, a paragraph that describes the idea, topic, expression, term, or process in the section on Bloom's *Taxonomy* that you find most difficult to understand.

▲ Cartoons and Diagrams

1. Provide a diagram that shows how Bloom's *Taxonomy* of the cognitive domain would apply to thinking critically about a controversial issue, such as the wisdom of assisted-suicide laws, the existence of intelligent extraterrestrial life, or the constituents of the best college education. In order to keep the diagram as simple as possible, ignore the details in sections I and II, limiting yourself to

---

4. Richard Paul, *Critical Thinking: What Every Person Needs to Survive in a Rapidly Changing World* (1990), p. 423.

5. Frank Smith, *To Think* (1990), p. 141.

6. Paul, *Critical Thinking*, p. 428.

what you consider the four most important elements of "knowledge" and the single most important element of "comprehension" in relation to the issue. Concentrate on the details of IV, V, and VI.

2. Draw a cartoon that shows the differences between knowledge, analysis, synthesis, and evaluation according to Bloom's cognitive domain.
3. Draw a cartoon that shows the differences between any three of the five aspects of Bloom's affective domain.
4. Provide a diagram that shows the hierarchical nature of Bloom's cognitive domain.

▲ Definitions of Key Terms

Provide a definition for each of the following terms as they are used in this chapter. Most of the terms are not defined in the chapter, although their meanings are described by the context in which they appear. You need to review the material (and a dictionary if necessary) to create the definition yourself.

Application	Cognitive Domain	Dispositions
Evaluation	Extrapolation	Hierarchy
Mnemonic Device	Synthesis	Taxonomy

▲ Short Essay Questions

Provide a response of approximately 200 words for each topic. Your responses should be well organized, grammatically correct, and neatly produced.

1. Explain the difference between an analysis of relationships and an analysis of organizational principles.
2. Explain the difference between knowledge and analysis.
3. Explain what "faith in the use of reasonable discussion" means.
4. Explain the difference between passive and active thinking.
5. Describe the difference between Bloom's cognitive and dispositional domains.
6. Describe the character of a person who has all five elements of Bloom's dispositional domain.

▲ Questions for Discussion

1. It is clear that Bloom's description of the cognitive domain is hierarchical. Do you find that the dispositional domain is also a hierarchy? Why or why not?
2. Bloom's *Taxonomy* provides a description of several dispositions involved in critical thinking. Do you feel that you possess all of the dispositions? Only a few? Provide examples of your behavior that explain which ones you have and which ones you don't have.
3. Frank Smith supports his claim that Bloom's *Taxonomy* is not accurate by stating that knowledge and comprehension almost always take place alongside, rather than before, application and evaluation, as the taxonomy's hierarchical structure would imply. Explain what Smith means. Does your own experience in knowing and comprehending support Smith's claim?

4. Examine a course you are currently taking (other than this one). List as many as possible elements of knowledge, comprehension, application, analysis, synthesis, and evaluation that are involved in the course.

5. According to Bloom's *Taxonomy*, memorization of specifics is the lowest element of knowledge, and knowledge of theories and structures is the highest. This claim of Bloom's *Taxonomy* has often been used as support for negative criticism of quizzes and tests that ask students merely to recall specific information without explaining the way the information is organized. Do you believe that such criticism displays a good understanding of Bloom's *Taxonomy*? Do you agree with the criticism? Why or why not?

▲ QUOTATION TO PONDER

> "It is possible to imagine a society or culture which is relatively fixed. Such a society represents a closed system in which it is possible to predict in advance both the kinds of problems individuals will encounter and the solutions which are appropriate to those problems."
>
> Benjamin S. Bloom, *Taxonomy of Educational Objectives. Handbook I: Cognitive Domain* (1956)

▲ JOURNAL TOPIC

> There are several types of hierarchies aside from taxonomies. Hierarchies organize items in ranks, grades, or groups by use of "ladders." Describe a hierarchy you have experienced, aside from Bloom's *Taxonomy*. What are your thoughts on the good and the bad aspects of hierarchical organizations?

THE *DELPHI REPORT*

From 1987 to 1989 a committee of forty-six higher education professionals, under the direction of Peter A. Facione, Dean of the College of Arts and Sciences of Santa Clara University, researched the topic "critical thinking" using the "Delphi Method." The "Delphi Method" is a research model that requires the formation of a committee of experts willing to share their knowledge and work toward a consensus opinion. The committee that studied critical thinking was made up of scholars from the disciplines of philosophy (52 percent), education (22 percent), social science (20 percent), and physical Science (6 percent).[7] The members responded to questions in a detailed, thoughtful way that reflected their expertise. The responses were discussed thoroughly by everyone. New questions were then provided, and responses were discussed. A total of six rounds of questions, responses, and discussions went into the project. The result of the two-year study was a report that stated the committee's consensus on the proper definition of critical thinking, along with descriptions of the skills and dispositions involved in critical thinking. A *consensus,* unlike a compromise, is a general conclusion arrived at by discussion with which everyone agrees. A *compromise* is a settlement, usually established by a vote, in which each participant

7. Facione, *Critical Thinking*, p. 3.

gives something in order to gain. The Delphi committee came to a consensus on their definition of critical thinking; that is, all of them agreed that their definition is the best definition of critical thinking. The definition truly has the appearance of a definition written by a committee; it is quite lengthy and more specific than most people would find necessary. However, it is a complete and thorough definition, worthy of our analysis.

> Critical thinking is purposeful, self-regulatory judgment that results in interpretation, analysis, evaluation, and inference, as well as explanation of the evidential, conceptual, methodological, criteriological, or contextual considerations upon which that judgment is based. . . . The ideal critical thinker is habitually inquisitive, well-informed, trustful of reason, open-minded, flexible, fair-minded in evaluation, honest in facing personal biases, prudent in making judgments, willing to reconsider, clear about issues, orderly in complex matters, diligent in seeking relevant information, reasonable in the selection of criteria, focused in inquiry, and persistent in seeking results that are as precise as the subject and circumstances of the inquiry permit.[8]

THE COGNITIVE SKILLS AND SUBSKILLS

The definition identifies "skills" and "dispositions" that the committee felt were essential to critical thinking. An analysis of both groups was provided in the report. The list of cognitive skills, including subskills, specific examples of the general skills follows:

Delphi Report
Cognitive Skills and Subskills

Skills	*Subskills*
Interpretation	Categorization
	Decoding significance
	Clarifying meaning
Analysis	Examining ideas
	Identifying arguments
	Analyzing arguments
Evaluation	Assessing claims
	Assessing arguments
Inference	Querying evidence
	Conjecturing alternatives
	Drawing conclusions
Explanation	Stating results
	Justifying procedures
	Presenting arguments
Self-Regulation	Self-examination
	Self-correction

---

8. Fascione, *Critical Thinking*, p. 2.

The *Delphi Report* and Bloom's *Taxonomy* on the Cognitive Dimension

The *Delphi Report*'s list of skills has some similarities with the description of the cognitive domain in Bloom's *Taxonomy*. For example, analysis and evaluation are included on both lists. "Inference" on the Delphi list seems to be similar to "application" on the Bloom list. *Delphi*'s "explanation" has striking similarities with Bloom's "synthesis." The differences between the lists are more interesting than the similarities, though. Bloom does not include "self-regulation" among the higher-order skills, and "interpretation" on the *Delphi* list seems to be regarded as "knowledge" and "comprehension" (lower-order cognitive skills) in Bloom's *Taxonomy*.

However, the most striking difference between the two studies is that the *Delphi* list of cognitive skills is *not* a taxonomy; it is not a hierarchy of skills, but rather a mere list. There is no claim in the *Delphi Report* that we need to have "knowledge" *before* we can be said to engage in critical thinking. In fact, the *Delphi* committee does not regard critical thinking as being separable from knowledge: "Although the identification and analysis of critical thinking skills transcend, in significant ways, specific subjects or disciplines, learning and applying these skills in many contexts requires domain-specific knowledge."[9]

The differences between Bloom's *Taxonomy* and the *Delphi* list reveal a change in what theorists thought about the nature of critical thinking between 1956 and 1990. Critical thinking was believed to be a "set of skills" at the time of Bloom's *Taxonomy*; once a person learned these skills they could "use" them. Bloom's *Taxonomy* seems to imply that critical thinking is a supplement to and an improvement in thinking. Critical thinking is not regarded as *rethinking*, as *reviewing, evaluating,* and *revising* different sorts of thinking, but as a *replacement* for all other types of thinking.

Chapter 1 pointed out that thinking (understanding, processing, and communicating) occurs in at least seven different ways. We think intuitively, mathematically, and scientifically, for example, in addition to the verbal and logical thinking that predominates in critical thinking. Bloom's *Taxonomy* implies, because it is a hierarchy, that thinking verbally and logically is by its very nature *better* than every other sort of thinking. The taxonomy encourages us to regard critical thinking as the *best* thinking; the sort of thinking that should replace every other sort of thinking.

The *Delphi Report*, on the other hand, does not describe critical thinking as a replacement for other sorts of thinking. Nor does it regard critical thinking as the best or only type of thinking.

> Not every useful cognitive process should be thought of as critical thinking. Not every valuable thinking skill is a critical thinking skill. Critical thinking is one among a family of closely related forms of higher-order thinking, along with, for example, problem solving, decision making, and creative thinking.[10]

---

9. Facione, *Critical Thinking*, p. 5.
10. Facione, *Critical Thinking*, p. 6.

The *Delphi Report* describes the cognitive dimension of critical thinking as a group of six skills, all of which are of equal importance in making judgments about the quality of thought. Critical thinking is one of the higher-order types of thinking, along with problem solving, decision making, and creativity.

THE DISPOSITIONAL DIMENSION: ATTITUDES

The *Delphi Report* describes two sorts of attitudes related to critical thinking. "Critical Thinking Dispositions That Affect Life in General" is a list of practical, day-to-day attitudes and habits of a critical thinker. These are broad descriptions of the sorts of attitudes the committee felt critical thinkers have in family life, in deciding how to vote on political and social issues, in academic study, and in their careers.

"Approaches to Specific Issues, Questions, or Problems" is a more specific list of attitudes that critical thinkers have when working on problems.[11]

Critical Thinking Dispositions That Affect Life in General

- Inquisitiveness with regard to a large range of issues.
- Concern to become and remain well informed.
- Alert to opportunities to think critically.
- Trust in the processes of reasoned inquiry.
- Self-confidence in one's ability to reason.
- Open-mindedness regarding different world views.
- Flexibility in considering alternatives and opinions.
- Understanding of the opinions of others.
- Fair-mindedness in appraising reason.
- Honesty in facing one's own biases, prejudices, stereotypes, egocentric or sociocentric tendencies.
- Prudence in suspending, making, or altering judgments.
- Willingness to reconsider and revise views where honest reflection suggests that change is warranted.

Critical Thinking Dispositions That Affect Approaches to Specific Issues, Questions, or Problems

- Clarity in stating the question or concern.
- Orderliness in working with complexity.
- Diligence in seeking relevant information.
- Reasonableness in selecting and applying criteria.
- Care in focusing attention on the concern at hand.
- Persistence though difficulties that are encountered.
- Precision to the degree permitted by the subject and the circumstance.

11. Facione, *Critical Thinking*, p. 15.

Interestingly enough, the committee of scholars who created the *Delphi Report* did not reach a unanimous consensus on the importance of the preceding dispositions to critical thinking. Only 60 percent of the participants believed that the dispositions are an essential aspect of critical thinking. Other members of the committee felt that critical thinking consists *only* of the cognitive skills and sub-skills. The attitudes have little to do with critical thinking, they argued, because the dispositions are characteristics of good critical *thinkers,* not critical *thinking.*[12]

The minority view on the role of attitudes in critical thinking is worthy of our attention. This view claimed that there is a difference between the *activity* of critical thinking and the *people* who partake of the activity. The activity itself, it said, has no emotional element. Only the people who carry out the activity can properly be said to have attitudes. The majority view, on the other hand, did not proclaim that there is no significant difference between the activity and the people who partake of it. Rather, the majority view claimed that the attitudes listed by the report are an essential part of critical thinking itself. The majority believed that these attitudes are equally as important to critical thinking as are the cognitive skills.[13]

As an illustration of the disagreement among the committee members, consider this question: Is a college student merely a person enrolled in an institution of higher learning? Or is a college student a person who attends class regularly, studies with diligence, and who has a commitment to learning? In other words, does being a college student consist only of being enrolled in a college, or is there more to it than that? The question is whether or not being a college student essentially involves attendance, study, and a commitment to learning. In the same way, does critical thinking essentially involve the attitudes listed by the committee?

CONCLUSIONS: THE *DELPHI REPORT* AND BLOOM'S *TAXONOMY*

We have examined the two major studies of critical thinking. What have we discovered?

Both reports agree that critical thinking has two dimensions: the skills, called the cognitive dimension, and the attitudes or feelings, called the dispositional dimension. The *Delphi Report* provides a more detailed and more coherent list of skills than Bloom's *Taxonomy,* and abandons the notion of hierarchy, which seems to be wise. The disagreement among the *Delphi Report*'s committee members with regard to the proper place of attitudes in critical thinking is interesting; but the more astute position seems to have been taken by the majority. After all, the brain (and the person) operates as a *whole.* As was discussed in Chapter 1, the whole person thinks, not just the cerebral cortex.

Both reports also agree that critical thinking is a review, evaluation, and revision of ideas. *Evaluation* is clearly described as central to critical thinking in

---

12. Facione, *Critical Thinking,* p. 14.
13. Facione, *Critical Thinking,* p. 13.

both. Although neither report specifically refers to *review* or *revision*, both discuss these activities using other terminology. Bloom's *Taxonomy* uses the term "analysis" to refer to review. The *Delphi Report* discusses review under the categories of "interpretation," "analysis," and "explanation." Both reports agree that a review interprets, analyzes, and explains the meaning of an idea.

Neither report thoroughly investigates the importance of revision, although both recognize it as essential to critical thinking. Bloom's *Taxonomy* regards synthesis as one of the three higher-order skills. A synthesis is the creation of a new idea from several old ideas. Bloom's *Taxonomy* refers to the new idea as a "unique communication." For example, after researching several articles on good study habits, you combine ideas from each one and write your own article. Your article is a synthesis of the articles you have read. Revision includes a synthesis; the improvement of an idea always results in the production of a "unique communication" after a review of many ideas, not just a review of the idea being revised. However, there is more to revision than synthesis. A revision makes use of an evaluation of each idea that is reviewed in order to produce an *improved* idea. A synthesis is not necessarily an improvement; a revision always improves. If your article were merely a combination of ideas taken from several sources, it would be a synthesis. It would be a revision only if it improved one or more of the ideas.

The *Delphi Report* does not examine revision but includes two dispositions among those "that affect life and living in general" that are important aspects of it. One, "flexibility in considering alternatives and opinions," is an essential attitude for revision. The other, "willingness to reconsider and revise views where honest reflection suggests that change is warranted," is equally important.

Revision requires flexibility and a willingness to reconsider. If we are to improve an idea, we must consider various interpretations of it, and we must be willing to change the way we feel about the idea if we are to change it for the better. For example, when you revise a written assignment, you must be flexible enough to consider ways of approaching the topic that you had not taken when you wrote the first draft. You must also be willing to consider your first draft to be inadequate. People who are inflexible and unwilling to reconsider what they have already done are not going to be able to revise anything! Hence the old saying, "A wise man changes his mind often, a fool never does."[14]

Our examination of Bloom's *Taxonomy* and the *Delphi Report* has given us a detailed picture of critical thinking that goes far beyond a definition. The terms "review," "evaluation," and "revision" have more meaning for us than they did at the conclusion of Chapter 1. In addition, we now understand that critical thinking includes attitudes as well as particular cognitive activities. Our next task will be to examine the standards of critical thinking.

---

14. Perhaps we should show some flexibility and willingness to reconsider! Let's revise this *old* saying to: "A wise person's mind is often changed, but a fool's never is." This seems to be an improvement in regard to its exclusive attitude regarding gender.

EXERCISES

▲ Most Intriguing Issue

Write a one-paragraph description of the most interesting idea, topic, or process described in pages 42–47. Be prepared to explain what you find interesting in class discussion.

▲ The Muddiest Point

Write a sentence or, if possible, a paragraph, that describes the idea, topic, expression, term, or process in pages 42–47 that you find most difficult to understand.

▲ Cartoons and Diagrams

1. Provide a logo for the cover of the *Delphi Report* that emphasizes its most important ideas.
2. Draw a cartoon that clarifies four of the "dispositions that effect life and living in general" listed in the *Delphi Report*.
3. Draw a cartoon that shows the difference between a consensus and a compromise.
4. Draw a cartoon that illustrates the meaning of "inference."
5. Draw a cartoon that illustrates the meaning of "self-regulation."

▲ Definitions of Key Terms

Provide a definition for each of the following terms as they are used in this chapter. Most of the terms are not defined in the chapter, although their meanings are described by the context in which they appear. You need to review the material (and a dictionary if necessary) to create the definition yourself.

Compromise	Consensus	Evaluation
Explanation	Inference	Interpretation
Persistence	Prudence	Self-examination

▲ Short Essay Questions

Provide a written response of approximately 200 words for each topic. Your responses should be well organized, grammatically correct, and neatly produced.

1. Explain the purpose of the *Delphi Report*.
2. Summarize the methodology of the *Delphi Report*.
3. Aside from the fact that one is a hierarchy and the other is not, what strikes you as the most important difference between Bloom's *Taxonomy* and the *Delphi Report*?
4. What strikes you as the most important similarity in the description of dispositions in Bloom's *Taxonomy* and the *Delphi Report*?

5. What does this sentence from the *Delphi Report* mean: "Although the identification and analysis of critical thinking skills transcend, in significant ways, specific subjects or disciplines, learning and applying these skills in many contexts requires domain-specific knowledge."

▲ QUESTIONS FOR DISCUSSION

Provide a written essay of 300–500 words that responds to each of the following questions which ask for your opinion. You should respond by stating it, and by providing thoughts, examples, and insights that support it. You should be willing to revise your response; you may change your opinion during or after a class discussion.

1. Both reports discussed in the chapter are *committee reports.* As such, they have strengths and weaknesses. What are some important strengths and weaknesses of committee reports in general?

2. Do you agree with the committee that the *Delphi Report's* division of dispositions into two categories is a good idea? Why or why not?

3. What are your thoughts on the question concerning the role of dispositions in critical thinking? Why do you suppose the committee made a distinction between *critical thinkers* (who have dispositions) and *critical thinking* (which is only a set of skills)?

4. Analyze and then explain the meaning of the *Delphi Report's* definition of critical thinking.

5. The chapter discusses several similarities and differences found in the *Delphi Report* and Bloom's *Taxonomy.* Analyze the summaries of the reports in the chapter and point out other important similarities and differences.

▲ QUOTATION TO PONDER

"There is a critical spirit, a probing inquisitiveness, a keenness of mind, a zealous dedication to reason, and a hunger or eagerness for reliable information which good critical thinkers possess but weak critical thinkers do not seem to have. As water strengthens a thirsty plant, the affective dispositions are necessary for the critical thinking skills identified to take root and to flourish in students."

Peter A. Facione, *Delphi Report* (1990)

▲ JOURNAL TOPIC

Committee reports have had, and continue to have, a strong role in our society. Briefly describe at least three important committee reports with which you are familiar aside from Bloom's *Taxonomy* and the *Delphi Report.*

STANDARDS OF QUALITY AND QUANTITY

Quality refers to how good or bad something is. The quality of a rose, for example, is judged by how closely it approximates a "perfect" rose in shape, fragrance, and color. It is very important to notice the distinction between quality and quantity. Quantity refers to size and its measurement. Quantity is judged by applying measuring instruments such as scales and rulers to things. These instruments provide us with conventional "standards of quantitative measurement." They are conventional because people around the world have agreed, or come to a consensus, on which standards of measurement to use. Most of the world uses the metric system to measure quantity: meters, grams, and liters, for example, to measure the quantity of length, weight, and liquid volume, respectively. In the United States, we use inches, ounces, and quarts to measure the same things. Quantitative measurement makes use of numbers by which to differentiate amounts. We can be very precise in measuring quantity; all we need is a precision instrument by which to determine the length, the weight, and so on, of a given object. We can use mathematics to estimate quantities that cannot be measured directly. For example, we cannot directly measure the length of distance from the earth to the sun, but we can estimate how far it is by using mathematics.[15] Scientific thinking and mathematical thinking are concerned exclusively with quantity.

The instruments used in scientific thinking are very precise, and the mathematics that is used to interpret and think about scientific measurements is quite complex, of course. However, we can best appreciate the nature of quantitative measurement by taking a quick look at a very simple instrument: the ruler.

A ruler is a piece of plastic (sometimes wood) that has been printed with at least twelve lines, usually more. Each of these twelve lines is one inch apart. Simple enough. However, how do the manufacturers of rulers know where to print those twelve marks? Well, they most likely use another ruler! But what about *that* ruler? How does the manufacturer know that the ruler being used to measure the places the lines are to be printed is accurate? Is there a "standard ruler" somewhere, a ruler that is exactly twelve inches long, and that has exactly one inch between each of its twelve lines? Of course there is. It is in Washington, D. C. and is kept in a vacuum-sealed jar. It is made of platinum. It is the "ideal ruler," the standard ruler that all others must "measure up to" in order to be quantitatively reliable.

At some time in history, people gathered together and came to a consensus about the length of an inch. That consensual, agreed-upon unit is now used to measure length in the United States. It is important to notice that quantitative measurement requires a *standard*. In order to make a judgment concerning quantity, it is necessary to have a standard, an ideal instrument, by which to make that measurement.

We also need standards in order to measure quality, which is not a measurement of "how much" or "how long" but of "how good" and "how bad" something is. Notice that instruments that measure quantity cannot measure degrees of good or bad. For example, we can quantitatively measure a rose's weight or length, the width of its leaves and petals, and so on. However, the

15. Astronomers calculate that the sun is approximately ninety-three million miles from the Earth.

question concerning "how good" the rose is can only be evaluated qualitatively. How is this accomplished? How can we make a judgment that the rose is a good one or a bad one? Is it simply a matter of opinion? In a way it is. Imagine that we are attending a rose show; there are hundreds of roses on display, and to the casual observer, they are all beautiful and of high quality. However, only a few of them have been awarded ribbons. Some have red, yellow, or blue ribbons, all of which were awarded by judges. In the judges' opinions, some roses are of better quality than others are. And one rose is the "best of the show." The judges use a standard of qualitative measurement in evaluating the roses. Each rose is judged on the basis of how well it compares with an ideal perfect rose. Rose lovers around the world have come to a consensus, an agreement, about the characteristics of good and bad roses. This agreement is not all that different from the sort of agreement scientists have made with regard to their standards of quantitative measurement.[16] Any judgment or evaluation, whether qualitative or quantitative, must be based upon a standard. If there is no standard, then we are left with a mere unsubstantiated opinion. Let's look at a few more illustrations.

There is a story told of a man who complained about a mouse in his soup. The waiter asked, "how big a mouse?" The man responded, "too big!" "Oh, come on, now," said the waiter, "how much soup can a little mouse eat?" Without a standard of quantitative measurement, the size of the mouse is a mere matter of unsubstantiated opinion. In the opinion of the customer, the mouse was "too big" and in the opinion of the waiter, the mouse was "small."

Another story: Two students were discussing their teachers. "Ms. Billingsgate is a horrible teacher," said Charles. "No she's not!" said Heather. "She's the best teacher I've ever had!" "She's horrid! She's the worst teacher I've ever had!" Charles exclaimed. "She's wonderful!" Heather retorted. The discussion turned into a dispute. "Give me one example of something wonderful that she's done," shouted Charles. "Give me one example of something horrid that she's done," Heather shouted back. "She makes us write term papers!" screamed Charles. "But that's why she's so wonderful," Heather yelled back. Without a qualitative standard of the importance of assigning term papers in determining what makes a good or bad teacher, Charles and Heather are merely exchanging unsubstantiated opinions.

Students are quite familiar with qualitative standards: grades. Grades only "mean something" if they are based on clearly determined qualitative standards. If a teacher assigns grades to students merely on the basis of his or her unsubstantiated opinion, the students have a reason to be unhappy. In this case, their grades, which are regarded by many people (potential employers, parents, and classmates) as the primary indicator of their academic performance, are assigned

---

16. Of course, there are some important differences, the most important of which is that scientific and mathematical thinking demand exact, rigid, and rigorous quantification standards. Qualitative standards, on the other hand, are more verbal and intuitive; thus they are more adaptable, richer, and more flexible.

without any qualitative standard. The grades are assigned in an arbitrary and capricious way.

STANDARDS AS IDEAL MODELS

Neither quantity nor quality can be judged or evaluated without standards. However, standards are not "discovered" by experience. They are ideals rather than things—ideas about perfection. An *ideal* bowl of soup is an idea of the perfect bowl of soup. An *ideal* teacher is an idea of the perfect teacher. Ideals are not real; they are imaginary ideas, which serve as goals, as inspirational depictions of perfection. Since standards are ideals, they need to be developed conceptually by people who have experience and expertise in whatever area to which the standard is applied. Roses are judged by how closely they approximate the standard "ideal rose." Teachers are judged by how closely they attain the level of performance achieved by an "ideal teacher." A grade of "A" is earned by an academic performance that approaches the "ideal." Standards of thought are qualitative ideals of "good thinking."

Bloom's *Taxonomy* and the *Delphi Report* both describe evaluation as one of the major tasks of critical thinking. Both acknowledge that evaluation is always done by the application of standards. However, neither report explicitly provides us with the standards we need in order to carry out an evaluation of the quality of thought. In order to develop those standards, we need to investigate the ideas of people who have experience and expertise in evaluating thought. Philosophers such as Aristotle, John Dewey, and Jürgen Habermas seem to agree about the sorts of standards we should use. Critical thinking theorists also provide advice. Robert Ennis, Blythe McVicker Clinchy, and Richard Paul, to name a few, are helpful in developing standards by which we evaluate thought.[17]

We sometimes hesitate to judge thinking; we feel that every person has a right to his or her own thoughts. Who are we to judge them? Critical thinking, however, does not judge *people*. Critical thinking judges *the quality of thinking*. There is a great deal of difference between the two! A person is worth our respect regardless of his or her quality of thinking. A "good person" can "think poorly," just as a "bad person" can "think well." Critical thinking evaluates (judges) the quality of thinking according to the standards of good thinking; it does not judge the quality of people!

---

17. Aristotle's classical work in developing standards of good thinking is found throughout his writings, but especially in "The Prior Analytics." John Dewey's *Logic, The Theory of Inquiry* (1938) and Jürgun Habermas, *Moral Consciousness and Communicative Action* (1993) are very helpful with regard to attitudinal standards. Richard Paul, *Critical Thinking: What Every Person Needs to Survive in a Rapidly Changing World* (1990), Blythe McVicker Clinchy, "On Critical Thinking and Connected Knowing" (1994), and Robert H. Ennis, "A Concept of Critical Thinking" (1962) are among the many important theoretical publications in critical thinking standards.

THE SEVEN STANDARDS OF GOOD THINKING

When we judge the quality of thinking, we must have some clear standards in mind regarding what we expect in good thinking. When we think critically, we review thinking with the standards in mind; if the thinking comes close to meeting our ideal expectations, we evaluate it as better thinking than that which does not come as close.

For centuries, philosophers and other authorities on the quality of thinking have agreed that thinking is best when it is *clear, accurate, specific*, and *significant*. Thinking that lacks these characteristics has been evaluated as being in need of revision. When thinking is not clear, it does not communicate well. When it is not accurate, it is incorrect. Thinking that lacks specificity is vague. When it is not significant, thinking is trivial. It makes a great deal of sense to agree with the traditional philosophical view that clear, accurate, specific, and significant thinking is *better* than thinking that does not communicate, is vague, incorrect, and trivial. Thinking is at its best when it understands, processes, and communicates ideas as clearly, accurately, specifically, and significantly as possible. The first four standards apply to what Bloom's *Taxonomy* and the *Delphi Report* call the cognitive domain. The last three are standards of the quality of the dispositions or attitudes of the thinker.

Attitudes about thinking are tendencies, motivations, and ways of approaching particular ideas. The last three standards apply to the "dispositional domain," which is recognized by both reports as essential in all thinking.

As was just mentioned, critical thinking judges the quality of thought rather than of the thinker. Perhaps the *Delphi* committee members who did not agree that attitudes should be included in a description of critical thinking had a point. Attitudes are possibly not characteristics of thinking, but of thinkers, and they did not want to judge the quality of people, but only of ideas. However, the *attitudes* people have are often detrimental to the quality of their thinking.

Controlled observations made by cognitive psychologists conclude that poor attitudes are actually more responsible for poor thinking than lack of information or lack of adequate thinking ability. According to these studies, seventy-five percent of the time when people score poorly on tests, are unsuccessful in solving problems, or fail to complete puzzles, they also display attitudes of lethargy and impatience. They are not persistent, and they seek immediate gratification.[18] A recent analysis of the thinking of many American politicians, journalists, and others concludes that their aggressive attitude of "ritualized devotion to criticism . . . and to destroying the opposition" seriously oversimplifies and misstates the complex problems the country faces.[19]

There is a difference between a person and his or her attitude about the thinking that he or she is doing. Critical thinking does not criticize people.

---

18. Delores Gallo, "Educating for Empathy, Reason, and Imagination," in *Re-thinking Reason: New Perspectives in Critical Thinking* (1994), p. 52.

19. Deborah Tannen, *The Argument Culture* (1998), p. 129.

However, in order for us to evaluate thinking completely, we need to judge the attitudes involved.

Critical thinking's expectations with regard to attitudes are that thinking should be *sincere in seeking the truth,* that it should *respect others,* and that it should *seek consensus.* Attitudes that lack these characteristics attempt to deceive, to demean, and to coerce others to agree by use of psychological or physical force. Thinking that is sincere, respectful, and seeks consensus communicates, processes, and understands ideas better than thinking that lacks these three attitudes. Deceptive, demeaning, and coercive attitudes usually result in thought that communicates poorly, is inaccurate, vague, and trivial. Here then are the standards of good thinking:

1. **Clarity**

   All thinking should be clear. That is, thinking needs to *communicate* well. Everyone involved with or affected by the ideas in question should be able to understand them. Vagueness, ambiguity, and logical and verbal incoherence should be avoided.

2. **Accuracy**

   All thinking should be accurate. Claims need to be supported by adequate evidence from appropriate disciplines, especially the natural and social sciences. Any lack of consensus by authorities should be clarified. Biased statements should be avoided.

3. **Specificity**

   All thinking should be specific. Definitions, descriptions, and explanations should be detailed and precise. Overgeneralizations and unwarranted assumptions should be avoided.

4. **Significance**

   Evidence and information provided as support for beliefs should be meaningful and should consider the complexity of the subject matter. Triviality, oversimplification, and irrelevancies should be avoided.

5. **Sincerity**

   Thinking should be motivated by a sincere attempt to discover the truth. We should struggle to discover the truth in spite of difficulties and obstacles. Deception attempts to exaggerate the evidence for one's own point of view and to understate the evidence for contrary positions should be avoided.

6. **Respect**

   Respect is the attitude of judging others' ideas, beliefs, and values by the same standards we use to evaluate our own, regardless of any advantages or disadvantages that may come to us. Biases in favor of or against gender, ethnicity, religion, race, age, and political persuasion should be avoided.

7. **Commitment to consensus**

   All thinking should have the attitude that a true, worthwhile idea, once it is well explained, and well understood, will be agreed upon by everyone.

Ideas that are understood and not agreed to are in need of revision. Force, either physical or psychological, should be avoided.

Each of these seven standards is an *ideal*. No act of thinking could possibly achieve any of them with perfection. Furthermore, different degrees of expectation apply in different contexts. We should not expect an elementary school student's speech on wolves to be as clear, accurate, specific, and significant as a graduate student's zoological report on the endangered status of the wolf. Standards are expectations relative to the purpose of the thinking and ideas being evaluated. Nevertheless, when we judge the quality of thought, no matter what the context, critical thinking determines how good or bad the thinking is by applying the ideals of clarity, accuracy, specificity, significance, sincerity, respect, and commitment to consensus.

EVALUATING THOUGHT

Critical thinking is composed of three elements: review, evaluation, and revision. The standards of verbal thinking are used to evaluate individual acts of thinking, such as a piece of writing. However, before we evaluate a piece of writing—an editorial in the newspaper, for example—we must first make sure that we understand it. Understanding is achieved by review; to review a piece of writing is to read it carefully enough to be able to define the terms it uses, to summarize and paraphrase its meaning, and to explain its ideas. A good critical thinking review also requires a close look at the quality and quantity of evidence used in the piece as well as an empathetic appreciation of the purpose of the piece. All of these aspects of review—definitions, summarizing, paraphrasing, explanation, evidence, and empathy—will be discussed in other chapters.

The goal of such an evaluation is the third element of critical thinking: revision of the piece. Revision usually consists of specific descriptions of improvements that can be made. An improvement, of course, is a change in the piece that brings it closer to the ideal standards. A piece that has trivial elements, for example, needs to be changed into a more serious, more significant one. One that is unfairly critical needs to be revised so that it is more respectful of opposing views.

It is important to remember that evaluation, the heart of critical thinking, always comes after review. Clearly, it would be inappropriate to attempt to measure the quantity of something we had not thoroughly examined. Imagine trying to measure the distance between the Earth and the Sun without knowing where either celestial body was located at the time of measurement! Or imagine someone attempting to measure the weight of a snipe, but not knowing what a snipe is! How would they find one? It is impossible to measure something if we do not know the location or the identity of what we are being asked to measure. In the same way, it is impossible to evaluate an act of thought or a piece of writing unless we understand what it means. Understanding is accomplished by reviewing a piece; we will study effective ways to accomplish a review in Chapter 3.

EXERCISES

▲ Most Intriguing Issue

Write a one-paragraph description of the most interesting idea, topic, or process described in pages 49–55. Be prepared to explain what you find interesting in class discussion.

▲ The Muddiest Point

Write a sentence or, if possible, a paragraph that describes the idea, topic, expression, term, or process in pages 49–55 that you find most difficult to understand.

▲ Cartoons and Diagrams

1. Provide a cartoon that illustrates the standard of clarity.
2. Provide a cartoon that illustrates the standard of accuracy.
3. Provide a cartoon that illustrates the standard of specificity.
4. Provide a cartoon that illustrates the standard of significance.
5. Provide a cartoon that illustrates the standard of sincerity.
6. Provide a cartoon that illustrates the standard of respect.
7. Provide a cartoon that illustrates the standard of commitment to consensus.

▲ Definitions of Key Terms

Provide a definition for each of the following terms as they are used in this chapter. Most of the terms are not defined in the chapter, although their meanings are described in the context in which they appear. You need to review the material to create the definition yourself.

Accuracy	Clarity	Commitment to consensus
Evaluation	Respect for others	Significance
Sincerity	Specificity	Standard

▲ Short Essay Questions

Provide a written response of approximately 200 words to each of the following. Your responses should be well organized, grammatically correct, and neatly produced.

1. Explain the standards you use in evaluating the quality of a pizza.
2. Explain the meaning of: "Standards are expectations."
3. Describe the difference between quality and quantity.
4. Explain the meaning of: "It is impossible to evaluate something if we do not understand it."
5. Describe each of the seven standards of verbal thinking in your own words, providing an example of how each could be achieved in a piece of writing.

▲ QUESTIONS FOR DISCUSSION

Provide an essay of 300–500 words that responds to each of the following questions which ask for your opinion. You should respond by stating it, and by providing thoughts, examples, and insights that support it. You should be willing to revise your response; you may change your opinion during or after a class discussion.

1. This chapter claims that standards of quantitative measurement are "conventional." Explain what this means. Provide some examples of quantitative measurement from the natural or social sciences. Explain how they are conventional.

2. Do you agree that all qualitative standards are conventional? How about the moral standards of right and wrong? If they are not conventional, then what sort of standards are they? If they are conventional, does that mean that they are unimportant?

3. Explain how you would define the qualitative standards of As, Bs, Cs, and Ds for this course.

4. The chapter emphasizes that critical thinking judges acts of thinking, but not the thinker. Is it really possible to evaluate the way a person thinks and not simultaneously make a judgment about that person? Write an essay that explains your point of view on this question.

5. This chapter provides "a closer look" at critical thinking that goes beyond the definition provided in Chapter 1. Write an essay entitled, "Critical Thinking," that synthesizes the main ideas from Bloom's *Taxonomy,* the *Delphi Report,* and the seven standards of verbal thinking. Your essay should provide a good description of what you understand critical thinking to be at this stage of the course.

▲ QUOTATION TO PONDER

"I believe that the mind can be permanently profaned by the habit of attending to trivial things, so that all our thoughts shall be tinged with triviality. . . . We should treat our minds, that is, ourselves, as innocent and ingenuous children, whose guardians we are, and be careful what objects and what subjects we thrust on their attention."

Henry David Thoreau, *"Life without Principle"*

▲ JOURNAL TOPIC

Review several "letters to the editor" in your local newspaper. Evaluate one for clarity, accuracy, specificity, significance, sincerity, respect, and commitment to consensus.

▲ PORTFOLIO PAPER

Review the piece you wrote on feminism and language use for the "Portfolio Paper" assignment for Chapter 1. Evaluate it for clarity, accuracy, specificity, significance, sincerity, respect, and commitment to consensus. Write a "self-evaluation" that describes the quality of the piece. Revise the piece accordingly.

CHAPTER THREE

THE NATURE OF LANGUAGE AND THE STANDARDS OF CRITICAL THINKING

THE NATURE OF LANGUAGE: FLEXIBILITY, RICHNESS OF EXPRESSION, AND ADAPTABILITY

Verbal thinking takes place in the medium of language, which can be defined as the use of words in an organized way that produces communication. More specifically, language is a system of conventionally defined and organized symbols that are of primary importance in the selection, organization, and interpretation of perceptual experience. Language is something like a game, such as chess. Words are similar to the pieces: the queen, king, knight, bishop, and so on. Each piece has a limited pattern of movement, according to the rules of the game. The limited pattern is similar to the limited meaning of words. Thus, the bishop can only move diagonally; it cannot move vertically or horizontally. In a similar way, the word "cat" has a limited meaning; it cannot mean, for example, "dog" or "tree." The rules of the game of chess are conventional; that is, they have been made up by human beings. The rules are not "natural" patterns, such as the climatic patterns of the weather or the developmental patterns of the

---

AFTER STUDYING CHAPTER THREE

You should be able to explain each of the three characteristics of language: flexibility, richness of expression, and adaptability. You should understand how linguistic interaction and confirmation help languages grow and develop, and how definitions help us avoid language's inevitable ambiguity and vagueness. Finally, you should be able to construct proper definitions, summaries, and paraphrases.

maturation of plants from seeds to blossoms. The meaning of words is also conventional. Language, like chess, is made up by human beings.

However, language is much more complex than any game. The rules of language limit the way words and the brain interact with each other. We know very little about these rules, just as we know very little about the brain and the nervous system in general. However, the rules of the "game of language" allow for a flexibility, richness of expression, and an adaptability found in no other game (not even in a computer game!) and in no other medium of thought, mathematics included. Psycholinguistics is the discipline that studies the rules of language, especially the ways in which the brain and nervous system create and follow them. It is a new and exciting science that researches the expanding knowledge we have about the way the brain works along with the ever-increasing amount of information available about the rules that every language follows.[1]

LANGUAGE'S FLEXIBILITY

Language has what psycholinguists call "multiple structures of meaning." That is, unlike the very limited patterns of movement of chess pieces (each must move exactly according to its pattern in every game) the meaning of words and sentences can have a variety of meanings in different contexts, and the same meanings can be achieved with use of different words and sentences. In chess, the queen can move various numbers of spaces horizontally, vertically, or diagonally. Only the queen can follow these patterns; it is the most flexible piece in the game. In language, every word or phrase has a large variety of meanings, depending upon the context in which it is used. Even a simple modulation of the tone of voice to give emphasis to different words in a single sentence can alter the meaning of the sentence. The sentence, "Alicia parked the car" can have at least three meanings, depending on voice modulation: "*Alicia* parked the car" has a different meaning than "Alicia *parked* the car," and a still different meaning than, "Alicia parked *the car*." In the first, we probably mean that Alicia, and no one else, parked the car. In the second, we could mean that Alicia parked the car instead of driving it around the block. In the third modulation, we most likely mean that Alicia parked the car instead of another vehicle, such as a pickup truck, motorcycle, or recreational vehicle.

Language's flexibility goes far beyond voice modulation. Imagine, for example, the different meanings of the sentence about Alicia and the car in two different contexts. One, a court of criminal law in which Alicia is on trial for aiding a bank robbery by driving the getaway car. "Alicia parked the car" could mean that there was a witness who saw her park the getaway car after the

---

1. There are about 3,500 different languages spoken around the world, all of immense complexity. There are no "simple" languages; those used by the most isolated communities follow the same general rules as those spoken by large masses of people. There are about twelve "major" languages, defined as those spoken by groups of fifty million people or more. English, Mandarin Chinese, Hindustani, Spanish, Russian, German, Japanese, Malay, Bengali, French, Portuguese, and Italian are the major languages.

robbery. The sentence indicates that there is evidence of her guilt. In the second context, the sentence is spoken by a hotel concierge who employs Alicia as an auto valet. The concierge is indicating that Alicia should be the recipient of the large gratuity left by a grateful hotel guest. The meaning of the sentence in this context is much different (especially as far as Alicia is concerned!) than in the courtroom. The multiple meanings of any word or sentence are not infinite, however. We cannot use "Alicia parked the car" to indicate that Bob loves fried potatoes, no matter what the context. The rules of language allow for great flexibility in the meanings of particular sentences but still provide definite limitations. Without limitations, there would be no meaning at all.

In addition to voice modulation and context, language's flexibility is demonstrated by its ability to use different words and sentences to communicate the same meaning. For example, we could describe one event—Jason eating his friend Bob's french fries in the school cafeteria—in three different sentences: "Jason ate Bob's fried potatoes;" or "Bob's fried potatoes were eaten by Jason;" or "Bob's fries? Jason ate them." All three sentences have the same meaning, even though they are different sentences. Different words give us the same meaning, too. We could refer to Bob's potatoes as "spuds," "french fries," or "shoestrings." All three words have the same meaning. There are many other ways to describe what Jason ate, each of which makes use of different patterns of the same words, or of different words and sentences altogether. Pieces in chess also have some flexibility in how they move. The pawn, for example, moves in ways similar to some moves allowed the rook, the king, the queen, and, under certain conditions, the bishop. Other pieces also share moves. This flexibility is important in chess. It is one of the factors that make chess such a fascinating, challenging game. However, the pieces in chess do not have the sort or degree of flexibility of words and sentences. The knight cannot move the way the bishop moves, and vice versa. Even the queen, the most flexible piece, cannot move in the knight's pattern. The pawn, even though it is flexible enough to move in ways that are similar to other pieces, cannot move exactly like them. Unlike the ability of different words and sentences to achieve the same meaning, different chess pieces cannot achieve the same pattern of movement. The multiple structures of meaning enable us to say different things in the same way, and to say the same thing in different ways. Obviously, this is a primary advantage of verbal thinking over all other sorts of thinking, since it can be as versatile and as flexible as language. However, the flexibility of language can also cause great confusion. Since different sentences can express the same meaning, difficulty in communication can arise. What one person said may seem to the casual listener to have a different meaning than what another said, but actually their meanings may be closer than they appear to be. In other words, we may think that two people are disagreeing about something, but in fact, they are not. In addition, since the same sentence can have different meanings, the meaning one person intends to say or write is sometimes not the same meaning another person understands. In these situations we may think that two people agree, while they are saying similar words, but in fact, they disagree, because they don't mean the same thing. Verbal thinking can easily become confused; the flexibility of language sometimes makes it very difficult to achieve clarity and specificity in describing ideas.

LANGUAGE'S RICHNESS OF EXPRESSION

In a game of chess each piece operates in its own way; pieces cannot "combine" and move in creative, completely unheard of, ways. For example, the bishop cannot be attached to the knight with duct tape in order to allow the "new" piece to move in a combination of both ways, diagonally (the bishop's pattern) and the "el-pattern" of the knight. There is a great deal of creativity involved in playing the game of chess, but it cannot be said that chess is "creatively rich." After all, a computer can be programmed to play chess very well. Every possible move and every possible combination of moves can be "taught" to the computer. The computer can also be taught to react to an opponent's moves in a way that accounts for a large number of possibilities. In fact, a computer can be programmed to learn every single possible move in the game of chess. IBM has programmed a computer ("Big Blue") that plays chess as well as, and even better than, many of the great chess players of our time. If the creativity in chess is so limited that a computer can be programmed to play it better than most human beings, then we cannot say that chess is "creatively rich." That is a term we will reserve for language.

Language's richness of expression resides in what psycholinguists call its "productivity." Language can be used to produce an infinite number of sentences from a limited supply of words, and can produce an infinite number of meanings from a limited supply of sentences. We can create meaningful sentences that we have not heard before; unlike "Big Blue," we do not have to have been programmed with specific instructions in order to use them. The computer cannot combine chess moves on its own. Even if we assume that every possible chess move has been programmed into a computer, it is severely limited in creativity in comparison with the speaker of a natural language. With language, we *routinely* create new sentences: sentences that have never been uttered, written, or heard. As an illustration, consider the sentences in this textbook. Comparatively few of them have ever been written before. The richness of language consists in its capacity to generate creative sentences and paragraphs that can be combined to stimulate us with completely new thoughts and ideas. In fact, as you read this book and reflect upon it, you may come up with some ideas of your own about critical thinking, ideas that have not occurred to the author or to anyone else. Language's richness of expression means that there are always new, creative ways to "put words together." There is a story that illustrates language's inherent creativity and richness of expression quite well. A psycholinguist was once asked, "If you were abandoned on a deserted island, which book would you like to have with you?" "Well," she responded with a smile, "I think I would want to have the dictionary, since it lists so many words. I would be able to combine them into any book I wanted to read!" Of course, the point of the story is that language's productivity allows for the creation of an infinite number of books from a finite number of words.

Verbal thinking is greatly enhanced by the richness of expression that language provides. Verbal thinking is not limited to any body of knowledge, any academic discipline, or even to any single natural language. Combining and associating words from any source at all, including translating ideas from one language into another, can create innumerable new ideas. We create poems, plays, novels, and movie scripts that no one in the past has ever considered, ever thought of. Moreover, it seems that richness of expression is self-generating; the more creative language becomes, the more creatively it can continue to grow and progress in improving the quality of thought.

However, the richness of language does not always provide magnificent, creative ideas such as those that we find in great literature and philosophy. The productivity of language can just as easily lead to confusion and ignorance as to enlightenment and progress. A new word or phrase does not always signify a new idea. For example, advertisers have created dozens of creative names for laundry and dish detergents, but all detergents are still composed of the same chemical compounds, no matter how they are named and packaged. Advertisers have given us many creative names for cigarettes that sound light-hearted and joyful ("Lark," for example), dignified ("Parliament"), tough and masculine ("Marlboro"), soft and feminine ("Eve"). However, cigarettes are not light-hearted, dignified, masculine, or feminine; over one-half million people die from cigarette smoking every year. Still, the richness of language allows cigarette companies to find more and more creative ways to advertise and sell more and more of their product. New words don't necessarily mean progress!

Unscrupulous politicians, business executives, journalists, and military leaders commonly come up with new ways of speaking and writing about very old, very horrible ideas or use language to mock worthwhile projects. Politicians describe the fact that millions of impoverished men, women, and children have no permanent place to live as a "housing shortage." They describe efforts to deny the availability of automatic antipersonnel weapons to civilians as "an infringement on constitutional rights." Government agencies that have responsibility to regulate the cleanliness of food, the safety of medications, and the quality of elementary education are called "bloated bureaucracies" and dismissed as irrelevant, irresponsible, and a waste of taxpayer's money. Shady business executives assure us that "it's not the steak that sells, it's the sizzle." By that they mean that business should not offer a good quality product; it should merely describe the product in enticing ways. "Tabloid journalism" routinely describes celebrities in exaggerated, completely irresponsible ways. One movie star is described as having a "torrid love affair" with another, even though they have only had lunch together. Professional athletes who step into a bar for a quick beer are described as "lushes" and "party boys." Military leaders around the world create euphemisms (pleasant sounding words for horrible things) for death, violence, and torture. The deaths of young people killed in battle are called "losses." Bombing raids that destroy entire communities are called "air strikes," and unspeakable tortures of prisoners of war are called "debriefings." These few examples are probably enough to make the point. The richness of language can obscure and trivialize perceptions as well as make them more accurate and more significant. The richness of language can make it very difficult to achieve the truth and depth of meaning that verbal thinking needs.

LANGUAGE'S ADAPTABILITY

Another comparison of the "game of language" with the game of chess will help explain language's adaptability. Chess can be played for several reasons. It can be used as a way to pass the time in a pleasant way, or as a way to meet new people. Chess can be used as a way of building up one's self-esteem (or of lowering it). It can be used to win prize money, or to enhance a one's reputation. Language can be used in several ways, too. That is, language can help us to achieve different sorts of purposes. In general, there are five tasks or functions for which language is commonly used: to represent, to direct, to commit, to express, and to perform. We will take a brief look at each task.

The Representative Function.   Language is most often used to represent ideas and beliefs. We use words to describe what we think, especially what we believe to be true. Of course, sometimes we want to describe ideas that we do not believe to be true, such as, "The moon is made of Brie." And sometimes we lie. "I did not eat the Brie you wanted for dinner." However, even if we are describing an idea we disagree with, or even if we are not telling the truth, we are nevertheless using language in order to represent our beliefs. Of course, the richness and flexibility of language is involved with representation. Thus, representations are rarely as simple as the Brie example; usually they are very complex, and sometimes they are quite vague and confusing. The truth is not always apparent. It is important to note that the representative function of language is *not* to represent *things* but to represent *ideas about things*. Language is always related to perception—not to things. If I say, "The Brie is in the refrigerator," I am representing my idea, my *belief* that the Brie is in the refrigerator and not the refrigerated Brie itself. Of course, my idea about the refrigerated Brie is not a fantasy. Like all ideas, it is based on a perception of sense-data.[2]

The Directive Function.   Language is used to direct people to do things. Words and sentences are used to provide instructions, to seek information, and to direct understanding. The "operating instructions" for setting up a VCR is an example of the directive function of language. Less obviously, a question such as "What is the correct answer to exercise six?" is also a directive task of language. The person being asked, in fact, is being directed to *respond* to the question. At times, directive language is used in order to stimulate thought and understanding. Rhetorical questions, such as, "Should every idea always be crystal clear?" are not meant to elicit responses, but to direct thoughts in a particular direction. Directive language can be subtle or blunt. Sometimes we may not even recognize that we are being told to do something. "Have a great day, eat at Joe's" is a directive slogan, and is quite clear. However, advertisers commonly use directive language in hidden ways. "You deserve a break today," is not a simple representation of a corporation's beliefs. It is a directive to purchase

---

2. More specifically, ideas are selected, organized, interpreted *memories* of sense-data.

a product. When a candidate running for political office proclaims, "My opponent is a home-wrecker and a dysfunctional parent," she is not describing her beliefs about the opponent. She is directing the audience not to vote for her opponent, but for her! Directive language can be vicious and manipulative. It can also be sincere and committed to consensus.

The Commitment Function.   Language can be used to make commitments. Promises, assurances, contracts, and pledges are examples of commitments made by the use of language. It is interesting to note that there is a difference between an actual commitment and a representation of the belief in that commitment. If someone says, "I promise to marry you," they have made a commitment. However, if he or she says, "I believe I will promise to marry you," that is a mere representation of an idea. Legal documents, such as real estate leases, are good examples of the commitment function of language. By signing one's name, one commits to the promises contained in the lease. If the lease claims that the person renting the property will mow the lawn, then the renter is promising to do so by signing the lease. As we know, legal documents are often written in vague and ambiguous language. The promises and commitments are not clearly described, or are described in an esoteric manner, that is, a way that does not correspond to the way most people use the language.

The Expressive Function.   The expressive function of language consists in the articulation or declaration of an emotion or feeling. Emotions are declared in obvious ways, "I am really depressed today!" and in rather subtle ways, "I don't seem to be interested in anything anymore." Notice that there is a big difference between expression and representation of emotion. An expression articulates an emotion in an intimate way; it puts the emotion into words. A representation is a detached description of an emotion. When a man says, "Science is the only hope of the world," he may be using the sentence as a way of expressing his feelings about the world situation, and not really representing his beliefs about scientific progress. That is, he may not believe that the idea "Science is the only hope of the world" is true. On the other hand, maybe he really does believe that science, and science alone, has the solutions to the world's problems. It is difficult to determine for which function the sentence is being used, especially since it is written, not spoken. If someone spoke the sentence, and we could hear him or her say it, the vocal modulations would give us an indication of which function was involved. Even then, it may be difficult to determine whether a person is using language expressively or as a representation of his or her ideas. The flexibility of language can also make it difficult, at times, for an individual to recognize the difference between representation and expression in his or her own use of language. It is common knowledge that we are not always aware of our own feelings. We often fail to recognize the impact our emotions have on our ideas. Unfortunately, this is especially true when we feel strongly about an issue. Political and social values, religious beliefs, and interpersonal relationships are always emotionally charged. It is virtually impossible to describe them in a purely representative way. Of course, this does not mean that there is something wrong with emotional language or that we should strive to reduce the emotional use of language. However, it does mean that it is difficult to understand and communicate well when emotional expressions are misinterpreted as representations.

The Performative Function.   Some uses of language actually accomplish things other than communication, and the processing and understanding of ideas. When the umpire puts his or her right hand in the air with the thumb extended and hollers, "You're out," well, there is no doubt about it. You are out. Simply *saying*, "you're out," makes you out. Even if you did touch the base before the first baseman caught the ball, and even if every person watching the game agrees with you about it, you are *still* out. Why? Because the umpire said, "you're out." That's all there is to it. Making use of the performative task of language is the only case in which "saying makes it so!"

THE CONVENTIONAL MEANING OF LANGUAGE

There are at least seven types of thinking, as we saw in Chapter 1. It is easy to forget that verbal thinking is a particular type of thinking because it is so prevalent. For most of us, speaking, reading, and writing are the primary ways we understand, process, and communicate ideas. Verbal thinking is primary because words have such flexible, rich, and adaptable meaning.

The meaning of words, as we discussed in Chapter 1, is both connotative and denotative. Connotative meaning is the meaning a term has as it is used within the language. The connotative meaning is the meaning definitions provide; we define the meaning of words by describing how they relate to other words. Denotative meaning is the meaning perception provides; it is the meaning determined by the perceptual reference of the word. Verbal meanings, and of course verbal thinking, always take place in a particular natural language. Since natural languages develop and change over time, the inherently rich and flexible meanings of words change, too. Both connotative and denotative meanings are *conventional*. That is, as the purposes of the people who use a language change, as their perceptions change, and as their relationships with the language develop, meanings of words also change and develop. The meaning of words, unlike the meaning of numbers, for example, or of scientific symbols, is not exact and rigid. Language acquires its flexibility, richness, and adaptability from the changes and development words go through in the cultures in which they are used. Of course, different natural languages use different words for naming things and thinking about ideas. The Spanish language uses the word "*gato*," the French language uses the word "*chat*," and the English language uses the word "*cat*" to represent the same animal. Obviously, no one of these words is "better" than another; the words are simply different. No one of them is the "real" word for the pet that purrs when we scratch its ears. Each is a conventional name used by people who share a natural language.

WORDS SHAPE THOUGHTS

Imagine that Melissa is walking through the park with her grandfather. It is a sunny day, the flowers and ornamental trees are in bloom, and Melissa and her grandfather are enjoying the pleasant environment, barely saying a word to each other as they stroll along. Suddenly her grandfather exclaims, "Look! A snake!" Immediately Melissa's attention, which had been directed at the unusually bright pink colors of the dogwood trees blooming along the path, is directed to the ground! She visually examines the tufts of grass carefully, organizing and interpreting each little bit of grass in a very serious attempt to locate the reptile. However, she can't find it. "Where is it: I can't see it!" she exclaims. "Right there," her grandfather says, pointing with his cane at a twig lying on the side of the path. Melissa feels immediate relief. "That's not a snake, Grandfather, it's only a twig." He stoops over, touches the "snake" with his cane, and says, "You're right. Only a twig."

In this illustration, Melissa and her grandfather initially had two different individual perceptual sets. He was watching the ground; she had her eyes on the trees. However, when he said, "Look!" the word caught her selective attention immediately. She is familiar enough with the conventional meanings of the English language to react quickly. The word "snake" also caught her attention since she has had previous frightening experiences with snakes. In fact, it was the word "snake" that directed her to search the ground carefully for the sort of visual sense-data to which she could correctly apply that word. However, since there was no snake, her eyes interpreted something that could have been a snake—the twig. Her grandfather was relieved to discover that what he had at first perceived to be a snake was merely a twig. However, he didn't make that discovery until she used the word "twig."

The illustration shows how we tend to forget that the way we use words shapes the way we think. Words are such common "attention getters" that we tend to take them for granted and forget how powerful they actually are. Melissa and her grandfather hardly noticed the word "snake." It's the real snake they were concerned with! Melissa and her grandfather share a conventional understanding of the connotative meaning of "snake," which, for both of them, is a scary slimy thing that slides along the ground in a very creepy way. When Melissa hears, "Look! A snake," the connotative meaning of the words has an immediate impact on her perceptual set. This shows that connotative meaning exerts an extremely powerful influence on perception. Melissa was, in fact, looking for a snake that wasn't there; both she and her grandfather were afraid of a snake that wasn't there! The word "snake" has that much connotative power. So do many other words. In fact, they are so powerful that we tend to take the words themselves for granted and to forget their power in shaping our beliefs and feelings.

WORDS AS "BRIDGES"

Verbalization, the use of language in understanding, processing, and communicating ideas, is the primary "bridge" between individuals. Our examination of the nature of perception showed that each person has his or her own "reality."

Each one of us selects, organizes, and interprets sense-data in our own way. Nevertheless, individuals share a common reality by "crossing over" to each other via the "bridge" of verbal thinking. The preceding example shows that words are "bridges" in two ways. First, bear in mind that a bridge provides passage between places that are separated. Human beings each have their own individual perceptual world; we are separated. Without language, there would have been no "bridge" between Melissa's perceptions and those of her grandfather, no *communication* between their individual perceptual worlds. The connotative meaning of the expression "Look! A snake!" which they both shared, was a bridge between Melissa's perceptions and those of her grandfather. If they did not speak the same natural language, then she wouldn't share the connotative meaning of the word "snake," and she couldn't "cross the bridge" to his perceptual set. Since they do share in the conventional connotative meaning of the expression, she can "cross over" to his perceptual world by using it. Words serve as connotative bridges.

Language also serves as a bridge between human beings and the world of sense-data. The denotative meaning of the word "snake" is the perception of the sense-data that makes up the snake. However, in the example, there was no such perception of sense-data. Melissa and her grandfather were unsuccessful in seeking a visual perception of the snake. Her grandfather was unable to determine that the twig was not a snake until she provided the word "twig" to influence his interpretation of the sense-data his receptors presented him. The sense-data did not change; rather, the interpretation of the sense-data changed. Words, then, are also denotative bridges. They "connect" us with real things by means of understanding and processing sense-data.

Verbal thinking is the bridge that provides a possible solution to the "two-world assumption" discussed in Chapter 1. Recall that the philosophical conundrum is based on the nature of perception. If each of us selects, organizes, and interprets sense-data in different ways, then how is it possible for us to think about the real world? How is it possible to "go beyond" our own perceptual set? How can we reach a consensus about things that are important to us? The solution to the puzzle may be that the real world is the world we all share by means of shared connotative and denotative meanings. Each of us moves beyond our own perceptual set and into a community by the use of language, by sharing meanings of words.

LINGUISTIC INTERACTION AND CONFIRMATION

All human beings have the neurological potential to use language. That is, the human brain and nervous system are "wired" in a way that makes it possible for young children to learn any number of languages. We call this neurological wiring the "deep structure" of language. The metaphor "hardware," drawn from the physical wiring of a computer, is often used to clarify this deep structure. Just as a computer is wired in a way that allows it to "speak" in any of the various "software programs" that are "installed," the brain's deep structure allows it to speak any language that is installed. The "surface structure," or natural language that is actually spoken, is the software that our brain speaks. Of course, brains do not speak—people do. Any person can learn any language at all, but the plasticity of the two-year-old's developing brain is especially receptive to learning language. As we age, our ability to learn new languages diminishes.

The deep structure is what allows us to think verbally. However, actual verbal thinking can take place only within a surface structure of a natural language. A computer has the hardware to "word process," but without a software word-processing program, no word processing will actually take place. In a similar way, the *linguistic interaction* a child experiences with family and the larger community is the installation of the software that allows the child to actually speak. Without the linguistic interaction, the child would remain a "potential" user of language, but would not actually speak. The use of language and the accompanying verbal thinking would be nonexistent.[3]

LINGUISTIC INTERACTION: HOW VERBAL THINKING DEVELOPS

Language acquisition emerges during the *interaction* between adults and children that developmental psychologists refer to as "baby talk" or "child-directed speech." Baby talk is not the chatter of the baby; it is the special language used by the *parent* in communicating with the infant. Observation results reveal that baby talk has a number of consistent features in every society in the world. No matter the culture or natural language of a community, baby talk is consistently similar in pitch (higher), intonation (more high-to-low fluctuation), vocabulary (simple, concrete), and sentence length (shorter). No doubt these are ways parents and other primary caregivers around the world use to attract the attention of their children, but many psycholinguists believe that there may be neurological features of children's brains that allow them to learn language more efficiently when baby talk is spoken. At any rate, everyone learns to speak a natural language by first learning to speak it in baby talk. The baby, for example, reaches for its mother and utters "maaaaa." The mother responds in a high-pitched tone, with an exaggerated clarity, "mommy." The mother goes out of her way to make speaking interesting and understandable for the child. Eventually the mother and child verbally interact in more conventional ways. Without this early verbal interaction, children would most likely not learn to use language, even though they are "hard-wired" to do so.

Of course, baby talk is much less complex than adult language. However, linguistic interaction does not stop with childhood; as adults, linguistic interaction allows our language use and verbal thinking to develop. We expand our understanding of our natural language (or if we are fortunate, of the several natural languages we speak) by interacting with new vocabulary, new ways of

---

3. The distinction between "deep" and "surface" structure of language was made by the linguist Noam Chomsky to explain, among other things, why children learn language at about the same age (twenty-four months) no matter what the child's language, nationality, race, or socioeconomic background.

putting words together, and with new ideas. Linguistic interaction expands our ability to make use of the richness and flexibility of the language, and we become more adept at verbal thinking as we become more adept at using the language. The more we read challenging pieces, engage in stimulating conversations, and stretch our limits in describing our thoughts and feelings in writing, our verbal thinking becomes richer, more adaptable, and more flexible. This development is possible only if we continually engage in linguistic interaction on a challenging level. Just as a baby would not move beyond simplistic baby talk without the extended and challenging verbal interaction with its mother and other caregivers, adults cannot move beyond the limits of childhood language without engaging in challenging verbal interaction with other adults. That is one reason reading and writing are given so much emphasis at all levels of education; we learn to develop a high quality of verbal thinking by interacting with high quality verbal thinking. When new vocabulary and new ideas challenge us in our reading, discussion, and writing, the deep structure acquires new "software." Our capacity to think verbally is "stretched" by this software. Education consists largely of acquiring higher quality linguistic software. Each subject that is studied, each work of literature that is read, each paper that is written, and each discussion in which we learn something new is very similar to the experience we had as an infant, speaking baby talk with our caregivers. Through this new, more sophisticated linguistic interaction, we are acquiring the software that allows us to engage in an increasingly higher quality of verbal thinking.

LINGUISTIC CONFIRMATION: HOW VERBAL THINKING UNDERSTANDS, PROCESSES, AND COMMUNICATES IDEAS AND FEELINGS

Linguistic interaction is kept alive by *confirmation* of linguistic, or verbal, meanings among its users. Confirmation is the tacit agreement that speakers of a language make between each other to accept conventional meaning of words, terms, and sentences. Confirmation *stabilizes* meaning; it provides an acceptance of particular meanings for particular words. Of course, the agreement is *tacit:* it is not written or spoken. Confirmation simply happens. Verbal thinking, and language itself, would be impossible if we refused to recognize that when people speak they mean the same thing that we mean when we use the identical words. As an illustration, if Heather says, "It is raining," we confirm her meaning by responding in a way that shows we understand what she said. We go to the closet and take out an umbrella. We are confirming, that is, validating Heather's communication as meaningful to us. What if she was playing a joke on us? What if she said, "It is raining," but actually the sun was shining? And what if, instead of going to the closet and reaching for an umbrella, we go to the window and look out, saying, "No it's not. The sun is shining!" We have still confirmed the *meaning* of what she said, even though we have not confirmed the *truth* of what she said. We confirm meaning whenever we respond in a way that shows we understand what has been spoken or written.

   Another example can illustrate how confirmation stabilizes meaning within a community. Marcus was having dinner with some friends at a restaurant he had not previously visited. It was an Austrian restaurant, with carvings of stags and other forest animals along the thick wood walls, Germanic script on the menu, and the lighting was dim. When he left his companions to use the restroom, he was confused by the gender identification signs on the restroom doors. Instead of the customary "Men" and "Women," the doors were labeled "Hansel" and "Gretel." Marcus had long forgotten the fairy tale and was unsure which name referred to the masculine and which to the feminine. He was too embarrassed by his ignorance to ask anyone directly, so he waited until someone exited from one of the doors. It so happened that in a few minutes a woman came out of the door labeled "Gretel," so his confusion was settled. The simple example shows the nature of confirmation in a rather profound way. Having no understanding of the connotative or denotative meanings of "Hansel" or "Gretel," Marcus was forced (by his embarrassment) to place his trust in the stranger who exited from one of the doors. In other words, he had to accept that there were conventional meanings of the terms, and that others in the restaurant knew what they were. His confusion was settled, in a very real sense, by an act of *confirmation*. The woman confirmed that the "Gretel" door was the door to the women's restroom by a performative use of language. Marcus knew that she understood the conventional meaning of "Gretel" because she used the "Gretel" door. The profundity of the example is this: It makes no difference whether "Hansel" referred to the male in the actual fairy tale. All that is necessary is that the people in the restaurant *conventionally agreed* that the door labeled "Hansel" was for the use of men. Even if all the patrons in the restaurant were mixed up, and men were using the "Gretel" door and women the "Hansel" door, it would make no difference in Marcus's thought process; connotative and denotative meaning is conventional. All that is necessary for meanings to be stabilized is the tacit agreement confirmation provides.

Here is a final illustration of how confirmation is essential to communication. Two people attend a production of Shakespeare's *Hamlet*. As they walk home they discuss what the character Hamlet meant to each of them, and how Hamlet's particular actions or speeches perplexed them. Their conversation might go this way:

> "I think that Hamlet was too sad."
>
> "I know what you mean, but after all, his dead father appeared to him in the form of a ghost and said he was murdered by his own brother! That would make anyone a little sad!"
>
> "Yes, but he doesn't really *do* much about it; he only . . . well, you know; he's so, well, satisfied with his own melancholy."
>
> "I'm not sure. He doesn't seem to enjoy being so morose. He doesn't act without thinking, but eventually he exposes his uncle."

Each playgoer *confirms* the meaning of the other's words about the character of Hamlet, even if they do not agree with each other. In fact, it is by *disagreeing* that the second playgoer confirms the meaning of the first. By disagreeing that Hamlet is "too sad," he confirms that the term is meaningful. Without confirmation, their conversation could not take place.

Verbal thinking understands, processes, and communicates ideas by reliance upon linguistic confirmation. In the first illustration, we understand the meaning of "it is raining" by confirmation. In the second, the young man is able to process his thoughts and make a socially acceptable decision on which restroom to use thanks to confirmation. In the last illustration, the two playgoers are able to engage in *communication* by confirming each other's meaning. Of course, thinking understands, processes, and communicates ideas simultaneously; the illustrations are not meant to imply that some linguistic confirmations result in understanding, others in processes, and others in communication.

LINGUISTIC INTERACTION AND CONFIRMATION: SOURCES OF VERBAL THINKING'S FLEXIBILITY, ADAPTABILITY, AND RICHNESS OF EXPRESSION

Of course, linguistic interaction is the continual "conversation" that occurs among those who speak and write a particular natural language. We learn new terms, develop new ways to use the language, and mature in understanding the language through interaction with other speakers and writers. The primary way we interact is by linguistic confirmation.

Confirmation is the means by which conventional meaning is established and maintained in a natural language. The connotative and denotative meanings of terms are stabilized over time by confirmations among the people who use the language. When we speak Spanish, we are confirmed by others who use the language that "*gato*" has a similar connotative and denotative meaning to the word "*chat*" used by those who speak, write, and think in French. When we speak English, we are confirmed by other English users that "*cat*" has the same meaning for all of us. Without confirmation, we would be in a perpetual quandary regarding the meaning of what we are saying, listening to, reading, and writing.

Over time, linguistic interaction and confirmation work together to create flexible, rich, and adaptable natural languages. For example, English has been developing and growing from its Germanic, Roman, and Greek roots for centuries. There are now over 450,000 words being used in the English language, three times the number of French words, and four times as many words as there are in Russian. English, French, and Russian, of course, all contain thousands of words that most people who use the language don't know. Every natural language has the potential to be used with much more flexibility and richness than most people develop. Nevertheless, the language is there, waiting for us to grow and develop in its use, and thereby to improve the quality of our verbal thinking.[4]

Certainly, verbal thinking can be as flexible, rich, and adaptable as the language it uses to understand, process, and communicate ideas. We have seen the same flexibility, richness, and adaptability that every natural language possesses

---

4. Our language is also waiting for us to help it grow and develop. By making use of the richness and flexibility of our language, we can create new words and phrases that can be eventually confirmed as part of the language, thereby increasing its richness and flexibility. For example, scholars estimate that William Shakespeare created more than 1,700 new words that are still in use.

become a source of confusion, lack of communication, and poor thinking. For example, we can believe we clearly understand a legal contract, but later on find out to our dismay that we didn't have as clear an understanding as we originally believed. The meaning of the contract was more flexible than we knew! Or it may appear on the surface that a political candidate is using words in rich, stimulating, inspiring ways, but upon reflection, we discover that everything he or she said is vague, trivial, and insincere. Sometimes a story in a newspaper or a report on television appears to be a clear presentation of the truth, but actually is inaccurate, perhaps even deceitful. The fact is that language is a two-sided coin. On one side it is the primary way that understanding and hope come into our lives. Great literary insights, religious inspirations, philosophical profundities—the wisdom of the past and present come to us through language. On the other side of the language coin we have the greatest source of human confusion and despair. Language can be harmful, dishonest, and ignorant. It can be used to trick and deceive, to confuse, and to perpetuate mistaken beliefs. Indeed, language use is as much the root of foolishness and ignorance as it is the heart of wisdom and truth. Lies, hatred, and prejudice verbally masquerade as insight, inspiration, and profundity.

When verbal thinking meets the standards of clarity, significance, accuracy, specificity, respect for others, sincerity, and commitment to consensus, the result is insight, inspiration, and truth. However, when the standards are ignored or avoided, the result is confusion, ignorance, and deception. We will examine how the first four standards apply to verbal thinking in the next section. Chapter 4 will discuss the remaining three.

EXERCISES

▲ MOST INTRIGUING ISSUE

Write a one-paragraph description of the most interesting idea, topic, or process described in the chapter so far. Be prepared to explain what you find interesting in class discussion.

▲ THE MUDDIEST POINT

Write a sentence or, if possible, a paragraph that describes the idea, topic, expression, term, or process in the chapter so far that you find most difficult to understand.

▲ CARTOONS AND DIAGRAMS

1. Provide a diagram that shows how flexibility, richness of expression, and adaptability work together in language.
2. Provide a cartoon that illustrates the conventional meaning of language.

3. Provide a cartoon that illustrates the flexibility of language—include the concept of "multiple structures of meaning."
4. Create a cartoon that shows the richness of expressive language—include the concept of "productivity."
6. Provide a cartoon that clarifies each of the five tasks (functions) of language.
7. Draw a cartoon that illustrates how richness of expression is related to linguistic interaction
8. Draw a cartoon that shows the way confirmation is related to linguistic interaction.

▲ DEFINITIONS OF KEY TERMS

Provide a definition for each of the following terms as they are used in this chapter. Most of the terms are not defined in the chapter, although their meanings are described by the context in which they appear. You need to review the material to create the definition yourself.

Adaptability	Conventional Meaning	Deep Structure
Flexibility	Linguistic Confirmation	Linguistic Interaction
Richness of Expression	Surface Structure	Verbal Thinking

▲ SHORT ESSAY QUESTIONS

Provide a written response of approximately 200 words for each topic. Your responses should be well organized, grammatically correct, and neatly produced.

1. Explain how Juliet's line from "Romeo and Juliet" displays Shakespeare's understanding of the conventional meaning of language: "What's in a name? That which we call a rose, by any other word would smell as sweet. . . ."
2. Explain each of the two ways in which language exhibits multiple layers of meaning by providing your own example of each.
3. Explain the linguist's joke (the dictionary and the deserted island), showing how it depends on an understanding of richness of expression.
4. Describe the difference between the representational and the expressive tasks (functions) of language. Use your own examples.
5. Explain how flexibility is involved with the directive function of language. That is, show how the same direction can be given in several ways and how several directions can be given in the same way. Use your own examples.
6. Explain how richness of expression is related to linguistic interaction. Use your own examples.
7. Explain how linguistic confirmation is involved with reading a piece of writing rather than in conversations.

▲ QUESTIONS FOR DISCUSSION

Provide a written essay of 300–500 words that responds to each of the following questions which ask for your opinion. You should respond by stating it, and by providing thoughts, examples, and insights that support it. You should be willing to revise your response; you may change your opinion during or after a class discussion.

1. Review the discussion of the role of cultural influence in Chapter 1. How is linguistic interaction and confirmation involved with this element of perceptual interpretation?

2. Review the discussion of the role of early childhood experience in Chapter 1. How is linguistic interaction and confirmation involved with this element of perceptual interpretation?

3. This chapter claims that, "In large part, education consists of acquiring higher quality linguistic software." Using your own examples, thoroughly explain this claim, then respond to the question, "If this is true of education 'in large part,' what is the 'smaller part' of education?" In other words, other than linguistic interaction, of what does education consist?

4. Review the illustration of Melissa and her grandfather's encounter with the "snake" in the park. Describe the different functions of language they use during the encounter. Does each sentence have only one function? Or can one sentence exhibit several functions at once? Why or why not?

5. Some students believe that once we recognize the complexity of language, it seems quite remarkable that we manage to communicate with each other at all. Why do they feel this way?

6. This chapter claims that language is so rich in expression that an infinite number of sentences can be created out of the limited number of words in a natural language. Does this mean that verbal thinking can, in principle, understand, process, and communicate every possible perception? Can human beings ever grasp reality completely? Why or why not?

▲ QUOTATION TO PONDER

> "When learning a foreign tongue we invariably have the impression of approaching a new world, a world which has an intellectual structure of its own. It is like a voyage of discovery in an alien land, and the greatest gain from such a voyage lies in our having learned to look upon our mother tongue in a new light. So long as we know no foreign languages we are in a sense ignorant of our own, for we fail to see its specific structure and its distinctive features."
>
> Ernst Cassirer, *An Essay on Man*

▲ JOURNAL TOPIC

If at all possible, observe a parent engage in "baby talk" with his or her infant. Describe the pitch, intonation, vocabulary, and sentence length used in the interaction. Do they conform to the descriptions in the text? Do you notice any instances of confirmation intermingled with linguistic interaction?

TWO MAJOR DIFFICULTIES WITH LANGUAGE: AMBIGUITY AND VAGUENESS

The flexibility, richness of expression, and adaptability of language can be a support and a hindrance to verbal thinking. As we have seen, all three are two-sided. Each functions to enhance understanding, processing, and communication, and yet each can also diminish the quality of thought. More specifically, language can be clear, significant, accurate, and specific, but it can also be ambiguous and vague.

AMBIGUITY

Ambiguity is the characteristic of words, phrases, or paragraphs that have more than one interpretation due to poor word choice, grammatical confusion, or incomplete comparisons. Ambiguous language is a direct result of the multiple layers of meaning that language's flexibility provides. We have seen that language inherently allows for different interpretations. Ambiguity, however, confuses connotative and denotative meanings unnecessarily. We learn a natural language's conventions regarding grammar and use of words as we grow and develop in our use of the language. Ambiguities can usually be avoided simply by adhering to conventional grammar and word usage. A grammatical or vocabulary change should be made whenever it can clarify language.

Sometimes ambiguity is amusing; puns, for example, usually depend upon ambiguous words or phrases. An example: "The captain told the sailor and the sailor tolled the bell." Ambiguity, when encountered in spoken language, is often due to poor word choice, most often to the use of homonyms.[5] However, homonyms are not the only case of ambiguous words. The written statement, "Management has decided to reinstate employee layoffs," could result in some serious misunderstandings at the workplace, especially if what management meant to do was merely "reinstate laid-off employees."

Both written and spoken language can be ambiguous due to poor grammatical constructions. For example, "Not all men are females," seems very controversial. So does "All men are not females." However, revising the grammatical structure eliminates the ambiguity: "No men are females." Another example of ambiguous grammatical structure: "Fifteen campers came down with food poisoning and their parents came to get them. This was a terrible thing." In this case, the ambiguity is due to the flexible meaning of the word "this." Does it refer to the food poisoning event or to the visit by the parents? One more example: "He loved fried foods and was very fond of long-haired cats." The incoherent grammar of this ambiguous sentence needs to be revised (and quickly, before the Humane Society finds out!). Incomplete comparisons lead to ambiguous meanings, too. "Samantha loves pasta more than her mother," should be revised to point out that "Samantha loves pasta more than her mother *does*."

The primary characteristic of ambiguous language is lack of communication, i. e., lack of clarity. As a result, its accuracy, specificity, and significance cannot be understood. It is impossible to determine how accurate "Samantha loves pasta more than her mother" is, as it is not clear whether Samantha loves pasta more than she loves her mother, or whether her mother doesn't love pasta as much as Samantha does. We cannot determine if the example is specific enough, because we cannot understand how much detail should be present if we don't

---

5. Homonyms are words that have similar pronunciations, but different spellings and meanings. In the example, the words "told" and "tolled" are homonyms.

understand what is being said. Is the example too trivial? Is it oversimplified? It is impossible to determine. The example does not communicate clearly: it is ambiguous.

VAGUE LANGUAGE

Vague language is imprecise because it lacks specificity, clarity, and accuracy. Some abstract words are inherently vague; good, bad, important, nice, thing, and stuff are words that overgeneralize unless they are clarified in a way that makes them more specific. For example, the sentence, "Mr. LaFran learned a lot of stuff in our school," is thoroughly vague; we have no idea of what Mr. LaFran learned or did not learn. Vague language is characterized primarily by lack of specificity. Specificity is an ideal standard that can never be perfectly achieved. The appropriate degree of specificity varies with the context and the particular purpose of the words being used. "Mr. LaFran did very well in his studies at our school," would be too imprecise for a letter of recommendation to a potential employer of Mr. LaFran. Such letters are meant to represent beliefs on the quality of a person's work. A more specific representation of the writer's beliefs is appropriate. Otherwise, the letter will not communicate well. However, the sentence might be specific enough in a casual conversation between people who know Mr. LaFran and are expressing their appreciation of his study habits. "Mr. LaFran did very well in his studies at our school," remarks one of his teachers to another during the graduation ceremony, and they both nod and smile.

Vagueness is sometimes an inadequate representation of a complex idea: "The economy of the United States is capitalist," is far too simple. The American economy is a very complex structure, and there are many forms of capitalism. Specific examples, distinctions, elaborations, and explanations are appropriate when complex ideas are represented in general terms.

Ambiguity and vagueness sometimes occur at the same time. "Charles is more overweight than he was," is an ambiguous sentence because it is an incomplete comparison. We don't know what Charles's weight "was" and don't know what period of time "was" represents. Hence, we don't understand how much overweight he supposedly is. The sentence is vague because it is imprecise in representing how much extra weight Charles is carrying. Ten pounds? Fifty pounds? Vagueness and ambiguity supplement each other.

Another example shows how vagueness and ambiguity can occur together, relative to the context. Steven asks, "How is the ice cream cone?" Jeff's response, "It's good," communicates well enough. However, if Steve's question is, "How do you feel about the recent price increase of ice cream?" Jeff's response, "It's good" would be unacceptably vague. It does not communicate a response at all; it is too imprecise. It is also ambiguous; does Jeff feel that the increase in the price of ice cream is good, or does he feel that the ice cream itself is good?

Of course, there is a difference between a vague sentence and a sentence with a demanding structure. The sentence, "An honest tale speeds best being plainly told" is not vague. However, understanding it requires some analysis, reflection, and thought. Upon review, the sentence does not exhibit any of the indications of ambiguity or vagueness. We should not be too quick to evaluate verbal thinking as ambiguous or vague. Most language communicates well enough for the purpose it is meant to accomplish.

In summary, the indications of ambiguity are poor word choice, grammatical confusion, or incomplete comparisons. The indications of vagueness are over-generalization and lack of clarification of inherently abstract words.

TOOLS OF CRITICAL THINKING: DEFINITIONS, SUMMARIES, AND PARAPHRASES

For critical thinking the most important of the five tasks of language is *representation*, the "putting of ideas into words." It is the primary way we understand, process, and communicate information. Expressive language is also important to critical thinking. Ideas are seldom, if ever, represented without a degree of expression of feeling. The representative-expressive function of language is carried out in both speaking and writing. Television, film, radio, lectures, public debates, and personal conversations are all examples of verbal thinking. Obviously, these "verbal" media are of immense importance. However, verbal communication comes and leaves quickly. We hear speech and it vanishes. It is very difficult to adequately review, evaluate, and revise the verbal media because, unlike writing, it is not permanently available on paper. Writing is permanent, it is "verbal thinking at rest." Writing is "always there," available for our repeated review, careful evaluation, and precise revision. Hopefully, the process of thinking critically about the written word will enable us eventually to become more adept with the verbal media.

Writing takes several equally important forms. Literary fiction and poetry are the subtlest, most flexible, and richest kinds of writing. However, the context of individual literary works and poems must be thoroughly understood in order to think critically about them. The connotative meaning of such works is extremely complex, and best dealt with after years of study. Writing also takes the form of nonfictional representational pieces: short and long essays, full-length books, even very short pieces of only a paragraph or two. These forms are the most common way that people communicate their representations of ideas as well as their expressions of feeling. In order to understand written pieces better (as we shall refer to representational writing) it is necessary to understand the vocabulary, the main ideas, and the support for the main idea. When we understand *what* is written (the vocabulary and main ideas), and *why* (the support) the main ideas are believed to be true, we understand the piece, and are in a position to evaluate and revise it. Definitions clarify the meaning of words and expose ambiguity and vagueness. Summaries are statements of the main ideas of a piece, as well as descriptions of the reasons given for their support. Paraphrases are restatements of the piece in a vocabulary and style that differ from the original, but which keeps the meaning of the main ideas and support intact.

We use tools to help us with physical tasks—we use shovels to garden, ovens to cook, and buses and trains to move from place to place. We also use tools to help with mental tasks. Definitions, summaries, and paraphrases are tools that are instrumental in critical thinking's review, evaluation, and revision of written pieces. First, each tool helps with the understanding of a piece (review). Second, each tool exposes inadequacies of the piece in regard to clarity, accuracy, specificity, and significance (evaluation). Third, each tool is essential to the creation of a good revision of the piece.

Good definitions, summaries, and paraphrases themselves must meet the standards of good thinking. A definition that is inaccurate, a summary that trivializes the original, or a paraphrase that is vague cannot help critical thinking. Each has a set of specific rules that, when followed, assure that critical thinking is reasonably clear, accurate, specific, and significant.

DEFINITIONS

Definitions are complete sentences in which the defined term is divided into its "primary designation" and "secondary designation." Note this definition: "A fish is a cold-blooded animal that lives exclusively in the water." The term being defined, "fish" is the subject of the sentence. The primary designation of "fish" is "animal." "Animal" is the name of the large group to which the "fish" belongs. Thus, "whale," "bird," "dog," and so on are all terms that have the same primary designation: animal. The secondary designation of the term "fish" is "cold-blooded," and "lives exclusively in water." The secondary designation describes the specific meaning of the word: how it is used differently than other words with the same primary designation. For example, "A whale is a large animal that lives exclusively in water, breathes air, is warm-blooded, and gives birth to live young." The primary designation is the same as that for "fish," namely, "animal." The secondary designations are "large," "lives exclusively in water, breathes air, is warm-blooded, and gives birth to live young." The definition of "bird" has the same primary designation, "animal," but its secondary designation is "warm-blooded, two-legged, with feathers and wings."

Term to Be Defined	Primary Designation	Secondary Designation
Fish	Animal	Cold-blooded, lives exclusively in water
Whale	Animal	Large, breathes air, is warm-blooded, gives birth to live young and lives exclusively in water
Bird	Animal	Warm-blooded, two-legged, with feathers and wings

We define a word by "placing boundaries" around its meaning. A definition is like a net, made up of the primary and secondary designations, placed over a word. As long as the word stays within the net, it has connotative and denotative meaning. However, if it has "gone beyond the boundary" of the net, it has been used in a way that does not communicate. The boundaries that a definition describes are conventional limits on the word's usage. Language is flexible and has an inherent ambiguity; words do not have exact, rigid meanings that can be completely captured in primary and secondary designations. The meaning of a word in a piece of writing is always, in varying degrees, relative to its context. Good definitions always reflect the way a word interacts with other words in the context of the writing.

For example, in "Eileen is fishing for trout" and "Eileen is fishing for the right idea," there are two different meanings of "fishing" and each meaning has its own definition. The "proper" definition is the one that clarifies the way the word is used in each context. Of course, words do have agreed-upon meanings of their own, no matter the context. The context cannot change that meaning beyond the primary and secondary designations without becoming hopelessly ambiguous and/or vague. "Eileen is fishing two cups of coffee" makes no sense. The word "fishing" has boundaries beyond which it has no meaning. No matter what the context, we cannot understand the sentence because "fishing" is not used properly, within its conventional boundaries. Over its long history, the word "fishing" has been used in many ways that make connotative and denotative sense. However, "fishing two cups of coffee" goes too far beyond those conventions.

Lexical Definitions.   Lexical definitions distinguish words by describing their conventional meanings. They establish the boundaries of words as they are normally used in ordinary language. "Fishing," for example, is defined as "the catching of fish for sport or a living." (The primary designation is "catching" and the secondary designation is "of fish" and "for sport or a living.") The sentence "Eileen is fishing for trout" uses the word "fishing" exactly according to the definition. However, "Eileen is fishing for an idea" uses the word "fishing" metaphorically. That is, it uses the word "fishing" as figure of speech.[6] In this way, its primary designation is "seeking," and the secondary designation is "without a plan or method." The boundaries of "fishing" also allow for the use of the word in this way. The sentence "Eileen is fishing two cups of coffee" pushes "fishing" too far: it pushes it out of the boundaries of its "net." There is no primary or secondary designation of the word "fishing" that allows it to be used meaningfully in that sentence.

Lexical definitions are found in dictionaries: they are descriptions of the way words are used according to current conventions. Dictionaries are written by lexicographers: people who describe and report on how words are being used.[7]

LEXICAL DEFINITIONS: GUIDELINES.   Lexical definitions describe the way terms are actually used in current ordinary language. That means they avoid *archaic* and *esoteric* meanings. An archaic lexical definition describes a word as it has been used in the past, not as it is *currently* used. To define the term "rake" as "a man

---

6. Metaphors are used in expressive as well as representational ways. They help clarify, explain, and describe in a way that exploits the flexibility and richness of language. We will examine metaphors more closely in Chapter 4.

7. In addition to the ordinary usage dictionary described here, there are many specialized dictionaries that provide disciplinary definitions, etymological definitions, and so on.

of low moral standards, especially in relation to women and drink," would be an improper lexical definition.

Lexical definitions also avoid being esoteric: being limited in meaning to a special, informed group of people. Esoteric definitions do not describe current *ordinary* usage. They describe the meaning of words the way special groups use them.

Lexical definitions are the best for clarifying words used in most pieces of writing. Conveniently, the dictionary contains thousands of very good lexical definitions and all we have to do is look them up. It is very important when clarifying meaning to be aware of the context of the word being defined. Dictionaries, especially ones recommended for academic work, always provide as many definitions as there are current meanings. The appropriate definition is usually apparent once the context in which it is being used is considered.

When reviewing a piece of writing, it is very important to look up the lexical definitions of words that appear to be vague or ambiguous. A vague word is one that lacks meaning because it is too general or too abstract, not one that only has an unclear meaning. A word is not vague simply because it is not in our current vocabulary!

When using lexical definitions:

1. Keep in mind that words can have several meanings; ordinary language is not rigid and exact.
2. In selecting the appropriate definition from the dictionary, always consider the context of the word in the piece of writing being reviewed.
3. Always look up words that seem to be vague; perhaps a lexical definition will clarify the meaning.

Disciplinary Definitions. Disciplinary definitions explain the way a term is used in a particular field of study (a "discipline") or activity. For example, the word "electron," can be defined lexically as "negatively charged particles that form a part of all atoms." However, if we are studying Astrophysics, we need a clearer, more specific definition of electron, one that we will not find in a dictionary of common usage. A disciplinary definition is esoteric to anyone seeking the ordinary use of the term.

Disciplinary definitions are found in glossaries of textbooks, as well as in other scholarly works such as professional journals, specialized encyclopedias, disciplinary dictionaries, and so on. A discipline is a special area of knowledge, most of which are studied in colleges and universities. Physics is a discipline, so are Composition, Sociology, and Art History. Each discipline has special terms that are used in particular ways within the area of study. Disciplines are actually specialized ways of describing perceptions, using terms and concepts particular to the interests and methods of the field of study. Since disciplines differ largely in how they describe experience, or perception, and in how they define the terms they use in those descriptions, they are referred to as "areas of discourse." Discourse refers to any use of language: reading, writing, and speaking. An area of discourse is a particular way of using language that is specific to a field of study. Every discipline, every academic subject, and every specialized approach to experience can be referred to as an area of discourse. Thus business, law, and economics are areas of discourse that use language in relation to matters that involve money and finance, but they do so in different ways. We can point out that different areas of discourse define the same term in different ways and often alleviate confusion and lack of understanding. For example, the term "trust" has different meanings in the context of ordinary language, business, and law. It carries the ordinary language meaning of "a disposition to have faith and feel secure about a person or process." In business, it refers to "a special sort of investment in which one person (trustee) manages holdings for another (beneficiary)." In law, the term means "a business practice that involves unlawful collusion and price fixing." In reviewing and evaluating a specialized piece of writing, it is very important to recognize the difference between lexical and disciplinary definitions. A word may be vague in relation to ordinary, lexical meaning, but if the disciplinary definition is made clear, it may be quite helpful in the context of the piece.

DISCIPLINARY DEFINITIONS: GUIDELINES.   The main thing to keep in mind about disciplinary definitions is that the words they define are esoteric. That is, for ordinary language the vocabulary of law, business, science, and other specialized terminology does not communicate well. The majority of people is not familiar with disciplinary meanings and considers them mere "jargon," when used in ordinary language.

Understanding an area of discourse requires understanding its vocabulary; otherwise we cannot communicate in the rigorous ways necessary. Disciplinary definitions are always more specific, more rigid, and more exact than lexical definitions. As a result, they are always more specific, clearer, and more significant than terms in ordinary usage.

However, some pieces of writing necessarily require disciplinary meanings. Unless the specialized terminology is lexically defined within the piece it invariably causes lack of communication. For example, a lease for student housing must be written in a way that establishes legal responsibilities for landlords and students, a purpose that can be achieved only with the use of a specialized legal vocabulary. However, the words should not be meaningful only to people with expertise in law; the students who sign the lease must be able to understand it, too! In order to avoid vagueness, the legal "jargon" should be defined lexically within the lease.

When using disciplinary definitions:

1. Jargon should be avoided. Disciplinary definitions of words should not be used outside of their specialized contexts; in ordinary language they are vague and ambiguous.
2. Within their area of discourse, disciplinary definitions achieve more clarity, specificity, and significance than lexical meanings and should be used whenever the context is appropriate.

3. In the few instances in which it is necessary to use disciplinary meanings in an ordinary language context, lexical definitions of the disciplinary terms should also be provided.

Stipulative Definitions.   A stipulative definition explains a word in a way that provides a temporary meaning for a particular group of people. It is an agreed upon, provisional meaning for those who use it in a rather narrow context. For example, three students, Holly, Jeremy, and Lisa are discussing the issue of "The Best President in United States History." They are having a difficulty with communication because they have not stabilized the meaning of the term "best president." Holly claims that President Lincoln was the best because of his courage during the Civil War. Jeremy says that President Roosevelt was best because of his ability to communicate well. Lisa believes that President Carter was the best president in American history because he provided moral direction to the country.

Of course, each student is using a different meaning of "best president." Lexically, their definitions are clear. Their definitions are also acceptable disciplinary definitions: each would find some support in political science and American history. However, their discussion is not going anywhere because "best president" remains a vague term. The students need to define "best president" provisionally, that is, they need to stipulate its meaning so that they can move forward in their conversation. After discussing each meaning of "best president," Holly, Jeremy, and Lisa stipulate that "best president" is defined as "the president who showed the most courage, communication skill, and moral direction during a period of crisis in the country." They decided to combine each meaning into one temporary meaning. The stipulative definition will not settle their discussion. They still need to decide which president had all three characteristics more than any other. The stipulative definition gives each student a clear, specific, significant definition of "best president." Their conversation will benefit from the definition since they have decided between themselves what "best president" means in the context of their discussion.

STIPULATIVE DEFINITIONS: GUIDELINES.   Stipulative definitions are used to clarify meanings when disciplinary and lexical definitions are not sufficient. If everyone agrees upon an acceptable definition, uncertainty about the meaning of terms is at least no longer an impediment to communication.

Stipulative definitions cannot simply be "made up." Care must be taken in choosing the primary and secondary designations. Of course, everyone immediately involved with use of the word should agree to the stipulation. It is of equal importance that the stipulative definition reflects established lexical and disciplinary meanings as much as possible. When creating stipulative definitions we should avoid slanting the definition so that it "resolves" discussion in a biased, or unfair way. In the example, if Lisa had insisted that the only definition she would agree to stipulate was "the best president is one who provided moral leadership," she would have slanted the definition to meet her own position in the discussion. This would not have encouraged communication.

Stipulative definitions that slant or bias meanings are called "persuasive definitions." They are meant to persuade and to manipulate people, not to clarify meaning and encourage communication. Persuasive definitions are sometimes encountered in advertising, political campaigns, and in discussions about moral and political values. For example the definition, "A caring mother is one who uses Softness brand disposable diapers," is persuasive because it unfairly stipulates the secondary designation "Softness user." The term "caring mother" is much more significant than that!

Stipulative definitions should:

1. be used sparingly, only when the clarification offered by disciplinary definitions is impractical and when lexical definitions are not precise enough for the purposes at hand.
2. adhere as closely as possible to the primary and secondary designations of lexical and disciplinary definitions.
3. be created only where there is a consensus on the wording among those asked to use it.
4. not be persuasive. That is, stipulated definitions should not be veiled deceptions that suit the purposes of a few individuals.

Creation of Definitions: Standards. Any good definition, no matter if it is lexical, disciplinary, or stipulative, meets the standards of good thinking. That is, every definition should be as clear, accurate, specific, and significant as possible.

1. **Clarity**

   The definition should be stated in a complete sentence, in which the term to be defined is the grammatical subject. It should avoid vague primary designations such as "thing," "object," or "word."

2. **Accuracy**

   The definition should correctly describe the meaning of the word in the context in which it is being used. Bias and persuasion should be avoided.

3. **Specificity**

   The secondary designation of the word should be as precise and detailed as possible. Overly general secondary designations should be avoided.

4. **Significance**

   The definition should be informative and useful. It should not repeat the defined term (or contain any synonyms) in the primary designation.

SUMMARIES

A summary is a brief, yet accurate description of a piece's main ideas and the supporting materials.

The main ideas of a piece are the central points it makes: what it believes to be true. The supporting materials for the main ideas are the reasons the piece provides the reader to show that the main ideas are true.

Summaries condense a written piece; only the main ideas and the reasons for them are included. Thus, summaries are not substitutions for the complete written piece; the full meaning is not present in the summary. Nevertheless, summaries are very useful for remembering and for understanding the meaning of a piece of writing.

A summary enables us to remember the meaning of a piece accurately and more clearly because it contains only the main ideas and supporting materials. Summaries are used as the basis of most discussions; it would be impractical to memorize complete written pieces. Perhaps more important than the benefits for memorization, though, is the fact that creating a summary can greatly help us in understanding a written piece. In fact, if we summarize it well, we can be certain that we understand it well.

If the material to be summarized is provided in a lecture, a video, or some other nonwritten format, notes should be taken or a transcript should be obtained. Accurate summaries can be constructed only from written documents. If we simply rely on our memory of what we heard or saw, it is virtually certain that we will not be able to capture the main idea and support of the original material. Our memory of the original will be incomplete and probably inaccurate.

Summaries are best constructed in a methodical way. The piece should be read very carefully several times, unfamiliar terms should be properly defined, and the main ideas and support materials should be identified in writing. The completed summary should be a brief, clear, accurate condensation of the piece. Creating a summary can be time-consuming; selecting the main ideas and their supporting materials requires a thorough understanding of the piece. A good way to begin a summary is "Briefly, the main points are. . . ."

The following is a list of steps in writing a summary.

1. Read the piece carefully, looking up lexical or disciplinary definitions of unfamiliar terms.
2. Reread the piece and write down the main ideas and supporting materials.
3. Combine main ideas and supporting materials into a clear and accurate paragraph or two.
4. Review the summary for accuracy, clarity, proper grammar, and spelling.

Standards for Construction of Summaries.   Summaries, while they are condensations, have a tendency to be less precise and to simplify (not oversimplify!) the meanings of the original piece. That is, usually the standards of specificity and significance are achieved in a lesser degree in the summary than they are in the original piece. Summaries should be clearer than the original, though, as only the main ideas and support are involved. Summaries should always accurately reflect the meanings of the original piece.

1. **Clarity**

   A summary should be clearer than the original piece. Any incoherence, ambiguity, and vagueness in the original should be reduced as much as possible in the summary.

2. **Accuracy**

   A summary should be relatively free of any distortion of the original piece's meanings. It should be as accurate a condensation as possible.

3. **Specificity**

   It is impossible for a summary to be as specific as the original piece, because it leaves out clarifications, most examples and illustrations, and provides only the main ideas and their supporting materials. Nevertheless, a summary should avoid unnecessary overgeneralizations whenever possible.

4. **Significance**

   Any irrelevant information in the original should be left out of the summary. Even though a summary cannot be as complex as the original piece, it should avoid trivializing and oversimplifying the ideas.

PARAPHRASES

A paraphrase is an accurate, significant rewording of a piece that changes its vocabulary and style and restates its meanings in order to achieve a specific purpose. There are three purposes of paraphrasing a piece: explaining, expanding, and understanding.

A paraphrase can explain a piece for an audience unfamiliar with the meanings of the original. For example, authors of software manuals paraphrase complex technical descriptions into terminology and style consumers can understand.

Paraphrases are also used to expand the ideas of the original piece to show its relevance to a topic not apparent in the original. For example, we can paraphrase "a stitch in time saves nine" (which is about "preventive sewing") into "careful eating and regular exercise helps avoid serious illness," a statement about preventive health care.

Finally, paraphrasing is helpful in achieving understanding by restating the original into our own words. We cannot truly understand something unless we can paraphrase it into our own terminology and style. A great deal of academic work consists of paraphrasing (and of summarizing, too); written assignments, quizzes, essay examinations, and research papers often ask students to summarize course material and "put it in your own words."

Paraphrase Construction: Standards. The main task of a paraphrase is to change the vocabulary and style of the piece in order to explain, expand, or understand its meaning more clearly. The first step in constructing paraphrases is similar to construction of summaries; a careful reading of the piece is followed by identifying its main ideas and supporting materials. However, in constructing a paraphrase, the second step is to identify key terms, the words or phrases in which the main ideas and support materials are expressed. Appropriate synonyms for these terms are selected and the paraphrase is written in a different style than the original piece. The purpose and audience of the paraphrase determine which synonyms and writing styles are appropriate. For example, a student could paraphrase Dr. Martin Luther King, Jr.'s "I Have a Dream" speech for two purposes. If she wanted to expand its meaning and make Dr. King's ideas more significant in relation to her term paper on affirmative action laws, her choice of vocabulary and style in paraphrasing Dr. King would parallel the style and terminology in her term paper. She would find synonyms for Dr. King's words that also occurred in the paper. Instead of using Dr. King's expressive rhetorical style, she would restate his ideas in the representational academic style commonly used in research papers. If she wanted to address a group of elementary school children on Dr. King, her paraphrase of the same speech would be in a style and vocabulary that the children would understand. The following steps can be used as a guideline in paraphrase construction. A good way to begin a paraphrase is with, "In other words, . . ."

1. Reflect on the purpose and audience of the paraphrase.
2. Read and reread the piece, identifying its main ideas, supporting materials, and key terms.
3. Identify appropriate synonyms and revisions of style, considering the purpose and audience of the paraphrase.
4. Write out the paraphrase, using synonymous terms or phrases and the revised style.
5. Check the paraphrase for clarity, accuracy, specificity, and significance.

Paraphrase Construction: Standards

1. **Clarity**
   A paraphrase should be free of vague and ambiguous words. It should have a style and vocabulary consistent with its audience and purpose.
2. **Accuracy**
   A paraphrase should faithfully restate the main ideas and support materials of the piece. The vocabulary and style of the paraphrase should not be biased or misconceived.
3. **Specificity**
   A paraphrase, unlike a summary, is as precise and as detailed as the original. A paraphrase should represent and express every idea of the original, but in a different vocabulary and style.
4. **Significance**
   Unlike a summary, a paraphrase should avoid simplification of the piece's meaning; all the depth and complexity of the original should be restated.

CONCLUSION

Language is the primary way we understand, process, and communicate meaning. The more clear, accurate, specific, and significant our language is, the more effectively it serves as the "bridge" between human beings and the world as well as the "bridge" between individuals. However, linguistic meaning is flexible, rich in expression, and adaptable. Words have multiple, evolving, and various meanings, all of which are stabilized only by interaction between the people who use them. Interaction stabilizes meaning by confirming conventional agreements on the definitions of words. However, the flexibility, richness, and adaptability of language are so powerful that meanings are often ambiguous and vague despite interaction and confirmation. There are at least three types of definitions, the lexical, the disciplinary, and the stipulative, which are used to stabilize meanings, and avoid ambiguity and vagueness. Each can be used to stabilize meaning, but the final authority on a word's meaning is always the context in which it is used. A great deal of verbal thinking takes the form of summarizing and paraphrasing written pieces. A summary is a condensation of a piece, in which the main ideas and support alone are described. Summaries are as clear and accurate as the original piece, but are simplifications, and always lack the original's detail. Paraphrases are restatements of written pieces in which the vocabulary and style are changed in order to explain, expand, or help understand the original piece.

Language is a system of conventionally defined and organized symbols that shapes our perceptions and ideas. Each of us is "born into" a natural language that will deeply influence our thoughts and feelings throughout our lives. However, our natural language constantly changes; its flexibility, richness, and adaptability are dynamic, not static, characteristics. The way a person uses their language also changes as he or she matures and develops special interests, ideas, and vocabularies. Each person contributes in varying degrees to the development of his or her language. Shakespeare created new words that we still use today. His contribution, like that of several other literary figures, was immense. Scientists and technicians have also given the language new words; with each insight and each new invention comes a new terminology. Screenwriters, television writers, journalists, songwriters, and others who provide the dialogues, buzzwords, and lyrics of popular culture all contribute to the growth of their language. When we use their new words in our own written work and in our conversations, we confirm the meaning of these words. We help stabilize them, and integrate them into the language. Meanwhile, older words and ways of speaking drop out of the language. The words of the past become archaic, and eventually die. The language itself, though, is alive. It grows, develops, and continues to shape ideas and feelings, continues to serve as the bridge between human beings and the world, and continues as the connection between individuals, who would otherwise be lost and alone within their own perceptual experience.

Can language really be that powerful? Is language a true bridge across the gulf between individuals, or is something more required? Meaning is conventional, slippery, and ultimately ambiguous. Miscommunication, misunderstanding, misrepresentation, and outright deception are common elements of the human experience with language. The power of language's richness and flexibility can go in either direction; it can help us understand the world and ourselves, and communicate our ideas about both. Or, it can encourage ignorance, lack of understanding, and lies. Sometimes we wonder if communication is really taking place. Each of us has our "own world," shaped by the selection, organization, and interpretation by our own nervous system. How can we be certain that we are communicating with another person, really sharing their experience?

Critical thinking's task is to guide us in the use of language so that understanding, truth, and genuine communication predominate in our lives. The activities of reviewing, evaluating, and revising what is said and written are meant to enhance the quality of thought. Definitions, summaries, and paraphrases are specific ways of making sure we really understand the thoughts and feelings another person is communicating. If we define their words well, if we summarize their main ideas and the support for those ideas, and if we are able to represent and express their ideas in our own words, then we can be certain that we understand them as well as possible. Our evaluations and recommendations for revision of what they have written will be based on a solid grasp of what they truly mean. Critical thinking is a guide along the bridge that language builds between us. Language cannot provide us with understanding, truth, and communication on its own—it must be guided by critical thinking.

EXERCISES

▲ MOST INTRIGUING ISSUE

Write a one-paragraph description of the most interesting idea, topic, or process described in pages 74–88. Be prepared to explain what you find interesting in class discussion.

▲ THE MUDDIEST POINT

Write a sentence or, if possible, a paragraph that describes the idea, topic, expression, term, or process in pages 74–88 that you find most difficult to understand.

▲ CARTOONS AND DIAGRAMS

1. Provide a cartoon that shows the difference between ambiguity and vagueness.
2. Draw a cartoon that shows how definitions, summaries, and paraphrases are tools of critical thinking.
3. Draw a cartoon that shows the way definitions stabilize meanings of words.
4. Provide a diagram or chart that shows the differences between definitions, summaries, and paraphrases.
5. Provide a chart (similar to the one on page 78) that shows the primary and secondary designations for each of the following terms. Follow the guidelines for creating definitions on pages 78–81.

Critical Thinking	Language	Linguistic Confirmation
Linguistic Interaction	Perception	Thinking

6. Provide a diagram that shows the differences in the lexical and any disciplinary definition of each of the following terms. You may have to think for a moment to come up with the disciplinary definitions of the terms. (A good dictionary will provide them as third or fourth meanings.)

"Nerve"   "Current"   "Plane"   "Water"   "Genius"   "Finish"

▲ DEFINITIONS OF KEY TERMS

Provide a definition for each of the following terms as they are used in this chapter (a disciplinary definition). Most of the terms are not defined in the chapter, although their meanings are described by the context in which they appear. You need to review the material and create the definition yourself. Be sure to follow the guidelines for creating definitions on pages 78–81.

Ambiguity	Disciplinary Definition	Jargon
Lexical Definition	Paraphrase	Piece of Writing
Stipulative Definition	Summary	Vagueness

▲ SHORT ESSAY QUESTIONS

Provide a written response of approximately 200 words for each topic. Your responses should be well organized, grammatically correct, and neatly produced.

1. Provide three disciplinary definitions from a course you are currently taking (other than this one). If you are not taking another course, provide the disciplinary definitions from your occupation or from an area of special interest.
2. Look up the term "critical" in your dictionary. Explain which meanings are appropriate for understanding "critical thinking" as used in this book.
3. Explain the difference between stipulative and persuasive definitions. Give an example of each (but not from the chapter; think up your own!)
4. Provide a definition for each of the following standards of verbal thinking. Follow the guidelines for creating definitions on pages 78–81.

"Clarity"   "Accuracy"   "Specificity"   "Significance"

5. Provide a summary of the first part of this chapter. Follow the steps and standards for summary creation on pages 83–85.
6. Provide a summary of the second part of this chapter. Follow the steps and standards for summary creation on pages 83–85.
7. Paraphrase the definition of critical thinking provided by The *Delphi Report* in Chapter 2 into your own words in order to understand it more thoroughly. Follow the steps and standards on pages 85–86.
8. Imagine that you have been asked to inform the incoming freshman class about critical thinking. Paraphrase the definition of critical thinking provided by The *Delphi Report* in Chapter 2 in order to expand its meaning into a vocabulary and style appropriate for your three-minute presentation. Follow the steps and standards on pages 85–86.

9. The chapter uses the metaphor of "tools" in describing the role of definitions, summaries, and paraphrases in critical thinking. Explain what this metaphor means.

10. Provide a written summary of the following in less than 100 words. Follow the steps and standards for summary creation on pages 84–85.

If you listen to American music, watch American television or movies, or read American magazines, you will probably agree that the most popular subject of these forms of entertainment is love. Romantic love always finds an audience in the United States. Falling in love, solving the problems of love, and achieving the happy ending—the big wedding—are subjects of interest to the adult as well as the teenage public. Millions of Americans celebrate Valentine's Day with special cards and gifts that announce their love to their mates, their friends, their coworkers, and their families. Popular songs tell us that ""All the world loves a lover." A popular saying is "Love conquers all." Numerous columns in magazines and newspapers offer advice to the lovelorn, to those with difficulties of the heart. To most Americans, romantic love is central to a happy life.

Not only do Americans believe in romantic love but they also believe that it is the best basis for marriage. Despite the high divorce rate in the United States, young women and men continue to marry on the basis of romance. Americans consider marriage to be a private arrangement between the two people involved. Young Americans feel free to choose their own marriage partners from any social, economic, ethnic, or religious background. The man or woman may have strong ties with parents, brothers, or sisters, but when he or she falls in love, the strongest feelings are supposed to be for the loved one. When an American couple marries, they generally plan to live apart from both sets of parents and build their own independent family. The goal of young people is to be each other's best friends and to increase the personal happiness of themselves and their children.

11. Provide a summary of the following in less than 100 words. Follow the steps and standards for summary creation on pages 84–85.

In many societies in the world, marriage is an important way to strengthen the main family line by uniting it with another family of the same social, economic, ethnic, and religious background. In these societies, there are many rules about whom a person can or cannot marry. Parents have a strong interest in seeing that their children continue the family's good reputation and position in society. They also want their children to have a good life. So sons and daughters are not free to choose their mates. By arranging marriages, parents can control the choice of a new member for the benefit of the children, the whole family, and the class to which they belong.

In India, for example, the ideal household includes the parents, the sons, and the sons' wives and children. In this type of arrangement, the strength of the family lies in the respect, loyalty, and cooperation among the children, and between the children and their parents. If a son is too interested in his wife, or if the wife is too independent or uncooperative, he or she may cause trouble by breaking the unity of respect and loyalty within the family. A good wife is one who is a good daughter-in-law. She is modest and obedient. She gradually breaks the ties with her own family and becomes completely interested in her husband's. In India many parents arrange a marriage for a son with the right kind of woman.

The son will meet with the woman once or twice before they marry. The families will exchange gifts of money and jewelry, and then there will be a great wedding ceremony. The couple will live together with the son's parents and family. The bride will be obedient and cooperative. If the sons' parents are kind people she will be well-treated and comfortable in her new home. She will provide company for her husband's mother and help in the management of the household. When her parents-in-law are away on vacation, she will take care of her husband's brothers and sisters. Someday she will have children of her own, and when her son is grown, she will look for a suitable bride for him.

12. Provide a summary of the following in less than 100 words. Follow the steps and standards for summary creation on pages 84–85.

> One afternoon, as I was leaving the subway at rush hour, trudging tiredly up the stairs, I felt a hand brush my rear. It was an ambiguous gesture, considering the size of the crowd, so I did nothing; but my heart began to pound and my face flushed. I felt a mixture of excitement (my first New York Pervert! Wait'll I tell the gang!) and fury (how dare this creep molest me). The hand struck again, this time unmistakably a pinch. I spun around, umbrella poised to strike a blow for womanhood and respect . . . and stared face-to-face with my husband. He took one look at my apoplectic expression and burst out laughing, which was a good thing, as I might have whomped him anyhow.
>
> This example shows the speed with which a single judgment—"this man is a friend with a rotten sense of humor, not a pervert"—transformed my apprehension and anger into delight. The arousal generated by adrenaline and noradrenaline is not enough to "cause" an emotion. It needs a psychological component before heat is transformed into hostility, uncertainty into fear, general distress into depression or rage. Adrenaline does not become the "anger hormone" until it is attached to a provocation, perception of injustice, or some interpretation of events.
>
> From *Anger: The Misunderstood Emotion* by Carol Travis (1982)

13. Paraphrase the following for the purpose of extending its meaning to the needs of a committee considering the grading policy at your college. Follow the steps and standards on pages 84–86.

> "If one's actions are not guided by thoughtful conclusions, then they are guided by inconsiderate impulse, unbalanced appetite, caprice, or the circumstances of the moment. To cultivate unhindered, unreflective, external activity is to foster enslavement, for it leaves the person at the mercy of appetite, sense, and circumstance."
>
> John Dewey, *How We Think* (1933)

14. Paraphrase the following in order to understand it more clearly in your own words. Follow the steps and standards on pages 85–86.

> Democracy ideally aims so to structure the arrangements of society as to rest them ultimately upon a freely given consent of its members. Such an aim requires the institutionalization of reasoned procedures for the critical and public review of policy; it demands that judgments of policy be viewed not as the fixed privilege of any class or elite but as the common task of all, and it requires the supplanting of arbitrary and violent alteration of policy with institutionally channeled change ordered by reasoned persuasion and informed consent.
>
> Israel Scheffler, *"Moral Education and the Democratic Ideal"* (1973)

15. Paraphrase the following in order to explain the passage to a group of parents of high school students. Follow the steps and standards on pages 85–86.

> "The rational person recognizes the power of reason, the value of disciplining thinking in accordance with rational standards. Virtually all the progress made in science and human knowledge testifies to this power, as so to the reasonability of having confidence in reason. To develop this faith is to see that ultimately one's own higher interests and those of humankind at large will be served best by giving the freest play to reason, by encouraging people to come to their own conclusions through a process of developing their own rational faculties."
>
> Richard Paul, *Critical Thinking* (1990)

▲ Questions for Discussion

Provide an essay of 300–500 words that responds to each of the following questions which ask for your opinion. You should respond by stating it, and by providing thoughts, examples, and insights that support it. You should be willing to revise your response; you may change your opinion during or after a class discussion.

1. The city council, of which you are a member, is scheduled to vote on the following resolution.

"Resolved: That all young people be not allowed to loiter late at night during the workweek."

What terms would you want to be defined before the council voted on the resolution? For which terms are lexical, disciplinary, or stipulative definitions appropriate? Remember that your task is not to express your view on the resolution; you are working to make it more understandable before an exchange of views takes place.

2. Respond to this statement: "Definitions don't solve problems; definitions are only words." What does it mean? Is it accurate? Is it clear? Is it specific? Is it significant? Do you agree with it? Explain.

3. Pablo Picasso is reputed to have once defined art this way: "Art is a lie that makes us realize the truth." This does not seem to be a proper definition. Why not? Some might claim that it is still a good stipulative definition of art. In what sense are they correct? In what sense are they not?

4. Adlai Stevenson, an unsuccessful candidate for president in 1952 and 1956, was reported as saying, "A free society is one in which it is safe to be unpopular." This does not seem to be a proper definition. Why not? Some might claim that it is still a good stipulative definition of a free society. In what sense are they correct? In what sense are they not?

5. When a summary misstates the original in a way that makes the original appear silly or inaccurate, it is often referred to as a "straw man" summary, or as the "straw man fallacy." ("Fallacy" is a term used in the discipline of Logic that refers to common mistakes in thinking.) Why do you suppose the term "straw man" is used?

6. Our society makes use of the word "hero" in many ways, some of which are vague and ambiguous. Explore the meanings of this word as it is applied to firefighters, police officers, soldiers, and cartoon characters (Superman, etc.). Also consider the actions of Lenny Scutnik, the man who dove into the icy Potomac River to save a woman from a plane crash a few years ago. Is it possible that Scutnik is more a hero than a police officer or soldier, who is, after all, doing his or her job? Provide a good definition of "hero," following the guidelines on pages 79–83.

7. Our society makes use of the word "role model" rather vaguely. Explore the meanings of this term as it is applied to professional athletes, teachers, business people, and parents. Provide a good definition of the word, following the guidelines on pages 79–83.

▲ QUOTATION TO PONDER

As one learns the language of a subject, one is also learning what the subject is. It cannot be said often enough that what we call a subject consists mostly, if not entirely, of its language. If you eliminate all the words of a subject, you have eliminated the subject. Biology is not plants and animals. It is language about plants and animals. History is not events. It is language describing and interpreting events. Astronomy is not planets and stars. It is a way of talking about planets and stars."

Neil Postman, *Teaching as a Conserving Activity* (1979)

▲ JOURNAL TOPIC

Thoroughly describe in writing two specific events in which you used summarizing or paraphrasing outside of this course within the past week. Did the activities improve your understanding, processing, and/or communicating of the ideas? In what way? If the activities did not help improve your thinking, why didn't they?

▲ PORTFOLIO PAPER

Compose a 500–700 word paper that describes how the use of proper definitions, summaries, and paraphrases play an important role in each of critical thinking's elements: review, evaluation, and revision.

CHAPTER FOUR

ATTITUDINAL STANDARDS AND EMPATHY

ATTITUDES

Every action we take, including speaking and writing, is motivated by an attitude or a feeling. Without motivation, there is no action. Actions include anything we do, even if we are doing nothing. Joe, who sits on the couch all day and "does nothing" is actually doing something. He is sitting and staring at the television; he is motivated to do this by an attitude. Perhaps he is depressed. No matter what he does, or doesn't do, there is an attitudinal component to his behavior.

There is more to verbal thinking than words. For instance, a conversation includes gestures, eye contact, and other bodily movements that substantially influence the meanings of the words being exchanged. Slight alterations in voice intonation can completely change the meaning of what is said even though the words themselves do not change. When David says, "I *can't wait* for my next midterm exam," and rolls his eyes to the ceiling, the meaning of what he says is quite different from Isabel, who is hurrying to the classroom as she says, "I

AFTER STUDYING CHAPTER FOUR

You should be able to empathetically evaluate pieces of writing in regard to the three ideal attitudinal standards of sincerity, respect for others, and commitment to consensus. You should understand the difference between empathy and sympathy. Finally, you should be able to detect attitudes in pieces of writing by reviewing metaphors, allusions, word choices, and prejudicial expressions.

can't wait for my *next* midterm exam." Language has multiple layers of meaning. These layers are not only the work of words: attitudes also have a significant role in establishing verbal meaning and thinking. After all, it is the contrast in David and Isabel's attitudes, not in their words, that make the difference in the meaning of what they say. The tones of voice they use are expressions of their different feelings about the upcoming midterm. David seems to be apprehensive; his sentence represents the idea, "I am not looking forward to this exam." Isabel seems to be excited; her words mean, "I am looking forward to this exam." The two students are representing two almost opposite ideas with the same words. The verbal *content* is the same, but the verbal *meaning* is different.

As this illustration shows, and as most people recall from their own similar conversations, attitudes are an essential part of verbal meaning. Studies confirm those feelings. As was pointed out in Chapter 2, cognitive psychologists believe that attitudes such as lethargy, impatience, persistence, and curiosity play a large role in the processing of ideas. Bloom's *Taxonomy* and the *Delphi Report* agreed that attitudes, or dispositions, are integral aspects of critical thinking. Critical thinking is not a mechanical, robotic activity, but a human endeavor that involves the whole person. Attitude not only affects the quality of thought; it also affects the meaning of the thought. That is, attitude plays a large role in the eventual clarity, accuracy, specificity, and significance of, for instance, a written piece. However, meaning is also effected. Our choice of subject matter, our vocabulary, our judgments, and our eventual conclusions are as much the result of our attitudes as our ideas.

In Chapter 3, we examined the first four standards of good thinking as they apply to verbal thinking's content. For example, our purpose in applying those standards to a written piece is to provide a qualitative measurement by which we can evaluate and eventually revise the piece. Standards, you will recall, are ideal models of perfection. No piece of writing can achieve them completely. In this chapter we examine the last three standards of good thinking as they apply to the attitudes involved with verbal thinking. These standards are also ideal models, the purpose of which is to give us a qualitative measurement of the attitudes behind the thought. We use them to evaluate and to make suggestions for revision in attitude. Detecting and evaluating the attitudes behind thought can also help us understand its meaning. The attitudinal standards are:

Sincerity
Thinking should be motivated by a sincere attempt to discover the truth. We should struggle to discover the truth in spite of difficulties and obstacles. We should avoid deception, attempts to exaggerate the evidence for our own point of view, and understating the evidence for positions contrary to our own interests.

Respect
Respect is the attitude of judging others' ideas, beliefs, and values by the same standards we use to evaluate our own, regardless of any advantages or

disadvantages that may come to us. We should avoid biases in favor or against gender, ethnicity, religion, race, age, and political persuasion.

Commitment to Consensus

All thinking should have the attitude that a true, worthwhile idea, once it is well explained and well understood, will be agreed upon by everyone. Ideas that are understood and not agreed to are in need of revision. We should avoid force, either physical or psychological, in seeking to gain agreement from others.

THE ATTITUDINAL STANDARDS: AN EXAMINATION

The seven standards of good thinking are interrelated. A written piece that is vague will suffer in significance as well as clarity. A piece that lacks specificity (for example, one that contains too many unwarranted assumptions) probably will suffer from oversimplification. A piece that results from an insincere attitude, such as one that attempts to deceive, will also lack clarity, accuracy, specificity, and significance in one way or another. A piece that lacks commitment to consensus will also be deficient in other ways. An attitude is "carried out" or "takes place" in the content of the written piece. When the attitude is seriously lacking in one or more of the standards, the deficiency will be reflected in the piece's lack of clarity, accuracy, specificity, and significance. This can occur in many ways. The following is a general description of the relationship of each attitudinal standard with each of the four cognitive standards.

Sincerity.   An attitude of sincerity or distortion motivates us, in general, to use language. We don't really communicate with others when we are being deceitful. Communication is an exchange of ideas, but insincerity hides the truth by distorting meanings, misrepresenting evidence, and avoiding precision and complexity.

An attitude of distortion usually occurs in one or more of these ways:

1. The deliberate use of ambiguous and vague words. An insincere attitude seeks to avoid a clear meaning. Vague and ambiguous words are left undefined, or given persuasive definitions in order to deceive others.
2. The deliberate misrepresentation of evidence. An insincere attitude seeks to overstate the quality of evidence that supports its position, and to disregard or minimize the value of evidence that does not support it.
3. The deliberate use of overgeneralizations. An insincere attitude does not clarify assumptions and avoids precision in order to misrepresent meanings of words, descriptions of evidence, and explanations of ideas.
4. The deliberate attempt to divert attention from the truth with insignificant representations and expressions. An insincere attitude seeks to misrepresent the truth by oversimplifying and trivializing complex ideas and evidence.

Respect.   Respect for others is the attitude that each person's perceptions, representations, and expressions are as valuable as our own. Whenever we encounter another person's words, we either respect them as inherently valuable and worth our attention, or we disrespect them as not worth our time. Lack of respect is often motivated by prejudice, the belief that another person is of less inherent value than oneself due to their gender, ethnicity, religion, race, age, or political values.

Disrespect usually takes place in one or more of the following ways:

1. The deliberate distortion of the meaning of another's written piece in a summary or paraphrase. Prejudice is one cause of an attitude of disrespect deliberately misrepresenting another's meaning.

2. An attitude of disrespect ignores the words of anyone considered "inferior," no matter how much support for his or her ideas can be found in appropriate disciplines. Only those who share common prejudices are cited as experts, even though there is no consensus on their qualifications among nonprejudiced authorities.

3. An attitude of disrespect stereotypes individuals as having only those characteristics prejudicially associated with their gender, ethnicity, religion, race, age, or political persuasion. Stereotypes of inferior groups are usually negative, while those of superior groups are always positive. Individual differences that cannot be attributed to prejudicial stereotypes are ignored. Only ideas and values that support the prejudiced stereotype are represented and expressed.

4. An attitude of disrespect trivializes the significance and depth of meaning represented and expressed by anyone perceived to be inferior. The complexity of the relationship of personal identity and gender, ethnicity, religion, race, age, and political beliefs is ignored.

Commitment to Consensus. A person who is committed to consensus has the attitude that in order for an idea to be true, it must be accepted as true by anyone who understands it. A commitment to consensus is an attitude that seeks to revise any idea that is not accepted as true by those who understand it, no matter what their status. Truth is regarded as the result of public dialogue and critical thinking, not as the private possession of a powerful elite.[1]

A lack of commitment to consensus is usually characterized by a willingness to resort to psychological and/or physical force to "uphold" a nonconsensual belief. For example, wars have been fought in order to force people to accept political or religious beliefs they do not believe to be true. The psychological force of advertising is often used to convince consumers that particular products are worth buying even if they do not need them.

---

1. An "elite" group is one that is deservedly recognized as more distinguished and capable than anyone else in a particular way. For example, there are elite surgeons and elite athletes. There are also elite students and elite parents. Elite groups do not necessarily disrespect other people, and there is nothing inherently wrong with being a member of an elite group. In fact, any person who regularly adhered as closely as possible to the standards of good thinking might be said to be a member of an elite group of thinkers!

The attitude that truth is nonconsensual can take place in one of more of the following ways:

1. Vagueness and ambiguity are used to convince and persuade others that beliefs should be accepted as true, even though the ideas have not been explained well and are not understood.

2. A nonconsensual attitude ignores evidence that does not support its own claims. It refuses to accept any evidence that supports claims with which it disagrees. A nonconsensual attitude selects and rejects authorities on the basis of whether they agree or disagree with the claims presented.

3. Nonconsensual attitudes resort to persuasive definitions and attempt to convince others without describing ideas in specific detail. They attempt to force others to accept their beliefs when they cannot persuade them.

4. A nonconsensual attitude often makes use of trivial "one-liners" that oversimplify complex issues. Irrelevant examples and illustrations portray ideas in simplistic ways in an effort to persuade others to accept beliefs and values they do not fully understand.

ATTITUDES ARE MOTIVATIONS

An attitude is a feeling: specifically, it is an emotional sense of approval or disapproval. Feelings of approval and disapproval lead us to act and think in particular ways. For example, Kate and Dave allow their children to watch violent television programs. One of the children's teachers tells them that studies have shown that children who regularly watch violent television shows tend to act more aggressively than children who don't view violent programs. Kate defends the programs as harmless. She has not actually seen the programs herself, and is not aware of the studies to which the teacher is referring. Nevertheless, she trivializes the studies as "a bunch of liberal mumbo-jumbo." She says that her children are no more aggressive than any other "healthy boys and girls." Are Kate's motivations sincere, respectful of others, and committed to consensus? Or is she motivated merely by the desire to defend her self-image as a good parent, even if in this instance she may not be parenting very well?

Attitudes motivate thinking in other, more complex ways. We care deeply about our religious, moral, and political values. However, most of them are accepted without much thought. The values our parents, church, and society display are initially accepted when we are children and soon become habitual. Our thinking is often motivated by a desire to preserve, protect, and defend our values. Or, if we are experiencing a rebellious stage, we can just as unthinkingly be motivated to cast them off, ignore them, or even attack them. Attitudes can motivate the way we think, even to the point of defending or attacking ideas without any real thinking at all, let alone any critical thinking!

HIDDEN ATTITUDES AND MOTIVATIONS

We usually don't know our own attitudes about values or ideas until we are challenged. Our attitudes are often established as part of our early childhood experience and tend to influence our perceptions without our actually being aware of them. As we know, habituation is a strong force in creating our perceptual sets. The attitudes that are established in early childhood play such a major role in how we feel and think as adults that we can be completely unaware that they are motivating us. For some people, it is only when their behavior becomes troubling to themselves or to society that they investigate their motivations with the help of a counselor or psychotherapist. For example, when we read in the newspaper about a heinous crime we may ask ourselves, "How could anyone do such a thing?" The people who committed the crime may very well be asking the same question of themselves! Their motivations could be as hidden from them as they are from us.

Psychotherapists, among other behavioral experts, try to help people become more aware of the attitudes that are motivating them to act and think in the ways they do. We tend to believe that only criminals or people with psychological problems need to examine their attitudes in this way. However, that may betray our own ignorance about the hidden nature of our own attitudes. True, we may not need a psychologist to help us unravel the attitudes and motivations behind our actions and thoughts because neither are "troubling" society or us, but this does not mean that our attitudes and motivations are causing no harm. For example, take the results of the study of poor thinking mentioned in Chapter 2. The attitudes of lethargy and impatience that motivated the people in the study to fail in solving the puzzles are, for the most part, hidden from them. They probably do not think of themselves as being lethargic and impatient; their failure was not the result of lack of information or lack of ability. Their attitudes of lethargy and of impatience caused them to fail. They did not have a sincere desire to discover the truth so they either accepted an easy answer or they simply quit. An insincere attitude seeks to oversimplify and trivialize complex ideas. In our earlier illustration, David was personified to be rolling his eyes while voicing his lack of enthusiasm about his midterm exam. Is David aware of his attitude?

THE DIFFICULTY OF DETECTING ATTITUDES

It is difficult to know our own attitudes, but it is even more difficult to understand the attitudes of other people. How can we determine if David has a lethargic attitude? How can we examine what he says and find his motivations? How can we find our own? This is an important question for critical thinking. Critical thinking does not need to examine the deepest and most hidden attitudes and motives in a writer's psyche. We can leave that to psychotherapy. Critical thinking does need to review and evaluate the attitudes that motivate verbal thinking. Without understanding the motivations behind a piece of writing, or without understanding our own motivations, we cannot evaluate them in relation to the three attitudinal standards of good thinking. If we cannot review and evaluate attitudes, then we cannot revise or change them for the better. Motivations are hidden, but can we nevertheless discover *something* about them? Can we at least recognize whether the attitude behind a piece of writing is as sincere, respectful of persons, and committed to consensus as it should be? We can find some help in this endeavor by reviewing Carl Rogers's idea of congruence.

Carl Rogers's "Congruence."   Carl Rogers, whose extensive work in psychotherapy qualifies him as an authority on the subject of attitude and motivation, believes that the more "congruent" a person's experience, self-awareness, and communication is, the more they will understand their own and others' motivations and attitudes. "Congruence" is Rogers's term for the harmony and "coming together" of three things: (1) an attitude, (2) awareness of the attitude, and (3) the verbal representation of the attitude. When a person can accurately and clearly be aware of and verbally represent their attitude, they are said to be a "congruent" person. Congruence is a sort of internal integrity. Rogers's point is that the more we understand our own attitude, and the more accurately and clearly we acknowledge that we have it, the more clearly and accurately we will be able to communicate it verbally. For example, an infant, when experiencing hunger, is aware of being hungry, and communicates this hunger by crying. The infant is congruent; he or she has hunger, acknowledges hunger, and communicates hunger.[2] Infants usually have little difficulty in being congruent; their simple motivations are obvious to themselves and others. However, as we mature, our motivations become increasingly private, and we lose awareness of them and of our ability to represent and express them in language. Adults are less congruent than they were as an infant.

> For an example of incongruence we must turn to someone beyond the stage of infancy. To pick an easily recognizable example take the man who becomes angrily involved in a group discussion. His face flushes, his tone communicates anger, he shakes his finger at his opponent. Yet, when a friend says, "Well, let's not get angry about this," he replies with evident sincerity and surprise, "I'm not angry! I don't have any *feeling* about this at all! I was just pointing out the logical facts." The other men in the group break out in laughter at this statement.[3]

Incongruence is the lack of a match between an attitude, awareness of the attitude, and representation of the attitude. Rogers's observations in counseling and psychotherapy led him to believe that it is relatively easy for us to *recognize* congruence and incongruence in others. With some people, we realize that what they represent is what they feel. We also recognize a facade when we see it. We understand that the incongruent person, illustrated by the angry man in the group discussion, has a hidden motivation. They laughed because they realized that he was verbally *expressing* something he refused to verbally *represent*.

2. Carl Rogers, *On Becoming a Person* (1961), 339.
3. Carl Rogers, *On Becoming a Person*, 339–340.

Language, we recall, is adaptive; it has at least five tasks or functions. One of these, representation, is the description of ideas or feelings. The other, expression, is the revelation of feelings. Incongruent people do not represent their attitudes or motivations; they may not even be aware of them. However, often these attitudes or motivations are expressed in tones of voice, facial movements, and gestures.

Rogers's idea of congruence helps explain how we can sometimes discover motivations. Congruent people represent and express their motivations verbally. There is no difficulty in detecting motivations if what people say is sincere, respectful of others, and committed to consensus because they are willing and capable of communicating their motives in words. However, the motives of incongruent people are much more difficult to detect.

People who are incongruent sometimes give themselves away in conversations, like the angry man in Rogers's example, by expressing their attitudes. An insincere car salesperson may *represent* that the car is "a real value," but we notice facial expressions and tones of voice that seem to express a lack of sincerity. Professor Johnson may represent to us that she has "an open door," and that she is anxious to hear the opinions of students. However, if she expresses lack of patience in listening to students' ideas (for instance, if she taps a pencil on the desk, and glances at her watch every two minutes) most students suspect that her door is not as "open" as she claims.

Less subtle actions than glancing at watches and tapping pencils also reveal attitudes. The hypocritical politician who represents himself as motivated by trust and honesty, and yet votes in the interests of the lobby from which he accepts thousands of dollars isn't as trustworthy and honest as he claims. His actions reveal his motivations to be more pecuniary than virtuous.

Aside from facial expressions, tones of voice, and contradictory actions, there isn't anything that reveals the motives of an incongruent person. Of course, people who are not in touch with their own motives cannot express or represent them in words. And if they don't know their own motives, or cannot accept them, they are probably hiding the motives from themselves as well as others. Detecting their motives can be virtually impossible.

However, a discussion with an incongruent person can often elicit an expression or representation of where they stand in regard to one or more of the three attitudinal standards of good thinking.

Detecting Attitudes in Pieces of Writing.   Attitudes can be detected in conversations from words, gestures, and other actions, including the ways people act that support or fail to support their expressed motives, such as the actions of the hypocritical politician. Pieces of writing have no gestures, no actions, and we often do not know much about the writer's life. This makes it difficult to determine the degree of sincerity, respect, and commitment to consensus present in a piece. Of course, sometimes the piece is clearly insincere, disrespectful, or lacks a commitment to consensus. For example, most advertising copy is so clearly an effort to persuade that the attitude behind it is easily detected. A phrase such as "You owe yourself a big bag of peanuts," written in large red letters on the side of a peanut vendor's wagon is certainly not seeking consensus! ("How do *you* feel about a bag of peanuts? Is it what you *really* want?") Political candidates who blatantly stereotype members of an opposing party as "ruthless opportunists" are obviously motivated by a lack of respect for their opponents. They do not regard their opponents' ideas as being as worthy of attention as their own. By calling their opponents "ruthless opportunists" they are attempting to trivialize the significance of their opponents' ideas.

The motivations behind most pieces of writing are not so obvious. On the one hand, some pieces are carefully written to intentionally deceive the reader. It can be very difficult to detect the attitudes behind them, because they are so well concealed. On the other hand, writers are sometimes not aware of their own attitudes. Their pieces may have a superficial appearance of sincerity and respect, but actually may be motivated by feelings of disrespect and a desire to distort the truth. We need to recognize that detecting the attitude behind a piece of writing is very difficult. We are always only speculating about the attitude; we can never know with any certainty whether a piece is motivated by sincerity, respect, or commitment to consensus.

When the attitude is not obvious, we can examine the piece to determine if perhaps an attitude is being displayed. There are four elements of written pieces that sometimes provide indications of attitudes: metaphors, allusions, loaded words, and prejudicial expressions.

METAPHORS. A metaphor is a word or phrase that describes something unfamiliar by comparing it to something more familiar, usually by describing the unfamiliar term in words usually used to describe the term that is more familiar. For example, carefully read Shakespeare's metaphor:

> "All the world's a stage,
> And all the men and women merely players.
> They have their exits and their entrances;
> And one man in his time plays many
> parts, . . ."[4]

Notice how Shakespeare describes the unfamiliar (the meaning of our lives) in a familiar way (a stage). His metaphor is meant to express his feeling that life, like a play, has a beginning and an exit, with some acting going on in between. His choice of the stage as a familiar description of the mystery of life reveals, to an extent, his attitude about the mystery of life. That is, it seems that Shakespeare felt that a person's life is no more (and no less) meaningful than the roles actors portray in the theater. An examination of the metaphor can reveal something (not everything, of course!) about Shakespeare's attitude, his feelings, concerning the mystery of life. Does he seem to be sincere, respectful, and committed to consensus? An examination of his piece shows that his attitude may

---

4. *As You Like It*, Act II.

not be committed to consensus. Perhaps the piece oversimplifies the mystery of life by describing it as a stage; maybe the description is trivial. Could Shakespeare be attempting to persuade us to accept his own beliefs about the mystery of life, even though he has not completely described them for us?

Obviously, Shakespeare's metaphor does not allow us to clearly detect his attitude. There is a great deal of room for speculation about it. However, sometimes an examination of the metaphors in a piece of writing can quite clearly reveal attitudes. For example, one of the more popular metaphors in our society is the war metaphor. We describe virtually every topic of discussion as a "war." We have the war on drugs, the war against poverty, even cola wars, and cereal wars. As one writer puts it:

> Americans talk about almost everything as if it were a war. A book about the history of linguistics is called *The Linguistics Wars.* A magazine article about claims that science is not completely objective is titled "The Science Wars." One about breast cancer detection is "The Mammogram War;" about competition between caterers, "Party Wars"—and on and on in a potentially endless list.[5]

War metaphors reveal an attitude of willingness to force others to accept beliefs whether or not they understand or accept them as true. When politicians refer to the "war on drugs," they are not motivated by an attitude of seeking consensus on a wise public policy regarding drug abuse and addiction. The metaphor reveals their attitude that the country is in a state of war; any policies other than their own are depicted as possible treason. War metaphors greatly oversimplify discussion about important ideas, making it appear that there are only two sides, which is never the case with complex issues. In doing so, they also reveal an attitude of disrespect for people who do not agree with either side of the issue. The so-called fringe views, or sometimes, off the wall views are not given consideration.

An examination of the metaphors used in a piece of writing can sometimes reveal a lack of sincerity. Television commercials and print advertisements often use metaphors to make obvious exaggerations about the nature of a product. A pick-up truck is a "rock," a soft drink is a "mountain dew," and a pet food is a "science diet." These metaphors clearly reveal that the attitude of the advertiser is insincere. They use misleading metaphors that are vague overgeneralizations about the qualities of their products in order to persuade consumers to consider purchasing them. Some metaphors used in commercials and advertisements oversimplify and trivialize important negative characteristics of products. For example, there is a great deal of difference between a caffeine-laden soft drink and the early morning dew on an alpine meadow! Advertisers are not defrauding consumers by using metaphors in this manner; they are merely attempting to stimulate interest in their products. However, it is important to recognize that the use of metaphors that obviously distort the quality of products reveals a lack of a sincere desire to assist consumers in discovering the truth

---

5. Deborah Tannen, *The Argument Culture,* pp. 13–14.

about them. In fact, consumers who seek the truth about products often read "the fine print" on labels or research consumer-oriented magazines.

ALLUSIONS.   An allusion is a casual or indirect reference to an idea or feeling that is suggested or insinuated by the piece, but which is not literally written down. Works of literature, films, and popular culture are often "alluded to" in written pieces without actually being referred to by words and sentences. For example, in the sentence "Jalon is not a rebel with a cause; he's not a rebel without one, either," there is an allusion to the film, "Rebel Without a Cause," an American movie made in the 1950's about adolescent alienation. The sentence has more meaning when we understand the allusion. Another example: "Jalon sure dropped the ball on his recent presentation to the class," alludes to games such as football and baseball in which "dropping the ball" is a mark of failure. Again, we understand the sentence more thoroughly if we are aware of the allusion.

Allusions don't only suggest things from popular culture, such as athletics and films. They can also hint at personal opinions, religious or political values, prejudices and narrow-minded views. Attitudes can sometimes be detected by examining these kinds of allusions. Consider this short piece:

> An age which can consider the scientist unfeeling, just because some of his findings have a validity independent of feeling, can obviously consider the artist unthinking. When the popular mind wishes to be friendly to the artist it makes of him an ethereal genius who does not descend to "mere" reason. When it wishes to be unfriendly, it makes of him a madman who could never rise to reason's sublime heights.[6]

First, we need to notice two allusions about the writer's personal opinions. The paragraph suggests that the writer feels that (1) there is something wrong with the belief that scientists are "unfeeling," and that artists are "unthinking." It goes on to suggest that the writer feels (2) that the "popular mind," depending on nothing more than how friendly it feels toward them, regards artists as being either geniuses or madmen. Neither personal opinion is literally written down. Both are only hinted at or insinuated. Nevertheless, the allusions allow us to detect an attitude of *disrespect* for the "popular mind," on the part of the writer. By alluding to (1) the popular mind's shallow evaluation of the role of feeling in science and thinking in art, the writer appears to be revealing his own feelings of superiority. When he refers to (2) the fickle way the popular mind decides whether artists are geniuses or madmen, the writer again seems to be alluding to his own superiority and the inferiority of the popular mind. The author's attitude seems to be rather narrow-minded. He stereotypes everyone but himself as the popular mind. Everyone, he appears to believe (except himself), thinks in the same shallow and fickle way.

Allusions to the writer's attitude can be found by "reading between the lines." That is, we can find attitudes that lay "behind" the piece by reflecting on

---

6. Eric Bentley, *The Life of the Drama* (1991), p. 103.

the allusions that the piece uses. We can sometimes detect an insincere attitude, or one that disrespects someone or that is trying to force its ideas on people.

LOADED WORDS.   Some words are loaded with attitude. A piece in a newspaper refers to a film actress as "cheerful on the set." That is not quite the same meaning as a popular tabloid's reference to the same celebrity: "frivolous in her approach to acting." Which is it? Is she "cheerful" or "frivolous"?

There is a subtle difference in meaning between the two words. To be "frivolous" is to be irresponsible, superficial, and even silly. Frivolous people are not in much demand in the film industry. Irresponsibility, superficiality, silliness? Who needs it? Being "cheerful," on the other hand, is to be pleasant and happy. There is nothing very controversial about these characteristics; in fact, most people see them as desirable traits that are not unusual on a movie set.

It is not uncommon to refer to pleasant, happy people as "cheerful." However, the word "frivolous" has a negative connotation for most people. It brings to mind words we use when disapproving of someone's actions, such as irresponsible, superficial, and silly. It seems to be used as an *expression of attitude* more than as a *representation of an idea*. The tabloid is using the expressive function of language, not the representative function, when it describes the actress as "frivolous." Expressive terms, when they declare attitudes of disapproval, are referred to as "loaded terms." They are "loaded with attitude."

Consider the following list of words. On the left are terms loaded with an attitude of approval. On the right are terms loaded with an attitude of disapproval. Each term could be used to represent an idea about the same individual or group. However, depending on which side of the list is chosen, the attitude is either positive or negative.

- Self-assured
- Dedicated
- Quiet
- Visionary
- Sympathetic
- Educated
- Generous
- Articulate
- Sincere
- Respectful
- Committed

- Arrogant
- Stubborn
- Dull
- Fanciful
- Lenient
- Bookish
- Extravagant
- Outspoken
- Zealous
- Submissive
- Inflexible

We can play a game with this list of loaded words. For example, select a person for whom you have positive feelings—your friend Kenneth. Kenneth is planning on donating several years of his life to work with the Peace Corps. He will be graduating "cum laude." He is also a critical thinker. So, you could say that Kenneth is visionary, educated, sincere, respectful of others, and committed to consensus. Or, taking the other side of the list, you could say he is fanciful, bookish, zealous, submissive to others, and inflexibly attached to consensus! Which is the real Kenneth?

Loaded words do not represent ideas or perceptions. They express attitudes about ideas or perceptions. The representation of Kenneth as "planning on donating several years of his life to work with the Peace Corps, graduating "cum laude," and "being a critical thinker" are representations of someone's perception of Kenneth. However, the loaded words are expressions of attitudes someone has about him. Loaded words convey meaning about the attitude of the person using them; they do not represent the person's perceptions or ideas.

Slang words are "loaded" with approval or disapproval. Slang is vocabulary used by people in order to identify with the values of a particular group. The vocabulary of the group allows members to communicate with one another in ways that reflect and reinforce their values. Group members, or those who identify with the group, feel slang terms express their feelings more adequately than those used in ordinary language.

Attitudes can often be detected by examining the loaded words in a written piece. If a newspaper editorial refers to the mayor's plans to build three more shelters for the homeless as a "generous project," a positive attitude can be detected. If her plan is described as an "extravagant scheme," then a negative attitude toward her plans is apparent.

In the brief piece about the "popular mind" we examined in the previous section (on allusions), we can note several loaded words that help display attitude. What if the "popular mind" had been expressed as the "prevailing view"? This would seem to be more respectful. What if, instead of referring to the belief that artists were either "ethereal geniuses or madmen who could never rise to reason's sublime heights," the writer had written, "discriminating intellectuals" or "distressed men who could never achieve reason's inspiration"? If the piece were revised, it could read this way:

> An age which can consider the scientist unfeeling, just because some of his findings have a validity independent of feeling, can obviously consider the artist unthinking. When the prevailing view wishes to be friendly to the artist it makes of him a discriminating intellectual who does not descend to "mere" reason. When it wishes to be unfriendly, it makes of him a distressed man who could never achieve reason's inspiration.

There are other suggestions for revision of this piece that would result from a review of word choice. One choice of words that may already be apparent is the use of "his," "him," and "man." Does this choice of words also express an attitude on the part of the writer that is important to a full understanding of the piece? These words are not "loaded" with attitudes of approval or disapproval. They are prejudicial expressions.

PREJUDICIALLY BIASED EXPRESSIONS. Attitude can be detected by examining a piece for words or phrases that indicate a biased attitude. Bias is an emotional attitude of partiality for a particular way of thinking and feeling. Our early childhood experiences, social interactions with peers, and cultural influences play a large role not only in shaping our perceptions, but also in establishing our inclinations to favor and disfavor particular ways of feeling and thinking. Prejudice and bias are not the same. "Prejudicial bias" (usually referred to as "prejudice") is a particular type of bias that was described earlier in this chapter as "the belief that another person is of less inherent value than oneself due to their gender, ethnicity, religion, race, age, or political values." Prejudicial expressions are a clear indication of an attitude that lacks respect for the targeted group.

No one can avoid bias completely. There are, it seems, an infinite number of ways to think and feel about experience. Each of us is developing our own style, our own ways of thinking and feeling. Our individuality, to a large extent, consists of these differences, these biases.

Prejudice should and can be avoided. In the first place, prejudice is simply unfair to people. Being the target of prejudice can have a devastating effect on an individual's life. Of course, it is severely damaging to self-esteem, especially for children. Prejudice is also at the root of many social, economic, and political problems on a global scale. Stereotyping and discriminating against individuals due to prejudicial biases *disenfranchises* them; that is, prejudice excludes targeted people from the opportunities others enjoy. All of us, as human beings, have a deep need for interaction with others. Most of the satisfactions life has to offer us are directly involved with attachment to other people. We need to be a part of things. Exclusion causes targeted individuals enormous frustration, alienation, and detachment.

Our own prejudicial biases can be overcome, as we shall see, by developing empathy with individuals and groups against whom we are prejudiced.

Prejudice in pieces written by others is often displayed in biased expressions. When the writer of the piece we revised earlier uses the masculine pronouns "his" and "him," he expresses a prejudicial bias against women. The expression reveals his attitude that men, not women, are scientists, and that men, not women, are artists. He expresses his prejudice again with the noun "man," which he uses to refer to all artists. The use of masculine pronouns to refer to men *and* women expresses a prejudice against women because such usage establishes men as the established representative of *both* genders. If "man" is believed to adequately represent women, then women must be believed to have less inherent value than men. If the piece were revised in a way to reduce its prejudicial bias against women, it would look something like this:

> An age which can consider the scientist unfeeling, just because some of his or her findings have a validity independent of feeling, can obviously consider the artist unthinking. When the prevailing view wishes to be friendly to the artist it makes of him or her a discriminating intellectual who does not descend to "mere" reason. When it wishes to be unfriendly, it makes of him or her a distressed individual who could never achieve reason's inspiration.

When the loaded words and prejudicial expressions of the piece are revised, its representational meaning becomes clearer, more accurate, more specific, and more significant. Of course, the actual author may not agree with our revision, he (Eric Bentley) may want to continue to express his negative feelings and prejudices. That would be a shame, but it is important to keep in mind that critical thinking reviews, evaluates, and revises *thinking*, not people. The detection of attitude in written pieces is meant to help with the understanding, processing, and communication of ideas, not to reform individuals. On the other hand, the more we overcome prejudicial thoughts and feelings, the more hope we can have that some day we can live in a world without prejudice.

Prejudicial expressions concerning ethnicity, religious beliefs, race, age, and political values also provide opportunities for the detection of attitude. When newspaper editorials refer to "Crafty Chinese Businessmen," or "Fanatical Iranian Moslems," they are showing an attitude of lack of respect for others and an unwillingness to seek consensus with those groups. As a result, the clarity, accuracy, specificity, and significance of the editorials are bound to suffer.

Detecting attitudes in written pieces is always speculative; whether a piece expresses a particular attitude can never be demonstrated with any certainty. The conclusions are always tentative. One way to improve the quality of a search for an attitude is to do some research on the life of the author of the piece. If we take a look at the life of Eric Bentley (who wrote the piece we have revised several times), we find that he was an American drama critic who taught at a prestigious university in the 1950s. His attitude seems to be representative of his social status and his era. It is possible for us to understand Bentley's ideas more thoroughly if we know something about him. More important, knowing something about Bentley's life allows us the opportunity to empathize with him. Empathy, which is taking on the perspective of another person, allows us, in a limited way, to share the perceptions of another person. We will examine empathy more thoroughly in the next section.

EXERCISES

▲ MOST INTRIGUING ISSUE

Write a one-paragraph description of the most interesting idea, topic, or process described in the chapter so far. Be prepared to explain what you find interesting in class discussion.

▲ THE MUDDIEST POINT

Write a sentence or, if possible, a paragraph that describes the idea, topic, expression, term, or process in the chapter so far that you find most difficult to understand.

▲ CARTOONS AND DIAGRAMS

1. Draw a cartoon that shows how attitudes of sincerity, respect for others, and commitment to consensus are expressed in actions.

2. Provide a cartoon that shows how attitudes are expressed in the subject matter and vocabulary of written pieces.

3. Create a cartoon that shows how attitudes are expressed in the judgments and conclusions of written pieces.

4. Create a cartoon that illustrates the ways deception is usually carried out in verbal thinking.

5. Provide a cartoon that illustrates the ways lack of respect usually takes place in verbal thinking.

6. Draw a cartoon that shows how a nonconsensual attitude can take place in verbal thinking.

7. Provide a cartoon of an incongruent person in a conversation with a congruent person.

8. Draw a cartoon that shows how metaphors in written pieces can be used to detect attitudes.

9. Create a cartoon that illustrates how allusions can indicate attitude in written pieces.

10. Create a cartoon that shows how word choice can reveal attitudes in written pieces.

11. Create a cartoon that illustrates the way prejudicial expressions can be used to detect attitude in written pieces.

▲ DEFINITIONS OF KEY TERMS

Provide a disciplinary definition for each of the following terms as they are used in this chapter. Most of the terms are not defined in the chapter, although their meanings are described by the context in which they appear. You need to review the material to create the definition yourself. Be sure to follow the guidelines for creating definitions on pages 78–81.

Allusion	Attitude	Disenfranchisement
Loaded Term	Metaphor	Motivation
Non-Consensual	Prejudice	Prejudicially Biased Expression
Stereotype	Verbal Content	Verbal Meaning

▲ SHORT ESSAY QUESTIONS

Provide a written response of approximately 200 words for each topic. Your responses should be well organized, grammatically correct, and neatly produced.

1. Describe the four ways attitude can be detected in written pieces.
2. Explain why it is much simpler to detect attitude in a conversation with a congruent person than to detect it in a piece written by an incongruent person.
3. Which attitudinal standard can be detected as in need of revision in each of the following? Explain how you came to your conclusion.
   a) A use of "one-liners" that oversimplify complex issues
   b) A deliberate use of imprecise description of evidence
   c) A prejudicially biased description of an individual
   d) A rejection of commonly accepted authorities who disagree with the conclusion of the piece

   e) A consistent use of negatively loaded words

   f) A clear attempt to psychologically force acceptance of an idea

   g) A minimization of evidence contrary to the piece's conclusion

   h) A deliberate distortion of meaning in a paraphrase

   i) A metaphor in a print advertisement: "Steve's Sausage is Hog Caviar"

   j) A metaphor in a business's name: "Ron's Perfect Used Car Paradise"

4. Examine the list of loaded words on p. 105. Create a single sentence for each pair, using the appropriate loaded term in each. (For example, *My professor is self-assured. My professor is arrogant.*) Explain how the different connotations of each loaded term express specific different attitudes for each pair. (For example, *"Self-assured" expresses the attitude that my professor is confident; "arrogant" expresses the attitude that my professor is egotistical.*

5. What allusions to personal opinions, religious or political values, prejudices or narrow-minded views are being made in each of the following? What attitudes do they express? Why do you think so?

   a) *"Men, be kind to your fellow men; this is your first duty, to be kind to every age and station, kind to all that is not foreign to humanity. What wisdom can you find that is greater than kindness? Love childhood, indulge in its sports, its pleasure, its delightful instincts."*

   (Jean-Jacques Rousseau, 1762)

   b) *"Our hopes for the future condition of the human race can be subsumed under three important heads: the abolition of inequality between nations, the progress of equality within each nation, and the true perfection of humanity. Will all nations one day attain that state of civilization which the most enlightened, the freest, the least burdened by prejudices, such as the French, the English, and the Americans have attained already? Will the vast gulf that separates these peoples from the slavery of nations under the rule of monarchs, from the barbarism of African tribes, from the ignorance of savages, little by little disappear?"*

   (Antoine Condorcet, 1795)

   c) *"I am sure that I never read any memorable news in a newspaper. If we read of one man robbed, or murdered, or killed by accident, or one house burned, or one vessel wrecked, or one steamboat blown up, or one cow run over on the Western Railroad, or one mad dog killed, or one lot of grasshoppers in the winter—we never need read of another. One is enough. If you are acquainted with the principle, what do care for a thousand instances and applications? To a philosopher all news, as it is called, is gossip, and they who edit and read it are old women over their tea."*

   (Henry David Thoreau, 1854)

   d) *"It is better to be a human being dissatisfied than a pig satisfied; better to be Socrates dissatisfied than a fool satisfied. And if the fool, or the pig, is of a different opinion, it is because they only know their own side of the question. The other part of the comparison knows both sides."*

   (John Stuart Mill, 1861)

   e) *"With satanic joy in his face, the black-haired Jewish youth lurks in wait for the unsuspecting girl whom he defiles with his blood, thus stealing her from her people. With every means he tries to destroy the racial foundations of the people he has set out to subjugate. Just as he himself systematically ruins women and girls, he does not shrink back from pulling down the* *blood barriers for others, even on a large scale. It was and it is Jews who bring the Negroes into Germany, always with the same secret thought and clear aim of ruining the hated white race."*

(Adolph Hitler, 1927)

▲ QUESTIONS FOR DISCUSSION

Provide a written essay of 300–500 words that responds to each of the following questions which ask for your opinion. You should respond by stating it, and by providing thoughts, examples, and insights that support it. You should be willing to revise your response; you may change your opinion during or after a class discussion.

1. The seven standards of good thinking are ideal models of perfection. No one can achieve them completely. Different pieces of writing should be expected to have different degrees of clarity, accuracy, specificity, and significance. For example, we expect less of each in an advertisement for a pizza restaurant than we do in a newspaper editorial. How about sincerity, respect for others, and commitment to consensus? Do we expect less of them in different pieces, too? Specifically, should we expect a lower degree of attitudinal standards in a pizza restaurant advertisement than in a newspaper editorial? Why or why not?

2. Is it possible for a piece of writing to fail in regard to sincerity, respect, and commitment to consensus, and yet be as clear, accurate, specific, and significant as it should be? Why or why not?

3. Attitudes are emotional senses of approval or disapproval, according to the chapter. However, isn't there also a "cognitive" element to attitudes? For example, Josh loves to read the classics of Western philosophy. He reads John Stuart Mill and Jean Jacques Rousseau late into the night. When asked what his motivation is, he replies that many of the ideas in these writings are profound truths, and that his motivation is a cognitive one, not emotional at all. Is Josh correct? Can cognitive factors alone motivate us? Can they play a role in motivating us?

4. What do you suppose is the larger obstacle in becoming a congruent person? Is it understanding our feelings? Is it acknowledging them? Is it communicating them? What are the specific differences between these three things? Are you a congruent person? How do you know if you are or if you aren't?

5. The chapter refers to "war metaphors," specifically the "war on drugs." Do you have any suggestions for a different metaphor, or is the present one satisfactory? Why or why not?

6. According to the chapter the exclusive use of masculine pronouns for gender expresses an attitude of disrespect to women. Do you agree? Why or why not? What about writers who rely exclusively on female pronouns for gender? Are they expressing an attitude of disrespect for men? Why or why not?

7. In relatively recent times, some educators and social critics have encouraged Americans to make changes in their language. They claim that the word "Blacks," for example, should be changed to "African Americans." The word "Indians" should be changed to "Native American." The word "Oriental" should be changed to "Asian American." Instead of "Homosexuals," we are encouraged to use "Gays," or "Queers." In place of "Handicapped," we should use "Physically Challenged." Other educators and social critics have discouraged these changes, claiming that language should develop on its own without our attempts to "police" it with demands for "political correctness." How do you feel about this debate? Are you on one side or the other, or do you feel there is more to the problem than the two "sides" consider?

8. Review the following editorials from imaginary college newspapers for metaphors, allusions, loaded words, and prejudicial expressions. What attitudes do you detect that you consider below the standards of good thinking?

a) Should Students Be Johns?

Last week, several jocks sent a letter to the editor begging the student body to "come and support us in our football games." The "student section is never full," according to the letter, "and there's hardly enough people to do the cards." Who wrote this letter? We know you guys scratched your "x's" on the bottom, but there weren't any spelling or grammatical problems. 'Fess up. One of the groupies did it; the same one that's writing all your English Comp assignments.

Let's face it. These "games" are bad, bad, bad shows. To get a ticket, you need to line up with the "fans:" mostly drugged out rock and roller types hoping for a glimpse of their fave sex icons. It's New Orleans on a Fat Tuesday. Three hours before the show, these drunks and meth freaks are screaming like savages at a mammoth hunt. There's even a little band of developmentally delayed boneheads with their bodies painted in school colors. Once inside, these howling hormone bags step up the action, groping for a bottle or a babe, no matter. It's "Leaving Las Vegas" meets "Planet of the Apes." They want to stick the other team in a big pot on a fire and dance around them naked. Somebody throw 'em a banana.

On the field of play, things aren't any better. The hookers look great at the start of the game in their tight shiny pants and buffed-up body padding, but are beaten, bloody, and bonkers by the end of the night. Yeah, hookers. These guys are steroid-bloated prostitutes and our university is their pimp. The Crazy Coach is the Big Madam in charge. He and his Boy-Toys have never seen the library; they don't read, don't even talk much. Well, that's not true if you count "Hey," "man," and "foo-baa," the only three words in their vocabulary. By halftime the stadium is Fort Apache and the cops are out for doughnuts. The savages spin out around the third quarter and head for the frat house liquor lounges. The place is empty by the time the guys in the white coats haul the hookers off the field in stretchers and body-casts. It's been another good night for Pimp U., our school.

Big Madam can't be bothered with his hacked-up hookers. He's long gone, cruising the bus station in his glitzy '75 Cadillac, eyeing nubile flesh for next year's stable.

Can you read this? Hey, man, no way, *no go to foo-baa.* No like. Too savage, too vile, too dumb, man, way too dumb.

b) Let's All Go to the (real) Movies

Last week's student council meeting was refreshing, gratifying, and pleasant. With no acrimony, no raised voices, and no rudeness, the student council voted to deny funding to the self-designated "College Film Society," thereby eliminating the most disruptive element on campus. All year long, this "society" has been an asteroid headed for campus values, a Godzilla out of control, a threat to what makes this college one of the few havens of moral values in our nation. Elitist film students, radical Bolsheviks to a man, plotted to crush the accepted values on campus by showing exploitative pornography, left-wing propaganda, and irresponsible hate-films (none of them from Hollywood, of course) such as students at this school have never seen. There have been many letters to this newspaper from defenders of family values and mainstream, law-abiding students denouncing and expressing well-spoken outrage at Carol Jones, leader of the propagandist purveyors of pornography who call themselves the "College Film Society."

Thank Goodness for the erudite conservatives and champions of the status quo who sacrificed their time to attend the student council's budget hearing last week. Some of these students, the best and brightest stars on campus, showed us what true freedom of expression really is: the defense of what is right and good. Of course, the wild-eyed fanatics and indoctrinated knee jerk liberals tried to turn dialogue into debate. But our student council Chairman, Ted Schultz, would have none of it! With all the finesse of a Ronald Reagan in his prime, Schultz guided his council in dedicated business student style. The council chamber had the atmosphere of a well-mannered corporate boardroom. With the wisdom of Socrates and the courage of Caesar, Schultz sent the multicultural antagonists scurrying back to whatever alleys they sleep in. Let's hope we see and hear from these free speech, free love, free *everything* addicts never again!

No longer does this newspaper feel it is on the deck of the Titanic, awaiting the disastrous assault on its principles that the ill-mannered film radicals had targeted next. Our sources verify our suspicion that if their funding had not been denied, they would have assaulted this paper next. But like a warm tub on a cold night, a fur coat in a snowstorm, this paper will now continue to stand for what is good and what is right. Here's a big thanks, men (and to the girls, too), you stalwart defenders of free enterprise, Gibraltars of fiscal responsibility, for standing up for the rights established by our founding fathers!

And let's everybody go see a *good* (Hollywood) movie tonight!

c) Quiet, please, some people are studying!

This is going to get some people pretty hot, as in angry, so if you count yourself among the Fem-Nazis you should stop reading right now. Wait a minute. What am I saying? Go ahead, make my day. Read on. I hope you get all steamed up, because I don't like you anyway.

This is the problem, gals. We have a library here on campus that has a lot of oblong-shaped things in it. These are called "books." A lot of people read them. That's what my friends and I were trying to do on Friday night when we were attacked by a horde of illiterates. Like a gaggle of geese seeking a warm Southern marsh, they descended on the third floor "Quiet Zone" squawking, squeaking, and squealing. Mating calls? Probably. Successful? I don't think so.

These Beach Blanket Bimbos had probably already been trying to snare men in the "meat market" bars that line the campus. Having found all the good-looking guys either already trapped or not available, they packed their makeup kits and headed for where they knew the future leaders and shakers (and moneymakers) were. The Quiet Zone on the third floor.

The literate man often spends his Friday evening in the Quiet Zone. It's a place of cultured good taste and intelligent relaxation; a place to get away from the gnawing televised idiocies going on in the "Recreation Rooms" of the dorms. By the way, those recreation rooms were a lot more peaceful before the dorms went coed. Anyhow, there we were, studying for our classes, like college students are supposed to be doing on a Friday night, when the Babes in Bookland made their entrance.

Immediately the Quiet Zone became a chicken coop; peck, peck, peck, cheep, cheep, cheep. A quick flight over to the magazine rack, no doubt to gaze at the latest Cosmo hair styles. (Successful cosmetology helps haul in that future husband!) It didn't take long for the Quiet Zone to take on the clatter and clutter of a sorority girl bash.

It was the Library of Alexandria all over again. The only thing they didn't do was build a fire. They probably couldn't work the matches.

I took things into my own hands and approached our own Marion the Librarian, who is paid to guarantee that the Quiet Zone be maintained as . . . quiet. Is that too much to ask? It appears to be! Marion immediately took the side of the banshees. Now I know that library science ain't rocket science, but don't they teach those people that Quiet Zones are supposed to be quiet? Marion didn't go to class that day, I guess. "The women are not making any more noise than you and your friends made last week, Mr. Clundey." I pointed out that she was mixing apples and oranges (or was it brains and berries?). "We were talking about the spectacular rise and lamentable fall of the Third Reich!" I exclaimed. "That's an event of great historical significance! These dyslexic dummies don't even know what the glories of the Third Reich were!"

She kicked me out. Me! She let the brain dead gossips stay. They played with their hair, exchanged fashion tips, and tried to seduce my friends.

What's my message? Stay away from the Quiet Zone, ladies. If you want to corral a stallion, stay in the bars. If you want to chatter about cosmetics, stay in your rooms. But whatever you do, stay out of the Quiet Zone. That's off limits; no illiterates allowed.

▲ QUOTATION TO PONDER

"This is how language works. It invisibly molds our way of thinking about people, actions, and the world around us. Military metaphors train us to think about—and see—everything in terms of fighting, conflict, and war. This perspective then limits our imaginations when we consider what we can do about situations we would like to understand or change."

Deborah Tannen, *The Argument Culture*

▲ Journal Topic

Review the "Letters to the Editor" page of a newspaper or newsmagazine for examples of metaphors, allusions, loaded words, and prejudicial expressions. Select one or two letters for a more thorough evaluation in relation to the three attitudinal standards of good thinking.

EMPATHY

Empathy is an emotional identification with the feelings, thoughts, and attitudes of another person. It is a "taking on" of another's perceptual set, "standing in their shoes." We can sometimes detect another's attitude and motivation by putting ourselves in their place. Consider the following illustration of empathy.

It is the first day of the new term. Sandy runs into her friend Jerome on the way to her first History of Western Civilization class. She tells him that she is worried about the course because she has heard that the professor, Dr. Hutchinson, is impatient with students.

> "I know what you mean," says Jerome. "I've had classes with impatient professors, too. But I had a course with Dr. Hutchinson, and I didn't find her to be impatient at all. She's a good teacher, very fair to everyone."
>
> Sandy replies, "Well, you are an honors student, Jerome. She probably thinks you're brilliant. How do you think I feel? I barely passed my English Composition course last term! I know she assigns essay questions for homework every week, including the first week!"
>
> "I understand," says Jerome. "I think I can relate to how you feel. You're really frightened that if you won't do well on your homework the first week of the term Dr. Hutchinson will think you are a bad student from then on."
>
> "That's right," says Sandy. "That's exactly how I feel."

Jerome has empathy for Sandy's feelings. He does not necessarily *agree* with her that Dr. Hutchinson is impatient. He doesn't even agree that Sandy's fear is warranted. He thinks Dr. Hutchinson is a good teacher, fair, and not impatient with anyone. Nevertheless, he can identify with Sandy's feelings. He can "get into" her perceptions, and share her views without agreeing with them. When we have empathy for someone, we perceive things the way he or she perceives them. We understand "where they are coming from."

Without empathy, Jerome and Sandy could not even have had a conversation. He had to be able to "put himself in her place" in order to understand her anxiety about Dr. Hutchinson's class. Without that understanding, he would not have been able to respond to her as well as he did, and no conversation would have taken place. For example:

Sandy: "I'm worried about this course, because I've heard that the professor, Dr. Hutchinson, is impatient with students."

Jerome: "What are you talking about? She's fine."

Sandy: "Well, you are an honors student, Jerome. She probably thinks you're brilliant. How do you think I feel? I barely passed my English Composition course last term! I know she assigns essay questions for homework every week, including the first week!"

Jerome: "I don't have the slightest idea of what you are talking about. I have no problem with her."

Sandy: "I have to go now, Jerome."

Jerome: "Huh? Oh, goodbye."

We need to have empathy with a person in order to communicate with them. However, we do not have to agree with them.

When we agree with a person's feelings, we have *sympathy* for them. In the first example, if Jerome had agreed that Dr. Hutchinson was impatient, not a very good teacher, and unfair, he would have been sympathizing, and not necessarily empathizing, with Sandy's perceptions. The words "sympathy" and "empathy" are often used as synonyms in ordinary language. When a person feels sympathy for someone else, it is usually the case that they empathize with that person, too. For example, if a friend has suffered from a death in the family, we sympathize with their sorrow because we agree that the death is a sorrowful event. We also empathize with them. We put ourselves in their place, and imagine how it must feel going through that sort of tragedy. We sympathize and we empathize. Since people often put themselves in the places of people they share sorrow with, it is understandable that ordinary language often treats the two words as synonymous.

It is important in critical thinking to keep their meanings separate. Understanding a point of view is impossible without at least a small degree of empathy, even if we don't agree with the opinion it represents. We cannot adequately review the meaning or the feeling of a written piece unless we at least have an elementary identification with "where it comes from." At the bare minimum, we need to be able to accept that the piece "comes from" a person who wrote it, and that it makes sense to that person. We may not know "*where* they are coming from," but we must at least empathize with them to the point that they are "coming from *somewhere*."

"But," someone complains, "what if they aren't coming from somewhere! What if they are just plain crazy?!"

The fact of the matter is that very, very few people are so crazy that they aren't coming from "somewhere." People, those with serious mental illnesses included, always write and speak in a way that represents and expresses their perceptions. When we accuse a person of being "crazy" and of making no sense at all, we are simply saying that we do not understand them. Individual people have very different perceptual experiences. As we saw in Chapter 1, each person lives within his or her own perceptual set. In Chapter 3, we learned that language allows us to "cross the bridge" from our own "world" to that of another person. However, even language cannot help us understand someone else unless we at first establish some empathy with him or her. After all, how can we confirm the meaning of another person's words if we don't at least recognize that that person is writing or speaking a language that makes sense to us?

Consider this far-fetched illustration. A space ship lands and an alien emerges to greet you,

"Take me to your leader."

"Sure," you say.

"Wait a minute!" says the alien. "What did you mean by that?"

"By what?"

"By that word 'sure?'"

"I meant what everybody means by it. I meant, 'ok,' I'll take you to my leader."

"Wait a minute," says the alien.

"What now?"

"What did you mean by that last sentence?"

"I meant what I said," you respond impatiently.

"What did you mean just now when you said 'I meant what I said?'" asks the alien with a skeptical look.

You are really losing patience now. "What if you said, 'I meant what I said?' What would *you* mean?"

"Well," says the alien, "I'd mean that what I said is what I mean."

"That's what I mean, too."

"Do you always mean what I would mean if I said what you said?" asks the alien.

"Of course," you respond. "How else would we communicate? Linguistic confirmation would be impossible without at least a small degree of empathy."

"What do you mean by 'empathy?'"

"Look here, alien," you say, "If you want to communicate with people on this planet, you're going to have to accept that when we say something, we mean what you would mean if you said it!"

"Ok, but tell me what empathy is," the alien says.

"Empathy is giving people a 'break,'" you say. "Empathy, at its least developed level, is assuming that when someone writes or speaks, they are representing ideas and expressing feelings they truly have."

"So this isn't one of those planets where everybody always lies?" says the alien.

"No, not all the time, or even most of the time" you say. "And even if people here do lie, it is possible to empathize with them a little. If my younger brother steals a cookie and lies about it, I can empathize with him. I don't agree that he should lie about stealing the cookie, but I understand, at least a little, *why* he lied. I can relate to where he is coming from. From his point of view, he was afraid of being punished."

"Tell me one more time what empathy is," says the alien.

"Empathy is the emotional identification with the feelings, thoughts, and attitudes of another person. It is a 'taking on' of another's perceptual set."

There is more to empathy than merely accepting that when other people use language that they are using it in the same way we do. However, without this very simple, very elementary form of empathy, linguistic confirmation and language itself would not be possible.

EMPATHY AND REVIEW OF WRITTEN PIECES

When reviewing written pieces, it is almost always possible to identify with the meaning of the words the writer has used to represent his or her ideas. If we understand the writer's vocabulary, we can identify with the meaning of what is written. Of course, we do not necessarily have to agree with it. For example, consider this short piece,

I'm only a seven-year-old boy, but I know that my favorite food, ice cream, is a health food. It has lots of milk in it, so it is high in calcium, which is good for your bones. It has sugar, too, which is a great energy food. I'd eat more ice cream, but my mother won't let me. She's not much of a health nut, I guess.

There is no difficulty in understanding the thoughts the young writer represents here. He believes ice cream to be a health food. It takes a minimum amount of empathy on our part to understand the meaning; all we need do is accept that the writer means what we would mean if we were in his place, and if we had written the piece.

It is important to notice that empathy is achieved by imagining that we are "in" the perceptual set of the person writing the piece. We don't achieve an empathetic standpoint by imagining that we are writing the piece from *our own* perceptual set. Rather, it is achieved by imagining that we are writing the piece from the perceptual set of the actual writer. We need to "put ourselves in the writer's place" and try to understand what is written from the *writer's* point of view. Otherwise, we cannot truly understand the meaning of the piece.

There is little or no difficulty in understanding the attitude displayed in the short piece. The writer is seven years old. Although he does not come out and express the feeling "I really like ice cream!" we know how he feels about it. He says that it is his "favorite food." We can "put ourselves in his place," imagine ourselves as seven years old, and recognize that his piece is a gentle plea for more ice cream in his life, not only because of its health value, but because he enjoys it. Our emotional identification with the boy's feelings about ice cream is empathetic. We are "taking on" his perceptual set. Of course, all of this does not mean that we agree with him about the nutritious value of his favorite food.

THE PURPOSE AND CONTEXT OF A WRITTEN PIECE

Understanding the purpose and the context of a written piece are keys to attaining empathy with it. We can "put ourselves into the shoes" of the piece by considering *why* and *how* it was written.

The Purpose of the Piece. The purpose of the piece consists in what the writer wants the audience to think and feel as a result of reading it. The writer may not have had the purpose clearly in mind during the writing process, although it is usually "in the back of his or her mind." The writer may have written the piece simply as a representation of thoughts and as an expression of feelings, without giving much consideration to how he or she wanted the audience to receive the piece's meaning.

Nevertheless, we can grasp the purpose of the piece by taking an empathetic stance with the writer. For example, when the seven-year-old boy writes that ice cream is a health food, we can grasp his piece's purpose by empathizing with his perceptual set. His purpose is to direct us to believe that he should be given more ice cream. That's what he wants us to think and feel as a result of reading his piece.

In Chapter 3, we discussed the five functions, or tasks, of language: to represent, to direct, to commit, to express, and to perform. The purposes of written pieces parallel these functions. That is, every piece's purpose consists of one or more of the tasks of language. By empathizing with the perspective of the piece, we can usually grasp its main purpose rather easily. In addition to the main purposes, there are more specific purposes. For example, the main purpose of the boys' piece on the dietary value of ice cream was to direct. More specifically, it was to persuade us of the truth of what he was representing. The following chart briefly describes the different purposes of written pieces.

Main Purpose	Specific Purposes
Representation	To describe an individual's perceptions, ideas, theories, fantasies, and opinions as well as to define words and to summarize and paraphrase another person's words.
Direction	An individual's orders, instructions, and attempts to persuade or convince. Most questions have the purpose of directing another person to respond.
Commitment	To make a contract, a promise, an assurance, or a pledge.
Expression	An individual's declaration of his or her moral, political, or religious values as well as the venting of emotions.
Performance	To cooperate with previously accepted rules or rituals in a game, ceremony, or social environment.

Most written pieces are representative; their specific purposes are to describe what we see, hear, and so on, as well as to describe our opinions. Definitions, summaries, and paraphrases are made in order to represent meaning. Another specific purpose of representation is to describe an individual's imaginary world in literature.

Pieces that direct have the specific purposes to convince the reader that an opinion should be accepted, or to show how to carry out particular tasks. Questions elicit responses.

Contracts, such as those made when people marry, lease property, or make agreements in other ways are among the specific purposes of pieces that are commitments. An assurance is a piece that is meant to guarantee that a commitment is still held.

Any piece about personal values, whether moral, religious, or political, is meant to express the writer's feelings. However, if the writer claims that the values go beyond the personal, and are values the reader (and perhaps everyone else) should embrace, the piece is also meant to persuade or convince. Of course, a piece that only describes values is not meant to express feelings or persuade.

Pieces that "meet requirements" have the purpose of performing a duty or carrying out an obligation. A great deal of academic written work carries out an assignment given by the teacher. As such, its specific purpose is to meet the requirements of a course. In addition, academic pieces may be meant to describe ideas and express feelings.

Context of the Piece.   The flexibility of language allows the meaning of a piece to change with its context, as we saw in Chapter 3. The context of a piece of writing consists of three elements that help shape its meaning: its cultural environment (in which the piece was written), its writing style, and its intended audience.

CULTURAL ENVIRONMENT.   The social, religious, economic, and political situation of a piece make up its cultural environment. A piece written in fourteenth-century Ireland has a much different cultural environment than one written in nineteenth-century France. In similar manner, a piece written about human rights in China in 1998 has a different cultural environment than one written on the same subject in the United States at the same time. The relationship of the writer with the cultural environment, if known, is helpful in evaluating attitude. A writer known to be a political dissident in China is in a different context than a U.S. Senator writing on the same subject. An author who is an acknowledged authority writes from a different context than one who is not.

WRITING STYLE.   Writing styles vary immensely; but usually a piece will be informal, formal, literary, argumentative, or scientific.[7] For example, informal styles are found in popular magazines, newspapers, and personal letters,. Specialized journals, academic studies, and institutional reports usually have a

---

7. "Writing style" here does not refer to an individual's personal manner of expression, but to the more general style in which the piece is written.

formal style. There are dozens of different literary styles, such as realism, classicism, and romanticism. There are many different genres, or types, of fiction: novels, short stories, poetry, screenplays, and so on. An argumentative style is an attempt to prove without any doubt that a belief is true or false. This is the style most often used in law, for example. Logical thinking, which is a different type of thinking than verbal thinking, is often represented in an argumentative style. It will be discussed in Chapter 5. Scientific style, like the argumentative style, is more logical than verbal. Examples of scientific style can be found in journals and reports from the social and physical sciences.[8] The style of a piece has a great deal to do with establishing its context. A piece on global warming found in a scientific journal has a much different style than one in a popular magazine.

AUDIENCE.   The intended audience of a piece is usually apparent from the publication source. The popular article on global warming found in *Time* has a different intended audience than one on the same subject in *Nature,* a journal that describes recent scientific research written by and for scientists around the world. Of course, the writing style of a scientific piece will be very different from one in *Time.* However, the writing style of *Time* and *Good Housekeeping* is the same: both are informal. Yet, the intended audiences are not; one is intended for a reader seeking information about the cultural environment, and the other is meant for those interested in domestic improvement.

"THE BENEFIT OF THE DOUBT:" EMPATHY IN APPLYING THE STANDARDS OF VERBAL THINKING

Empathy, as we have seen, is essential in reviewing a piece, especially in understanding its meaning and attitudes. It is also essential to the *evaluation* of a piece's meaning and attitudes. The standards of good thinking are ideal models. No piece should be expected to be perfectly sincere, respectful, and committed to consensus any more than it should be expected to be perfectly clear, accurate, specific, and significant. The appropriate degree of all seven standards varies, depending upon the purpose and context of the piece.

Evaluation is an empathetic activity; it is a consideration of how well the piece meets our expectations, considering its purpose and context. We cannot evaluate or even detect attitudes in metaphors, allusions, word choice, or prejudicial expressions unless we have an empathetic relationship with the piece. That is, only when we have an understanding of its purpose and context, can we review and evaluate the piece properly. Every piece of writing was written by a *person* with a purpose in mind. Every piece was written by a *person* in a particular context.

The best way to recognize this human element in all written pieces is to review and evaluate them empathetically. Actually, this is quite easily done. Instead of demanding that the piece demonstrate that it is sincere, respectful,

---

8. Some of the major differences between the social and physical sciences will be discussed in Chapter 6.

and committed to consensus, we should "give it the benefit of the doubt," and assume that unless we can detect clear, specific instances of an *absence* of these standards, the piece is attitudinally acceptable. This is the proper role of empathy in critical thinking. We inform ourselves, as much as possible, of the purpose and context of the piece. Then, with those two elements in mind, we review the metaphors, allusions, word choices, and prejudicial expressions to detect any instances of a *lack* of sincerity, respect, and commitment to consensus. Empathetic evaluation does not allow us to put demands on the piece to "prove itself" any more than empathy allows us to put demands on people to "prove" that their words make sense.

We also need empathy to properly evaluate pieces for the first four standards (clarity, accuracy, specificity, and significance) of good thinking. A piece does not have to be *clear;* it merely needs not to be *unclear.* In the same way, the piece does not have to be accurate, it only needs to *avoid inaccuracies.* A piece should *avoid* overgeneralizations and unwarranted assumptions; it does not have to be completely detailed and precise. Pieces should *avoid* triviality and oversimplification; they don't have to achieve significance.

The seven standards of verbal thinking are *ideal models;* they need to be applied empathetically, that is, with the recognition that written pieces represent and express the perceptions of individual human beings. A piece should be given "the benefit of the doubt;" it should be evaluated as in need of revision only if any of the standards of good thinking are clearly lacking. In the next chapter, we will investigate logical thinking, which is a much more rigorous, exact, and rigid way of understanding, processing, and communicating ideas than verbal thinking. We will notice, however, that even logical thinking requires empathy.

EXERCISES

▲ MOST INTRIGUING ISSUE

Write a one-paragraph description of the most interesting idea, topic, or process described in pages 105–122. Be prepared to explain what you find interesting in class discussion.

▲ THE MUDDIEST POINT

Write a sentence or, if possible, a paragraph, that describes the idea, topic, expression, term, or process in pages 105–122 that you find most difficult to understand.

▲ CARTOONS AND DIAGRAMS

1. Provide a cartoon that shows the difference between empathy and sympathy.
2. Create a cartoon that shows how sympathy and empathy often occur together.

3. Provide a cartoon or diagram that illustrates the different purposes and contexts of two different pieces, both titled, "Hunting Bear in Alaska." Include the main purpose, at least one specific purpose, and all three elements of context.
4. Provide a cartoon or diagram that illustrates the different purposes and contexts of two different pieces, both titled, "A Day at Disneyland." Include the main purpose, at least one specific purpose, and all three elements of context.
5. Provide a cartoon or diagram that illustrates the different purposes and contexts of two different pieces, both titled, "Growing Your Own Tomatoes." Include the main purpose, at least one specific purpose, and all three elements of context.
6. Provide a cartoon or diagram that illustrates the different purposes and contexts of two different pieces, both titled, "Credit Cards and College Students." Include the main purpose, at least one specific purpose, and all three elements of context.
7. Do some historical research if necessary. Draw a cartoon or diagram that shows all three elements of the context of each of the following: Adolph Hitler's *Mein Kampf*; Marx and Engles's *Communist Manifesto*; Betty Friedan's *The Feminine Mystique*.
8. Draw a cartoon or diagram that shows all three elements of the context of each of the following: Henry David Thoreau's *Walden;* Harriet Beecher Stowe's *Uncle Tom's Cabin*; Alice Walker's *The Color Purple*. Do some literary research if necessary.
9. Draw a cartoon or diagram that shows all three elements of the context of each of the following: *Fortune* Magazine, *Wired* Magazine, *The Nation* Magazine. Do some research in popular culture if necessary.

▲ DEFINITIONS OF KEY TERMS

Provide a disciplinary definition for each of the following terms. Most of the terms are not defined in the chapter, although their meanings are described by the context in which they appear. You need to review the material to create the definition yourself. Be sure to follow the guidelines for creating definitions on pages 78–81.

Audience	Context of a Piece of Writing	Cultural Environment
Empathetic Evaluation	Empathy	Main Purpose of a Piece of Writing
Specific Purpose of a Piece of Writing	Sympathy	Writing Style

▲ SHORT ESSAY QUESTIONS

Provide a written response of approximate length for each topic. Your responses should be well organized, grammatically correct, and neatly produced.

1. Explain the difference between empathy and sympathy, using your own examples.
2. Describe the difference between the purpose and the context of a piece of writing.
3. Describe two possible specific purposes of each of the following:
   a) The manual that comes with a new video camera

    b) The menu in a café
    c) A screenplay
    d) A textbook
    e) The "Pledge of Allegiance" (to the American flag)
    f) A novel
    g) The lyrics to a popular song
    h) A cookbook
    i) A letter to your favorite professional athlete
    j) A letter to your congressperson

4. Explain why empathy is necessary to evaluate a piece for clarity, accuracy, specificity, and significance.

5. Explain why empathy is necessary to evaluate a piece for sincerity, respect, and commitment to consensus.

6. Paraphrase in your own words for the purpose of a more thorough understanding: "A piece should be given 'the benefit of the doubt;' it should be evaluated as in need of revision only if any of the standards of good thinking are clearly lacking."

▲ QUESTIONS FOR DISCUSSION

Empathetically evaluate each of the following pieces according to the three attitudinal standards of good thinking following these steps: (1) Specifically describe which metaphors, allusions, word choices, and/or prejudicial expressions helped you detect the piece's attitudes (2) Discuss the purpose and context of the piece as much as you feel is appropriate (3) Thoroughly explain whether you think the piece achieves a proper degree of each of the three attitudinal standards. You may also comment on how well it achieves the four skill standards.

1. The Death Penalty in America

I was amused the other day by an editorial I read in a weekly newsmagazine. The author said that the time between sentencing a man to death and the carrying out of the sentence is way too long. According to him, it takes about ten years before the state's commitment to kill a man is carried out. He was upset that in the meantime, the man goes on living on death row at great expense to the state. It costs about $25,000 a year to keep a man there. So that means a quarter of a million dollars is spent by the taxpayers on a man they are going to kill anyway. The editorial said that was stupid. Why spend all that money? It's like you go out and buy a new car, then push it off a cliff. He wants criminals who've been convicted of capital crimes to be executed right away, without any appeals and without any time in prison. Maybe right there in the courtroom, I guess.

The editorial is about the dumbest thing I've ever read. The writer probably was a spoiled rich kid who went to college and never got in trouble with the law because his daddy knew the right people. If he had ever been arrested, he would realize how unjust and prejudiced the system really is. He would know how cops beat up innocent people and plant drugs on them. If he had ever been in prison he would know that the money all goes to the guards and to the sleazy politicians. The convicts don't see anything of it. It probably costs about $5,000 a year to keep somebody locked up. The other twenty goes to pad the pockets of the real crooks.

As for no appeals, has he ever thought about how corrupt the cops and judges and the whole criminal justice system is? It's a railroad to hell, and if you ever get caught in it, it will take you there. Nobody gets off. If you are innocent, they can prove you did something anyway. If you are guilty, they can prove you did something worse. They don't care if you are guilty or not; as far as the system goes, anyone who comes into it is going to stay in it. You can be sure.

If there were no appeals, hundreds more men would be murdered by the state every year. Don't get me wrong here. There's no hope in the appeals. The only reason the system allows them is to get more money into the hands of corrupt lawyers and judges.

So let me explain something to you. See, it's a game called "cops and robbers." Both sides are in it for the money. The robbers take the money from the chumps— that's you. And the cops and judges take the money from—you guessed it, chump—from you. Only they call it "taxes." The robbers at least call it what it is: stolen goods. So don't go moaning and groaning about spending a quarter million to keep slimes like me alive for ten years before you kill me. It ain't going to me. It's going to the real thieves and the real robbers: your "public servants." I've done seven years on death row, and according to the writer, that means I have three to go before they kill me. You know something? I think they might even make it four or five.

2. The Language of Dogs

Human beings are not the only creatures that use language. As the companion of three German Shepherds, two Doberman Pinschers, and a Rottweiler, I can attest to their ability to communicate. Since anyone reading this magazine already has or is planning on acquiring a dog, I know I do not have to explain why I do not call myself a "dog owner," but their "companion." My dogs are my friends.

Talking with dogs is not the same as with people. Dogs don't literally speak our language. They have their own; I call it "Dogese." Dogese is spoken with the mouth, like human language, and with the eyes, ears, tail, and whole body. Human beings only use their mouths to speak, but dogs use everything they have. They are very good communicators. If we pay attention, we can understand them very well.

When a dog barks for a long time with short intervals in between, it means that the dog is lonely. You should spend some time with her. If she barks continuously without any short intervals, then she is warning you. Maybe an intruder is in the neighborhood. When she gives one short high-pitched bark she is alerting you to something fun or interesting. My dogs do this when I give them their meals. At first, you may not notice the differences between the barks, but if you pay attention, you will soon be able to identify them. Your dog will reward you with more barking when you do.

A dog communicates with growls, too. A low-pitched, soft growl means that something is very disturbing and that she is telling you that she may need to attack. A high-pitched growl combined with a short bark means that she is frightened. When she growls but does not show her teeth, she is saying that she's having fun. If you play tug-o-war with your dog, you'll notice this growl.

The dog's tail communicates her feelings very well. Everyone knows that a dog is happy when she wags her tail. There are several ways of doing it, though, and each means something different. The faster she moves her tail, she is saying she's getting more and more excited about something. When her tail is barely wagging, she is saying "hello." A medium wag, especially of a tail at the midposition, means that she is trying to understand something. I've noticed this many times when I am asking my dogs to talk with me. Their tails go back and forth at a steady rate, and when they finally get what I'm saying, they wag them faster and faster. A happy dog wags its tail rapidly and often.

When the dog's ears are erect or bent slightly forward, it means that she is paying close attention. If her head is bent to the side while her ears are in this position, she is telling you that she is confused about something. If her ears are bend slightly back, it means that she doesn't like what you are doing, or what is going on. If they are bent all the way back to a position on the top of her head, she is warning you that she may attack. Any intruders who ignore the communication and keep coming onto the property will probably wish they had stayed home!

When a dog looks at you straight in the eye, she is telling you that she feels like she is your equal. She is completely confident in your friendship. If she looks sideways or downwards, she is saying that she accepts you as her mistress.

Dogs speak with their whole body. When she pokes her rear end into the air and stretches her chest down to the ground, with her paws pushed out in front, she is saying that she wants to play. This is usually accompanied with a rapidly wagging tail. When she rolls over on the ground and gazes at you with big brown eyes, exposing her belly, she wants you to rub it. This is a friendly, loving way of telling you that she trusts you completely. When she places her paw on your knee or paws the air in front of you, she is telling you that she is in need of affection.

Dogese is easy to learn. If your dog can learn to speak it with other dogs, why not with you? We all know that dogs learn our language. They understand the words "come," "sit," "heel," "lay down," and dozens of others. They have taken the first step in communication by learning our language, and we can take the next step by learning a little Dogese.

3. Student Voter Registration

All students! Everyone welcome! Free snacks and soft drinks for every student with a current ID!

Thursday at 7:00 P.M. in the college cafeteria! Come and have a free meal on us, your One Nation Student Voter Registration Committee!

Meet some of the candidates for The Associated Student Body Government (ASBG) offices! All approved One Nation candidates will appear and speak!

Every responsible, intelligent student realizes the importance of getting out and voting for the candidate of your choice. Last year less than fifty percent of American Voters went to the polls! How many were college students? Were you among them? Were you registered to vote?

It is a scandal that our college, like our country, is being overrun with foreign intruders who are not truly cooperating with the American way of life. They do not socialize or do business with Americans, but stick with their own kinds, do business with their own kinds, and hire their own kinds. Americans are becoming second-class citizens in their own country. The aliens from Asia, The Middle East, South America, and Eastern Europe are turning our country into a Foreign Country!

The One Nation Learning Group is the only study group on our campus who cares enough about the foreign invasion to sponsor the educational and public-spirited Free events on Thursday at 7:00 P.M. in the cafeteria. Come one, come all!

Registering to vote is an important duty that every true American must carry out. Are you registered? Will you vote in the upcoming Campus ASBG Elections? Have you met the ASBG Candidates?

Do you know Lars Racketts? The tall, handsome candidate for ASBG President is a Junior. He has attended seven colleges already, so he has major experience with being a leader among students. Lars has traveled the country, observing the Foreign Invasion of Asians and other nonAmericans into our Nation's Colleges.

Says Lars Racketts, "It is time to stem the tide!" Lars knows better than anyone how easy it is for Foreigners to invade American colleges. "They just pretend to be American," he says. "Before you know it, they are overrunning the classrooms and flooding the job market."

Our candidate for Vice President is Bob "Bang-Bang" Bangerling, a well-liked Sophomore from a town only eighty miles from this very campus. "I'm a local guy," says Bang-Bang, "and I played football for my high school team." On the field, Bang-Bang saw lots of violence. "I have seen what happens when young men get really pumped up," he says. "I could tell you stories that would chill your soul!" Bang-Bang is going for a sack when it comes to America. "This country is our country. It is time for us to take control and Push Back the Foreigner Attack. I am getting pumped for being Vice President of the ASBG!"

The Secretary job of ASBG is going to belong to Vanessa Johnson if you and other students take your right to register to vote seriously! And what a great secretary she will be. Vanessa says, "These shameless runaways from foreign countries, I mean, why did they come here? I mean *really?*" We know what you mean, 'Nessy! How about it? What happens to a foreign sweetheart when she manages to tie the knot with an American Hunk? Oh, yeah, it's the citizenship game! "I know for a fact that over eighty percent of the Foreign female freshmen who come to our country to go to college are only interested in getting married to American boys," she says. Meet Vanessa at the Free Voter's Registration sponsored by the One Nation's Voter Registration Committee!

Last, but not least, meet the coolest Business Administration Major you will ever, ever, have the pleasure of knowing, Sam Dash. Sam—yeah, that's his real name, ain't it cool!—Dash wants to take a good close look at the financial books the previous ASBG left behind. "They had some Foreigners on their staff," says Sam, "and somebody responsible has to do a little checking up on their work. There's probably some missing funds that they've taken back to wherever." Sam is a happy guy, but he has a deadly serious side when it comes to terrorism.

"I had a close relative who had a very near miss with a terrorist bomb," Sam told us. "I cannot tell you anything more about it, because it's classified information. But terrorism is a threat to all of us in our One Nation." As ASBG Treasurer, Sam will do all he can to expose terrorists on campus before they strike. "When I think of all the damage they have done, it makes my blood boil," he says. "They come here for one reason—to destroy our One Nation!"

What is One Nation? Come to the Voter Registration in the cafeteria on Thursday at 7:00 P.M. You'll have a great time meeting these four fine candidates for ASBG and you'll like the food, too. There is no need to register for voting in ASBG elections; your student ID is enough. So if you can't come, just vote for Lars, Bang-Bang, Vanessa, and Sam in the upcoming ASBG election. As far as voting in noncampus elections, no registrations will be handled at the meeting.

Come one, come all! Keep our One Nation free and pure! Stem the Terrorist Tide! Have a Good Time and Vote ONE NATION!

4. Fall is the Most Wonderful Time of All

What's your most favorite season? Mine is Fall, and I want to tell you why in two hundred words. Some people call it Autumn, and I think that's a very pretty word. It reminds me of my friend, Autumn Spinoza. We both go to Fairmont Jr. High School together. We live only two blocks from each other. She lives over on the corner of Fourth Street and Larch Avenue. I love Autumn because she is my best friend. I like Fall because when the leaves fall from the trees they cover the street and sidewalk with wonderful colors. That's why it's called Fall. The leaves.

Another reason I love Fall is because the air is so clean. You can breath in the crisp cool puffs just like they have come in straight off the ocean. It is that fresh. There is no pollution in the Fall.

The last reason I love Fall is because it is when school starts and that means I can come to Fairmont Jr. High School and be in the class with Mrs. Berry, my favorite teacher ever. I love her too, but not as much as Autumn, or Fall.

▲ QUOTATION TO PONDER

"Democratic society also depends on our developing the habit of stepping into the shoes of others—both intellectually and emotionally. We need literally to be able to experience, if even for a very short time, the ideas, feelings, pains, and mindsets of others, even when doing so creates some discomfort."
Deborah Meier, *Phi Delta Kappan,* 1996

▲ JOURNAL TOPIC

Review the "Letters to the Editor" page of a newspaper or newsmagazine for examples of metaphors, allusions, loaded words, and prejudicial expressions. Select one or two letters for an empathetic evaluation in relation to the seven standards of good thinking.

▲ PORTFOLIO PAPER

Review your paper on the relation of definitions, summaries, and paraphrases to review, evaluation, and revision from Chapter 3. Revise the paper, adding 300 words on your thoughts on the importance of the attitudinal standards when defining, summarizing, and paraphrasing.

CHAPTER FIVE

ELEMENTS AND ORGANIZATION OF ARGUMENTS

THE MAJOR DIFFERENCES BETWEEN VERBAL AND LOGICAL THINKING

Verbal thinking is highly flexible, rich in meeting human needs, and adaptable to a variety of purposes. Logical thinking does not have those three qualities: its one purpose is to evaluate arguments. Specifically, its purpose is to *distinguish trustworthy arguments from untrustworthy arguments.* Trustworthy arguments are clear, specific, reasonable, and truthful enough to offer us great practical value. Untrustworthy arguments lack clarity, are unreasonable, and/or are based on false claims. Trustworthy arguments can alleviate confusion, provide direction, and guide understanding even when issues are complicated and difficult. Untrustworthy arguments can deceive us, can confuse us, and can lead us into misguided opinions and dupe us into believing foolish ideas or even lies. Distinguishing between the trustworthy and the untrustworthy argument is the task of logical thinking.

To accomplish its task, logical thinking must be more *exact* than verbal thinking; meanings of words and sentences must be absolutely clear. The reasoning process in logical thinking is much more *methodical* than in verbal thinking; ideas are expected to follow each other in reasonable ways. Logical thinking is *rigorous* in testing arguments to determine whether they are trustworthy or not.

AFTER STUDYING CHAPTER FIVE

You should be able to distinguish arguments from explanations, and practical logic from pure logic. You should understand the nature of implication and know the conclusion and premise indicators listed in the text. You should be able to identify the conclusions, premises, and hidden premises in arguments.

The three characteristics of logical thinking are (1) *exactness of expression,* (2) *rigid adherence to proper methodology, and* (3) *rigorous testing of the quality of reasoning.* Unlike verbal thinking, which is concerned with understanding, processing, and communicating ideas and feelings, logic is limited to one particular process: the evaluation of arguments. Of course, logical thinking also understands and communicates ideas, but in a very limited way. It is only concerned with understanding and communicating its own processes. Logicians (experts in logical thinking) study and discuss logic's vocabulary and concepts, and in doing so, they understand and communicate ideas. However, for the most part, to think logically is to process ideas: that is, to *organize* and *evaluate* them. Logical thinking organizes ideas in a methodical way, and then evaluates them according to standards of reason. Verbal thinking and logical thinking, then, are quite different. One is flexible, adaptable, and is used to communicate, understand, and process; the other is much narrower. Logical thinking is limited to organizing ideas into arguments that are then evaluated as trustworthy or untrustworthy.

Logical thinking is much narrower in scope and purpose than verbal thinking. Human beings constantly use verbal thinking. Logical thinking is used more sparingly. Like mathematical or scientific thinking, most people use it when they feel a need to prove that something is reasonable. In addition, logical thinking's exact, rigorous, and rigid way of processing ideas can become so intricate and complicated that few people have the time, energy, or interest to pursue it thoroughly. Logicians are similar in this way to experts in the fields of Physics, Chemistry, Astronomy, and Mathematics; they spend years and years studying the processes involved with the organization and evaluation of arguments.

Critical thinking reviews, evaluates, and revises thinking; it is more exact, rigorous, and rigid than most verbal thinking. It is also logical. As we have seen, critical thinking establishes standards by which it evaluates and suggests revisions in verbal thinking: it seeks out and provides definitions for vague and ambiguous terms; it summarizes and paraphrases; and it evaluates written pieces according to the seven standards. In all of these activities, critical thinking is processing ideas in a logical way. That is, it is organizing and evaluating them. However, critical thinking is broader than logical thinking. It does much more than organize and evaluate arguments. Critical thinking is *both* verbal *and* logical. Sometimes it is more one than the other; it depends on the specific type of thinking involved. For instance, scientific research should be reviewed and evaluated more logically than editorials in daily newspapers. However, critical thinking cannot completely abandon logical thinking when dealing with the newspaper editorial. The task of critical thinking is to improve *all* types of thinking; sometimes this is accomplished with more attention to the verbal standards, sometimes to the logical ones. A written piece that attempts to prove a point, to demonstrate, without any doubt, that its conclusion is true, should be evaluated in a logical way. A written piece that seeks to provide a point of view, or to make its opinion known, but is not attempting to "prove" anything, should be evaluated according to the standards of verbal thinking. Most written pieces are mixtures of verbal and logical thinking, and need to be organized and evaluated in both ways.

Previously, we used the term "idea" as a general term for any kind of mental activity. However, our discussion of logical thinking needs to clearly distinguish between statements that represent perceptions and those that express emotions. Logical thinking is concerned only with representative statements, and not with expressions of emotion.

We will need to make use of three stipulative definitions in order to make our discussion of logical thinking as clear as possible. We will stipulate that the word "feeling" refers to expressions of emotion. The stipulated definition of "idea" is a representation of a perception. We will stipulate that the word "belief" means a general term referring to either or both ideas and feelings. We will also use the words "feelings," "ideas," and "beliefs" for feelings, ideas, and beliefs that someone has, but does not express.

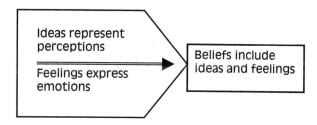

The term "belief," then, refers to an idea or a feeling, or to ideas that are interwoven with feelings. "The beautiful American flag is flying above the courthouse," is an example of an idea mixed in with a feeling; the perception of the flag flying above the courthouse is interwoven with the feeling that the flag is beautiful. Verbal thinking is mostly made up of beliefs; we understand, process, and communicate both ideas and feelings.

THE HEART OF LOGICAL THINKING: IMPLICATION

Logical thinking organizes and evaluates the *implication* relationship between ideas. Implication is the relationship one idea has with another when one idea *supports* the other idea. To *support* an idea is to "demonstrate" or "prove" it to be meaningful. For example, the ideas "All dogs are animals" and "Lassie is a dog" *imply that* "Lassie is an animal" are meaningful. These ideas support, or imply, the idea "Lassie is an animal." Implication is a relationship in which one idea is "explicitly pulled out" of one or more other ideas that implicitly already contain it. To be "explicit" is to be obvious; to be "implicit" is to be hidden. Imagine a dog kennel with dozens of dogs inside; it is not obvious that Lassie is one of them. She is implicitly in the kennel. However, when you take Lassie out of the kennel, you are explicitly "pulling her out" and she is no longer hidden. She was "implied by" the kennel all along, and when you "pulled her out" you proved that she was there. She was implicitly there; now she is explicitly there.

Logical implication is the "pulling out" or "proving" that an idea is implicitly contained in other ideas. The idea, "Lassie is an animal," is implicitly contained (hidden) in the two ideas, "All dogs are animals," and "Lassie is a dog." It is not explicitly contained, not obviously contained, but it is there. How do you know? By thinking logically! That is, by organizing the ideas in a way that makes the implication more obvious. Here is a diagram of the implication relationship of these ideas:

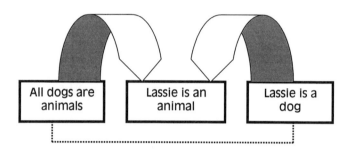

In the diagram the two side boxes *implicitly contain* the middle box. The two arrows represent that the side boxes *imply* the middle box. The middle box is "hidden" in both of them, shown by the dotted line.

The two ideas, "Lassie is a dog," and "All dogs are animals," when considered together, *prove* that the idea "Lassie is an animal" is as meaningful as the other two ideas. That is, since the middle box is already contained in the side boxes, it is not taken from someplace else and "added on" to them, but is already implicit within them. It is not a new idea; it is implied by the "side" ideas. So, it is as meaningful as they are. This next diagram may help to clarify how implication "proves" ideas to be meaningful.

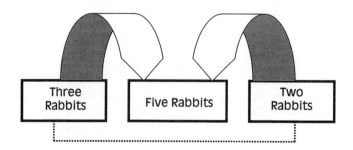

In this diagram the two side boxes prove that the middle box is as meaningful as they are. Three rabbits and two rabbits, taken together, "prove" that there are five rabbits. In this case, though, the "proof" is mathematical, not logical. Imagine that there are two real boxes, each of which contains rabbits; one has three, the other has two. Without a doubt, there are five rabbits all together. This diagram does not really need the middle box. We already know that there are five rabbits because of the dotted line, which connects the box containing three rabbits with the two rabbits in the second side box. It is quite obvious that they imply the middle box.

Implication, like addition, is used to prove that ideas are meaningful. If we ask, "How many rabbits are there?" the mathematical response is to prove that there are five. Verbal thinking could respond, "There's quite a few rabbits," because verbal thinking is not as exact and rigid as mathematical thinking. In the same way, if we ask "Is Lassie an animal?" verbal thinking can respond simply by saying, "Of course; everybody knows that!" However, logical thinking, being more exact, rigorous, and rigid than verbal thinking, seeks to prove that "Lassie is an animal" by organizing and evaluating the relationship of the ideas that imply it.

When an idea is implied by other ideas, it is as meaningful as they are. If the "side boxes" are not meaningful ideas, or even if only one of them isn't meaningful, then implication between them and the "middle box" cannot be meaningful. For example:

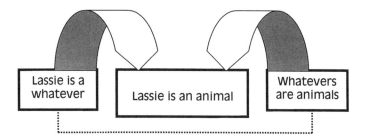

"Lassie is a whatever" is too vague to be meaningful because there is no known meaning for "whatever." "Whatevers are animals" isn't meaningful, either. As a result, the implication is meaningless. Notice that it is the *implication* that is meaningless, not the middle box. It makes sense on its own. How are we to decided if it is "implicit" in the side boxes if we do not know what they mean? It is impossible to determine if the implication is a meaningful one when we cannot determine the meaning of the side boxes. *An implication is meaningful only if the implied idea is clearly implicit within the ideas that imply it. If the meaning of any of the ideas is vague or ambiguous, the implication is meaningless.*

The implication is also meaningless if the idea in the middle box is not implied by the side box ideas. For example, the idea "Lassie is an animal" is not implied by the ideas "Lassie is a celebrity" and "All celebrities are famous." Even though all three are meaningful ideas, the side boxes do not implicitly contain "Lassie is an animal." This is indicated by the absence of the dotted line between the boxes. They are both *logically irrelevant* to the idea, since they have nothing to do with "being an animal." They do *not* imply that "Lassie is an animal."[1]

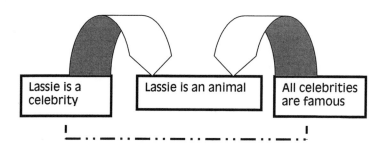

Two Kinds of Implication

When an idea is "implicitly contained" in other ideas it is "implied" by them. There are two sorts of implications: deduction and induction.

Deduction is an implication process in which the meaning of ideas alone is considered. That is, deduction, or deductive implication, is a process of deriving implicit ideas from others by examining *only* the meaning of the ideas, with no concern at all for their truth. The fact that an idea is deductively implied by other ideas does not demonstrate that the idea is true; it only proves that it makes sense, or has meaning.

An idea can be meaningful, and not be true. For example, "Lassie is a dog" is meaningful because we understand it. However, "Lassie is an elephant," which is not true, is nevertheless meaningful. We understand what it means. That's how we know it is false. There are many examples of meaningful, but false ideas. They are ideas that make sense, but for which we either have evidence that they are false ("Lassie is an elephant") or no evidence that they are true ("Elvis is alive and well in Las Vegas").

Without evidence, we cannot logically determine whether an idea is true or false. Evidence is the information base that confirms or verifies beliefs. False ideas are those that are shown to be untrue by appropriate evidence. True ideas are those that are supported by the appropriate quantity and quality of evidence. For example, "Lassie is an animal" is true if we have appropriate evidence that she really exists, and that she really is an animal. As most people realize, several dogs were used to play "Lassie" on the television series. So, it is really not

---

1. These two ideas do imply that Lassie is famous, though.

true that "Lassie is an animal." The truth is that "Lassie" is a role in a television series. However, "Lassie is an animal" is meaningful, nevertheless.

Logical thinking is also concerned with the implications evidence provides, known as induction. Induction is very much concerned with whether ideas are true or false. A true idea is one that is inductively implied by other true ideas. An idea can be inductively implied, or implicit, in the evidence that supports it. For example, social scientists have observed that nine out of ten young people who begin to smoke cigarettes during their teenage years become addicted to them. What idea is implicit within this evidence? Imagine that you observe your brother, Jackson, who is seventeen years old, begins to smoke cigarettes today. Does that inductively imply that he will become addicted to nicotine? How strong is the evidence that he will become an addict? Induction evaluates the type and various components of the evidence in order to decide how strong or weak the evidence is for Jackson's eventual addiction.

Induction is the implication relationship between evidence and the strength or weakness of the conclusions drawn from it. There are different types of evidence, and different components of evidence, both of which play important roles in evaluating the strength or weakness of the claims about truth implied by them. We will discuss evidence in Chapter 8. This section will examine deductive implication, which is the same as a deductive argument.[2]

ARGUMENTS ARE NOT DISPUTES

Logic's disciplinary definition of "argument" is "a group of statements, some of which claim to meaningfully imply others." Ordinary language uses the word "argument" quite differently. For example, we would normally think of the following as an argument:

"You said you would turn off the stove and you didn't!"
"Oh, so what, you nagging baboon!"
"Get out of the house, you irresponsible creep."

However, in the way logical thinking uses the term, the example is not an argument. It is a "dispute," or an emotional disagreement between people. Sometimes, when people have a dispute, they try to prove that they are right and that the other person is wrong, usually by raising their voices or calling one another names. Logical arguments are also efforts to prove something, but not in the same way as disputes. The logical sense of the term "argument," in fact, has nothing at all to do with emotional disputes. It is a disciplinary term that is used to describe implication relationships.

A deductive argument is a group of statements, the meanings of which are claimed to imply the meaning of another statement. (An inductive argument is

---

2. "Argument" in this chapter will always refer to "deductive argument," unless a specific reference to induction is made.

a group of statements describing evidence that is claimed to imply the truth of another statement.) The way logical thinking uses the term "argument," there is no dispute between people at all. Deductive arguments are pieces of writing that claim implications between ideas. The following is an example of a deductive argument:

All dogs are animals, and Lassie is a dog. Therefore, Lassie is an animal.

There is no dispute going on here; the argument consists of a piece of writing that is claiming to prove "Lassie is an animal." It is doing so on the basis of meaning alone; there is no evidence presented. The task of logical thinking is to decide if the argument is meaningful or not. Logic is not concerned with winning arguments; only with evaluating them.[3]

Arguments Are Made Up of Statements, Not Utterances. Because logical thinking is much more exact, rigorous, and rigid than verbal thinking, it has a more limited view of the meaning of sentences. In strictly logical thinking, only "statements" are meaningful. "Statements" are sentences that represent ideas in arguments. Statements are the *only* logically meaningful sentences. As far as purely logical thinking is concerned, any sentence that is not a statement is logically meaningless.

Statements are defined as "sentences that are either true or false." This may seem to be an odd definition, because we have noticed that deduction is not concerned with truth, only with meaningfulness. However, deduction is not at all concerned with *whether* a statement is true or false: only that it *can be* either true or false. The disciplinary definition of "statement" means that for logical thinking in its purest form, statements are *clear representations of ideas.* They are *never* vague representations, expressions of emotion, never directives, never commitments, or performatives. As we discussed in Chapter 3, language has a representative function, in which ideas are represented (clearly or not) in words. An idea can be clearly represented in an accurate, or true manner, or in an inaccurate, or false manner. A representation of an idea does not need to be true in order to represent an idea; it can represent false ideas, too! For example, all of the following are statements:

The moon is not a planet   The moon is a planet

Mars is a planet   Mars is not a planet

Each of them is a representation of *either* a true idea or a false idea. The argument,

The moon is a planet, and a Mars is not a planet.
Therefore, the moon is not Mars

---

3. We sometimes use arguments in order to win disputes, however. For example, attorneys present arguments in court in their attempt to win cases. Academic researchers use arguments to prove that their theories are correct.

contains only statements. "The moon is a planet" and "Mars is not a planet" is false, and "The moon is not Mars" is true.

This argument contains all statements,

> Since all bears are fish, grizzly bears are not mammals,
> because fish are not mammals

even though it contains two false representations. While it is false that "all bears are fish," and that "grizzly bears are not mammals," the sentences are all *either* true or false.

Any sentence that is not a statement is defined as an "utterance." An utterance is any sentence that is neither true nor false. Directive and expressive language are both "utterances." All utterances are logically meaningless. As far as purely logical thinking is concerned, there are only two sorts of sentences: statements and utterances.

A statement is a sentence that is either true or false:

THE MOON IS NOT A PLANET // THE MOON IS A PLANET

An utterance is a sentence that is not a statement:

LOOK AT THE MOON // THE MOON IS SPLENDID

These are both disciplinary definitions, appropriate for logical thinking at its "most pure."

PURE AND PRACTICAL LOGIC

There is a distinction between *pure* logical thinking and *practical* logical thinking that needs to be recognized at this point. Pure logical thinking is the exact, rigorous, rigid organization and evaluation of purely conceptual arguments. Pure arguments are not actually encountered in our daily lives; they are "pure" because they are made up of statements that have no connection to practical affairs. Pure arguments are of purely theoretical interest to logicians. Pure logic's disciplinary definition of "statements" reflects its purely conceptual interests by *excluding* expressive and directive sentences.

Practical logic, on the other hand, organizes and evaluates arguments that are found in daily life. These are the arguments found in newspaper editorials, television talk shows, and news programs, as well as in daily conversations. In practical logic, the disciplinary definition of "statements" *includes* expressive and directive sentences along with representative sentences. Much of what people try to prove in practical arguments is expressed in emotional and directive language.

Critical thinking is much more concerned with practical logic than with pure logic. We will discuss the difference between the two much more thoroughly later in this chapter.

STATEMENTS IN PURE AND PRACTICAL LOGIC

Pure logical thinking, which is extremely exact, rigid, and rigorous, defines statements as meaningful and all other sentences as meaningless utterances. There are many examples of utterances, some of which may appear at first glance to be statements. For example,

1. The coffee is as hot as the Fourth of July
2. The Fourth of July is a great holiday
3. Meet me at Cami's new apartment on the Fourth of July
4. I promise to be there on the Fourth of July

The first utterance is a metaphor: it is an expression of an emotion. It represents a feeling, but it is neither true nor false. How hot *is* the "Fourth of July?" Doesn't it depend on where you are? Independence Day may be hot in most parts of the U. S. A., but it is not very warm at the Arctic Circle on that date, or any other date! Of course, as a metaphor it represents the belief that the coffee is hot. However, it does not represent it in a way that can clearly be determined to be true or false. As with most metaphors, it is very personal, and depends upon our individual experience for its representational and expressive meaning. Logical thinking, whether pure or practical, requires more exact meanings than does ordinary language. If Bob and Ann are having coffee at the Corner Café, and Ann takes a sip and says, "The coffee is as hot as the Fourth of July," Bob understands what she means, especially if he has any capacity to empathize with her perspective. Arguments are concerned with *implication*, not with the vague representation of beliefs or expression of feeling, which it regards as meaningless. This is a good illustration of the difference between logical and verbal thinking.

The second utterance is clearly an expression of emotion. It cannot be said to be true or false. If someone responded, "No it's not. The Fourth of July is not a great holiday," they would not be disputing the *truth* of what had been said. They would have been disputing the appropriateness of the expressed *emotions*. Some people like the holiday, and some do not. When logical thinking is purely exact, rigid, and rigorous, it attempts to detach the representation of meaning as much as possible from the expression of emotion. Expressive language is far too ambiguous and vague to meaningfully imply ideas. For example, expressions are so vague that two people can initially believe that their feelings are at opposite ends of the spectrum, and a few minutes later, believe that they are intimately united. For example:

Steve: The Fourth of July is a great holiday!
Mindy: No, it isn't. The Fourth of July stinks!
Steve: Do you really feel that way? Don't you love hot dogs and apple pie?
Mindy: Sure I do, but I can't stand all that patriotic baloney.

Steve: Me neither, but I sure do love the food my mom makes for the family picnic! Want to come over?

Mindy: Sounds great! I'll be there in red, white, and blue!

As far as pure logic is concerned, Mindy and Steve's conversation did not contain any statements. Their vague expressions initially appeared to indicate that they felt differently about the holiday, and later they discovered that they felt the same way about it. The point here is that expressions of emotion are too vague and too ambiguous to provide the exact meaning necessary in arguments. They are, for the purposes of pure logic, meaningless.

Practical logic, on the other hand, accepts expressive sentences as statements; it does not regard them as meaningless. In daily life, emotion is sometimes quite relevant to us in demonstrating a belief. For example:

Sam: The park board closed the children's pool last week for cleaning, and still hasn't opened it. I think that's a shame! What are they thinking about? Don't they realize that the kids need a place to swim on these hot summer days? They need to clean the pool immediately!

Schaka: I agree. We should write a letter to the editor of the *Daily Bugle* and complain. That's the only way to let people know our problem and get the park board into action!

Sam: I'm glad you feel that way, Schaka. Let's write it together!

Pure logic would not accept Sam and Schaka's expressive sentences; they would be too vague for its rigorous conceptual purposes. Practical logic would accept them as meaningful; its concern would be whether they are clear enough to be understood empathetically, and whether they are relevant to what is being demonstrated. Since Sam wants to demonstrate the need to clean the pool, his emotions would be accepted as relevant to practical logic.

The third example is a directive, and the fourth is a commitment, neither of which represent ideas clearly enough for pure logical thought. They are not true or false. A statement always represents an idea; a directive gives instructions that may be helpful in different degrees. For example, someone may give us good directions on how to find the library. However, good directions are not true representations; they are helpful instructions. For example:

- Take the Number Twelve bus from anywhere on Isaac Avenue, get off at the corner of Boyer Avenue and Park Street, and go up the large concrete stairs. Walk past the pond and enter the library by the side door.
- Penrose Library is about a half-block down Boyer Avenue, on the left side of the street.
- Go down Poplar Street until you come to a stoplight, and turn left. Go one block, then turn right on Boyer Avenue. Penrose Library is about a half-block down on your left.

The first example contains no statements; every sentence is a directive, which may or may not be helpful. The second example is a statement; it is either true or false. The third example contains both directives and a statement. The last sentence is a statement. Of course, the directives that precede it determine the context of its meaning. However, if you follow the directions, the last sentence represents an idea that is either true or false.

Practical logic often accepts directives as meaningful statements. For example, in the example about cleaning the swimming pool, Schaka says

"We should write a letter to the editor of the *Daily Bugle* and complain."

Since the directive follows from what was said before, it makes enough sense to be accepted as a statement as far as practical logic is concerned.

Commitments are utterances. Note these three examples.

"I vow that I will never eat at that restaurant again."
"I am going to eat yogurt every morning from now on."
He swore he would never eat at "Joe's Café" again;
he says he's going to eat yogurt for breakfast.

The first two examples are commitments; they may or may not be serious, or wise. We make good commitments, and we make poor ones. However, commitments are never true or false. They are utterances. The last example is a statement, a description of a commitment. It represents a meaningful idea, and it is either true or false.[4]

Of course, performative utterances are ceremonial expressions that accomplish tasks.

"With this ring, I thee wed."
"This court finds you innocent off all charges."
She didn't get married, and the court found her guilty. What a bad day for her!

The first and second examples are performative utterances; the last contains a statement that represents an idea about the ceremonies or official functions that took place. It could be false or true. The last example also contains an expressive utterance.

Arguments and Explanations. Logical thinking's disciplinary definition of "argument" is "a group of statements, some of which claim to meaningfully imply others." This definition holds for both pure and practical logic. Arguments, as we have seen, are made up only of statements. However, this

---

4. As far as practical logic is concerned, if commitments are understandable, they are statements.

does not mean that any group of statements is automatically an argument. There must be a relationship of implication between the statements; the meaning of some of the statements must *implicitly contain* the meaning of another. As we have seen, when one idea implies another it *supports* or *proves* its meaningfulness. Without an implication relationship, a group of statements is not an argument. This is the case whether we are thinking logically in a pure way or in a practical way. Consider this example:

Some skydivers are grandparents and a few are great-grandparents.
Physically challenged individuals skydive. So do visually impaired people.
There are more people skydiving now than ever before.

Every sentence in the paragraph is a statement, but there is no demonstration, no implication relationship between them.

Let's examine the paragraph more closely by putting each statement in a numbered box.

#1 Some skydivers are grandparents and a few are great-grandparents.

#2 Physically challenged individuals skydive.

#3 So do visually impaired people.

#4 There are more people skydiving now than ever before.

Each sentence is a statement; each clearly represents an idea that is either true or false. However, the group of statements is not an argument. None of the statements *imply* any other. None of them are *implicit* in any other. None of them *prove* that any other statement is meaningful. There is no *demonstration* of any statement as being meaningful. Of course, there is a group of statements, and taken together, they represent some ideas (some may be true, some may be false; it doesn't matter which) about skydiving. However, they do not imply each other. There is no relationship among them that we could represent with the arrows that we used to show implication in a previous example:

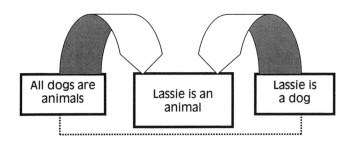

In this example, the arrows show that the side boxes imply the middle box. The side boxes implicitly contain the middle box's meaning. They prove that the middle box is meaningful. However, in the skydiving example, there is no implication, and we wouldn't have the slightest idea where to draw the arrows. Since logical thinking is concerned only with arguments, groups of statements that do not have an implication relationship are of no interest to logical thinking.

The skydiving statements have a common theme, though. They describe details and specific aspects of the activity. They *explain* a general idea, or theme, about skydiving. #4, "There are more people skydiving now than ever before," is the main idea. The other three statements are *explanations* of the main idea. There is a great deal of difference between an explanation and an argument. Explanations do not demonstrate or prove the meaningfulness of a statement. They provide specific details that *clarify* a statement; they describe details, define terms, summarize, and paraphrase statements in order to provide a "new look" at an idea. They are often quite imaginative, providing examples and illustrations to help clarify meaning, but they do not demonstrate or prove that a statement is meaningful; they *clarify* it. This is an example of an explanation:

> A skydiver is someone who jumps out of an airplane with a parachute. He or she often falls through the sky at blazing speed before opening the parachute and gently floating to the ground. Sometimes skydivers form groups and hold hands thousands of feet up. Some do acrobatics while "free-falling." Skydivers come in all ages, from all occupations, and need not be athletic. Individuals skydive for many different reasons, but most likely all of them find it exciting because they realize it is dangerous.

Explanations can be difficult to separate from arguments. Explanatory clarifications can appear to be demonstrations. The example directly above is an explanation; it *clarifies* the idea that skydiving is done by a diverse group of people who find it exciting. Consider this example, which attempts to *demonstrate* or *prove* the same idea:

> Some skydivers jump once or twice a week, others go every day. There are also those who go much less often, maybe once or twice a year. A few are very athletic; they often do acrobatics in the air. Others do it for the companionship. Some

skydivers are in their sixties or even older. The youngest are in their late teens. Both men and women skydive. Therefore, skydivers are a diverse group of people.

The last statement concludes that the previous group of statements demonstrates or proves that skydivers are a diverse group. Since it claims to be demonstrating the meaningfulness of the last statement, it is an argument. Without that claim, however, it is an explanation.

The most important difference between explanations and arguments is the element of demonstration or proof. Arguments attempt to prove that an idea is meaningful; they do not merely provide details or clarify. Arguments, if they are of good quality, prove that even though we may not want to accept an idea as meaningful, we must do so. When people refuse to accept what a good argument has proven, they have to recognize that they have no good reasons for doing so. That's why arguments are so powerful; they are used in academic and scientific research, in the legal system, and in many other areas in which proof, not mere persuasion, is required. Arguments are usually quite easy to separate from explanations: if someone has written an argument, they usually make it relatively clear that they are trying to prove a point. The best way to decide, then, if a group of statements is an argument or not is to seek its claim of proof. As we shall see in the next section, this claim is always present in an argument, although it may not always be obvious.

EXERCISES

▲ Most Intriguing Issue

Write a one-paragraph description of the most interesting idea, topic, or process described in the chapter so far. Be prepared to explain what you find interesting in class discussion.

▲ The Muddiest Point

Write a sentence or, if possible, a paragraph that describes the idea, topic, expression, term, or process in the chapter so far that you find most difficult to understand.

▲ Cartoons and Diagrams

Cartoons are drawings that characterize or symbolize ideas, processes, or expressions in imaginative ways. Diagrams are drawings, tables, or charts that show how specific details of an idea, process, or expression are interrelated.

1. Provide a diagram that shows the main differences between logical thinking and verbal thinking.
2. Draw a diagram or cartoon that shows how critical thinking makes use of verbal and logical thinking.

3. Provide a cartoon that illustrates your own example of deductive implication.
4. Draw a cartoon that illustrates the difference between an argument and a dispute.
5. Provide a diagram that shows the general similarities and differences between utterances and statements, according to both pure and practical logic.
6. Provide a cartoon that shows the similarities and differences between two similar sentences, one an expression and the other a statement. Create your own sentences.
7. Provide a cartoon that shows the similarities and differences between two similar sentences, one directive, and the other a statement. Create your own sentences.

▲ DEFINITIONS OF KEY TERMS

Provide a disciplinary definition for each of the following terms as they are used in this chapter. Most of the terms are not defined in the chapter, although their meanings are described by the context in which they appear. You need to review the material to create the definition yourself. Be sure to follow the guidelines for creating definitions on pages 78–81.

Belief	Deductive Argument	Deductive Implication
Explanation	Feeling	Idea
Logical Proof	Logical Thinking	Practical Logic
Pure Logic	Statement	Utterance

▲ SHORT ESSAY QUESTIONS

Provide a written response of approximate length for each topic. Your responses should be well organized, grammatically correct, and neatly produced.

1. Explain why critical thinking uses both verbal and logical thinking.
2. Why is implication "the heart" of logical thinking?
3. Describe the similarities and differences between deductive and inductive implication.
4. What is an argument? Why must arguments be made up of statements, not utterances?
5. What are the differences between an explanation and an argument?
6. For each of the following, explain what type of sentence it is: representative, expressive, directive, commitment, or performative. Briefly indicate whether it is a statement or an utterance according to pure logic and according to practical logic.
   a) You will find the cafeteria if you go to the Student Development Center and turn to the right.
   b) The cafeteria is next door to the Student Development Center.
   c) The cafeteria serves very spicy black bean burgers that are the best vegetarian fare on campus.
   d) Black bean burgers are made of soybeans, spices, and chicken.
   e) The parking lot is never full on Tuesday afternoons.
   f) I promise to wash your car if you buy me one of those spicy black bean burgers from the cafeteria.
   g) I promised to wash his car in exchange for a black bean burger.

h) Ralph, wash my car this afternoon at three o'clock.

i) Debbie's midterm exam in psychology was unfair.

j) Debbie's midterm exam in psychology was printed on red paper.

k) Debbie's grade on her psychology midterm was so low that she quit going to class.

l) Don't ever quit, Debbie.

m) My psychology professor is very attractive.

n) Superman lives next door to my cousin.

o) My cousin's name is Lois Lane.

p) Lois, go ask Superman to help Ralph wash my car.

q) Three professors are teaching one course in geology.

r) The geology course is a pain in the neck.

s) One of the professors who teaches the geology course is very easy to understand, but the others are hard.

t) I'm going to buy my psychology professor a black bean burger for lunch.

7. List the characteristics of explanations and of arguments. Then show why each of the following is one or the other.

a) The moon is a planet. The moon floats around in the sky and orbits around the earth. It isn't as far away as the other planets, which orbit the sun. It affects the tides, too.

b) Johnson committed the crime. It can be proven beyond a reasonable doubt. He had the opportunity. He had the means, and he had the motive.

c) Johnson's crime was not premeditated. That is, it wasn't planned. He came into the store waving a loaded handgun. The clerk said he acted "half-baked." When she asked him what he wanted, he said that his car was out of gas and he needed money to fill it. When she asked him why, he said, "Because I'm feeling like I want to rob this place and I need to drive away fast!"

d) Apples are conducive to digestion. They also have a crisp texture and taste most people find enjoyable. They stay crisp for six to eight months in cold storage. Apples, then, are an appropriate fruit for school lunch programs.

e) Apples are an appropriate fruit for school lunch programs for three reasons. The well-known saying, "An apple a day keeps the doctor away" has some basis in fact. Apples are conducive to digestion. They also have a texture and taste most people, children included, enjoy. They can be conveniently stored for months.

f) Children who watch television over twenty hours a week have shorter attention spans than average. The type of shows they watch makes no difference. Children who watched cartoons tested in the same range as those who watched soap operas.

g) Children who cannot sit still and read for more than a few minutes have short attention spans. The normal child is able to sit quietly and read a story for at least forty-five minutes.

h) Viewing television cartoons is the major reason behind children's short attention spans. Television viewing fatigues the eye. The images on the screen come and go very quickly, stimulating the child every few seconds. Cartoon story lines are simplistic and obvious, requiring no effort on the part of the child. As a result, children are tired, overstimulated, and lethargic.

i) Every Peace Corps volunteer has lived and worked in an impoverished place. No one could do that and still vote for Henry Plummer for sheriff. Plummer won't be getting any votes from any Peace Corps veterans.

j) Henry Plummer won't get Ron's vote. Ron was in the Peace Corps in Mali for two years. He saw a lot of poverty there, as well as sickness. He couldn't possibly vote for Plummer, even though they are cousins.

▲ QUESTIONS FOR DISCUSSION

Provide a written essay of 300–500 words that responds to each of the following questions which ask for your opinion. You should respond by stating it, and by providing thoughts, examples, and insights that support it. You should be willing to revise your response; you may change your opinion during or after a class discussion.

1. Logical thinking is characterized by exactness of meaning, rigid adherence to its one task of evaluating arguments, and rigorous evaluation of meaning. Verbal thinking is richer, more flexible, and more adaptable than logical thinking. What benefits can logical thinking provide us that verbal thinking cannot? Why?

2. Some social critics believe that logical thinking is the cause of dissension and distrust in our society. Everyone demands that others prove that their ideas are meaningful, showing a lack of trust. These critics believe that logical thinking has a negative influence on empathy, and in turn on communication in general. What do you think about these ideas? Why?

3. Pure logical thinking finds meaning only in statements; that means it regards all other functions of language as meaningless. Some believe that a legal system that is purely logical would be an excellent one, able to achieve justice with perfection. Why do you suppose they think this way? Describe their position as if it were your own.

4. Many people believe that if most people around the world thought in a purely logical way, we would have fewer disputes and that war would be eliminated. Why do you suppose they think this way? Describe their position as if it were your own.

▲ QUOTATION TO PONDER

"Logical consequences are the scarecrows of fools and the beacons of the wise."
Thomas Huxley, 1874

▲ JOURNAL TOPIC

Watch a television talk show in which a political, social, or moral discussion takes place. Describe the disputes you notice, as well as any arguments that are presented.

PURE LOGIC AND PRACTICAL LOGIC: A CLOSER LOOK

Deductive logic, as we have seen, is not concerned with whether statements are actually true, but only if the premises in an argument imply the meaningfulness of the conclusion. Inductive logic evaluates whether or not an argument's premises are true, and whether they imply the truth of the conclusion. The discipline of Logic is the study of the implication relationships of deductive and inductive arguments without any concern for the way that they are used in everyday life. This is the study of "pure logic," usually referred to as "formal logic." Pure logic is similar to mathematics. When the mathematician studies the formula for the area of a rectangle (A=LW) she does not concern herself with any specific plots of land, any of the rectangular-shaped shoeboxes in her closet, or any other rectangles encountered in our daily lives. As a mathematician, she is only interested in pure mathematics: not in the practical uses of it. In the same way, formal logic is not concerned with actual arguments that take place in daily life.

Formal logic is the study of the pure relationships of meaning and truth in nonpractical arguments. In the previous section of this chapter, we examined implication as if it had no practical application at all. Deduction was separated from induction. Deduction evaluates arguments with no concern at all for the truth of what is stated. Deduction is exact, rigid, and is inflexible in applying its rules; it has no concern for practical results. This may seem odd: why would anyone want to study arguments that have no practical benefit? The best response to this question is that pure logic is very challenging and extremely intriguing. It is, along with mathematics, the most purely rational activity anyone can possibly undertake. As a matter of fact, mathematicians and logicians often get together and compare notes on their discoveries and creations. There is an old story about the mountain climber who was asked by a reporter why he climbed the mountain. What practical benefits are there in mountain climbing? The mountain climber responded, "I climb the mountain because it's there." Mathematics and Formal Logic are "mountains" of abstract relationships. Their laws and formulas are very difficult to fully comprehend. However, there is a great deal of satisfaction in both disciplines, and, though it may sound odd to the uninitiated, mathematicians and logicians find a profound beauty in what they do. So do mountain climbers. Our concern, however, is with Practical Logic: the study of implication as it applies to arguments actually made in daily life. Students study pure mathematics when doing their homework in arithmetic. They apply the rules of pure mathematics when they balance their checkbooks or figure out their gas mileage. They are then doing practical mathematics. Practical Logic is the application of the rules of deductive and inductive pure logic to arguments people actually make.

Practical Logic identifies, reviews, and evaluates arguments as they occur in the context of everyday conversations and pieces of writing. Reflect for a moment on how much of our lives are involved with arguments. For example, Beverly watches the morning news while she has breakfast. It is full of arguments about the value of political programs, social values, and cultural events. Should the president's new taxation package be accepted by Congress? There are arguments in favor of, against, and for reforms. Should high schools routinely test athletes and band members for illegal drug use? There are arguments presented for several different positions on the issue. Should the city build a new arena for its professional soccer team? Again, there are many different positions, many different arguments being made. Later in the day Beverly attends her college classes, and professors present arguments in favor of the answers they accept for the great questions in History, Sociology, or Psychology. Was the United States wrong in using nuclear weapons in the bombing of Hiroshima and Nagasaki? Did John F. Kennedy make a mistake when he decided not to support the Bay of Pigs invasion? Should health agencies provide free needles to drug addicts with AIDS? Does freedom of speech extend to using "hate language" in public? Do long prison sentences reduce crime? Should businesses provide day care for employee's children? After school, Beverly goes to her part-time job at the mall, where she encounters arguments about which is the best basketball team, whether teenagers should be allowed to have credit cards, and how much higher the minimum wage should be (an argument in which she has a lot of interest!). By the time Beverly goes home and starts to study for the next day, she has encountered dozens of arguments. Practical logic is concerned with each one. How seriously should she take her professor's argument that the United States was justified in using nuclear weapons? Should she accept her friend's argument that short prison sentences would be as effective in deterring violent crime as long ones? And is her boss right when he argues that the minimum wage should not be raised? Is his argument a good one?

Unlike pure deductive logic, practical logic is significantly concerned with whether the statements in arguments are true. An argument that is meaningful, but which contains false statements is not acceptable to Practical Logic. That's why it is "practical." In our daily lives, we want arguments to be meaningful *and* truthful. We don't want to be misled by unscrupulous people who attempt to manipulate us with tricky arguments. We want to be able to review and organize arguments in order to evaluate them as meaningful in a *practical* way. We want to know if we can trust an argument, if we can accept what it claims to prove. The main characteristic Practical Logic seeks in arguments is whether or not they are *trustworthy*.

For example, Practical Logic would not accept the "Lassie argument" as trustworthy. Since several dogs played the role of Lassie, it is not true that "Lassie is a dog," and not true that "Lassie is an animal." Practically speaking, a person who believes those statements has been misinformed. Of course, the fact that pure deductive logic finds the argument meaningful is important. Implication is at the heart of practical arguments as well as at the heart of formal logic. However, in daily life, we need more than what formal logic can offer. We need practical arguments we can trust: arguments that are both truthful and sensible.

Practical Logic: Directive and Expressive Sentences.   As we have seen, directive and expressive sentences are often acceptable in practical arguments, and are referred to as "statements." This is a major difference between practical and pure arguments: practical arguments regard representative sentences as the only statements. In practical arguments, expression of emotion is sometimes relevant to the conclusion. Of course, sometimes emotion can be manipulative and distracting, in which case it is not acceptable. Almost every practical argument directs us to believe something, or to do something. For example, Beverly's professor wants her to believe his conclusions about the use of nuclear weapons by the United States. Her boss wants her to vote against raising the minimum wage. That's what often makes the arguments we encounter on a daily basis *practical*: they contain directive statements. They attempt to prove to us that we should believe or do something.

Of course, the bulk of practical arguments are made up of representative statements. And while practical logic accepts expressive and directive statements as meaningful, they are often troublesome and irrelevant to what is being demonstrated. Expressive statements can be especially manipulative and distracting.

In the next few sections, we will examine the elements and organization of arguments. Then we will discuss the ways practical arguments are evaluated.

ELEMENTS OF ARGUMENTS: PREMISES AND CONCLUSIONS

The statements that make up arguments, whether practical or formal, either support the implication or are supported *by* the implication. The statements that support it are called *premises*. Premises provide evidence or reasons that are given in support for the demonstration of the main point of the argument, called the *conclusion*. For example, in the very simple argument:

Lassie is an animal because Lassie is a dog and all dogs are animals

One premise is:

Lassie is a dog

Another premise is:

All dogs are animals

The conclusion is:

Lassie is an animal

Notice that the premises imply the conclusion. The conclusion is "implicitly in" the premises. The meaning of *Lassie being a dog* and *dogs being animals* "contain" the meaning of *Lassie being an animal.*

In the previous section of this chapter, there are several diagrams that illustrate the nature of implication. Here is one that is quite familiar by now:

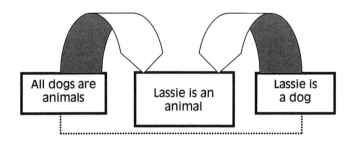

The conclusion of this implication is "Lassie is an animal." The two premises, seen in the side boxes, support it. The premises of an argument support the conclusion; they are the reasons behind the meaningfulness of the conclusion. The conclusion is the statement that is proven or demonstrated by the premises. Every argument has a conclusion and at least one premise. Most arguments have several premises.

When referring to both the premises and the conclusion of an argument at the same time, we say, "the statements," meaning the conclusion *and* premises. In practical arguments, the premises are usually representations of ideas, but are sometimes expressions of emotion. The conclusion, as we have seen, is often a directive. For example:

> Those who do not study history are doomed to repeat it. Anyone who knew much about history would not want to repeat it; the past is full of horrible events. So, study your history, learn from it, and liberate yourself from your ancestors' foolish errors.

Of course, it is very important to distinguish the premises from the conclusion of an argument. The first step in understanding an argument is to identify the conclusion. After that, the premises are relatively easy to find. The conclusion of the above argument is:

> Study your history, learn from it, and liberate yourself from your ancestors' foolish errors.

The premises are:

> Those who do not study history are doomed to repeat it. Anyone who knew much about history would not want to repeat it; the past is full of horrible events.

In some arguments the conclusion and premises are not as clearly distinguishable as in the example. If we mistakenly decide that the conclusion is a premise, then we miss the argument's point. Knowing what is being demonstrated—the conclusion—is obviously a very important aspect of understanding the argument. The conclusion should be identified first. The best way to separate the conclusion from the premises is to ask the questions, "What is the argument trying to prove? What advice is the argument giving? What does it want me to do?"

Unfortunately, it is not always easy to distinguish premises and conclusions. When the argument presents a difficulty, we can make use of the following "indicator terms" to help identify premises and conclusions. These terms often point out, or "indicate" that the statement that *follows them* is a conclusion or a premise. Premises *follow* the premise indicator term and the conclusion *follows* the conclusion indicator term. Not every argument contains both premise and conclusion indicator terms, and some contain neither.

However, memorizing at least the first five indicators in each column will help immensely in organizing arguments.

Premise Indicators	Conclusion Indicators
Because	Therefore
For	Means That
Since	So
Seeing That	It Must Be That
Inasmuch As	It Follows That
In View Of The Fact That	Hence
For The Reason That	Thus
Follows From	Implies That
Owing To	Is Evidence That
As Shown By	May Conclude That
As	Consequently
May Be Inferred From	May Infer That
Is Proven By	Proves That
Is Indicated By	Indicates That

Indicators can be very helpful in identifying conclusions and premises. Consider the following example, in which the conclusion and premises are impossible to distinguish.

> All Sociology professors do statistical analysis. Many Sociology professors use computers. Computers are very helpful in analyzing statistics in Sociology.

Our first step in reviewing the argument should be to identify the conclusion. Which statement is the "main point"? Which is being demonstrated, and which ones are supporting the demonstration? We can tell that the first statement is probably a premise. Which of the remaining two is the conclusion? Notice how helpful an indicator term can be:

> All Sociology professors do statistical analysis. So, many Sociology professors use computers. Computers are very helpful in analyzing statistics in Sociology.

The addition of the conclusion indicator "so" makes it very clear that the conclusion is "Many Sociology professors use computers." Here is another example of the argument, with different indicators:

> All Sociology professors do statistical analysis. Many Sociology professors use computers. For computers are very helpful in analyzing statistics in Sociology.

The premise indicator "for" helps us identify the premise "Computers are very helpful in analyzing statistics in Sociology." After that, we are on our own! We don't have a conclusion indicator, so we have to decide which of the two remaining statements is the conclusion. How do we decide? We need to be empathetic. We read the entire argument, and try to figure out what we would be trying to prove if we had written it.

Empathy, which was discussed in Chapter 4, is placing ourselves in another person's place: "walking in their shoes." As Chapter 4 made clear, empathy is an essential aspect of verbal communication. Here, we see that it is an important part of logical thinking as well. Later in this chapter, we will find further uses of empathy. For now, however, we need to recognize the importance of empathy in identifying conclusions.

Which statement do you feel that *you* would be trying to demonstrate if *you* had written the above argument? Notice that this question is asking you to empathize with the argument. You are not being asked what you think the conclusion *should be,* but what it *would be* if you were in the place of the person who wrote it the way he or she did. Wouldn't you try to write the argument in a way that made the most sense? And doesn't it make the most sense if "Many sociology professors use computers" is the conclusion? The order in which the premises are arranged seems to be an "empathetic clue" to which is the conclusion and which is the remaining premise. "All Sociology professors do statistical analysis" wouldn't be demonstrated very well if it were the conclusion. It doesn't make much sense that someone would try to prove that Sociology professors do statistical analysis by pointing out that they use computers and that computers are good for that task! Computers are good for a lot of things besides statistical analysis. On the other hand, it does make sense that someone would try to demonstrate that Sociology professors use computers because they do a lot of statistical analysis and that computers are good for doing that sort of work.

We often need to engage in this sort of empathetic thinking in seeking the conclusions of arguments. Some arguments don't have any indicators. And sometimes, it can appear that an argument has an indicator, but it really doesn't.

The simple fact that one of the indicators appears in an argument does not always mean that it is functioning as a premise or conclusion indicator. For example, the word "since" is listed as a premise indicator. However, in the following argument "since" is *not* a premise indicator.

> In the past, meals consisted of either chunks of meat eaten with knives or soup taken directly from bowls. In the mid-nineteenth century forks were first used to supplement knives. Spoons came into use in the late 1880s. In the last one hundred

years, meal preparation has become much more diverse as sauces, bite-sized deli-
cacies, and vegetables predominate our diet. Since 1900, the utensils have influenced the way food is prepared.

The conclusion is: "Since 1900, the utensils have influenced the way food
is prepared." Even though the word "since" appears, it does not function as a
premise indicator, but as a reference to a period of time. In fact, the word "since"
appears in the conclusion! Here is an argument in which the conclusion indicator "so" does not indicate the conclusion:

So many salmon die on the fish ladders meant to facilitate their passage over the
dams that the number of those who spawn upstream is greatly reduced. Many fish
that do make it are so injured that they do not spawn. The dams are detrimental
to the life cycle of the salmon.

The conclusion here is: "The dams are detrimental to the life cycle of the
salmon." Even though the conclusion indicator "so" appears twice in the argument, it does not function as one. It refers to the quantity of fish, and the seriousness of their injuries.

We cannot discern the premises and conclusions of arguments in a mechanical way; even premise and conclusion indicator terms need to be empathetically understood. The word "and," for instance, often appears between two
premises. However, on occasion it can also function as a conclusion indicator. In
this example "and" is between two premises:

Since so many salmon die on the ladders and those who are merely injured do not
spawn, we may conclude that the dams are detrimental to the life cycle of the
salmon.

However, it is a conclusion indicator here:

Many salmon die on the ladders, while those who are injured do not spawn, and
the dams are detrimental to the life cycle of the salmon.

Again, the key to the proper conclusion (and premise) identification is to
imagine that you are in the place of the person writing the argument. What
would you mean to be the conclusion *if you were the one who had written it*?

Allusions and Hidden Premises.   Not every premise in an argument is always
literally stated in words. Sometimes the premises are *allusions*. As we have seen
in Chapter 4, an allusion is a casual or indirect reference to an idea or feeling
that is suggested or insinuated, but which is not literally written down.
Allusions often indicate a written piece's attitude. In arguments, allusions usually indicate hidden premises as well. Premises are sometimes suggested or insinuated; they may not be directly stated in the argument. When premises are
not directly stated, but are *alluded to* they are called "hidden premises." Finding
hidden premises can be a very important part of argument analysis. Sometimes

the hidden premises supply very important support for the conclusion. Once they are identified, they can also be important in evaluating the trustworthiness of an argument. An argument can appear to be rather convincing as long as its hidden premises remain hidden. Once they are identified, though, the argument can sometimes be recognized as inadequate. For example, notice this argument, which you have probably already heard in the media or in conversations.

> It would be a good idea to enact the death penalty for possession of illegal drugs because executing people for possession of drugs would do away with most crime.

The above argument clearly contains the conclusion: "It would be a good idea to enact the death penalty for possession of illegal drugs." The argument offers in support the stated premise: "Executing people for possession of drugs would do away with most crime." Notice the premise indicator "because."

However, there is more support for the conclusion than the premise states. A very important allusion is present:

> Possession of illegal drugs is the *major cause* of crime.

The allusion is a *hidden premise*. We find it by noticing "something missing" between the stated premise and the stated conclusion. There is a gap between them that the hidden premise fills.

We know that this is a hidden premise because the argument concludes that most crime would be done away with if we executed people convicted of drug possession. That means that the argument is alluding to more support that it is stating. It is assuming that drug *possession* is the *major* cause of crime.

We have not changed the argument by identifying the hidden premise; we have merely clarified it. We have "filled in the gaps" by *stating* what the argument has *hidden*. The argument now states:

> In view of the fact that possession of illegal drugs is the *major cause* of crime, it would be a good idea to enact the death penalty for possession of illegal drugs because executing people for possession of drugs would do away with most crime.

Stating the hidden premise reveals that the conclusion is supported by a doubtful allusion. Criminologists do not agree with it; they believe that drug possession is *a* cause, but not the *major cause* of crime. The identification of the hidden premise reveals a weakness in the argument's reasoning that was always there.[5] It just wasn't as obvious.

It is always important to expose hidden premises. Sometimes an argument is strengthened by identifying a hidden premise. For example, consider this argument:

---

5. Specifically, the hidden premise is an oversimplification of the issue. There are many more causes of crime than drug possession! Chapters 6 and 7 examine oversimplifications and other reasoning errors (fallacies).

Men can be feminists just as easily as women since they can believe in and advance causes that help reduce unfair discrimination against women.

The premise indicator "since" helps us identify the stated premise:

Men can believe in and advance causes that help reduce unfair discrimination against women.

There is no conclusion indicator, but there is only one other statement, and it seems to be the conclusion:

Men can be feminists just as easily as women.

This is a rather controversial conclusion. Many people would disagree with it because we normally associate feminism with women. The stated premise, though, indicates that from the argument's point of view, men can believe in and advance causes that help reduce unfair discrimination against women. One hidden premise is:

Anyone who believes in and advances causes that help reduce unfair discrimination against women is a feminist:

Another hidden premise is:

It is not necessary to be a woman in order to be a feminist.

The argument can be restated with the hidden premises included.

Seeing that it is not necessary to be a woman in order to be a feminist, and because anyone who believes in and advances causes that help reduce unfair discrimination against women is a feminist, and since men can believe in and advance causes that help reduce unfair discrimination against women, it follows that men can be feminists just as easily as women.

Many people may not have initially agreed with the conclusion of this argument because of its hidden premises. Once they are identified and stated, however, the argument is clearer. Some people will now be able to reflect and agree that the conclusion makes sense, even though the argument did not appear reasonable when they first read it. Of course, others may still disagree, but it is now much easier for them to explain why. The premises are all "out in the open."

The important point for critical thinking is not whether we agree with the conclusion or not, but that we give the argument an empathetic review. Hidden premises should be identified and stated as closely as possible to the way the person behind the argument would state them.

Of course, an empathetic review does not mean a *sympathetic* review. We should *not* state hidden premises in a way to make them stronger or weaker than they are. It is not proper to state an allusion in a way that makes the argument seem weaker than it is because to do so is to "put words into someone's mouth" that they really did not mean to say or write. If we make the argument appear to be ignorant of well-known facts, or if we make it appear to be more unreasonable than it is, we are pretending that the person who wrote it is more ignorant and more unreasonable than he or she really is.

On the other hand, neither should we state hidden premises in a way that makes the argument seem stronger than it is. If the stated premises display an ignorance of facts, or if they are unreasonable, the hidden premises should not be stated in a way that corrects either failing.

Empathy is essential in stating hidden premises; once they are identified, they should be stated in the way the writer of the argument would state them, if he or she were present.

Some arguments allude to the conclusion. Usually this occurs in a context that makes the unstated conclusion rather obvious. For example, if these statements appeared in an article titled "Not All Feminists Are Women," the conclusion would be quite apparent:

> A feminist is anyone who believes in and advances causes that help reduce unfair discrimination against women, and some men believe in and advance those causes.

Even though there are no premise indicators in this argument, the missing conclusion can be identified by considering its context. Of course, unstated conclusions should be empathetically identified. We should never make an argument appear to be more or less trustworthy than it really is.

Organizing Arguments.   Once the conclusion and the stated and hidden premises have been identified, the argument needs to be organized into a coherent whole. Organizing the argument requires us to restate it in a particular pattern. The conclusion should be clearly labeled and stated first. Then the stated premises should be stated, and finally the hidden premises. Most arguments can be organized rather easily. For example, note how this rather complex argument is organized. First, the way the argument is originally presented:

> Seeing that love can be present without a marriage license, it follows that any couple, whether gay or heterosexual, should be recognized as being married. Some people disagree, but think about it. The legal, social, and other benefits of married life should not be denied because of narrow-minded bias.

The first step in organizing the argument is to identify the conclusion. After a careful reading, it appears that the conclusion is:

> Any couple, whether gay or heterosexual, should be recognized as being married.

The conclusion indicator, "it follows that" helped us find the conclusion. Now we understand what the argument is trying to demonstrate, or to prove.

The next step is to list the stated premises. This can be done in any order; what is important is to list them all, and not to list anything in the argument that is not really meant to be support. For example, in this argument, the sentence, "Some people disagree, but think about it," is not supporting the conclusion. It is simply a sentence that the writer included to encourage us to reflect on what the argument has to say. It is not a premise, and should not be listed.

There are two stated premises. They are:

Love can be present without a marriage license.

The legal, social, and other benefits of married life should not be denied because of narrow-minded bias.

The hidden premises of this argument are allusions that fill in the gaps between the conclusion and the premises. If we empathetically consider what the writer of the argument means, we will come up with these hidden premises:

Love is the primary qualification for being married.

Narrow-minded bias is the only reason a marriage license would be denied to heterosexual or gay couples who love each other.

People are sometimes biased against heterosexual and gay couples who love each other.

There are no important distinctions to be made between heterosexual couples and gay couples with regard to being married.

We are now ready to put the argument in a well-organized format, with the conclusion and premises properly labeled:

Conclusion

Any couple, whether gay or heterosexual, should be recognized as being married.

Stated Premises

Love can be present without a marriage license.

The legal, social, and other benefits of married life should not be denied because of narrow-minded bias.

Hidden Premises

Love is the primary qualification for being married.

Narrow-minded bias is the only reason a marriage license would be denied to gay couples who love each other.

People are sometimes biased against gay couples who love each other.

There are no important distinctions to be made between heterosexual couples and gay couples with regard to being married.

The argument is now organized in a format that will allow us to evaluate whether or not it is trustworthy. We will continue with this argument in the next chapter.

CONCLUSION

Logical thinking is rather dry when contrasted with verbal thinking. It lacks verbal thinking's richness, flexibility, and adaptability. In their place, it has rigor, rigidity, and exactness. The contrast between them is like that between two cousins. One is lively, friendly, and has a home filled with singing and storytelling. The other is plodding, secluded, and lives in a well-organized, clean, but unimaginative house. However, neither cousin functions very well independently of the other. Verbal thinking needs the rigor and exactness of logical thinking in order to achieve excellence. Its clarity, accuracy, specificity, and significance are all greatly enhanced by logical thinking. In its turn, without verbal thinking, logical thinking is not practical. Its rigorous attention to proper organization, its exactness in meaning, and its rigid concentration on proper inferences cannot be applied to the world of human concerns unless logical thinking is supplemented by verbal thinking.

Practical logic is a harmony of logical and verbal thinking. They do not have equal roles; the major tasks of practical logic are logical, not verbal. However, without the verbal element, practical logic would not be of any use; it would not be practical.

EXERCISES

▲ MOST INTRIGUING ISSUE

Write a one-paragraph description of the most interesting idea, topic, or process described in the chapter in pages 146–158. Be prepared to explain what you find interesting in class discussion.

▲ THE MUDDIEST POINT

Write a sentence or, if possible, a paragraph that describes the idea, topic, expression, term, or process in pages 146–158 that you find most difficult to understand.

▲ CARTOONS AND DIAGRAMS

1. Provide a diagram that shows specific differences between formal logic and practical logic.
2. Draw a cartoon that shows the importance of empathy in selecting the correct conclusion.

3. Draw a cartoon that shows the importance of empathy in restating hidden premises.
4. Draw a cartoon that shows the differences between premises, hidden premises, and conclusions.

▲ DEFINITIONS OF KEY TERMS

Provide a disciplinary definition for each of the following terms as they are used in this chapter. Most of the terms are not defined in the chapter, although their meanings are described by the context in which they appear. You need to review the material to create the definition yourself. Be sure to follow the guidelines for creating definitions on pages 78–81.

Conclusion	Conclusion Indicator	Hidden Premise
Practical Argument	Premise	Premise Indicator

▲ SHORT ESSAY QUESTIONS

Provide a written response of approximate length for each topic. Your responses should be well organized, grammatically correct, and neatly produced.

1. Describe three important differences between practical and formal logic.
2. Explain why directive and expressive sentences are not regarded as statements in formal logic, but are accepted as such in practical logic.
3. Explain three ways in which you can identify the difference between the premises and conclusion of an argument.
4. Explain why empathy is often necessary in identifying the hidden premises of an argument.
5. The chapter claims that there is a difference between a "dispute" and an "argument," and says that critical thinking is not involved with disputes. However, isn't it true that some disputes do involve arguments? Provide an example. Explain how critical thinking could help resolve the dispute.
6. Using the premise and conclusion indicators, identify the premises, conclusions, and at least one hidden premise of each of the following.
   a) The car being out of fuel, we may infer that we will be late to class.
   b) The car being out of fuel may be inferred from our being late to class.
   c) The lack of success of "binge diets" is evidence that a daily diet of limited intake is the best way to lose weight.
   d) The lack of success of "binge diets" follows from evidence that a daily diet of limited intake is the best way to lose weight.
   e) Owing to the lack of an experienced goalkeeper, the women's soccer team won't win the tournament.
   f) In view of the fact that the women's soccer team did not win the tournament, they must lack an experienced goalkeeper.
   g) The large number of students in the library on any weekday afternoon is indicated by the fact that the students on this campus take their task very seriously.
   h) The large number of students in the library on any weekday afternoon indicates that the students on this campus take their task very seriously.

  i) The dormitory rules are not being followed. This may be inferred from the noise after 11:00.

  j) The dormitory rules are not being followed. Hence there is noise after 11:00.

  k) The number of dogs on campus has increased inasmuch as there are more students who own dogs.

  l) The number of dogs on campus has increased implies that there are more students who own dogs.

  m) As you were driving over the speed limit, you must pay the fine.

  n) As you must pay the fine, you were driving over the speed limit.

  o) Professor Torres's excellence as an instructor means that she should receive the Teaching Award at commencement.

  p) That she should receive the Teaching Award at commencement proves Professor Torres's excellence as an instructor.

  q) The cafeteria is the best place to eat seeing that a dietician plans the meals.

  r) The cafeteria is the best place to eat; it must be that a dietician plans the meals.

  s) The parking lot is full implies that we will be unable to find a place to park.

  t) The parking lot is full as shown by our inability to find a place to park.

  u) Seeing that the pond is frozen, the temperature is below freezing.

  v) It must be that the pond is frozen; the temperature is below freezing.

  w The space station is a success because many different nations helped build it.

  x) The space station is a success thus many different nations helped build it.

  y) The cat is on the windowsill means that my grandfather is not home.

  z) The cat is on the windowsill for the reason that my grandfather is not home.

▲ QUESTIONS FOR DISCUSSION

Identify the conclusion, stated premises, and hidden premises and organize each of the following arguments. Identify each statement as representative, expressive, or directive. Pay special attention to hidden premises; paraphrase them accurately.

1. The college grading system should be changed from the current letter system to a more detailed number system inasmuch as the number system gives students a more accurate description of their performance and gives teachers the opportunity for a more detailed assessment of student work.

2. The income provided the city from a new convention center should be very high; consequently, everyone should vote for it.

3. Inasmuch as the new convention center will be a stimulus to an increase of crime, it follows that no one should vote for it.

4. Other cities with comparable populations that have convention centers have higher crime rates than we do; consequently, a vote for the convention center is a bad idea.

5. In view of the fact that there is great interest in the convention center, and that other cities have done very well financially by attracting the sorts of activities convention centers bring in, a vote for the convention center is a good idea.

6. It must be that laws against assisted suicide are violations of privacy. People should be able to make their own decisions about important things in their lives without governmental interference.

7. Governments have serious responsibility to their citizens and because the government is the guardian of the people's welfare, laws against assisted suicide are necessary and right.

8. Dying is terribly important, so people should be able to die as they please, without any government laws prohibiting assisted suicide.

9. Dying people are often in pain and very distressed, and cannot make important decisions rationally, and that proves that laws against assisted suicide are good ones.

10. Owing to the fact that democratic societies rely on the good judgments of their citizens, high quality public education is essential to their survival.

▲ QUOTATION TO PONDER

"The ability to critically analyze issues that affect personal, social, and political decision making will distinguish those who feel in control of their lives from those who do not."
Allison King, "Inquiry as a Tool in Critical Thinking," 1994

▲ JOURNAL TOPIC

Carefully observe and reflect upon the classroom discussions you have experienced during your years in formal education. How often do students argue in these discussions? How often do they engage in disputes? What would be a good strategy for you to follow in encouraging more argument and less disputes during these discussions?

▲ PORTFOLIO PAPER

Write a 300–500 word essay that explains the difference between arguments and disputes. Clearly describe the elements of arguments. Describe the specific ways disputes lack these elements.

CHAPTER SIX

EVALUATING ARGUMENTS: VAGUE TERMS AND FALLACIES

EVALUATING PRACTICAL ARGUMENTS: THREE PROCEDURES

Once an argument has been properly organized, it can be evaluated for trustworthiness. A trustworthy argument will be clear and reasonable enough to offer us some practical value. An untrustworthy argument will be of little or no value if it contains key terms that are too vague or ambiguous to be clearly and specifically understood, or that contains serious reasoning errors. There are three procedures in deciding whether an argument is trustworthy enough to be of practical value to us. First, we need to evaluate the key terms for vagueness and ambiguity. Second, we evaluate the argument for specific serious errors in reasoning, called "fallacies." Third, we make our decision: considering the results of the first two procedures, is the argument trustworthy or not? Could it benefit from revision? Is it so untrustworthy that it should be rejected?

This diagram of the three procedures involved in argument evaluation may be helpful. Although it is a general overview, a more detailed, step-by-step description of evaluation of arguments will be discussed in this chapter.

AFTER STUDYING CHAPTER SIX

You should understand the difference between trustworthy and untrustworthy arguments and be able to recognize vague and ambiguous key terms in an argument. You should understand what fallacies are, and should be able to identify and explain the straw man fallacy and the fallacies of inappropriate authority, attacking the person, appeal to force, and oversimplification.

Trustworthy Arguments	Three Procedures Taken in Argument Evaluation	Untrustworthy Arguments
Clear and Specific; Understandable	Identify and Evaluate Key Terms	Vague or Ambiguous Key Terms
Truthful and Reasonable	Identify Fallacies	Serious Errors of Reasoning
Worth Serious Consideration	Evaluation of Trustworthiness	In Need of Revision or Rejection

A trustworthy argument is one that we can rely upon to give us good advice in making practical decisions. It is clear, well balanced, truthful, reasonable, and worth our serious consideration. In the final step, we need to judge the practical value of the argument.

IDENTIFYING VAGUE OR AMBIGUOUS KEY TERMS

Vague language is imprecise: it lacks specificity, clarity, and accuracy due to overgeneralization. Ambiguity is the characteristic of words and sentences that have more than one interpretation due to poor word choice, grammatical confusion, or incomplete comparisons.[1]

Formal logic is extremely exact; it does not allow any ambiguity or vagueness whatsoever in arguments. Practical logic, though, while it deals with arguments in a less formal way, is willing to accept some of the inevitable ambiguity and vagueness characteristic of ordinary language. However, practical logic will not allow the *key terms* of an argument to be ambiguous or vague. The key terms of an argument are those words, phrases, and sentences involved directly in the implication.

There are four points to consider in evaluating an argument for vague and ambiguous terms:

1. Key terms that are so vague or ambiguous as to interfere with the argument's inference should be identified.
2. Some terms can be satisfactorily defined by empathetically considering the context of the argument, or by considering information acquired from outside the argument.
3. Even though some terms cannot be satisfactorily defined from a consideration of context or outside information, it may be appropriate to simply point out the specific way the ambiguous or vague terms interfere with the argument's clarity.
4. If the key terms cannot be satisfactorily defined, and if the argument's inference is obviously untrustworthy because of it, it is appropriate to point out that the argument is not trustworthy due to its vague or ambiguous terms.

---

1. Chapter 3 provides a more extensive discussion of vague and ambiguous language.

Before an argument can be evaluated for vague and ambiguous terms, it must be properly organized. The first point in organizing it is to identify any vague or ambiguous key terms This is not done in a mechanical manner; empathy is involved. Even if a key term is not defined in the argument, if it is understandable in the argument's context, it should not be identified as vague or ambiguous. Likewise, vague or ambiguous terms that have little impact on the implication should not be identified: they are not *key terms*.

Here is the argument, organized in the proper format:

Conclusion

Any couple, whether gay or heterosexual, should be recognized as being married.

Stated Premises

Love can be present without a marriage license.

The legal, social, and other benefits of married life should not be denied because of narrow-minded bias.

Hidden Premises

Love is the primary qualification for being married.

Narrow-minded bias is the only reason a marriage license would be denied to gay or heterosexual couples who love each other.

People are often biased against gay or heterosexual couples who love each other.

There are no important distinctions to be made between heterosexual couples and gay couples in regard to being married.

The conclusion seems to have one vague key term. "Couple" is not clear. What is the definition of a "couple" in the context of the argument? An empathetic reading of the conclusion reveals that the word is being used to mean "two people who have a relationship" of *some special* sort. It seems to be clear that two people attending a movie together, for example, would not be defined as a "couple" by the argument. If we look further into the argument, we see that in the first stated and hidden premises, "love" is related to "marriage." This indicates to the empathetic reader that the argument is presuming that the "couple" in the conclusion is one that has a relationship of "love." The term, then, is not as vague as it first appeared. Even though the conclusion literally states "any couple," it is clear from the *context* of the argument that it defines the term as "two people who love each other." A nonempathetic reading of the conclusion would miss the contextual meaning of the term "couple" and would simply label it "vague." This would not be proper. On the other hand, the word "love" has several meanings and may be in need of further definition.

The term "recognized" in the conclusion is also without definition. An empathetic reading of the argument, however, shows that in the second stated premise, "legal, social, and other benefits" helps clarify its meaning. The conclusion must mean "legal and social recognition." What are the "other" benefits? Do they also impact the meaning of "recognition?" It does not appear that the term "other" is a key term in the argument. It does not play a role in the implication relationship between the premises and conclusion.

The conclusion, once clarified by an empathetic consideration of the argument's context, is:

> Any couple in a loving relationship, whether gay or heterosexual, should be socially and legally recognized as being married.

The only other key term in the argument that seems to be vague or ambiguous is in the second stated and second hidden premises: "narrow-minded bias." An empathetic reading of the argument cannot find a definition of the phrase in the argument's context. All we are told is that narrow-minded bias is the only reason the benefits of marriage would be denied to these couples. If we go to outside information, however, we will find some help in defining its meaning. The argument is probably referring to the well-known fact that many people in our society have serious reservations about gay marriages. In the light of this outside information, we could define narrow-minded bias as "prejudice against gay marriages." But this adds confusion, not clarification, to the argument. Clearly, the stated and hidden premises, and the conclusion, which is implied by them, are describing gay *and* heterosexual couples, not *only* gay couples. While there is obviously much more bias against gay couples than heterosexual couples in society, the key term "narrow-minded bias" appears to be ambiguous. It could refer to gay couples alone, or to both heterosexual and gay couples. Since it is a key term, it should not be as ambiguous as it is.

In addition, outside information is not clear in regard to the term "narrow-minded bias" in relation to people who have reservations about gay marriages. Are their reservations truly "narrow-minded"? Is it possible that there are some people who have good reasons for their reservations about gay marriage who are not narrow-minded at all? Of course there are! Some people believe that gay couples should be recognized legally and socially, and should be allowed the rights of married couples, such as sharing health and life insurance benefits, credit ratings, tax liabilities, and so on. However, they do not believe that marriage is the proper way to acknowledge these rights. Some of these people do not believe that gay couples should be allowed to adopt children, an inherent right of married couples. Others, however, do not object to gay couple's adopting children. They feel that marriage is too traditionally heterosexual to be practical for gay couples. They believe a new tradition should be created to acknowledge the love gay couples have for each other.

Outside information shows that there are many points of view on gay marriages. Those that do not approve of them are not *necessarily* examples of "narrow-minded bias." "Narrow-minded bias" is obviously being used in an ambiguous manner in this argument.

We may *suspect*, at this point, that the argument is not trustworthy. But are we certain? A review of the third and fourth points from page 163 to be considered in evaluating vagueness and ambiguity is appropriate here.

3. Even though some terms cannot be satisfactorily defined from a consideration of context or outside information, it may be appropriate to simply point out the specific way the ambiguous or vague terms interfere with the argument's clarity.

4. If the key terms cannot be satisfactorily defined, and if the argument's inference is obviously untrustworthy because of it, it is appropriate to point out that the argument is not trustworthy due to its vague or ambiguous terms.

At this point in our evaluation, the third point seems more appropriate than the fourth. "Narrow-minded bias" is seriously ambiguous. However, the argument is not *obviously* untrustworthy simply because of this term's ambiguity. It is enough, at this point, to simply point out that the argument's clarity suffers because of the ambiguous term's confusion of bias against gay couples with a bias against heterosexual couples, as well as its confusion in regard to the bias against gay marriages as always due to narrow-mindedness. We need to note this serious ambiguity and proceed with the next step in the evaluation.

FALLACIES

"Fallacy" means "a serious error in the quality of an implication." The word "fallacy" is a synonym for "serious error in reasoning." A fallacy is an error or a deliberate deception that can make an untrustworthy argument appear to be trustworthy.

Whether an argument contains ambiguous terms or not, it may be untrustworthy because it contains one or more fallacies. There are many such errors that are commonly made. For example, celebrities often appear on television commercials endorsing products they obviously know nothing about. Imagine that your friend Bob sees a commercial in which a professional football player, Tyler Hansel, endorses the Thrifty Mortgage Company. If Bob then argues that Thrifty is the best mortgage company because Hansel endorsed it, Bob has committed a common error in reasoning. He has argued that because Hansel is a football celebrity, he is therefore an authority on mortgage companies. This is the "fallacy of inappropriate authority." Bob's argument has not proved that Thrifty Mortgage Company is the best because his argument is based on a fallacy.

In Bob's case, the fallacy was probably a simple error in reasoning. Bob may have become too enthused over Hansel's football exploits to actually reflect on the quality of his own argument. Fallacies are often simple errors that are made out of carelessness.

On the other hand, the Trusty Mortgage Company may not be as innocent as Bob. They may have deliberately created the commercial and hired Tyler

Hansel in order to deceive innocent television viewers into believing that their company is better than it is. Trusty's fallacy may be deliberate. They intended to disguise an untrustworthy argument as a trustworthy one that would deceive some people.

How would Bob have reacted to Trusty's commercial if, instead of the well-known and well-liked Tyler Hansel, the spokesperson was someone he had never heard of? Most likely, he wouldn't have paid any attention to it! But let's say that he did watch it rather carefully. Wouldn't Bob have inquired further into the company before he accepted that Trusty is the best mortgage company? Of course. But Trusty doesn't want Bob to inquire any further into their company; Trusty wants Bob to rely on Hansel's endorsement. They deliberately deceived Bob with their fallacious commercial.

Of course, few people would be fooled by the Trusty commercial. It is offered here only as a simple example to help explain the way fallacies work. They are often much more subtle and much more complex than the example. In evaluating arguments, it is important to keep every fallacy in mind; they are sometimes well hidden.

Fallacies are not always intentionally created in order to deceive. They can also be errors of judgment. However, unintentional fallacies are sometimes just as difficult to detect as intentional ones. Logical thinking rigorously seeks out fallacies in arguments. The best way to detect them is to examine every argument carefully for one of the ten fallacies listed here. Even if it at first appears that the argument is completely trustworthy, we nevertheless must rigorously examine it. Sometimes an argument can appear to be perfectly trustworthy, but a close examination of it reveals a well-hidden fallacy.

You will be able to complete the evaluation of the argument that claims to demonstrate the appropriateness of gay marriages after a discussion of ten fallacies.[2] In this chapter we will examine the first six; the remaining four will be discussed in Chapter 7.

Ten Fallacies

- The fallacy of INAPPROPRIATE AUTHORITY
- The fallacy of APPEAL TO FORCE
- The fallacy of ATTACKING THE PERSON
- The fallacy of OVERSIMPLIFICATION
- The fallacy of SHIFTING THE BURDEN OF PROOF
- The fallacy of THE STRAW MAN
- The fallacy of MINDLESS CONFORMITY
- The fallacy of IRRELEVANT EMOTION
- The fallacy of OVERGENERALIZATION
- The fallacy of UNWARRANTED ASSUMPTION

---

2. There are many fallacies; some logicians claim that there are over one hundred different ones. The ten we study seem to occur most often.

THE FALLACY OF INAPPROPRIATE AUTHORITY

We must rely on experts and authorities for much of our knowledge. How many of us are capable of the scientific research, the experimentation, and the assimilation of data necessary to assemble evidence on our own? No one can possibly research and test everything we need to know in this complex world. Specialists in various disciplines authoritatively communicate their findings to us, and we accept what they say. But when someone speaks with *inappropriate* authority, their views do not provide good reasons to believe the offered conclusions. Simple examples of inappropriate authority fallacies abound in television "testimonial" commercials. Sports figures (authorities in playing football, baseball, and so on) give apparently expert advice on shoes, breakfast cereals, and, as we saw earlier, mortgage companies. Why should we accept the conclusions of a basketball player when he or she tells us that a particular brand of shoes is worth our purchase? What does a basketball player know about shoes? *Podiatrists* know about shoes! (Podiatrists are specialists in the care of feet.)

More serious cases of inappropriate authority can occur when authorities are paid to represent special interests. Thus, an authority in nutrition who is paid by a soft drink corporation to testify at congressional hearings on the proper role of sugar in the diet should not be accepted without question.

Appropriate authorities are experts in the area of which they speak or write; they usually have credentials, such as academic degrees, licenses, or certificates of qualification. Appropriate authorities are always acknowledged as experts by their peers. However, when a person who has appropriate authority in one area speaks "with authority" outside his or her area of expertise, he or she engages in the fallacy of inappropriate authority. Here is a sobering example from Nobel Prize winner Johannes Stark, who was an authority in physics. Here, Stark is writing *outside* his area of expertise:

> Natural science is overwhelmingly a creation of the Nordic-German blood component of the Aryan peoples. The Jewish spirit is wholly different in its orientation. True, Heinrich Hertz made the great discovery of electromagnetic waves, but he was not a full-blooded Jew. He had a German mother, from whose side his spiritual endowment may well have been conditioned.

Johannes Stark was an appropriate authority in one area; he won the Nobel Prize in physics. His claims that only "Aryan peoples" were capable of scientific thinking, and that Jews are not able to think scientifically, while very popular in Stark's Nazi Germany, are claims about genetics and history of science, neither of which are areas in which Stark was an appropriate authority. The fact that Stark was an appropriate authority in physics was most likely seen by some people as a good reason to accept his pronouncements in genetics and history of science as reasonable support for Hitler's racist political values. Stark spoke with inappropriate authority. His support was not reasonable at all.

We rely on authorities to sincerely and accurately provide their expertise. And for most people, it is difficult to understand the limits of an expert's authority. Authorities and experts have a serious responsibility to publicly acknowledge the limits of their knowledge. Unfortunately, authorities do not always have the integrity to take that responsibility seriously. We have to carefully examine arguments that cite authoritative claims. The support appropriate authorities provide *within* their area of expertise is trustworthy. But arguments that rely on premises provided by inappropriate authorities are always fallacious. Perhaps a good rule to follow is an old one: "Question Authority!"

THE FALLACY OF APPEAL TO FORCE

An argument always attempts to prove that the conclusion is worthy of belief. Trustworthy arguments do this by providing clear and reasonable support for the conclusion. They rely solely on the power of reason. Whenever an argument relies on any other type of power to support its conclusion, it commits the fallacy of appeal to force.

The most obvious sort of force is the physical threat of violence or harm. The argument distracts us from a critical review and evaluation of its premises and conclusion by putting us into a defensive position. Here is an example of an obvious appeal to force:

> You should give me an "A" in this course, Professor Karmy. I haven't done much work. I don't understand any of the material. I have received no grade higher than a "D." But consider this: If you don't give me a final grade of "A," I will break your arm.

Notice that the last premise is very distracting to Professor Karmy. The other premises clearly do not support the conclusion, which is the directive statement, "You should give me an 'A' in this course." The only support for the conclusion is the threat of physical violence and harm.

But appeals to force are not always physical threats. Appeals to psychological, financial, and social harm can be no less threatening and distracting. Notice the appeal to financial and social harm in this example:

> Professor Karmy, my father is visiting the campus this week and he would like to meet you. He will be busy on Tuesday, since he's spending the day playing golf with the College President, his old roommate. And on Wednesday he is meeting with the Endowment Office, where he plans to give a $100,000 check to the college. You should meet with Dad on Monday and assure him that I will be getting an "A" in this class. It will probably make your life a lot easier.

Appeals to psychological force can be very distracting. Rather than provide clear and reasonable support for a conclusion, a threat to disrupt a person's emotional life is made.

> Professor Karmy, I will be calling you this evening, and every evening to remind you that you should give me an "A" in this course. I will be entering your apartment when you are not home, and will leave notes to that effect in your bedroom

and kitchen. I'll be going through your office files here at the college while you are in class. I will be watching your every move as you carry out your day. I have bugged your telephone. I will read your mail. You will never be free of my surveillance. Or, you can avoid the whole thing and give me an "A."

Not all appeals to force are obvious. Even a subtle reference to harm can distract us from giving a thorough review of the argument's clarity and quality of reason.

Professor Karmy, do you know what it is to "key" a car? It's when someone uses a key to scratch a long ugly line along the doors. It can really destroy the appearance of a nice new car. Hey, speaking of nice cars, I really like your new Ford! I saw it in the parking lot this morning on my way to class. You know, Professor Karmy, I want an "A" in this course very much. I know I haven't done much work in here. But I want an "A" so much, well, I don't know *what* I'd do if I didn't get one.

It is important to notice that the appeal to force is always made to the person who is listening to (or reading) the argument. However, this can be done directly or indirectly. An indirect appeal to force is one that threatens someone with whom the individual reading the argument is emotionally attached. The most obvious indirect appeal to force is the "ransom note":

If you ever want to see your cat alive again, Professor Karmy, you'll give Melissa Ramsey an "A" in this course!

People who are in subordinate positions are often the target of appeals to force. For example, sexual harassment is often characterized by direct appeals to force. Consider this telephone call:

Miss Ramsey, this is Professor Karmy speaking. I would like you to accompany me to a three-day meeting next week. We'll be staying in the same room at the hotel; you'll love it. I don't see how I can possibly give you an "A" in this course if you don't come along with me. I sure can give you an "F" if you don't.

Appeals to force are more common in conversations than in written arguments, probably because they are so obvious when they are in writing.

THE FALLACY OF ATTACKING THE PERSON

This fallacy supports its conclusion by demeaning, insulting, or sometimes merely making a demeaning reference to an individual's character, intelligence, or personal circumstances. For example,

John is a dirty rat, so don't believe him.

is an argument that relies on the fallacy of attacking the person. There may be some good reasons for not believing John, of course. But calling him a "dirty rat" is not one of them. Acceptance of a conclusion as reasonable requires more supportive premises than mere name-calling.

Attacking the person is common in political speeches. There is an attempt to demean the target of the attack and portray his or her opinions and arguments as untrustworthy:

My opponent is a thief and a liar, so don't vote for her!

Not every political case of attacking the person is so blatant. During the Senate confirmation hearings of Supreme Court Justice Clarence Thomas, Anita Hill accused him of sexual harassment. Thomas denied the accusation. The controversial hearings held the public attention for weeks. In an effort to discredit Anita Hill's accusations, defenders of Thomas presented evidence to the confirmation committee that Hill had made eleven telephone calls to Thomas from 1983 to 1987, which was the year Thomas married his wife, Ginni Lamp. The number of phone calls in itself was not persuasive. Eleven calls in four years are not good evidence for anything. But the Thomas camp told the press that it was:

"We have eleven phone calls initiated by her from 1984 through the date of Clarence Thomas's marriage to Ginni Lamp, and then it all ended. What does that say about Hill's behavior?"[3]

The insinuation was clear; Hill had called Thomas because she was romantically attracted to him. She stopped calling after he was married. Her claims of sexual harassment by Thomas were the irrational ravings of an unrequited lover. This attack on Hill's personality led the public, and the Senate committee, to believe that her accusations were groundless.[4]

The demeaning attack on her character was unreasonable. During the hearings Hill, a graduate of Yale Law School and a tenured professor of Law at Oklahoma State University, was labeled "a fantasizer," "a spurned woman," "an incompetent professional," and a "perjurer."[5] Opinion polls revealed that fewer than 25% of the public believed Anita Hill's claims.[6] Did the Senate committee, as well, accept the personal attacks as good reasons to come to the conclusion that Hill was lying? We can only hope that they thought more critically than that!

---

3. Jill Abramson and Jane Mayer, *Strange Justice: The Selling of Clarence Thomas;* (1994), pp. 281–282.

4. In fact, the story of Hill's unrequited love did not mention that Diane Holt, the person who kept notes on Thomas's phone log, stopped working for him almost immediately after his wedding. There are no records of any phone calls—from Hill or anyone else!—after the wedding! Abramson and Mayer, p. 282.

5. Abramson and Mayer, p. 295.

6. It is interesting to note that after the hearings were concluded and more information about the personal attacks on Hill came out in the media, public opinion on her credibility rose to 44%, and only 34% believed Thomas. Abramson and Mayer, pp. 345, 352.

In any case, the Thomas confirmation hearings illustrate that attacks on the person can be quite subtle and, to some, convincing.

Personal attacks are usually meant to demean a person in order to make their opinions and arguments appear to be untrustworthy. Groups can also be attacked for the same reason. For example:

> Anita Hill and that whole crowd of fem-nazi spinsters whine and whimper about being sexually harassed. But not one of them is good-looking enough for any man to give 'em a second look. It's all fantasy, all dreamed up. They just want a man and they can't get one, folks. That's all there is to it.

The poor reasoning in the fallacy of attacking the person is often quite obvious. However, if we are prejudiced against a person or group, we are especially vulnerable to the fallacy. Our biases can blind us to an attack; from our biased point of view, it may seem quite reasonable. Of course, the best way to avoid this vulnerability is to reduce our own biases and develop our capacity for empathy. How much differently would the Thomas confirmation hearings have gone if the American public had been less prejudiced against Anita Hill and more empathetic with her point of view?

EXERCISES

▲ MOST INTRIGUING ISSUE

Write a one-paragraph description of the most interesting idea, topic, or process described in the chapter so far. Be prepared to explain what you find interesting in class discussion.

▲ THE MUDDIEST POINT

Write a sentence or, if possible, a paragraph that describes the idea, topic, expression, term, or process in the chapter so far that you find most difficult to understand.

▲ CARTOONS AND DIAGRAMS

1. Provide a cartoon that shows the difference between an empathetic evaluation of vague terms in an argument and one that is not empathetic.
2. Provide a cartoon that shows the differences between appropriate and inappropriate authorities on over-the-counter cold remedies.
3. Provide a cartoon that shows the differences between appropriate and inappropriate authorities on pick-up trucks.
4. Provide a cartoon that illustrates the fallacy of inappropriate authority.
5. Provide a cartoon that illustrates the fallacy of appeal to financial force.
6. Provide a cartoon that illustrates an indirect appeal to force (but not a ransom note!)
7. Draw a cartoon that illustrates the fallacy of appeal to psychological force.

8. Draw a cartoon that shows the difference between the fallacy of the indirect appeal to force and the fallacy of attacking the person.
9. Draw a cartoon that illustrates at least three ways the fallacy of attacking the person takes place.
10. Illustrate a combination of the fallacy of inappropriate authority and of attacking the person in one cartoon.
11. Illustrate a combination of the fallacy of appeal to force and of attacking the person in one cartoon.

▲ DEFINITIONS OF KEY TERMS

Provide a disciplinary definition for each of the following terms as they are used in this chapter. Most of the terms are not defined in the chapter, although their meanings are described by the context in which they appear. You need to review the material to create the definition yourself. Be sure to follow the guidelines for creating definitions on pages 78–81.

Appropriate Authority	Demeaning Reference	Fallacy
Fallacy of Appeal to Force	Fallacy of Attacking the Person	Inappropriate Authority
Key Terms	Trustworthy Argument	Untrustworthy Argument

▲ SHORT ESSAY QUESTIONS

Provide a written response of approximately 200 words for each topic. Your responses should be well organized, grammatically correct, and neatly produced.

1. Explain the difference between an empathetic evaluation of vague key terms and one that is not empathetic.
2. What is a trustworthy argument? Can a trustworthy argument ever have vague key terms? Explain.
3. What is an untrustworthy argument? Can an untrustworthy argument have no vague terms? Explain.
4. Can a trustworthy person ever make an untrustworthy argument? Explain.
5. Describe an example of a television commercial that commits the fallacy of inappropriate authority. Explain how the fallacy makes the commercial untrustworthy.
6. Provide an example of a conversation in which you took part and noticed an argument in which the fallacy of inappropriate authority was committed.
7. Explain how a professor might make an appeal to force in an argument about the value of grades in his or her course. What type of appeal to force would be made?
8. Explain how a parent might make an appeal to force in an argument directing a child to study. What type of appeal to force would be made?
9. Explain the difference between demeaning gossip about a person and the fallacy of attacking the person.
10. Provide an example of an argument you noticed in the media in which the fallacy of attacking the person was made. How subtle was the attack? What specific sort of attack was it?

▲ Questions for Discussion

Provide an essay of 300–500 words that responds to each of the following questions that ask for your opinion. You should respond by stating it, and by providing thoughts, examples, and insights that support it. You should be willing to revise your response; you may change your opinion during or after a class discussion.

1. Properly organize each of the following arguments. If possible, empathetically revise any vague or ambiguous terms. Explain where and why you detect a fallacy of inappropriate authority, appeal to force, or attacking the person. Be specific about the fallacy. Do not simply name it in general; explain which type you think it is. If the argument is a combination of fallacies, explain which fallacies are involved.

a) Since Dr. Anderson is a clinical psychologist of great reputation, he must have a good idea about the sort of grapes that go into making a good wine. I don't know anything about wine, and only buy what he tells me. You should too.

b) The philosopher Frederich Nietzsche wrote several well-known books that have had a great deal of influence. A lot of people don't realize that he had syphilis, though. I don't believe anyone who lived a life of such low morality should be read anymore. Therefore, Nietzsche's books should be removed from the college library.

c) Professor Wagner: Students, I suggest you all study much harder. You have gained the distinction of being the worst class I have ever been forced to teach. I think it might be appropriate for me to mention that the college does allow me to give an "F" to anyone I think is not doing passing work.

d) There's nothing like "Vita-Grow" for your lawn. It's the best stuff since the chickens and the cows left the city for the farm. And "Vita-Grow's" got a lot better in the last couple years, too. Just ask anyone who uses it. They know how good "Vita-Grow" is for your lawn. Pick some up today at your favorite store.

e) There they go again! The city council is on a rocket ship to the moon! They want to raise taxes again, like they don't care if tomorrow ever comes. They need a good spanking, that's what. Let's have a recall vote on every one of the bums! I agree with the talk show host on the radio; he says that if they raise taxes, throw 'em out on the street. Let's take his advice; he knows what he's talking about.

f) Biff: Betty, I don't think you should keep up with your dance lessons. I don't like the looks of that skinny little guy that's teaching you. I'm not going to pay for them anymore. And if you pay for them yourself, you have to answer to me, and you won't like that, I can guarantee you, babe. So forget ever going again.

g) Babe Ruth was the greatest baseball player who ever lived. He drank a lot of alcohol, smoked cigars, abused women, and in general led a life that these political correctness police would hang him for. Babe knew what life was about; I think these "Pc'ers" should shut up. They don't know what life's about.

h) Your honor, I want to say a few words about the defendant. First of all, he doesn't have a job, he hasn't had a shave or haircut in months, and he smells like he hasn't had a bath in six weeks. He swears that he's telling the truth about his whereabouts on the night of the burglary, but I don't believe a man like him, and you shouldn't either.

i) Mr. Arnott? This is the Acme Pool Service calling. We know you have a very nice swimming pool, and want to compliment you on how clean you keep it. I know you want to keep it that way. We have a truck that goes by your home once a week. You should hire us. There's been a lot of vandalism in your area, Mr. Arnott. People dumping dangerous chemicals into pools. How about hiring us to make sure your pool stays clean?

j) Hi there, folks. You all know me, because you see me play a doctor in the great show, "Hospital Hunks." I love taking care of all the patients on the show. When they get tired and worn down, I always prescribe "Energize." You don't need a prescription, though, because you aren't on television! Stop by your grocer, your drugstore, or anyplace, really. But buy a jar of "Energize" today!

2. The chapter claims that individuals in subordinate positions are often the targets of appeals to force. Describe some situations you have read about or seen on television news programs in which this seems to have happened.

3. The fallacy of attacking the person sometimes takes the form of "character assassination." For example, this is what appears to have happened to Anita Hill in the Clarence Thomas hearings. Describe a case of character assassination in history or contemporary times of which you are aware.

4. The fallacy of inappropriate authority occurs when someone who is not an acknowledged authority in the field is accepted as if he or she was a legitimate expert. However, sometimes it is difficult to decide what are the credentials of an appropriate authority. What sort of credentials would you accept as a mark of expertise in the following?

a) What college you should attend.
b) What sort of car to buy.
c) Which dentist to visit.
d) Which bank to open a checking account.
e) Which, if any, church to attend.
f) How to choose an appropriate spouse.
g) How to decide what *really* caused the American Civil War.
h) Whether sexism is a serious problem in our society.
i) Whether racism is a serious problem in our society.
j) Whether or not you should become a vegetarian.

▲ QUOTATION TO PONDER

"Of course, an expert's judgment is not conclusive proof; experts disagree, and even in agreement they may err, but the expert opinion is surely one reasonable way to support a conclusion."
Irving Copi, *Introduction to Logic*, 1990

▲ JOURNAL TOPIC

According to a traditional description, war is "the last step in diplomacy." What are your thoughts about this description? What is it attempting to say about the diplomatic relationships between nations and appeals to force?

THE FALLACY OF OVERSIMPLIFICATION

There is little need to demonstrate conclusions that are common knowledge, and usually we can make simple inferences without the need for an argument. Arguments are usually constructed to prove or demonstrate a conclusion about a complex issue. There are always several different points of view on these issues. An argument is an attempt to demonstrate that one conclusion (out of many other possible conclusions) is worthy of trust: that it, and not the others, should be felt emotionally, acted upon, and/or believed. As a consequence, most arguments are forced to *simplify* the complex ideas contained in their premises and conclusions.

To simplify an idea is to interpret an idea in a way that makes it less complex. For example, it is impossible to summarize or paraphrase without simplifying the ideas to some extent. A summary simplifies an idea into its main point and its support material. A paraphrase can simplify terminology if its purpose is to make an idea more accessible to an audience. If we did not simplify complex ideas, we could not think about them unless we were authorities in the subject areas involved. For example, imagine how impossible it would be to understand the complex technical concepts involved with space probes, undersea exploration, and experiments in genetic engineering if we did not simplify them. We must simplify ideas if we are to discuss them. Arguments, being part of the process of communication, must also simplify ideas.

However, an argument can go too far in simplifying ideas; when it does so, its reasoning becomes untrustworthy due to the fallacy of oversimplification. *The fallacy of oversimplification misrepresents the complexity of complex ideas by reducing them to trite, bland statements.* A trite statement is one that has been used so often that it has lost its ability to represent an idea well. Oversimplifications are bland because they are lifeless; they tend to take the energy out of complex issues and render them dull and uninspiring. One of the most noticeable characteristics of the fallacy of oversimplification is its tendency to use "one-liners" in arguments instead of statements that reflect the complexity of an issue.

For example, there have been many arguments proposed in the United States about ownership of firearms, especially handguns. Some people feel that legal prohibition of all firearms would lower the senseless violence that plagues our urban areas. Others feel that not all firearms should be prohibited, but that some—inexpensive handguns most commonly used in crimes—should be. Still others feel that registration of firearms is the answer. There have been suggestions that a large tax on firearms and ammunition could lower the number of such weapons in the wrong hands. There are arguments that ammunition for automatic weapons and other antipersonnel weapons should be prohibited, or made available only to those with special licenses. Still others have suggested that longer prison sentences for those who are convicted of crimes in which firearms are used would deter the use of firearms.

There are thousands of people in the country who enjoy using firearms for recreation, especially target shooting and hunting. These people have never used a firearm to harm anyone and have no intention of doing so. There are people who collect firearms as a hobby; they enjoy the precision and craft involved in the manufacture of firearms. Some of these people do not even fire the guns. They see them as concrete illustrations of the history of our country's battles with the wilderness and its international enemies. Still other people feel that their own safety and the security of their family necessitates ownership and competence with handguns.

Our society is very diverse; some live in rural areas where hunting is the primary recreation. Others in small towns or rural areas love to drive a few miles into the countryside and "do a little shooting." Others live in areas of high crime, where they can hear automatic weapons firing in the middle of the night. There are people who live confined in their inner city homes, frightened by the gunfire as they would be by a war going on in the streets. Clearly, the issue of the proper role of firearms is a very complicated one for Americans.

The fallacy of oversimplification trivializes this highly emotional and complex topic with trite one-liners. "Guns are for killing people, and killing is wrong," is an oversimplification of the issue. Of course, guns are for killing; but as indicated above, they are also used for a great many other purposes. If guns were *simply* used for killing people, and if that were *all* they were used for, the whole issue would be much simpler than it is. The toxins used in chemical warfare, such as anthrax, are used for killing people. These toxins are *only* used for killing. As a result, nations all around the world have limitations on the availability of anthrax. Since people do not have hobbies or recreational pursuits that involve the use of anthrax, there is no perceived need for demonstrating its proper role in American life. The trite statement, "Anthrax is for killing people, and killing is wrong," is not controversial. However, when the oversimplified statement "Guns are for killing people, and killing is wrong" is used as a premise in an argument claiming to prove that the possession of all firearms ought to be made illegal, a fallacy of oversimplification has taken place.

In the same way, the hackneyed slogan, "When guns are outlawed, only outlaws will have guns" is another obvious oversimplification. Both one-liners are meaningless statements that conceal the vibrant issue at the heart of the many disagreements in our society regarding the role of guns.

When these and other trite, bland statements are used as premises of arguments, they have a strong tendency to make the issues appear much more dull and lifeless than they actually are.

The fallacy of oversimplification *minimizes* an issue. That is, it makes an issue appear to be "smaller" than it is in two ways.

In the first way, oversimplification reduces a complicated topic to a much less complicated issue that it really is. When the premises of an argument are oversimplifications, the conclusion actually has little to do with the complex issue it claims to address. Unfortunately, the mass media—especially television news programming—is guilty of oversimplifying issues every day. The complicated problems of the world cannot be described very well in two or three minute "reports." The causes, repercussions, and inherent intricacies of national and international concerns must be ignored; the reports consist of a series of oversimplifications. Later in the news program, when experts are asked to comment and provide support for their opinions about these events, their arguments are quite often untrustworthy due to the fallacy of oversimplification. As a result, the television audience does not hear and does not understand the complexity of the problems being discussed. Oversimplification has minimized the issues: it has made them smaller than they are.

The second way that oversimplification minimizes complex issues is by *marginalizing* any opinion that is not firmly "for" or "against" an oversimplified solution to the complex issue. "Marginalizing" an opinion means placing it "on the margin" of the page, not in the center. That is, oversimplified opinions that are "in favor" or "against" an issue are regarded as the *only* opinions. They are, metaphorically speaking, placed at the center of the page. Any opinion that is not an oversimplified one is marginalized: put aside as unimportant. When the media oversimplifies complex issues, and then minimizes them by acknowledging only two mainstream positions, one "pro" and the other "con," every other opinion automatically becomes marginalized. No one ever hears of them. As a result, many people who attempt to become informed by watching the "Evening News" are actually subjected to oversimplified reports and opinions! There are many important details involved with the issues that are never covered, and dozens of marginalized opinions that are never given any attention.

Of course, the fallacy of oversimplification is not limited to the mass media. Any argument that demonstrates its conclusion by minimizing an issue with trite, bland premises—especially "one-liners"—commits the fallacy of oversimplification.

THE FALLACY OF SHIFTING THE BURDEN OF PROOF

Every argument attempts to *prove* that its conclusion is true. In order to do so, it must "carry the burden" of providing its own proof. It cannot "shift" its burden, or give the responsibility of proving its conclusion to another argument. The *fallacy of shifting the burden of proof claims that unless an opponent can disprove its conclusion, the conclusion must be accepted as proven.* It is always the task of an argument to present support for its own conclusion. Arguments that commit this fallacy simply point out that there is a *lack* of proof that the conclusion is false, and that the conclusion follows from that. For example,

There must be ghosts in the closet since it cannot be proven that there aren't any.

The *lack* of proof that there is no ghost (and how could there be any, as ghosts are invisible, etc.?) is not good support for the claim that there *are* ghosts. The name of the fallacy comes from the way it shifts the task of proving that ghosts are in the closet to other arguments, specifically to those who deny that there are ghosts. Because they cannot prove that there are not any ghosts, the fallacy asserts that it has proved that there *are* some ghosts. In this way, the fallacy actually claims that the argument's conclusion follows from an *absence* of support. The fallacy claims that:

No one can prove that my conclusion is not true or not reasonable, therefore my conclusion is true and reasonable.

Here is an example:

No one has ever been able to prove that Alma, the famous telephone psychic, is not able to forecast the future. Therefore she can forecast the future.

The shifting the burden of proof fallacy is often committed in arguments that attempt to prove that a controversial religious, moral, or political value should be followed. A well-known occurrence of the fallacy is found in attempts to demonstrate that God exists. For example:

God must exist; for years and years people have tried to prove that there is no God, and no one has ever been successful. If there were no God, certainly there would have been proof of the fact by now.

On the other hand, the shift of the burden of proof also occurs in arguments that attempt to demonstrate the atheistic position:

God must not exist; for years and years people have tried to prove that God exists, and no one has ever been successful. If God existed, certainly there would have been proof of the fact by now.

The fallacy is also common in moral and political issues:

No one has ever satisfactorily shown that animals do not have souls, and anything with a soul has rights. Therefore, animals have the same rights as human beings.

Issues such as the "animal rights controversy" are extremely complex, difficult philosophical problems. For centuries philosophers and others have been puzzling over questions about how we should properly relate to animals. As with many issues involving moral values, there is no "proof" that any particular position is correct. The discussions provide a forum for debating the various "positions." These philosophers not only provide arguments, but also engage in disputes. As a result, people become more interested in "winning the debate" than in finding a consensus about the best solution. In their zeal to win, they easily fall into committing the fallacy of shifting the burden of proof. "I can't prove I'm right, but you can't prove I'm wrong, either!" Unfortunately, too many of our discussions about values are debates. We need to learn that no one ever wins a debate. The only way anyone wins in these situations is when everyone comes to a consensus and agrees on the best approach to the problem—for everyone involved.

Sometimes it is difficult to determine which "side" in a discussion has the burden of proof. For example, which is more reasonable: that those who believe animals have rights supply the proof, or that those who do not believe in animal rights supply it? Is the burden of proof on those who support the existence of God, or with the atheists? How about the death penalty? Should those who oppose it carry the burden, or those who favor it? Whenever difficult issues such as these are being discussed, it is best that each point of view supply its own proof. Neither point of view has a clearer responsibility than the other to bear its own responsibility to demonstrate its own claims.

However, when very controversial conclusions are asserted, the general rule of thumb is that the conclusion needs to shoulder the burden of its own proof.

For example, conspiracy theories are almost always very controversial. A conspiracy theory is an explanation of social or political events that bases its conclusions about their causes on premises that there are secret, illegal, evil groups of people (or, alas, aliens from outer space) plotting and executing destructive plans. Conspiracy theories should be reviewed very carefully for the fallacy of shifting the burden of proof. Often an argument attempting to prove the presence of a conspiracy will "shift the burden" to those who deny it.

> The Central Intelligence Agency is a gang of murderers. No one can prove that they are not behind the deaths of Stalin, Krushchev, and Mao-Tse Tung. They killed the Kennedy brothers, too. Anyone who denies this must confront the evidence, the strongest of which is that there is not a shred of proof that the CIA was not in on these killings.

Note that the argument shifts the burden of proof *away* from its own "evidence" *to* those who deny its conclusion. This fallacy often makes reference to premises that support its conclusion, but the primary support is always the *lack* of evidence anyone else has to "prove it wrong." In most conspiracy theories, the fallacy of the burden of proof is used to call into question the standing of anyone who would question the conspiracy:

> The Central Intelligence Agency is a gang of murderers. No one can prove that they are not behind the deaths of Stalin, Krushchev, and Mao-Tse Tung. They killed the Kennedy brothers, too. Several historians have denied that there is any conspiracy involved. For example, Dr. Michael Kiefel, a well-known historian, has written a book in which he provides evidence that there is no connection between the assassinations of the Kennedys and the CIA. However, Kiefel has not shown he is innocent himself; he has most likely been working for the CIA. He does not deny any connection to "The Company" in his book.

One of the most devastating conspiracy theories to grip the United States in this century was the "Red Scare" of the 1950s. Joseph McCarthy, a U.S. Senator from Wisconsin, gained fame by using the fallacy of shifting the burden of proof. In early 1950, at the start of the cold war with the communist government in Russia (the Soviet Union), McCarthy accused the United States Department of State of being "infiltrated" with communist agents bent on the destruction of the country. He was challenged to demonstrate his claim, but refused to provide support, claiming it was "secret." He merely increased the vehemence and range of his accusations. By 1952 he was chairing a Senate committee that had taken on the task of "exposing communists" in all areas of

American government. McCarthy doggedly pursued those he regarded as "Reds"; people's careers were destroyed and reputations were ruined when they could not "prove their loyalty to the United States government" to McCarthy's committee. McCarthy never provided any support for his accusations, but relied almost exclusively on the fallacy of shifting the burden of proof. When asked to provide evidence for his charges that a particular person was a "communist," McCarthy would typically respond,

> "I do not have much information on this, except for the general statement of my investigators that there is nothing to disprove communist affiliation."

McCarthy shifted the burden of proof. Even though he was presenting a conclusion ("Jones is a communist"), he offered no support for it. He merely offered *lack* of support for the denial of his conclusion ("there is no evidence Jones is not a communist"). McCarthy's argument style was so consistent that a new term was coined in his name: "McCarthyism" means "to make accusations of political disloyalty without support."

An argument should always support its own conclusion. McCarthy engaged in poor quality reasoning when he accused people of "communist leanings" without also providing support for his charge. However, he did more than reason poorly; his unreasonable accusations devastated many innocent people's lives.

McCarthyism is actually a combination of two fallacies. The fallacy of shifting the burden of proof is combined with that of attacking the person: to accuse a person of disloyalty, and then claim that the burden is upon them to prove that they are loyal. For example, here is a less political, more personal example of combining the two fallacies:

> You are a dysfunctional parent; prove that you are not!

The American criminal justice system is very aware of the dangers posed by the fallacy of shifting the burden of proof. In our system, a person accused of a crime does not have to prove his or her innocence. It is the task of the government to prove their guilt. That's why a person accused of a crime does not have to speak to the police, does not have to cooperate at all with a criminal investigation. The burden of proof is on the accusers. This seems fair, considering that the government has hundreds of law enforcement professionals, attorneys, and forensics experts helping to gather evidence and create reasonable arguments that prove the accused is guilty. The accused person is only one individual, usually with minimal resources, at least compared to those of the government.

THE FALLACY OF THE STRAW MAN

A "straw man" is a "scarecrow," not a real man, but a weak imitation of a man. Gardeners use scarecrows to frighten crows; they do a fairly good job for a short period of time. It doesn't take the crows very long to catch on. The gardener is soon frustrated by the view of several crows pecking at the corn, while two or three others wait their turn, perched on the scarecrow's shoulders.

The straw man fallacy gets its name from the scarecrow. *The straw man fallacy occurs when a premise misquotes, misrepresents, or oversimplifies another person's point of view in order make it easier to criticize it or even dismiss it as completely unreasonable.* The misrepresentation of the other person's point of view is not their "real" point of view; it is a "weak imitation" of their point of view.

The straw man fallacy is often the result of a lack of empathy on the part of the person criticizing a point of view. For example, this argument misquotes the famous Inaugural Speech of John F. Kennedy, and then proceeds to criticize Kennedy's point of view:

> Kennedy said, "Do not ask what you can do for your country, but ask what your country can do for you." For that reason, Kennedy is obviously the most selfish president this country has ever had.

To misquote another person's statements and then use the misquotation to criticize him or her is a straw man fallacy; it is very poor reasoning. To do so intentionally is also deceptive. But the straw man fallacy also occurs when the argument misrepresents the other person's point of view, even though it may quote him or her faithfully. For example:

> Kennedy said, "Do not ask what your country can do for you, but ask what you can do for your country." Kennedy was attempting to encourage young men to join the armed forces with this directive. He wanted to start a war and conquer Laos and Vietnam and he needed a lot of young men and women to help him succeed in the war in Southeast Asia, which he was obviously planning at the time of his inauguration.

This argument is not referring to the "real" John F. Kennedy, but to a "straw man," a "pretend" Kennedy. It quotes his Inaugural Speech faithfully, but then proceeds to misrepresent the meaning of the quotation. Even the most cursory examination of the speech reveals that Kennedy was not specifically referring to military service in the quotation, but to a more general attitude of caring for others. The argument proceeds from the misrepresentation to "demonstrate" that Kennedy was secretly planning to start a war in Southeast Asia at the time of his inauguration.[7]

The straw man fallacy often misrepresents the context from which a quotation is taken. More often, however, it takes place without a quotation; the straw man usually occurs when the point of view is paraphrased or summarized:

> Kennedy, in his Inaugural Address, expressed the hope that Americans would pay higher and higher taxes in order to support his plans for a bigger and bigger

---

7. The argument may be heading toward a "conspiracy theory" in relation to the Kennedy administration! If so, we can anticipate that may eventually "shift the burden of proof."

government. In his famous "Ask not" remark, he directed the American people to not ask for tax refunds, but to ask to pay more taxes than they were required by law to do. For this reason, Kennedy is the first liberal "tax and spend" president.

When the summary of a point of view is a complete misrepresentation, the straw man fallacy is usually at work:

> While John F. Kennedy was president, he used the federal government to control colleges and universities by providing hundreds of thousands of students low interest loans, by giving grants to faculty in every area of study, including the arts and humanities, and by visiting college campuses around the country personally. He was trying to gain the loyal affection of the professors and students so that he could control their minds. Therefore, the Kennedy Administration is one of the most tyrannical of any in American history.

The straw man fallacy can also be used to oversimplify a person's point of view.

> Kennedy's presidency was seen by him merely as a way to extend the power his rich family already had in New England over the rest of the country, and, he hoped, over the entire world.

All oversimplifications ignore details and make complex issues appear to be less complicated than they are, as we have seen. When a fallacy of oversimplification is used explicitly to make a person's point of view appear less complex than it really is, the straw man fallacy is usually at work.

The straw man fallacy is sometimes a deliberate attempt to misrepresent or oversimplify a point of view with the intention of deceiving others. However, more often, it is an example of the poor reasoning that comes from a lack of empathy. For example, the arguments in this section about John F. Kennedy all conclude with negative assessments of his political career. In seeking support for that conclusion, the arguments commit the straw man fallacy because Kennedy's Inaugural Speech and administrative policies have not been empathetically studied. The speech and policies have not been allowed to speak for themselves, but have been twisted to meet the needs of the arguments' conclusions. Of course, an empathetic reading of Kennedy's speech and policy documents does not need to be sympathetic. However, it needs to read the material in a way that "stands in the shoes" of *Kennedy*, and not in the shoes of the purposes of the arguments' conclusions.

It is possible to provide empathetic, reasonable arguments that conclude with negative assessments of John F. Kennedy's political career. However, it is not reasonable to base such conclusions on "straw man reasoning." Reasonable arguments do not tailor "scarecrow suits" for "straw man" premises that fit a previously determined, biased conclusion. Reasonable arguments give an empathetic representation of the premises, and tailor the conclusion to fit the arguments of a real man or woman.

Arguments are attempts to demonstrate or prove that the conclusion is reasonable. In order to do this successfully, the argument's premises must infer the conclusion clearly and reasonably. The best way to determine if the argument is a good one is to evaluate it for vague and ambiguous terms as well as for fallacies. If the argument does not have any fallacies, and if it does not contain any vague or ambiguous terms, then we are able to trust that its conclusion is reasonable.

Chapter 4 describes empathy as very important in evaluating the quality of verbal thinking. A piece does not need to prove that it is clear, accurate, specific, and significant. It merely needs not to be *unclear, inaccurate, unspecific,* and *insignificant.* We give the written piece the "benefit of the doubt."

In a similar way, we do not demand that an argument prove that it is reasonable. All we ask is that it is not *unreasonable.* We evaluate the argument for clarity of terms, much in the same manner as we do written pieces. We do not demand that they be perfectly clear, only that they not be vague and ambiguous. When we evaluate the argument for fallacies, we do not demand that it be perfectly reasonable. All we ask is that it not contain any fallacies. If the argument is not unreasonable, we give it the benefit of the doubt. We evaluate it as trustworthy.

Reasonable people can disagree. So can trustworthy arguments. Not all trustworthy arguments agree with each other. There are several arguments, each of which is reasonable, about most of the pressing social, political, and personal issues that confront us.

For example, there are several reasonable arguments about the best way to achieve high-quality health care in our society. Some acknowledged authorities argue that national health insurance is the best way. Others argue that private health insurance is best. Still others argue that Health Maintenance Organizations (HMOs) are the best bet. Some people argue for a combination of several solutions. It would be quite closed-minded to claim that one, and only one, of these arguments is reasonable. There are reasonable arguments for each of these points of view.

An argument that we have determined to be reasonable is worth our trust. But that does not mean that it is worth our compete acceptance. There are also other trustworthy arguments. We can trust them: that means we can discuss them without fear of deception or innocent mistakes in reasoning.

The fact that a person is reasonable and understandable means that he or she can be trusted; but it does not mean that he or she has the right answer. In fact, many trustworthy people disagree. The more they discuss issues, though, the closer they will come to a consensus, to an agreement. Arguments are like that. We need to accept that the more reasonable arguments we listen to, the more likely we will find a reasonable answer of our own.

EXERCISES

▲ MOST INTRIGUING ISSUE

Write a one-paragraph description of the most interesting idea, topic, or process described in pages 176–184. Be prepared to explain what you find interesting in class discussion.

▲ THE MUDDIEST POINT

Write a sentence or, if possible, a paragraph that describes the idea, topic, expression, term, or process in pages 176–184 that you find most difficult to understand.

▲ CARTOONS AND DIAGRAMS

1. Draw a cartoon that illustrates the difference between a simplification and an oversimplification.
2. Provide a cartoon that shows how the fallacy of oversimplification "marginalizes" opinions.
3. Provide a cartoon that illustrates the fallacy of shifting the burden of proof.
4. Draw a cartoon that illustrates the straw man fallacy.
5. Draw a cartoon that shows the lack of empathy in the straw man fallacy.
6. Provide a cartoon that illustrates a straw man fallacy combined with a fallacy of attacking the person.
7. Provide a cartoon that illustrates the fallacy of oversimplification combined with the fallacy of appeal to force.
8. Draw a cartoon that shows the fallacy of shifting the burden of proof combined with the fallacy of attacking the person.

▲ DEFINITIONS OF KEY TERMS

Provide a disciplinary definition for each of the following terms as they are used in this chapter. Most of the terms are not defined in the chapter, although their meanings are described by the context in which they appear. You need to review the material to create the definition yourself. Be sure to follow the guidelines for creating definitions on pages 78–81.

Complex Issues	Conspiracy	Conspiracy Theory
Hackneyed Slogans	Marginalize	McCarthyism
Minimization	Oversimplification	Simplification

▲ SHORT ESSAY QUESTIONS

Provide a written response of approximately 200 words to each of the following. Your responses should be well organized, grammatically correct, and neatly produced.

1. Explain the difference between a summary of a book that simplifies the book and one that oversimplifies it.
2. Provide an example of an argument that commits a combination of the straw man fallacy and the fallacy of oversimplification.
3. What is a "marginalized opinion"? Is the network television news the only cause of marginalized opinions?
4. Why are conspiracy theories often troubled by the fallacy of shifting the burden of proof?
5. Explain how the straw man fallacy and the oversimplification fallacy both suffer from a lack of empathy.

6. List three "hackneyed slogans" that oversimplify complicated issues. Explain in detail why they are examples of the fallacy of oversimplification.

7. Provide an example of a student committing the straw man fallacy in explaining low grades to his or her parents.

8. Provide and explain an example of a salesperson committing the fallacy of shifting the burden of proof in trying to convince a consumer to purchase a used car.

9. Can the "shifting the burden of proof" fallacy be caused by a lack of empathy? Why or why not?

10. Explain how the shifting of the burden of proof fallacy is also an oversimplification of an issue.

▲ QUESTIONS FOR DISCUSSION

Provide an essay of 300–500 words that responds to each of the following questions which ask for your opinion. You should respond by stating it, and by providing thoughts, examples, and insights that support it. You should be willing to revise your response; you may change your opinion during or after a class discussion.

1. The chapter claims that television news programs routinely commit the fallacy of oversimplification in two ways, by misrepresenting complex issues as overly simple, and by marginalizing opinions. Do you feel that some television news programming is less guilty of oversimplification than others? Do you feel that some are not at all guilty? Investigate several news programs before you respond; remember, not all television news is on local channels or the "Big Three" networks.

2. If television news programming routinely oversimplifies complex issues, where can we turn for more reliable information about the world? Where can we go to become aware of "marginalized opinions"? What are your specific suggestions?

3. What are the characteristics of McCarthyism? Are there any examples of it in contemporary America? If you know of one, provide enough detail to explain why it is an example of McCarthyism. If you do not believe there are any examples of McCarthyism today, explain how our society has managed to avoid it.

4. What if there really is a conspiracy "out there"? How would you go about finding it without engaging in the fallacies of oversimplification, shifting the burden of proof, and the straw man fallacy?

5. The United States Constitution's Bill of Rights establishes that every citizen has a right to be considered innocent until they are proven guilty in a legal proceeding. The constitution makes it very clear that the burden of proof is on the government to prove the guilt of the accused. But there is dissatisfaction with this aspect of the Bill of Rights; some feel that too many guilty criminals are going free. How do you feel about this question? Should the Bill of Rights be amended so that people accused of particular types of crimes (or even of any crime at all) be required to prove their innocence? Should the burden of proof be on the accused instead of the government?

6. Not every slogan is an oversimplification. But many advertising slogans are actually fallacies of oversimplification. List at least three and explain why they are fallacies, and not merely slogans.

7. Which argument bears the burden of proof on the debate about whether or not there is nonterrestrial intelligent life? Why?

Properly organize each of the following arguments. Empathetically revise any vague or ambiguous terms if possible. Explain where and why you detect a fallacy of oversimplification, shifting the burden of proof, or the straw man fallacy. Be specific about the fallacy and explain which type you think it is. If the argument is a combination of fallacies, including fallacies discussed earlier in the chapter, explain which ones are involved.

a) When the Bible says that Jesus went among the people doing good, that means he cured the sick and taught people how to be happy. The Bible does not say Jesus went around being good. There's a difference. You don't have to be good. But you should do good if you want to be a Christian.

b) Socrates once said, "The unexamined life is not worth living." He therefore had a very low opinion of the value of human life. He felt anyone who wasn't a philosopher should be put to death; after all, their life "is not worth living."

c) Folks, unless Mrs. Calhoun can demonstrate that she did not steal the missing funds, we have no choice but to recall her from office. Anyone who would stoop so low as to pilfer our petty cash has no business being the president of this club! She is a low-life, a common thief.

d) This country isn't what it used to be; kids having kids, that's the problem! They should all be kicked off welfare. Let them fend for themselves! They and those like them are the cause of this nation's moral crisis!

e) The cold, hard fact, Mr. Rogers, is that you cannot prove you didn't cheat on your last quiz. Since I caught you cheating on this one, I must conclude that you also cheated on the last one.

f) Einstein once said, "God does not play dice with the universe. There is order in everything." His opinion is only one opinion. However, Einstein was a great man. His opinion on this matter should be taken seriously. It proves he felt that gambling is morally wrong.

g) Professor Hong is a racist, and I can prove it. He said that human beings are not the same. He said that African Americans are not the same as European Americans in their skin color or their ethnic backgrounds.

h) Murderers deserve the death penalty. They have taken a life, and so their life should also be taken away. How could anyone believe otherwise? How could anyone show that a murderer does not deserve to die?

i) There are many serious disagreements going on in the world today. Israel and the Palestinians are always on the brink of war. The Irish are plagued with terrorism and civil strife. North and South Korea are engaged in a bitter struggle for economic superiority. There is only one answer to these problems. People need to love each other.

j) I know that you did not write this paper yourself, Miss Martinez. I also realize you are a clever liar, but you will never be able to convince me that it is your own work. I am going to call your coach and have you removed from the team. That is the punishment you deserve for being a cheater and a liar!

k) The Internet is a curse, not a blessing. It's full of child pornography and other horrid material. Sex criminals use the Internet to seduce young boys and girls. It doesn't belong in a decent home. Those who say it's a matter of privacy are simply perverts, that's all. Privacy! They want pornography and filth, not privacy!

l) Anyone who believes in religion is an ignorant dope. Of course, there are plenty of believers who will deny that they are ignorant, and will deny that they are dopes. Their denial is itself proof of just how stupid they really are.

m) Anyone who is in favor of the right to have an abortion is a baby-killer. There's no more to the issue than that; either you believe killing children for your own convenience is right or you don't.

n) The invasion of our planet by aliens from outer space started in Egypt at the time of the Pharaohs. How else were the pyramids built? The wise religious leaders of the ancient world were aliens: Moses, Lao-Tsu, Jesus, Buddha, and Mohammed. How else can you explain the marvelous truths these leaders gave humanity?

▲ QUOTATION TO PONDER

"You have the right to remain silent and not say anything which might incriminate yourself. Anything you say can and will be used against you in a court of law. You can stop answering questions I ask you at anytime. You have the right to have a lawyer with you when you go to court or during questioning. If you cannot afford a lawyer, one will be appointed for you."
The *Miranda Warnings,*
which clarify the Burden of Proof in American Criminal Law

▲ JOURNAL TOPIC

Watch two television news programs on the same evening. One should be a half-hour network program. The other should be the "The MacNeil-Lehrer Report," or a similar program—one that is a full hour in length and that covers only three or four events. Describe the simplifications and oversimplifications you notice in each one's coverage of the same events.

CHAPTER SEVEN

FALLACIES AND THE EIGHT STEPS OF ARGUMENT EVALUATION

The first group of fallacies we studied in Chapter 6 all make unreasonable references to people in some way. The fallacy of inappropriate authority misrepresents people as authorities or experts. The fallacy of appeal to force psychologically induces fear in a person whom the argument is trying to convince. The fallacy of attacking the person tries to support its conclusion by demeaning someone.

The second group of fallacies shared the characteristic of being misrepresentations of meaning. The fallacy of oversimplification, which is often found in summaries or paraphrases, ignores important specific details. The fallacy of the straw man, which also is common in summaries and paraphrases, misrepresents meaning. The shifting the burden of proof fallacy transfers the responsibility of proving its conclusion to another argument, thus misrepresenting the poor quality of the first argument's inference.

In this chapter, four fallacies are examined. The first two, the fallacy of mindless conformity and the fallacy of irrelevant emotion, are related to the emotional life of the person who is creating the argument; specifically, to his or her need for social acceptance or to more general emotional distractions. The last two fallacies, the fallacy of overgeneralization and the fallacy of unwarranted

AFTER STUDYING CHAPTER SEVEN

You should be able to identify and explain the fallacies of mindless conformity, irrelevant emotion, overgeneralization, and unwarranted assumption. You should be able to understand and follow the eight steps in argument evaluation. You should be able to review, organize, and evaluate arguments as trustworthy or not trustworthy.

assumption, both lack specific reference to details involved with the support or evidence provided by the premises.

THE FALLACY OF MINDLESS CONFORMITY

Conformity is our psychological need for the acceptance and approval of other people. Conforming is acting according to what we perceive to be the expectations of others. It is the basis of social cohesion; the laws, rules, customs, and arrangements that allow us to live our lives in routine ways. If we did not conform, there would be no society. We wouldn't have any legitimate expectations concerning the behavior of others, and they wouldn't be able to expect consistent behavior from us.

Imagine how difficult life would be if we didn't conform to accepted behaviors in something as simple as going to the library to study. The library staff might be playing loud music and dancing on the tables. Students could be throwing books out of the windows, setting fire to the journals, and pouring soft drinks into the computer terminals. Perhaps some chickens and ducks would be laying eggs in the newspaper racks. It would be impossible to study.

Conformity is a social necessity that provides personal stability. We need to feel that we "fit in" with others. On a more profound level, conformity is an essential aspect of linguistic interaction; those who use the same natural language "conform" to the way others speak, read, and write. Conformity gives our lives more satisfaction and more coherence.

However, conformity can sometimes make no sense at all. Doing something harmful "because everyone else does it" is still harmful, not satisfying. For example, several cults have made the news in the last few years with their "suicide pacts." Individual members of these groups initially find the pacts to be satisfying. The pacts provide them with a strong feeling of belonging. However, when the day comes for the group to commit suicide, many individuals have second thoughts. They have to decide if conforming in this particular act is *really* going to give them the satisfaction of belonging. After all, they will soon be dead!

When we read about mass suicides and other dramatic examples of harmful conformity, we often ask, "Why do people do such thoughtless things?" Psychologists believe that group pressure can exert subtle influences on us to "mindlessly conform" to behavior we realize is foolish or harmful. We can also "mindlessly conform" to other people's opinions without thinking.

The "Asch Conformity Experiments" were devised by the psychologist Solomon Asch to determine if people would conform to a clearly incorrect judgment if they were subtly pressured to do so by group behavior. As one of the subjects, you arrive at the experiment location in time to take a seat at the end of a row where four people are already seated. The experimenter asks which of the following three comparison lines is identical in length to the standard line.

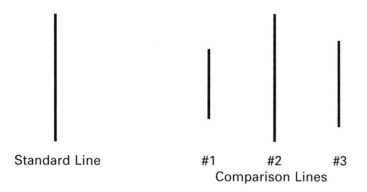

Standard Line   #1   #2   #3

Comparison Lines

You clearly see that the correct answer is "Comparison Line #2" and wait for your turn. You begin to get a little bored when the next set of lines proves to be equally easy. But during the third trial, in which the answer is as clear as the first two times, the first person gives what you feel is a wrong answer: "Comparison Line #3." When the second and third people give the same obviously incorrect response, you sit up and give the lines a good hard look. When the fourth person also says, "Comparison Line #3," your stress level rises even more. The experimenter looks at you, waiting for your answer. You are torn between the unanimity of your four fellow subjects and the evidence before your own eyes. You hesitate before answering, not sure of what you should say. If you mindlessly conformed to the group and said that comparison line #3 is equal in length to the standard line, you acted in the same way as *over one-third* of the subjects in the Asch Experiment.

Other psychologists have followed up on the Asch Experiment, using the same test under more controlled conditions. They have found that people tend to conform mindlessly if they feel unsure of themselves in the group, if the group is unanimous, if they admire the status and prestige of the group, and if others in the group seem to be watching them.

Mindless conformity has been shown to play a large role in courtroom jury deliberations, voting in political conventions, and other activities in which people in groups make choices.

The fallacy of mindless conformity consists of pressuring the reader or listener to agree to the conclusion by referring its the popularity with others. The popularity of the conclusion is its only support.

A simple example:

Murphy's Hamburgers have sold billions; they are the best hamburgers in the country.

Note that the connection between the popularity of Murphy's Hamburgers and their quality is not at all clear. We are being asked to accept the idea that the hamburgers are "the best" on the grounds that they are popular. The fallacy is quite obvious. Here is a more subtle fallacy of mindless conformity in an argument defending television network children's cartoon programs.

> We recognize that most children's television programming is violent, gender-biased, and offers no learning opportunities. There have been several studies to substantiate these facts, and we do not dispute them. However, we also realize that the programming in question is very popular with large numbers of children We must be doing something right. We are not going to change our children's programming; it is simply too successful as it is.

The conclusion of this argument is the directive, "The children's programming should not be changed." There are two stated premises, which can be paraphrased as, "Children's programming is violent, gender-biased, and educationally without value," and "Children's programming is popular." The conclusion is supported by the second. The first premise does not support the conclusion at all; in fact, it clearly supports the idea that the programming should be changed. The subtlety of this example is found in the *hidden* premise, "popularity with children is the most important factor in making decisions about children's programming." This is an appeal to mindless conformity; "the children love the programming, and so should you."

The fallacy of mindless conformity is more prevalent than we might suspect. The popularity of an idea with the masses of people, or with a smaller group perceived to have status and prestige, is not enough to support a conclusion on its own. Imagine this argument, which could have been made several hundred years ago:

> The world is a flat disk, and if a ship sails too far out to sea, it will fall off. Since everyone believes this, including the most prestigious minds of our time, it is true. Anyone who sails far out to sea will fall off the earth.

We may be amused by mindless conformity from the distant past, but keep in mind that fallacious reasoning is still with us today:

> Sexual abstinence is the one sure way to avoid unwanted pregnancies and sexually transmitted diseases. But no teenager who's cool really believes that sexual abstinence is possible today. Therefore, young adults should be encouraged to have sex outside of marriage.

The claim "no teenager who's cool really believes that sexual abstinence is possible today" is not adequate support for the conclusion. The "cool teenagers" may be a prestigious group, but so were those who claimed that the earth was flat. The popularity or prestige of a belief is not enough for it to reasonably support a conclusion.

We should keep the Asch Experiment in mind when we review arguments with premises that refer to how "popular" or "unpopular" particular ideas are with masses of people, with high status groups, and with high prestige groups. If we are as susceptible to the pressure to conform as the experiments indicate, we are also very susceptible to being manipulated in our beliefs by those who appeal to our need for conformity. Labeling ideas as "unpopular" or "out of fashion" is one way of appealing to our need for conformity.

We need to ignore claims about the popularity and prestige of a belief. Critical thinking requires that we focus our attention on an empathetic understanding of ideas, whether they come from popular sources or from marginalized areas of society. One of the major problems in our society is that we have a tendency to ignore ideas that come from what the popular media calls the "fringe." We label "fringe" ideas as "weird," or as "crazy." And yet, it is quite obvious that many of the popular ideas people now accept are ideas that at one time were quite unpopular! For example, it was once thought to be "weird" to exercise on a regular basis; people who jogged, lifted weights, or took brisk walks were regarded as "health nuts." Only a few years ago, vegetarianism was viewed with much suspicion: more "health nuts." "Interracial" dating and marriages have increased in acceptance, yet both practices that were very unpopular only a generation ago. There are many examples of unpopular ideas becoming popular; the point here is to recognize that the popularity of an idea is not a demonstration of its value.

We need to be wary of nonempathetic reviews of unpopular ideas or people in the mass media. Keep in mind that popular ideas about complex issues are often based on oversimplifications by network television news programs. Unpopular ideas, on the other hand, are very often marginalized; they haven't received the media attention and discussion they deserve. Popular ideas are sometimes based on arguments that commit the straw man fallacy and that shift the burden of proof. Too many people would rather have "an opinion" that "fits in" with those of their peers than to go to the trouble of investigating unpopular ideas.

It is easy to mindlessly conform, "join the crowd," and criticize unpopular, unfashionable ways of perceiving the world. However, it is not reasonable. A popular conclusion that relies on mindless conformity may win friends and influence people; it may sell magazines and raise television ratings, but it will not help anyone think more clearly or more empathetically.

THE FALLACY OF IRRELEVANT EMOTION

No elements in an argument should distract attention away from the relationship between the support and the conclusion. The implication relationship is the heart of any argument. Expressive statements can easily distract us from giving close attention to the quality of support provided by the premises. Our concentration wavers. We get "caught up" in our emotions and lose track of what point the argument is really trying to make.

The fallacy of irrelevant emotion consists in eliciting emotions such as fear, pity, anger, and so on *in the person to whom the argument is presenting its demonstration.* For example,

> "I am not responsible for the traffic accident because I am a poor college student without any money to have my car repaired."

is an obvious case of irrelevant emotions being presented instead of support. The traffic officer, to whom the argument is directing its proof, is being distracted from the accident by a feeling of pity for the student. That, at least, is the intention of the argument. Very few people (and *no* traffic officers!) are taken in by arguments that are this blatant in making use of irrelevant emotion.

This is not to say that emotion has no place as support for a conclusion. In some cases, expressive statements can be quite relevant. For example, expressive statements are sometimes used to support conclusions that direct us to accept moral values. For example, feelings of pride, anger, and love are often relevant in arguments about what is morally right and wrong. This argument does not make an *irrelevant* use of emotion:

> Wife abuse, helpless women being beaten by the men they most need for support, is horribly wrong. In ninety-nine out of a hundred cases, the husband is much stronger than the wife. She has no way to avoid his violent rage. She scurries about like a terrified animal, often on hands and knees, trying to escape the kicks and blows of the man who claims to love her. She ends up bruised, bloody, and psychologically devastated. Angela Browne's well-known 1993 study of wife-beating concludes that injuries range from bruises, cuts, black eyes, concussions, broken legs and backs, miscarriages, permanent damage to joints, partial loss of hearing and sight, and even death. More than half the women murdered in this country are killed by their husbands or partners. What is the cure for this tragedy? That is a very difficult question. But it is not at all difficult to conclude that wife abuse is terribly, terribly wrong.

The emotions of anger and pity we feel in relation to battered women are legitimately involved with the conclusion, "wife abuse is terribly, terribly wrong."

It is often difficult to determine the degree of relevance between an expressive premise and the conclusion of an argument. Expressive statements are often vague; it is difficult to decide if they actually support the conclusion or detract our attention from a lack of support. As a rule, however, if the expressive premise is not clearly in support of the conclusion, it should be regarded as irrelevant.

In other words, the *burden of proof* is on the *argument* to clearly point out the relevance of the emotion it is using as support. This is done in two ways. First, the expressive statement must not be vague or ambiguous. Second, in order for an expressive premise to be relevant to the argument's conclusion, appropriate representative premises must supplement it.

The expressive statement, "wife abuse is terribly, terribly wrong" is not so vague as to be irrelevant to the conclusion. We can understand its meaning with little difficulty. The representative premises from Angela Browne's study support the expressive statements as well as the conclusion.[1] The study supplements the expressive statements; we can understand *why* the emotions are relevant to the conclusion. The argument seems to meet its responsibility in

---

1. The statistics, regrettably, are real. Angela Browne, "Violence against Women by Male Partners," *American Psychologist,* 48 (1993).

accepting the burden of proof in pointing out the relevance of the emotions of anger and pity to its conclusion.

The fallacy of *irrelevant* emotion occurs in arguments in which emotion is stated vaguely and/or has no supportive statements.

Consider the following excerpt from a short essay entitled "Pardon Me if I (Still) Smoke," which concludes that public policies that restrict smoking actually increase smoking.

> In 1997, smoking sets you apart—literally. At restaurants we are seated back by the kitchen door, where we dine to the music of busboys clattering silverware into milky dishwater. At work we smoke huddled in the rain and snow, risking pneumonia for (we are told) the sake of public health. The unintended consequence of each new restriction has been to make smoking a badge of honor—a sign of one's refusal to give in. And now, with last week's agreement (that increases the powers of the Federal Food and Drug Administration over cigarettes)—with this consensus arrived at by America's cynics, pundits, and buttinskies—the attractions of smoking can only grow.[2]

The support for the conclusion of this argument consists of an attempt to arouse the emotions of pity and reverence for cigarette smokers. The smokers have poor seating in restaurants, have to smoke outside in foul weather, and so we should pity them. The smokers' "badge of honor"—their "refusal to give in" should instill an emotion of *reverence*. These feelings of pity and reverence are offered in support of the conclusion that restrictions increase "the attraction of smoking."

The expressive statements in the argument are not so vague as to defy an empathetic understanding. It may be difficult to feel pity for a person who is forced to sit at a poor table in a restaurant. That doesn't seem to be very serious. But we have all noticed smokers coughing outside in bad weather, and a feeling of pity for them is not inappropriate. We can feel sorry for them, huddled against the wind and rain, as they strain to suck in another toxic "lungful."

The expressive statement "the consequence of each new restriction has been to make smoking a badge of honor—a sign of one's refusal to give in," is rather vague. An empathetic reading of the argument may result in a feeling of pity for a smoker beset with bad restaurant seating, and who is forced outside for a cigarette break in a driving rainstorm. But where does the "badge of honor" come in? We usually reserve such badges for those who sacrifice for others, not sacrifice for *themselves*. Perhaps the argument wants us to recognize that the smoker is saving the public from "second hand smoke" by taking the bad table and by smoking outside. Does the smoker deserve a badge of honor for that? A rigorous and empathetic reading of the argument, however, shows that the argument does not perceive "second hand smoke" as a serious public health hazard. By claiming that the reason cigarettes are not allowed in public is,

(we are told) for the sake of public health

---

2. Andrew Ferguson, "Pardon Me if I (Still) Smoke, *Time*, June 30, 1997, 32.

the argument rejects any support from that direction. It actually belittles the idea that second hand smoke is a health threat. There is no supplementary support for the emotion of reverence that the argument seeks. The expressive appeal to reverence and "badge of honor" is irrelevant to the conclusion.

There are no supportive statements in the argument, and for good reason. Cigarette smoking has actually *decreased* in the last twelve years, a period of increased restrictions on smoking in public. In fact, there are ten percent fewer smokers now than when restrictions were first put in effect. Of course, this does not prove that restrictions have actually caused the decrease in smoking. Indeed, smoking could have decreased even more if restrictions were not in effect. The burden of proof, however, is on the argument. It must support the quite controversial claim that restrictions on public smoking have increased the attractions of smoking.

The emotional appeal that is made in the argument, while not completely vague, is irrelevant to its conclusion, which we can paraphrase as "Restrictions on smoking help make smoking more popular." If the argument wants to claim that restrictions on smoking play an important role in increasing the attractiveness of smoking, more relevant support of its expressive statements is necessary.

Fallacies, as we have seen, often occur in combinations. For example, this argument, in addition to the irrelevant emotion fallacy, also commits the "attacking the person" fallacy when it engages in name-calling; the "cynics, pundits, and buttinskies" who "helped increase FDA powers." Name-calling is a way of demeaning people, and the argument is certainly even less reasonable because of the presence of this fallacy.

EXERCISES

▲ Most Intriguing Issue

Write a one-paragraph description of the most interesting idea, topic, or process described in the chapter so far. Be prepared to explain what you find interesting in class discussion.

▲ The Muddiest Point

Write a sentence or, if possible, a paragraph that describes the idea, topic, expression, term, or process in the chapter so far that you find most difficult to understand.

▲ Cartoons and Diagrams

1. Provide a cartoon that shows some important differences between conformity and mindless conformity.
2. Draw a cartoon that illustrates mindless conformity to a conclusion due to the perceived prestige of accepting it.

3. Provide a cartoon that shows how peer pressure is involved with mindlessly conforming to a fallacy of inappropriate authority.
4. Provide a cartoon that shows the relationship of the fallacy of mindless conformity to marginalization.
5. Provide a cartoon that shows how the fallacy of irrelevant emotion distracts a person from the argument's inference.
6. Draw a cartoon that shows how the fallacy of irrelevant emotion can be combined with the fallacy of attacking the person.
7. Draw a cartoon that shows how the fallacy of irrelevant emotion can be combined with mindless conformity.
8. Draw a cartoon that shows how the fallacy of irrelevant emotion can be combined with the appeal to force.

▲ DEFINITIONS OF KEY TERMS

Provide a disciplinary definition for each of the following terms as they are used in this chapter. Most of the terms are not defined in the chapter, although their meanings are described by the context in which they appear. You need to review the material to create the definition yourself. Be sure to follow the guidelines for creating definitions on pages 78–81.

Conformity   Expressive Premises   Fallacy of Irrelevant Emotion

Fallacy of Mindless   Mindless Conformity   Representative Premises
  Conformity

▲ SHORT ESSAY QUESTIONS

Provide a written response of approximately 200 words for each topic. Your responses should be well organized, grammatically correct, and neatly produced.

1. Explain the importance of the Asch Conformity experiments to an understanding of the fallacy of mindless conformity.
2. Describe how a person's need for prestige in the business world could result in fallacious reasoning about the value of a government plan to raise taxes on business.
3. Describe how a film student's need for status could result in fallacious reasoning about the quality of a movie.
4. Provide an example that shows how the fallacy of mindless conformity can combine with the fallacy of irrelevant emotion.
5. Provide an example that shows how the fallacy of irrelevant emotion can combine with the fallacy of oversimplification.
6. Explain in your own words the two ways to decide whether or not an expressive statement is relevant or irrelevant to an argument's conclusion. Provide some examples to clarify your short essay.

▲ QUESTIONS FOR DISCUSSION

Provide an essay of 300–500 words that responds to each of the following questions which ask for your opinion. You should respond by stating it, and by providing thoughts, examples, and insights that support it. You should be willing to revise your response; you may change your opinion during or after a class discussion.

1. The Asch Conformity Experiments took place in the early 1950s. Do you believe that the experiments would have similar results if they were performed today with students at your school? Why or why not? You may want to discuss this question with a psychology professor or student.

2. Some social critics believe that jury trials are simple exercises in mindless conformity. The juries are so anxious to come to a decision that they rush too quickly through complex evidence and come to a decision that is based more on oversimplification and mindless conformity than on reasonable deliberation. These critics believe that jury trials should be abandoned in favor of three-judge panels. It is assumed the judges would be more reasonable than juries made up of ordinary citizens. What do you think about this?

3. The relationship of the fallacy of mindless conformity to marginalization is discussed briefly in the chapter. What particular "marginalized points of view" can you describe in relation to the issue of legalization of marijuana as it is discussed in the mass media?

4. The appeal to irrelevant emotion fallacy is commonly used in advertising. Examine at least five different print advertisements for cigarettes or alcoholic beverages. Discuss the specific emotions that you think are being appealed to by the advertisements.

5. View the commercials of several different prime-time entertainment television programs. Notice that many of the commercials contain fallacies of appeal to emotion as well as appeals to mindless conformity. Explain specifically how three particular commercials commit one or both of these fallacies.

6. Ask at least ten students why they have chosen to attend your school. You can ask each of them to write down his or her response or you can take written notes. Review the responses carefully; explain whether or not you find the fallacies of appeal to mindless conformity and /or appeal to irrelevant emotion in at least seven of them. Turn in the written responses as well as the results of your review.

7. At times it is very difficult to determine if an expressive statement is a support for or a distraction from the argument's conclusion. The chapter advises that the burden of proof be on the argument. If the argument does not clearly meet the two requirements for an expressive statement to support the conclusion, we should consider the reasoning to be fallacious. It is probably not wise, however, to always follow this advice. Provide an example, including an argument and a context, in which it would be more reasonable not to follow the chapter's advice.

8. Some social critics believe that the two-party system—the Democrats and the Republicans—encourages too many fallacies of mindless conformity and oversimplification in our national political discussions. Why do you suppose they believe this? Do you think our country would benefit from more political parties? Why or why not?

9. Properly organize each of the following arguments. Empathetically revise any vague or ambiguous terms if possible. Explain where and why you detect a fallacy of mindless conformity or of irrelevant emotion. Be specific about the fallacy; explain which type you think it is. If the argument is a combination of fallacies, including fallacies discussed earlier in the chapter, explain which ones are involved.

a) We used to attend church on a regular basis, but now that we have moved to this new neighborhood, we don't go anymore. The people here are better off financially than our old friends and, for whatever reason, they just don't go to church. It's hard enough being accepted by these people; I don't want them to think I'm a Bible Beater, too! So it just doesn't make any sense to go to church anymore.

b) I work hard all day, breaking my back. I'm entitled to a couple beers when I get off the job. When I come home I want my dinner on the table, and I want it hot! I don't care what time it is; you have it ready, do you hear me?! You better do it nice, too, or I'll slap you around!

c) Dave and I are getting married secretly next week. It's a really good idea, because Dave says we shouldn't wait another day! I'm so excited, I can hardly wait! Dave's a really great guy, and I'm sure I love him. We've known each other for over a month.

d) Vegetarianism is the only way to go now. All my friends are "veggies." Think about the animals that are killed by all the fascist meat-eaters. Poor little cows and chickens and pigs. I don't feel too sorry for the pigs; they are so ugly! But I like the cows and chickens.

e) Eat at Burger Heaven: the most spiritual burger you've ever had in all eternity! Join the hundreds of thousands of Happy Heavenly Burger customers. If it's good for them, it can't be bad for you!

f) My Uncle James says that foreign cars are a lot better than anything made in the United States. He's a cool weatherman on t. v. and wouldn't even get in one of those things! Neither will my mom or dad. None of us in our family like American cars, and that's why a foreign car is best for me, too.

g) I'm so tired of weirdo cigarette smokers! I can't stand the way they all stand in front of restaurants and blow smoke on your clothes when you walk in. And they cough so much that you think they're going to die right there on the spot. I'd never go on a date with a smoker. If any of my friends saw me with one, I'd just die of shame!

h) We are all going to cheat on the next test, Jose, and if you know what's good for you, you'll cheat too. There's no other way to pass this course, and no other way to keep your friends, either.

i) A modern woman is independent, thinks for herself, and she looks it, too! So smoke Village Girl Cigarettes, the choice of the fun, liberated go-girl who knows where it's at!

j) How much longer are we going to put up with Senator Walters? He should have been voted out of office years ago! He votes for all the really horrible things, like that ridiculous taxation bill, and then he turns around and votes against all the wonderfully splendid things. And where on earth does he get those clothes? And that hat? Oh, he just embarrasses us!

▲ QUOTATION TO PONDER

"When we're in a group, we tend to think as that group does; we may even have joined the group to find 'like-minded' people. But we also find our thinking changing because we belong to a group. It is the hardest thing in the world to maintain an individual dissident opinion, as a member of a group."
Doris Lessing, *Prisons We Choose to Live Inside*, 1987

▲ JOURNAL TOPIC

Ask your psychology or sociology professor about the "Milgram Experiment." If you are aware of the experiment, or if you want to find out about it on your own, you can review it in almost any introductory psychology textbook, and in many sociology texts. Write down your reflections on the experiment; what does it say about our tendency to mindlessly conform?

THE FALLACY OF OVERGENERALIZATION

A *generalization* is a representative statement about a group that describes characteristics held by some or all of its members. Generalizations are usually preceded by the words "some," "many," "a majority," "a very large number," "all," or by a specific number ("ten dogs," "one-hundred dogs," etc.). Of course, there are other words used to generalize but all refer to quantity.

We generalize whenever we make a "general" or "broad" statement. "Dogs are friendly animals" is a generalization that describes all dogs in a broad, general way. Indeed, it is an overgeneralization: a statement that exaggerates a characteristic of a group. There are some dogs that are not friendly at all. There are some reclusive dogs, some depressed dogs, and even some vicious dogs. The generalization, then, would be more accurately phrased if were not so broad. "Most dogs are friendly" would be better.

Prejudicial descriptions of people are sometimes called "biased overgeneralizations." They are similar to name-calling. Thus, "college students are brilliant, dedicated students" is, unfortunately, an overgeneralization. "College students are party-hungry spoiled brats" is a biased overgeneralization. It is also an attack on the person, since college students as a group are demeaned by the name-calling.

Generalizations in arguments are often found in the conclusion. Reasonable general conclusions follow a pattern: the more general the conclusion's claim, the more support in the premises. The argument is fallacious only when conclusions go *beyond* the premises' support.

The *fallacy of overgeneralization* occurs when the premises are too limited to support the extent of the conclusion's generalization.

Overgeneralizations are among the most common reasoning errors. Arguments often "overstate" what their premises support. For example, an argument in a popular magazine concludes

Schools seem to have lost sight of their historical role in helping children through adolescence.

It provides the following four premises:

1. Sex education textbooks describe genitalia, masturbation, sexual intercourse, sexual abuse, sexually transmitted diseases, and alternative family structures.
2. Elementary school children are "encouraged to use scientific terms—like *anus* and *buttocks* instead of words that are perfectly apt for a six-year-old's vocabulary."
3. "Middle-schoolers may learn not only about abstinence but also about condoms, other forms of contraception, and abortion."
4. Teachers don't discourage mutual masturbation, sexual intercourse, and other sexual expressions, but encourage students to discuss the topics and decide for themselves.[3]

The four premises are not capable of supporting the generalization: "Schools seem to have lost sight of their historical role in helping children through adolescence." How many schools are doing this? The conclusion indicates that all of them are. Furthermore, even if all schools are letting children down in sex education courses (and there is little evidence here that they are really doing that) there is no evidence that schools have lost sight of their role in helping children through adolescence in other ways. The argument is an example of the fallacy of overgeneralization in both ways. The conclusion is a much more sweeping indictment of schools than the premises support. Let's examine the overgeneralizations in this argument more specifically.

Generalizations require support, the more sweeping they are, the more support they need. For example, this conclusion can be adequately supported by a study of the schools in one county:

> The *schools of St. Louis County* do not provide enough direction for children's adolescent sexual decisions.

However, this conclusion is a broader generalization. It needs support from studies of the whole state:

> The *schools of the entire state of Missouri* do not provide enough direction for children's adolescent sexual decisions.

The conclusion we are considering is much broader than one state, or even several states:

> *Schools* have lost sight of their historical role in helping children through adolescence.

This is an extremely broad overgeneralization. It seems to claim that

> *Every school in the United States of America seems* to have lost sight of its historical role in helping children through adolescence.

---

3. Barbara Dafoe Whitehead, "What They Want to Teach Your Child about Sex," *Reader's Digest* (February 1995), 155–160.

Even though the conclusion does not literally claim to describe "every school" in the country, an empathetic reading of the argument leaves no alternative. Nowhere in the argument is there any indication that the conclusion is limited to a specific city, county, or state's schools. The conclusion clearly is referring to all American schools. There is not enough support in the premises for such a generalized conclusion; it is a poorly reasoned argument due to its fallacy of overgeneralization.

In addition, the conclusion of this argument commits another fallacy of overgeneralization in its claim that schools

> have lost sight of their historical role in *helping children through adolescence.*

Every premise discusses sex education. Nothing else is referred to about "helping children through adolescence." There is no mention of the schools' successes or failures in helping with children's psychological, physical, or intellectual development. Certainly, these three areas are of immense importance in adolescence, as well as in every developmental stage of life. The conclusion claims that schools have lost sight of their historical role in helping children *through adolescence.* However, the premises do not support such a broad generalization. This lack of support indicates once more that the argument is not reasonable due to another fallacy of overgeneralization.

An empathetic reading of the argument would suggest that the conclusion be revised. It needs to limit its assertion. It could be revised to read

> Schools do not provide enough direction for children's adolescent sexual decisions.

Now the conclusion limits its assertion to sexual decisions, which the premises have more capacity to support. However, the conclusion is still far too general in regard to the number of schools it discusses. Its premises do not provide enough information to support a claim about every school in the country.

Perhaps the conclusion should be further revised to

> The schools examined in this study do not seem to provide enough direction for children's adolescent sexual decisions.

This much more limited claim would be a more reasonable conclusion; it does not exceed the support provided by the argument's premises.

One final point about the conclusion; notice that it uses the phrase "do not seem," rather than the bolder, "do not." "Seems to be the case" is a "qualifying term." These phrases soften the argument's claim about how certain it is about the conclusion. There are other qualifying terms that "soften" conclusions; among them are "it appears to be the case," "it is possible that it is the case," "it is probable that it is the case," "it could be the case," "it may be the case," and "there are good reasons to believe it is the case." The use of qualifying terms is a good way to avoid conclusions that are too strongly worded for the degree of demonstration provided by their premises. An argument rarely achieves absolutely certain proof of the conclusion's accuracy. The use of qualifying terms acknowledges its limitations.

THE FALLACY OF UNWARRANTED ASSUMPTION

Unwarranted assumptions are *controversial or false hidden premises.* Almost every argument has some hidden premises; an argument is not expected to state every support for its conclusion in a premise. The *fallacy of unwarranted assumption* occurs when the conclusion is *primarily supported* by a *controversial* or *false* hidden premise.

Any support that is not commonly known to be true should be stated, not hidden. Any support that is not commonly accepted by authorities, but which is believed to be true by a few of them should be stated, not hidden. Of course, false assumptions provide no support at all for the conclusion, whether they are hidden or stated. Many arguments that contain unwarranted assumptions are actually relying on *false* statements. They are attempts to deceive. Some unwarranted assumptions, however, simply result from a lack of research or a failure to consider how complicated an issue may be.

It is important to recognize that a simple assumption on the part of an argument is not a fallacy of unwarranted assumption. The word "warranted" means "a characteristic of something that has the force of proof." In an argument, a hidden premise that is a "warranted assumption," is one that has the "force of proof." It is hidden, but not unwarranted. To be "unwarranted" is to be "groundless," "without foundation," and "flimsy." An unwarranted assumption is a hidden premise that provides groundless, flimsy support; it leaves the conclusion "without a foundation."

The sex education argument examined earlier in the section on the fallacy of overgeneralization contains an unwarranted assumption.

Here is its conclusion, empathetically revised:

Many schools do not seem to provide enough direction for children's adolescent sexual decisions.

The controversial hidden premise is

Nothing that is being done in many schools, including (1) the use of scientific terminology in discussion of sex, (2) the lack of discouragement of specific sexual practices, and (3) the encouragement to discuss sexual topics, helps children make good decisions about sex when they become adolescents.

This hidden premise is controversial because authorities in the area of sex education are not unanimous in regard to its truth. As a matter of fact, many sex educators (and parents!) believe that the use of scientific terminology in discussions about sex alleviates the vagueness and ambiguity that characterizes the slang and "baby talk" that characterizes much of our talk about sex. They also believe that discouragement of specific sexual practices "mystifies" them; if children are told to "never, never" explore particular practices, research shows that they have a tendency to do so as soon as they find the opportunity! Sex educators and most parents also believe that open discussion about sexuality, in fact, does help people make mature sexual decisions. The fact that most sex educators believe these things does not mean they are absolutely true. Sexuality is a complex aspect of human life; no one understands it completely.

But the argument *assumes* that the current practices are not good ones. It should not assume that claim in a hidden premise. It should clearly and openly represent its belief in a stated premise. The assumption is *controversial*, it needs to be "out in the open."

The fallacy of unwarranted assumption sometimes involves a hidden premise that assumes a general principle applies in a questionable situation. For example,

> The more a person knows, the better off they are. Therefore, the more a child knows about sadistic sexual practices the better off he or she is.

This is an inappropriate use of a general principle; it is assumed that the principle applies to the situation, but the situation has particular characteristics that the hidden premise has left out. The above argument's hidden premises are:

> The principle, "the more a person knows, the better off they are," is true for *every* sort of knowledge and for *every* person. This includes knowledge that could psychologically traumatize a child.

The hidden premises' assumption that the principle applies to this instance is controversial. Very few sex education experts would agree that children would benefit from knowledge about sadism. The fallacy, like all fallacies, is an error in reasoning that indicates the untrustworthy nature of the argument.

EIGHT STEPS IN THE EVALUATION OF ARGUMENTS

The one task of logical thinking is the evaluation of arguments. Everything discussed in this chapter, as well as in Chapters 5 and 6, is directly related to this task. As you progress in evaluating arguments, try to keep in mind as much specific information as possible. You should refer to Chapter 5 in order to remind yourself of the details involved in steps one through four. Steps five through eight are covered in this chapter.

Steps one and two are rather straightforward. Don't forget that the identification of hidden premises (step three) requires an empathetic review of what the argument is attempting to imply.

Step four should be carried out carefully. The more accurately the argument is organized, the more effective your evaluation will be. Step five is simple, but important. Knowing the type of statements in the argument can be a great help in understanding the argument, as well as in detecting fallacies in step seven.

Step six requires a careful empathetic evaluation of words and phrases. Vague or ambiguous terms should be pointed out, and suggestions for revision, if appropriate, should be made.

The seventh step requires a rigorous evaluation of the relationship between the premises (both stated and hidden) and the conclusion. You should always explain as thoroughly as possible *why* you feel a specific fallacy has been committed. That is, describe exactly where the fallacy occurs in the argument, and explain why you think that the fallacy is the one you indicate. Be aware that fallacies often occur in combinations. For example, a straw man fallacy may occur with an attack on the person whose words are being misrepresented.

Step eight asks for your judgment about the overall trustworthiness of the argument. Review your evaluations in steps six and seven. Is the argument untrustworthy due to vagueness, ambiguity, or fallacious reasoning? Perhaps you have suggestions for revision that would make the argument more trustworthy. If so, specifically point them out. Explain why they help the argument. Keep in mind that an empathetic revision does not change the meaning or intention of the argument; it merely clarifies words and phrases and/or improves the argument's reasoning. In your judgment, the argument may appear to be trustworthy as it is, with no need for revision. If that is the case, mention any small problems you notice. If the argument strikes you as an excellent one, now is the time to point that out.

Keep in mind that no two people are going to evaluate an argument in exactly the same way. Individuals may notice different fallacies, clarify terms, and revise statements in slightly different ways. However, an untrustworthy argument will always be exposed if the eight steps are followed carefully.

The purpose of critical thinking is to improve thinking. Argument evaluation, an important aspect of critical thinking, shares in that purpose. Thinking is improved when we identify an argument that is untrustworthy; we alert ourselves and others that its conclusion should not be taken seriously. When we revise an argument we improve it by pointing out its failings and providing revisions that make it more valuable. Identifying a good or excellent argument also improves thinking; it gives us an example of the sort of argument we can trust.

Steps to Follow in the Evaluation of Arguments

1. Identify and state the conclusion
2. Identify and state the stated premises
3. Identify and state the hidden premises
4. Organize the argument
5. Identify and label each statement as representative, expressive, or directive
6. Describe the evaluation of every statement for vague or ambiguous terms
7. Describe the evaluation of the argument for fallacies
8. State whether or not the argument is trustworthy

FOLLOWING THE EIGHT STEPS: A MODEL

We first encountered this argument in Chapter 5:

> Seeing that love can be present without a marriage license, it follows that any couple, whether gay or heterosexual, should be recognized as being married. Some people disagree, but think about it. The legal, social, and other benefits of married life should not be denied because of narrow-minded bias.

After careful review, we went through steps one through four and organized the argument with the conclusion and premises properly labeled. We continue here with step five, and appropriately label each statement.

Conclusion

Any couple, whether gay or heterosexual, should be recognized as being married. (DIRECTIVE)

Stated Premises

Love can be present without a marriage license. (REPRESENTATIVE)

The legal, social, and other benefits of married life should not be denied because of narrow-minded bias. (EXPRESSIVE)

Hidden Premises

Love is the primary qualification for being married. (EXPRESSIVE)

Narrow-minded bias is the only reason a marriage license would be denied to gay couples who love each other. (REPRESENTATIVE)

People are sometimes biased against gay couples who love each other. (REPRESENTATIVE)

There are no important distinctions to be made between heterosexual couples and gay couples in regard to being married. (REPRESENTATIVE)

The conclusion is clearly a directive: it advises us to do something. The first stated premise represents an idea; namely, that people can love each other and not have a marriage license. Of course, love is an emotion but the first premise is not expressing the emotion, it is describing an idea about it. The second stated premise expresses the feeling that there is something wrong ("narrow-minded bias") with denying the benefits of marriage. It also seems to direct us not to deny them out of narrow-minded bias. However, the statement is primarily an expression of outrage that anyone would do this, not a directive to avoid doing it. The first hidden premise, unlike the other three, is not a representation of ideas about marriage and love, but an expression of feelings about the immense importance of love in marriage. The last three hidden premises represent ideas. They do not express emotions, nor do they give us directions or advice.

We worked on step six in Chapter 6, where we reviewed and evaluated the argument for vague and ambiguous terms. As a result, we found several such terms, but only "narrow-minded bias" appeared to be so seriously ambiguous that we decided that it could not be empathetically understood.

Rather than reject the argument as untrustworthy due to the ambiguity of the term, however, we decided simply to point out that the argument lacked clarity because of it. The ambiguous term confused bias against gay couples, which is rather common, with bias against heterosexual couples, which is not. The ambiguous term also implied that the bias against gay marriages is always due to narrow-mindedness. That did not seem to be obviously true.

Step seven is best carried out by evaluating the argument for each fallacy, starting with the first and ending with the tenth.

The fallacy of inappropriate authority is not present. The argument does not refer to any authorities for support of the conclusion.

The fallacy of appeal to force is not present, either. Nowhere does the argument threaten in any way.

The fallacy of attacking the person may be present in a minor way. The argument, in claiming that "narrow-mindedness" is the only reason that anyone would be biased, indirectly attacks anyone who would disagree with its conclusion as "narrow-minded." This is name-calling.

The fallacy of oversimplification is present in the argument. "Love can be present without a marriage license" trivializes the relationship of love and marriage. While true, it is rather trite, and insignificant to the conclusion. There are several legal prohibitions that keep some heterosexuals (and presumably, some gay couples as well) who love each other from getting married. For example, there are age limitations as well as residency requirements, blood tests, and so on. It may seem obvious, but people who are already married to someone else cannot marry someone "new," no matter how much they love him or her, unless they have obtained a divorce. The point is that while love *can* be present without a marriage license, there *are* reasons why some couples, gay as well as heterosexual, should not be allowed to marry.

This trite treatment of the relation of love and marriage goes further. The argument also oversimplifies in the last hidden premise.

> There are no important distinctions to be made between heterosexual couples and gay couples in regard to being married.

This premise, like the previous oversimplification, may very well be true. On the other hand, there are some differences between gay and heterosexual couples in many people's *perceptions* that are relevant to the conclusion. To overlook them is unreasonable; they are at the center of the controversy about gay marriages. How important is it that gays cannot themselves bear children? How important is it that gays are perceived by some as unfit to adopt children? Is it important that some people believe marriage to be based on religious values; the same values that regard gays as "sinful"? Even though these are biased misperceptions, the argument should not marginalize those who hold them by oversimplifying the "differences" between gays and heterosexuals. It should acknowledge that some people (mistakenly) believe that there are such distinctions; to acknowledge them does not at all imply agreement with them.

The fallacy of shifting the burden of proof is not present in the argument. Neither is the straw man fallacy. There is no fallacy of mindless conformity; the argument is actually concluding with an unpopular point of view.

There is no fallacy of irrelevant emotion. The expressive statements in the argument do not seem to be irrelevant to its conclusion. The expression of outrage that people with "narrow-minded bias" would prohibit marriages between people who love each other expresses a value that is relevant to the conclusion's directive.

The fallacy of overgeneralization is not obviously committed in the argument. The premises do not go beyond the support. There is no need for a qualifying term in the conclusion of this argument, which is a generalization, but not an overgeneralization.

Finally, the fallacy of unwarranted assumption is considered. The hidden premise that may commit this fallacy is

> Narrow-minded bias is the only reason a marriage license would be denied to gay couples who love each other.

We already noted that this premise comes very close to an attack on the person. It is also an unwarranted assumption; the premise is too controversial to be offered in support of the conclusion. Again, the premise may be true. But the argument's task is to *prove* the conclusion to be reasonable, and it cannot do that unless it addresses the topic's controversial aspects. To simply assume that anyone who disagrees with the conclusion is "narrow-minded" is clearly unwarranted.

In step eight, we need to point out whether or not the argument is trustworthy. After a review of our evaluation, we find that the argument's main difficulty is with the term, "narrow-minded bias." This term is ambiguous, it seems to attack those who do not agree with the argument's conclusion by name-calling, and it reveals an unwarranted assumption that the only reason anyone would disagree with the conclusion is that they are "narrow-minded." In addition, the argument suffers from an oversimplification of the relationship between love and marriage. Thus, the argument commits at least two, perhaps three, fallacies and contains a seriously ambiguous term.

For those reasons, the argument is not trustworthy. The attacking the person and unwarranted assumption fallacies could be eliminated if the argument were revised to eliminate the ambiguous term "narrow-minded bias." However, the argument would still suffer from oversimplification. Gay marriage is a complex issue, and deserves a more thorough demonstration.

It is important to realize that even though we have found this argument to be untrustworthy, that does not mean that there are no reasonable arguments that demonstrate that gay marriage should be allowed. An argument with a similar conclusion but with clearer terms and better reasoning is not difficult to imagine. The following is not a perfectly reasonable argument, but it is more reasonable than the one we have evaluated.

> Gay couples are made up of individuals, just like heterosexual couples. Currently, people marry for an enormous number of different reasons. Some marry as a sacred religious event, others as merely a financial convenience. Each couple has its own unique reasons for marrying, and gay couples are no different in this regard. One of the best reasons to marry, of course, is love. And many gay couples who want to marry do love each other. In conclusion, society should not prohibit gay marriages.

CONCLUSION

Arguments play a powerful role in our lives. They are used to *demonstrate* and to *prove* conclusions. We change the way we think about things when we accept an argument, and when we change the way we think, we change the way we act.

When we are not sure about how we think or feel about an important issue, whether it is personal or social, arguments help us make up our minds. Arguments carry the rigor, exactness, and rigid methodology of logical thinking. We feel we can trust them. Logical thinking is a secure haven amid the storms of confusion and controversy that surround us. We can trust it because it is reasonable.

Of course, to be perfectly reasonable is an ideal. Purely logical thinking reaches as close to perfection in reasoning as any human activity. Like mathematics, it is detached from the world of human perception and carries out its reasoning in a "pure world" where absolute certainty is possible. Even the elementary school student realizes that "3+3=6" is absolutely certain. Of course, the elementary student also knows that there is a big difference between the absolute certainty of a pure mathematical equation and the practical world of human experience. The certainty that "$3.00+$3.00=$6.00" is one thing in the world of pure mathematics. In the practical world, it doesn't mean much if you don't have any dollars at all in your pocket!

In other words, there is a difference between the way things come out in "pure reasoning" and the way they are in our daily lives. The world of pure reasoning is simpler than our lives—which have many more details and complexities than pure mathematics or pure logic.

Nevertheless, we find through experience that we can trust reason more than anything else to provide us with truths we can trust. An argument that is clear, reasonable, and that has accurate premises provides us with a trustworthy conclusion. That does not mean that logical thinking *always* gives us the right answer to the perplexities of our lives. However, it does mean that logical thinking will *usually* relieve those perplexities, if we do it well. Of course, as was pointed out in the "Conclusion" of Chapter 6, finding reasonable arguments is actually the beginning of a reasonable discussion, and it is by no means the completion of the search for truth.

Logical thinking requires a great deal of discipline on our part. Words cannot be allowed to be vague or ambiguous. Ideas cannot be loosely arranged, but need to be rigidly organized into clearly stated premises and conclusions. Hidden premises need to be identified and clearly brought out in the open. The argument has to be rigorously tested to make sure it contains no fallacies. Then, and only then, can we be said to have reasoned well. Then, and only then, can we trust the conclusion.

Unscrupulous individuals attempt to clothe their selfish grabs for power, fame, and wealth in the "garb of reason." They are aware of the power of arguments, and so they try to delude us, dupe us, and swindle us by hiding their deceptions behind fallacious reasoning.

Well-intentioned, but uninformed people often promote their beliefs without due attention to the rigors of logical thinking. Unlike the deceivers, they do not intend to beguile us or lead us astray. They sincerely believe their conclusions and they want us to believe them, too. But sincere arguments are not enough. People are misled by them, act upon them, and then find themselves confused and uncertain where to turn. They sincerely believed that their arguments proved their most cherished beliefs to be true. However, their conclusions were built upon premises with vague and ambiguous terms, and their reasoning was fallacious.

Arguments are powerful. However, they are trustworthy only if they are composed of nonambiguous, clear statements and only if they are free of fallacies. A trustworthy argument can clarify confusion, provide direction, and alleviate confusion. An untrustworthy argument can deceive us, confuse us, and betray us to deception and gullibility.

Chapter 6 points out that there are three elements in the evaluation of arguments: The evaluation of terms for vagueness and ambiguity; the evaluation of inferences for the presence of fallacies; and the final judgment concerning an argument's trustworthiness. We are now in a position to carry out the task of argument evaluation. As you can see from the last three chapters, the task requires patience, attention to detail, and an appreciation of the nature of logical thinking's exactness, rigor, and rigid adherence to methodology. Thinking is hard work!

However, there is even more to thinking than argumentation. Thinking should be more than clear and reasonable; it should also provide the *truth*. In Chapter 8, we will examine truth and, more specifically, evidence.

EXERCISES

▲ MOST INTRIGUING ISSUE

Write a one-paragraph description of the most interesting idea, topic, or process described in pages 200–210. Be prepared to explain what you find interesting in class discussion.

▲ THE MUDDIEST POINT

Write a sentence or, if possible, a paragraph that describes the idea, topic, expression, term, or process in pages 200–210 that you find most difficult to understand.

▲ CARTOONS AND DIAGRAMS

1. Draw a cartoon that shows the difference between a generalization and an overgeneralization.
2. Provide a cartoon that illustrates a biased overgeneralization.
3. Draw a cartoon that shows the difference between an unwarranted assumption and an assumption.
4. Provide a diagram that shows the rule of thumb "the more general the conclusion, the more support it needs."
5. Provide a diagram or cartoon that illustrates the eight steps to follow in the evaluation of arguments.

▲ DEFINITIONS OF KEY TERMS

Provide a disciplinary definition for each of the following terms as they are used in this chapter. Most of the terms are not defined in the chapter, although their meanings are described by the context in which they appear. You need to review the material to create the definition yourself. Be sure to follow the guidelines for creating definitions on pages 78–81.

Assumption	Biased Overgeneralization	Fallacy of Overgeneralization
Fallacy of Unwarranted Assumption	False Assumption	Generalization
Qualifying Term	The Power of Arguments	Warranted Assumption

▲ SHORT ESSAY QUESTIONS

Provide a written response that follows the eight-step method suggested in the chapter to each of the following. Your responses should be well organized, grammatically correct, and neatly produced.

1. Evaluate the following argument; follow the eight-step method suggested in the chapter.

   "Everyone in my church group agrees: Parents and libraries, as well as schools should not provide books on scientific subjects to children. Most scientific books fail to mention that God created the world. Over ninety percent of children's books on dinosaurs contain misleading information."

2. Evaluate the following argument; follow the eight-step method suggested in the chapter.

   "Most cases of date rape happen when the couple has been drinking alcohol. Thus, if the legislature would only increase the penalty for underage alcohol use when it takes place at parties with both men and women present, we would never have to worry about date rape again!"

3. Evaluate the following argument; follow the eight-step method suggested in the chapter.

   "To get rich, keep an eagle eye on things! Real estate investment requires supervision and maintenance of the property, or else the investor will lose money. For this reason, you should always invest in property no further than one-half hour's drive from your home. You can't keep an eagle eye if you are too far away!"

4. Evaluate the following argument; follow the eight-step method suggested in the chapter.

"Newspapers get your hands dirty and are hard to manage. They flop all over the place. Television news shows are easy to watch and always warn you if a distasteful picture is about to appear. So, television is a much better source of information about the world."

5. Evaluate the following argument; follow the eight-step method suggested in the chapter.

"Animal rights advocates are wrong when they demonstrate against medical experiments on dogs. Everyone knows that animal experimentation is essential to medical progress. Animals don't feel pain the same way humans do, anyway. And in the Bible it says that we are masters of the animals; we can do with them as we please."

6. Evaluate the following argument; follow the eight-step method suggested in the chapter.

"As mother of three darling little ones, I was sitting in my office at work, and suddenly had a vivid image of my home on fire. I immediately called home and awoke the sitter who excitedly reported smoke coming from under the bedroom door. The sitter extinguished the fire, saving my little children's lives. This is an excellent example of hundreds of cases of Extrasensory Perception (ESP) that happen every day. No one who disputes the fact of ESP can prove that it did not occur in my case or hundreds of others."

7. Evaluate the following argument; follow the eight-step method suggested in the chapter.

"Without a doubt, every convicted murderer should be executed. Certainly, all bleeding-heart liberals will disagree; they think all murderers were abused as children or were victims of social injustice. The liberals care more about the murderers than the victims! As Mr. Collins, my chemistry teacher, says, "Capital punishment is every murderer's reward."

8. Evaluate the following argument; follow the eight-step method suggested in the chapter.

"I am the only candidate for governor who will do what is right for our state. I was born in a small town, was raised by two loving parents, and will instill the values of small towns and two-parent families into the lives of my wife and children. I have never spoken out against anything that good, morally righteous people favor. Unlike my opponent, who is unmarried and dating men half her age, and who finds pleasure in the fast life of the city, I am just like you, rural, honest, and simple. She, on the other hand, is a fast-talking lawyer who will say anything to get elected.

9. Evaluate the following argument; follow the eight-step method suggested in the chapter.

"Being young is a time for partying, meeting people, and developing social know-how. Studying and being serious about world affairs is for older people; they're the only ones who can do anything about that stuff, anyhow. Sure, the old geezers will say I am wrong, but that's just their opinion. My opinion is as good as anyone's. Give me a break, I'm only twenty-two! I have my whole life ahead to be serious and miserable."

10. Evaluate the following argument; follow the eight-step method suggested in the chapter.

    "Friends, it is clear that my opponent in this election is trying to destroy our beloved country. He has consistently voted to raise our taxes to the point where an honest business can no longer prosper. No decent person would deny that his well-concealed extramarital affairs are permanently damaging the moral values of our greatest asset, our young people. He has even been involved in crimes, such as the unsolved murder of his speechwriter. I have asked him on several occasions to prove that these allegations are false, but he merely hides behind what he calls "reasonable arguments." Well, we all know a reasonable argument when we see one, and what's reasonable here is that nobody can argue that he is a traitor to us all!

11. Evaluate the following argument; follow the eight-step method suggested in the chapter.

    "Well-known actor Biff Loman has authenticated the telekinetic powers of Ba-Room-Boi. 'Ba-Room can do more than twist spoons and toss lamps to the floor,' says Biff. 'I have witnessed amazing feats of tele-kine-cogni that really blew my mind! Ba-Room-Boi has shown me how to improve my life by actually changing other people's minds by use of his amazing 'tele-kine-cogni' method!' Do your children disobey you? Is your spouse reluctant to give you what you want? Is your boss unappreciative of your hard work? Change their minds! Ba-Room has helped many with his powers, but perhaps you haven't yet benefited. You owe it to your family and yourself to purchase his video, *Tele-Kine-Cogni: The Method of Mental Control.*"

12. Evaluate the following argument; follow the eight-step method suggested in the chapter.

    "Everyone knows how easy it is to criticize others, but it isn't as easy to take a good hard look at yourself. All these self-described "critical thinkers" should stop being so critical and start believing in the tried and true ways of right living. Why are they so intent upon criticizing? Why are they so negative? Why do they want to tear down everything? Why don't they have a good word for anything or anybody? Because they think they are better than we are, that's why. They think they are superior to those of us who know that what's true is true, what's right is right, and what's good is good."

▲ QUESTIONS FOR DISCUSSION

1. Evaluate the following argument; follow the eight-step method suggested in the chapter.

   "The men's basketball team at the college builds character and healthy bodies for the athletes. It also provides entertainment for the students. The team won the championship last season. The mathematics, science, and humanities programs do nothing for the athlete's health, and they are not entertaining at all. Students of math, science, and the humanities have won no championships. The basketball team would benefit from new uniforms, a really nice new bus, and free meals at fine restaurants. Therefore, the basketball team has the right to the same amount of budgetary funding as do the college's combined instructional programs in mathematics, science, and the humanities."

2. Evaluate the following argument; follow the eight-step method suggested in the chapter.

   "A serious world population problem exists today. The ideal solution is for everyone to be responsible in deciding whether he or she should reproduce. However, few people make that decision in a reasonable way. They let emotions interfere with proper family planning. The least talented and least intelligent people always have the most children. It's common knowledge. And if we are not careful, these people could set the process of evolution in reverse! The only practical solution to this overwhelming problem is to identify inferior people and force them to be sterilized at puberty."

3. Evaluate the following argument; follow the eight-step method suggested in the chapter. This is the argument introduced in Chapter 5. Before you proceed, review your work on it and make revisions, if necessary.

Seeing that love can be present without a marriage license, it follows that any couple, whether gay or heterosexual, should be recognized as being married. Some people disagree, but think about it. The legal, social, and other benefits of married life should not be denied because of narrow-minded bias.

▲ QUOTATION TO PONDER

"Now for some people it is better worth while to seem to be wise than to be wise without seeming to be."

Aristotle, *On Sophistical Refutations*

▲ JOURNAL TOPIC

Identify at least three fallacies that you have noticed in conversations, in reading the news, or in watching television during the past week.

▲ PORTFOLIO PAPER

In this chapter you have studied how fallacies interfere with implication. You should understand that the implication relationship between premises and conclusions is disrupted by fallacies. Fallacies get in the way of good arguments, and rupture communication. No doubt, fallacious reasoning often causes disputes. Review the paper you wrote on the difference between arguments and disputes while studying Chapter 5. Revise the paper, and add another 300–500 words that explain how fallacies can cause disputes in personal and public life.

CHAPTER EIGHT

EVIDENCE

PERCEPTION: THE BASIS OF ALL KNOWLEDGE

Our discussion of perception and the brain in Chapter 1 concluded that every perception has been selected, organized, and interpreted. We examined the two-world assumption, the philosophical puzzle that rests on the recognition that everything a person knows is "in his or her mind," but that everything one knows *about* is "outside of the mind." We studied the relationship of the body's receptors (the senses of vision, sound, smell, taste, and touch) with "sense-data." We pointed out that people sense the world in their own way, perceive their sensations in their own way, and "live in their own world." We are isolated from each other. Each one of us has his or her own individual perceptual world. Yet we share each other's perceptual worlds through communication, primarily through language. Language, as we discussed in Chapters 3 and 4, is the "bridge" between human beings. Language, the conventional system of words and their meanings, allows us to represent perceptions and express feelings to other people.

We also noticed that language is the "bridge" between the outside world and ourselves. Language, while it is an essential aspect of our cultural experience, is one of the primary factors in the interpretation of sensation. That is, the natural language that we speak is more than a communication system. It also plays

AFTER STUDYING CHAPTER EIGHT

You should be able to describe the difference between public confirmation of beliefs and mindless conformity. You should be able to clearly distinguish each of the three components of evidence, as well as each of the four types of evidence, describing the strengths and weaknesses of each type.

a role in the interpretation of experience. The language we use to speak about the world also influences the way we perceive the world.

However, what is the "world"? What is "out there"? What is the world like *before* and *apart from* any human knowledge of it? What are the facts about "reality"? What is it *really* like? One of the most difficult lessons for critical thinking is that we do not know the answer to that question. We never will know what the world is like before and apart from our own knowledge of it. We would have to be able to know the world as it is *without* our knowing it! That is not possible.

For example, try to name something that you have not perceived. Remember that perception is the selection, organization, and interpretation of sensation. Therefore, the question is asking you to name something you have not seen, heard, smelled, tasted, or felt. Keep in mind that anything you have read, any films you have seen, any conversations you have been in, and any emotions you have felt are all perceptions! Thus, when you are asked to name something you have not perceived, you are being asked to give a name to something of which you have no experience at all. It is impossible to do that. Even if we come up with a purely imaginary being—for example, "a Martian housecat"—we must admit that we created this imaginary cat out of our perceptions. We combined our experience of Mars, which may come from seeing sci-fi movies or from studying astronomy, both of which are perceptions, with "housecat," which is obviously based on our perceptions.

On the other hand, if we are asked to name something we know about, but do not know the *complete truth* about, our task is much easier. We don't know the complete truth about any of the things we know about; for example, we don't know if there are or are not any housecats on Mars. We don't know the complete truth about how many grains of sand there are in the Sahara Desert. We don't know completely why we catch colds. We know about these things; we just don't know *all* about them. To know the *complete truth* about something is to know *all* about it: to know *everything* that could *possibly* be known about it. A human being cannot have the complete truth about anything.

Nevertheless, we do know the *partial truth* about many things. That is, we know that there is a planet Mars. Astronomers know a lot more than that about it! We know that housecats have unique personalities. Of course, zoologists know a lot more about housecats than most of us do. We know that the Sahara is the world's largest desert, and that it is located in northern Africa. Of course, geographers know more, much more, than that. Moreover, some mathematicians might know how much sand it consists of, give or take a few million grains! Immunologists still do not know how to cure the common cold, but they know a lot more about it than the average person. The point here is that while human beings cannot know the complete truth, we can know a great deal about things. However, we can know only what we have perceived. The more we perceive, the more we know.

TRUTH CORRESPONDS WITH PERCEPTIONS AND COHERES WITH BELIEFS

Truth is a characteristic of beliefs and statements: not a characteristic of things. We don't say, "the housecat is true"; we say that our *beliefs about* the housecat are true. Sometimes we use the word "truth" metaphorically, as an expression of our feelings about someone or something. For example, Eva says, "Kim is a true friend." However, Eva does not mean that Kim is literally "true." Eva means that her perception of the way Kim acts *corresponds* to what she believes are the essential characteristics of friendship. Eva means that Kim is a good friend because she perceives that Kim acts the way she believes a good friend acts.

We could ask Eva whether her idea about the way that a good friend acts is true or not. Her response might surprise us.

> "I know that my beliefs about what a good friend is are true for several reasons. First, I have developed them by observing the way people act in friendships. Second, I have listened to my parents' advice on friendship. Third, I have read stories and seen films about friendship. Fourth, I have studied friendship in my social psychology course. I don't know everything about friendship, but I believe I know a good friend when I see one."

Eva is telling us that she believes her ideas about friendship are true because they all *connect* with other ideas about friendship that she believes to be true. The advice from her parents, the observations she has made on her own, the studies done by the social psychologists, and the stories and films all *cohere,* or come together, in her ideas about friendship.

Truth corresponds with perceptions and coheres with ideas. True beliefs always *fit with perceptions* and *connect with other true beliefs.* Eva knows the truth about Kim's friendship because her ideas about the friendship *correspond* to her perceptions of it. In turn, she knows the truth about friendship because her ideas about it all *cohere.* Let's take a more detailed look at these two characteristics of truth.

TRUTH CORRESPONDS WITH PERCEPTIONS

To *correspond* with a perception is to "fit" or to "harmonize" with it. A true idea about a cat is one that fits, or harmonizes with, perceptions of the cat. Of course, the zoological perception of a cat is much more complex and detailed than a child's perception. The child's ideas about the cat may be partially true ("The cat is soft and furry") but the zoological ideas are more complete than those of the child ("The cat is extremely flexible, very agile, an excellent swimmer, and a faster runner than any other mammal").

A false idea does not correspond with perceptions. If the child believes that the cat cannot swim because it displays a dislike of water, her ideas are false. The child does not have a perception that corresponds with her idea. She has an idea that goes beyond her perceptions. The zoologist, who has perceived cats swimming, can correct her. The zoologist can also direct the child to *evidence* that will allow her to revise her idea. Evidence in this example could be videotape of cats swimming.

TRUTH COHERES WITH OTHER TRUE BELIEFS

True beliefs *cohere* with other truths. This means that true beliefs always make sense in relation with other true beliefs. That is, true beliefs "stick together." In other words, true beliefs are always reasonably related to other true beliefs. A true idea about a cat is one that agrees with other true ideas about cats. For example, we know that cats are mammals. From that true idea we can infer with confidence that cats nurse their young. This means that the idea that its mother nursed the child's cat at one time is true. The child does not have to actually perceive the cat to know that this idea is the truth. Arguments make use of the coherence feature of truth. If the premises of an argument are true, and if the argument is reasonable and clear, then the conclusion is always true.

If the child asks us, "Did my cat's mother nurse it as a kitten?" we can confidently respond with a trustworthy argument:

> Your cat is a mammal, and all mammals are nursed by their mothers. Therefore, its mother nursed your cat.

Since true ideas always cohere with each other, we do not need to personally experience the correspondence of every idea with a perception. If that were the case, we would have a very limited number of truths. Human knowledge could not progress; each person's ideas would have to correspond with his or her own personal perceptions. For example, each of us would have to perceive a cat nursing in order to know that "its mother nursed your cat" is true. Each of us would have to leave the planet in a space ship in order to know that "the earth is flat" is false. Truth's inherent coherence means that once we gain a body of true knowledge, we can make inferences from what we already know and expand our knowledge.

Of course, true ideas have *both* characteristics of coherence and correspondence. That means that we cannot decide that an idea is true simply by creating a reasonable argument that shows it coheres with other true ideas. The idea must also correspond with perception. Let's look more closely at these two characteristics.

Coherence with Beliefs — **TRUTH** — **Correspondence with Perceptions**

***Rashomon:* A More Detailed Look at the Two Characteristics of Truth.**   In 1950, the influential Japanese filmmaker, Akira Kurosawa, directed *Rashomon*. Authorities on film regard Kurosawa as one of the best directors in history. His *The Seven Samurai* was remade into *The Magnificent Seven,* a very influential Western movie. *Yojimbo* has been remade several times, first as Clint Eastwood's *A Fistful of Dollars,* and later as *Last Man Standing,* starring Bruce Willis. *The

Hidden Fortress is acknowledged by George Lucas to be one of the primary inspirations of *Star Wars.*

Rashomon is so influential that it has been remade twice. In 1964 Paul Newman starred in *The Outrage,* and in 1996, Meg Ryan and Denzel Washington starred in *Courage Under Fire.*

Rashomon is a story about truth told through a series of flashbacks that tell of a woman's rape and a man's murder, possibly by a bandit. A woodcutter witnessed the events and, with the help of a priest, he puzzles over the truth about what really happened. In the four flashbacks, each character relates his or her perception of the events. In the bandit's account, he accepts the blame for the murder, but denies that the woman was raped, saying it was an act of mutual consent. The woman's story is that she was raped, but she hints that she may have murdered the husband. The dead man's story (told by a medium) is that his wife was raped, and that he committed suicide. The woodcutter's tale is a composite of the other three, and the viewer is left to wonder if the woodcutter actually saw anything at all! Each story is compelling and plausible, but each one also has something about it that makes it unbelievable. The film never reveals what really happened. The viewer is left with four perceptions, none of which is the complete truth, but each of which is a partial truth.

Rashomon isn't a puzzle or a "who done it?" It is a film that explores the nature of truth focusing on the inability of any one person to know the complete truth, no matter how clearly his or her perceptions may seem. By the end of the film, the viewer realizes there is no such thing as *the complete truth* about what happened in the woods. There are only the four partial truths, four perceptions.

Each person interprets the events in the woods differently. Even though each one's ideas correspond with his or her own perceptions, they do not correspond with those of anyone else. This helps point out an important characteristic of truth; it is usually not enough that an individual's ideas correspond only with his or her own perceptions. Ideas of this sort are only "subjectively true." Ideas that are accepted by others are "objectively true." *In order to be objectively true, our ideas must also correspond with the perceptions of other people.*

For example, Martin and Roberto are waiting for the bus. Martin believes that he sees their mutual friend Leroy driving his car. "Hey, Roberto, look! It's Leroy! He can give us a ride!" he exclaims. Roberto looks in the direction Martin is pointing. "No, that's not Leroy," he says. "That guy has longer hair than Leroy." Martin looks again, and realizes that his idea was not true. For a moment, he thought it was. However, Roberto did not confirm the idea; it was not objectively true.

In *Rashomon*, each person has his or her own perceptions that correspond with his or her own beliefs. The bandit believes that no rape took place; his perceptions correspond with his belief. These are subjective, not objective, truths. The woman believes that a rape did take place. Her perceptions correspond with her belief, and her beliefs are subjectively true. However, that does not mean her belief is *objectively* true. Unless a belief corresponds with the perceptions and feelings of others, we do not have an objectively true belief.

The film also portrays the nature of coherence. Coherent beliefs "hang together." They are related by implication or in some other reasonable way. The characters' narration of their experience in the woods is subjectively coherent. For example, the bandit's story, which is the first one, is consistent; every event he describes makes sense in relation to every other event. When he is finished, we feel that his story, because it is so coherent, must be objectively true. Then we see the woman's, which is also subjectively coherent. Nevertheless, it does not cohere with the bandit's tale. As each character narrates, we become more and more aware that there is no objective truth in any one of their descriptions.

SUBJECTIVE AND OBJECTIVE CORRESPONDENCE.   Correspondence between an idea and a perception is said to be subjective when an individual's idea fits only with his or her own perception. For example, Martin perceives, and believes, that the driver is Leroy. His idea corresponds with his perception. It is subjectively true for Martin that the driver is Leroy. Roberto, on the other hand, believes that the driver is not Leroy. His idea corresponds with his perception and is also a subjective idea. It is subjectively true for Roberto that the driver is not Leroy.

However, Martin's idea is not objectively true; no one else confirmed that Leroy was driving the car. Martin, if he does not communicate his idea to anyone, will never know the objective truth.

Subjective correspondence is the theme of *Rashomon*. Each person's ideas only correspond with his or her perceptions. However, since there is no public confirmation, there is no objective truth. We, the audience, are in the same situation as the characters in the film; we are limited to our own subjective truths.

Subjective correspondence becomes objective correspondence when people confirm with one another that their perceptions and beliefs correspond in the same way. This process, called "public confirmation" of beliefs, is an aspect of linguistic confirmation, which was discussed in Chapter 3. Linguistic confirmation is the tacit agreement that speakers of a language make between each other to accept the conventional meaning of words. It stabilizes linguistic meaning. Public confirmation of subjective correspondence stabilizes beliefs. It is usually done through oral communication. For example, Roberto tells Martin, "I believe that this bus coming now is the one we should take." Martin responds, "Yes, it's our bus." Martin has publicly confirmed Roberto's subjective correspondence by using words. However, perhaps Roberto does not say anything; he sees the bus coming, believes it is the one that he and Martin should catch, and moves toward the street. Martin sees the bus and moves with him. That gesture confirms Roberto's perception. Either way, in gestures or words, Martin's confirmation of Roberto's perception moves Roberto's subjective correspondence to the level of objective correspondence.

THEORETICAL AND EMOTIONAL COHERENCE.   Beliefs cohere (make sense or stick together) with each other in two primary ways: theoretically and emotionally. A theoretical coherence occurs when ideas are related by inference. We examined inference in Chapter 5. An argument is a good example of a theoretical implication. However, theoretical implications occur in ways other than arguments. Beliefs cohere in narratives, which are nonargumentative stories or accounts of ideas and feelings. For example, a film is a narrative: a series of images that are "glued together" by the story and characters. Many written pieces are narratives; they discuss a theme and express an opinion that makes sense in relation to the discussion.

Theoretical coherence is subjective if the beliefs cohere for only one person. If the beliefs are shared with others, and others find them coherent, then the beliefs are objectively coherent. The process of public confirmation of coherence is the same as with correspondence. A person must share their narrative with others in order to obtain the theoretical confirmation that moves their subjective truth to the level of objective truth. This process occurs whenever we share an essay, a story, or a film with an audience. In effect, we say, "This belief makes sense to me. Does it make sense to you?" If the audience confirms that the belief makes sense, it is objectively coherent. Of course, the wider the audience, the more objectively coherent the belief.

EMOTIONS AND BELIEFS

In Chapter 1 the brain was described as a family of three. The reptilian complex, which takes care of the primitive survival responses such as seeking food to satisfy hunger, was the grandfather. The neocortex, which does creative and cognitive tasks, was the child. The mother, who balances the family by restraining the primitive impulses of the grandfather and the wild experimentation of the child, is the limbic system. The limbic system is the emotional component of the brain. The brain always works as a unit. Our beliefs and perceptions always involve an element of survival instinct, cognitive meaning, and emotion. As a result, every belief and every perception has an emotional component.

It is easy to understand the connection between the emotions and primitive survival responses. For example, a starving person feels anxiety and fear. If an individual is threatened in any way, his or her response will be emotionally charged. It is common to associate emotions with survival responses. However, we need to recognize that emotions are also present in all of our brain activities, including those of the neocortex. Emotion is not separate from thinking; it is an inherent aspect of it.

Of course, sometimes the emotions can distract us from clearly focusing on our cognitive tasks. For example, it is very difficult to study if we are anxious about something in our personal life. Emotions can also cloud our judgment. The fallacy of irrelevant emotion, studied in the last chapter, is an example of feelings interfering with the reasoning process.

Because of this interference, some scientists and philosophers claim that the emotions always and only distract thinking. They deny that emotions have *any* cognitive benefit. They *insist* that any belief that has the slightest emotional tinge is "complete nonsense!"[1] However, these same individuals are quite *emotional* about their claim. They are *adamant* about it! In other words, their belief, contrary to their claim, has an emotional aspect itself. All beliefs have an emotional aspect.

---

1. Some believe that these scientists and philosophers are committing the fallacy of oversimplification. What do you think?

For example, some beliefs about moral values are highly emotional. Others are much less emotional, even insignificantly so. In some beliefs the emotions are coherent, and in others they are not.

Coherent and Incoherent Emotions. Ideas cohere *theoretically* by inference. Emotions, however, cannot be said to "infer" each other. Emotions are not ideas; they are feelings.[2] When they make sense, or cohere, emotions are in accord. Most of the time, an individual's feelings are *subjectively coherent;* they tend to be consistent. For example, if Barbara is disgusted by candy, she is also unhappy to receive the gift of a box of chocolates from Terry. However, if she finds Terry attractive, she may change her feelings and be overjoyed by the gift. For a period, she may be both happy and unhappy about the gift; her emotions are not coherent. This does not mean that there is something emotionally wrong with Barbara; it simply means that she hasn't "sorted out" her feelings about the gift. The great majority of the time, though, emotions are subjectively coherent.

It is not unusual, however, for the emotions of one person to be different from those of another in relation to the same thing. A very simple example of this is Barbara's disgust for candy, and most people's attraction to it. Barbara's subjective emotion about candy is not *publicly confirmed.* A publicly confirmed emotion is a subjective emotion that most people feel about something. Thus, a subjective attraction to candy is publicly confirmed. Disgust at candy is not. We can say, then, that an attraction to candy is "objectively coherent." This is not a normal way of describing emotions, and the term is rather clumsy. However, it points out that emotions, as well as ideas, can be subjectively coherent, yet, not be shared by other people. An objectively coherent emotion is shared.

For example, a person may say, "I feel angry about the new tax laws." If she is the only person in the country that feels anger about them, we can say that her emotion is subjective. If others also feel anger about the tax law, then they confirm her subjective feeling, and we can say that her subjective emotion is objectively coherent. When a person expresses a feeling that finds no public confirmation at all, it is a good indication that their idea is limited to subjective truth.

As was mentioned earlier, emotions are especially important in beliefs about values. Imagine this conversation:

Charles: I am so happy that there is a war going on in the Middle East! It thrills me to watch the news and see the bombing and destruction. I am especially elated about the terrorism.
Jonathan: How can you feel that way? I am disgusted by that war!
Esther: So am I!
Katherine: Me too!

---

2. A reminder: We stipulated (Chapter 5) that "ideas" are representations of perceptions, and that "feelings" are expressions of emotions. "Beliefs" are mixtures of ideas and feelings.

Michael: I am filled with grief whenever I hear about it.

Brad: There is nothing worse than war; I hate it!

Charles: But war is a good thing!

All: No it's not! War is horrible!

Charles: Well that's not how I feel about it. It makes great TV.

All: You are entitled to your feeling, Charles, but we do not share it.

As this example indicates, emotions that do not have public confirmation are not objectively coherent. This does *not* mean that there is something *wrong* with them. There are many cases in which a single person's feelings and ideas are, for a time, more reasonable than those held by the great majority of people. Eventually, over time, if others come to share the subjective ideas and feelings of that one individual, then the subjective beliefs acquire more *completeness* than if they had remained subjective.

Subjective and Objective Coherence of Beliefs. As discussed earlier, emotional coherence can be subjective or objective. Subjective *theoretical* coherence is usually described as "internally coherent." (The term "subjectively coherent" is reserved for emotions.) Theoretical coherence is a "reasonable connection" of ideas with one another. Subjectively coherent feelings that go through the process of public confirmation become objectively coherent.

An internally coherent theory, like an argument that has no fallacies, is a group of ideas that are reasonably related. As long as a theory is not compared or contrasted with other theories, it remains only internally coherent. However, if there are other theories on the same topic that reasonably cohere with this theory, then it becomes objectively coherent as well.

The subjects studied in school, such as psychology, literature, and so on, are composed of objectively coherent theories. When a new internally coherent idea is presented, it is evaluated to see where it objectively coheres. If it fits in with theories in psychology, it is integrated with the other psychological theories. If it is a theory that fits in with theories in literature, then it becomes a coherent part of that subject. Of course, the process is much more complicated than this.

Each area of study actually has various "schools of thought" that approach the subject matter in internally coherent, but different, ways. For example, in psychology there are several different theories about the human mind. The Behaviorists have one theory, the Gestaltists another. The Behaviorist theory is a group of theories about human knowledge, each of which coheres with every other. The Gestaltist theory is also made up of a group of coherent theories. When a psychologist publishes a new theory, others in the field evaluate it. The first thing they look for is whether the newly published theory is internally coherent. If it is, then it is examined for objective coherence. The Gestaltists will accept the new study if it coheres with their coherent group of theories. If the study does not cohere with the Behaviorist theories, they will not accept it as objectively coherent. In other words, each school of thought is made up of its own internally coherent theories. A new theory is accepted only if it coheres with them.

You may wonder if there are any theories that are accepted by *every* school of thought in psychology. If there are, then those theories are "objectively coherent" in the fullest sense of the term. At present, there do not seem to be any significant theories in psychology with that degree of objective coherence. Thus, if you ask a question about the nature of the mind in psychology class, the teacher is likely to respond, "Well, it depends on how you look at it." What he or she is saying is that there are several different psychological schools of thought about the mind. The theoretical response to your question from one of those schools of thought will be coherent in relation to it, but not to others.

Some subjects have fewer schools of thought than others do. Mathematics, chemistry, biology, and physiology are examples of areas of study that have only a few. Philosophy has more schools of thought than any other area of study; it is literally composed of hundreds of internally coherent theories that have no objective coherence with each other. The more objective coherence an area of study has, the more conceptual unity it possesses, and the more objective truths it will have. For example, philosophy contains no objective truths at all. Philosophy is actually composed of many different methods of approaching knowledge.

Public Confirmation and Completeness of Truth.   At the beginning of this chapter it was pointed out that no one knows the complete truth. Partial truth is all any of us ever know. Nevertheless, through public confirmation, individual subjective truths are integrated with others, and eventually a coherent body of knowledge develops. For example, every subject matter studied in school was once a mere *subjectively* coherent, *subjectively* correspondent, truth. They were isolated ideas and individual feelings. For example, the science of chemistry only began to be an objective body of knowledge about 1700, with the work of Robert Boyle and others. Prior to that time, there were very few, if any, objectively coherent, publicly confirmed truths in chemistry. Of course, there were many subjective truths. Some chemists believed that there were only four chemical elements—air, earth, water, and fire. Others believed that lead could be turned into gold. However, none of these ideas could be publicly confirmed, and there was no objective coherence among them. Boyle and other early chemists established a unified group of theories that were publicly confirmed as well as objectively accepted as coherent, and the science of chemistry began. Other subjects have gone through similar processes in the development of truth.

It would be an oversimplification to claim that the development of truth takes place without mistakes. At times, theories and ideas have been publicly accepted by an entire generation, only to be shown to be untrue later on. The path to truth and knowledge is not a straight line! Truth takes "two steps forward, one step back" on a path with many twists, turns, and dead ends. In fact, scientists and scholars can easily spend their entire lives trying to find public confirmation for only one truth. They are often disappointed even in that. As a recent example, consider the scientific hunt for a cure for the AIDS virus. A generation of immunologists from all over the world has been seeking the truth about the causes of AIDS. Their successes have been far outnumbered by their failures. That is the true nature of public confirmation and the search for objective truth; it is frustrating, exhausting, and very hard work.

Nevertheless it is public confirmation that moves us beyond subjective to objective truths. When others agree with our perceptions, and when our theories coherently fit with theirs, then we have gone beyond our own limited world and crossed the bridge to the world of objective truths.

Public confirmation integrates partial truths with others, and consequently human knowledge increases and deepens. Partial truths are seen to confirm and to cohere with other partial truths, and truths become more and more complete. As truths grow and develop, as we learn more and more, our intellectual lives become richer. As we deepen our understanding, we have more opportunities to improve our physical, psychological, and social health. It is not possible to achieve complete truth, but we can make truths more complete than they are.

Critical Thinking and Public Confirmation.   It is very important to understand that public confirmation is not at all the same as "public acceptance." Mere acceptance of popularity of beliefs, whether ideas or feelings, is not a reasonable way to determine if they have gone beyond subjective truth to objective correspondence and coherence. Just as we cannot accept an argument as trustworthy simply because it is popular, we cannot accept an idea as objectively true simply because a large number of people accept it! Critical thinking, not mindless conformity, is the central element of public confirmation.

In fact, critical thinking and public confirmation are identical processes. Only when ideas and feelings—beliefs—are reviewed, evaluated, and revised in a *critical* manner, can they become clearer and more reasonable. Of course, critical thinking combines verbal and logical thinking to review and evaluate beliefs. As we have seen, both of these activities are done in a methodical way. A review of ideas involves defining terms, summarizing main ideas and support, as well as paraphrasing. Each of these activities has specific guidelines that must be followed. Many theories are in the form of arguments. Critical thinking identifies these elements and organizes them. Thus, when critical thinking reviews ideas and feelings, it does so in a rigorous manner. It follows a reasonable pattern.

Ideas in written pieces are evaluated for clarity, accuracy, specificity, and significance. Feelings are evaluated for sincerity, respect for others, and commitment to consensus. Inferences in theories are evaluated for vague terms and for fallacies. Only when beliefs meet the expectations of critical thinking are they granted public confirmation.

In this section, we have discussed one of the most difficult topics in the history of humanity. Philosophers, scientists, poets, and others, no matter where or when they have lived, have always struggled with the question, "What is truth?" The struggle continues in our time. We have only a partial understanding of truth. To claim otherwise would be arrogant and foolish. Nevertheless, we do know something about truth.

CONCLUSION

Truth is not a characteristic of things, but of ideas and feelings, both of which are based on perception. Whether we have observed something ourselves, read someone else's description of an observation, read someone else's theory, seen a film, or found out about a belief in the mass media, the only way we can come to be aware of anything is through perception. Beliefs are always interpreted by our cultural experience, most often by language.

Truth, no matter how extensive, is always only partial. No individual could possibly know the complete truth. The world is too complex for that. In addition, each person interprets experience, and no matter how complex his or her beliefs, they are always limited by the person's perceptual interpretation of them.

A true belief is one that corresponds with perceptions and coheres with other beliefs about the same subject. Feelings are an integral part of beliefs; we never have a belief without feeling something about it. Beliefs about values are especially laden with feeling. Subjectively coherent feelings are consistent within the emotional life of the person who has them. Objectively coherent feelings are those that are shared by others. Coherent groups of ideas about the same subject are called "theories." Theories can be subjectively or objectively coherent. Subjectively coherent theories are known as "internally coherent." An objectively coherent theory is one that connects reasonably with other theories about the same thing. Groups of these theories are organized into various subject matters, for example, chemistry, history, or music theory. They are studied and used as the background knowledge for new investigations.

As long as a belief, whether an idea or a feeling, remains subjective, it remains partially true. It may be true only for the one person who believes it. An idea moves from being subjectively true to objectively true by going through the process of public confirmation. Critical thinking, not mindless conformity, establishes whether an idea has been publicly confirmed. Critical thinking uses its standards to review and evaluate ideas. Mindless conformity simply relies on popularity. Critical thinking continually reviews, evaluates, and revises ideas, even those that have been publicly confirmed in the past.

The premises of arguments are statements that support conclusions. The support statements in pieces of writing are beliefs that support a main idea. The more completely true the belief, the better the support. Another term for "support" is "evidence." In the next section, we will examine the components and types of evidence. Evidence is the perceptual, emotional, and theoretical support for a belief. There are four types of evidence: experimental, observational, testimonial, and anecdotal. Our examination of evidence should provide us with a more complete understanding of arguments as well as of more common pieces of writing.

EXERCISES

▲ Most Intriguing Issue

Write a one-paragraph description of the most interesting idea, topic, or process described in pages 200–226. Be prepared to explain what you find interesting in class discussion.

▲ The Muddiest Point

Write a sentence or, if possible, a paragraph that describes the idea, topic, expression, term, or process in pages 200–226 that you find most difficult to understand.

▲ Cartoons and Diagrams

Cartoons are drawings that characterize or symbolize ideas, processes, or expressions in imaginative ways. Diagrams are drawings, charts, or tables that show how specific details of an idea, process, or expression are interrelated.

1. Draw a cartoon that shows the difference between subjective and objective correspondence of an idea and a perception.
2. Draw a cartoon that shows the difference between an idea that has objective correspondence and one that does not.
3. Draw a cartoon that illustrates subjective and objective coherence.
4. Provide a diagram that shows the relationships between coherence (both subjective and objective) and correspondence (both subjective and objective) with partial and complete truth.
5. Draw a cartoon that illustrates subjective and objective theoretical coherence.
6. Provide a cartoon that illustrates objective theoretical incoherence.
7. Provide a cartoon that shows objective emotional incoherence.
8. Draw a cartoon that illustrates the nature of public confirmation.
9. Draw a cartoon that shows the relationship between a publicly confirmed idea and one that is not.
10. Draw a cartoon that illustrates the general development of subject matters and schools of thought.

▲ Definitions of Key Terms

Provide a disciplinary definition for each of the following terms as they are used in this chapter. Most of the terms are not defined in the chapter, although their meanings are described by the context in which they appear. You need to review the material to create the definition yourself. Be sure to follow the guidelines for creating definitions on pages 78–81.

Truth	Partial Truth	Complete Truth
Subjective Coherence	Objective Theoretical Coherence	Objective Emotional Coherence
Objective Correspondence	Subject Matter	Public Confirmation

▲ Short Essay Questions

Provide a response of approximately 200 words to each topic. Your responses should be well organized, grammatically correct, and neatly produced.

1. Provide a clarification of the diagram at the conclusion of the section.
2. Explain the difference between partial and complete truth. Are some partial truths "more partial" than others are? Explain.
3. Describe the difference between a true idea and a false idea.
4. Explain the difference between feelings and ideas.
5. Provide and explain an example of a position on a moral issue that has attained objective emotional coherence in our society.
6. Provide and explain an example of a position on a moral issue that has not attained objective emotional coherence in our society.
7. Explain the difference between internal and objective theoretical coherence.
8. Explain the importance of objective theoretical coherence and objective correspondence in building a subject matter.
9. Explain the difference between public confirmation and public acceptance of a belief.
10. Explain what this means: "A school of thought is a coherent group of beliefs that cohere internally and with those of a subject matter. They do not necessarily cohere with those of other schools of thought within the same subject matter."

▲ Questions for Discussion

Provide an essay of 300–500 words that responds to each of the following questions which ask for your opinion. You should respond by stating it, and by providing thoughts, examples, and insights that support it. You should be willing to revise your response; you may change your opinion during or after a class discussion.

1. This section begins with the claim that "one of the most difficult lessons of critical thinking" is that we cannot know reality, but only our perceptions of reality. Explain what the claim seems to mean within the context of the chapter as well as you can, and then describe your feelings about it. Do you find this claim depressing, binding, exciting, liberating, or just plain confusing?
2. All three films mentioned in this section are available on videotape. View one of them and discuss how several specific scenes illustrate some ideas about truth covered in the chapter.
3. According to the chapter, a moral idea that has attained public confirmation is a more complete truth than one that is held subjectively, without any (or with very limited) objective coherence. Yet, many moral leaders are individuals who criticize their own society's accepted values. How do you explain this?
4. Review a subject you are currently studying, other than Critical Thinking, and describe several schools of thought it has. (You should discuss this question with an authority in the subject.)
5. Describe your thoughts on this very speculative question. "All knowledge is based on perception, and all perception is based on sense data. What is reality? Is sense-data the same thing as reality? On the other hand, is perception reality? Or is knowledge reality?"

6. The chapter claims that public confirmation changes subjective truth into objective truth, and partial truth into more complete truth. However, isn't it possible for one person to know the truth and for everyone else to be wrong? In that case, wouldn't subjective truth be more complete than objective truth? Explain your thoughts on this issue.

7. The chapter discusses the difference between true and false ideas, but does not mention the difference between true statements and lies. What are some differences between lies and false ideas?

▲ QUOTATION TO PONDER

"Objectivity is a matter of intersubjective consensus among human beings, not of accurate representation of something nonhuman."
Richard Rorty, *Achieving Our Country,* 1998

▲ JOURNAL TOPIC

There is a great deal of discussion about UFOs in the media; there are television programs, videos, tabloid accounts, and web sites devoted to the topic. Review one of these discussions for subjective and objective truth. For example, is the discussion internally theoretically coherent? Objectively coherent? How much objective correspondence is present?

TRUTH AND EVIDENCE

Beliefs are represented or expressed in statements. Some statements are offered as support for other beliefs. To support a belief is to provide reasons, or groups of reasons, to show that the supported belief is true. For example, the premises of an argument are statements that claim to support the conclusion. They claim to reasonably and clearly infer the conclusion's truth. If the premises of a reasonable and clear argument are true, then its conclusion is also true. Beliefs that support other beliefs, whether as premises in an argument or in some other way, are called "evidence." The terms "support" and "evidence" are synonymous.

Evidence is made up of perceptual, emotional, and theoretical *components.* These components parallel ideas (perceptual and theoretical) and feelings (emotional). Evidence, like truth, is best when it corresponds with perceptions and coheres with other ideas and feelings. Evidence can be offered in representational statements that offer perceptual and theoretical support, or it can be offered in expressive statements that offer emotional support. Evidence has all three of these components, but in varying degrees depending on the specific type of evidence involved.

Evidence that is partially true or subjectively true is not as strong as evidence that is more completely true. Of course, ideas are evaluated as more or less partially or completely true. Evidence, however, is most often composed of many beliefs (that is, by many statements that represent perceptions and express feelings). Some of the statements that make up the evidence may be more or less completely true than the others. Evidence is very rarely provided in only one or two statements. Often, there will be several paragraphs (or more) of evidence. For example, the evidence of some very complex ideas such as those offered by science and social science may consist of thousands of pages of research that describe hundreds of experiments and observations.

Evidence, then, is not evaluated as "complete" or "partial." We use those terms exclusively for the statements and beliefs that make up the evidence. Instead, we use the terms "strong" and "weak." These terms are similar to the terms "complete" and "partial," but refer to the entirety of the evidence offered by the argument or piece of writing. The more subjective and partial the evidence is, the weaker it is. The more objective and complete it is, the stronger it is. Strong evidence has more public confirmation than weak evidence.

There are four different *types* of evidence and the type of public confirmation that makes each one stronger or weaker distinguishes that type of evidence from the other. The four types of evidence are experimental, observational, testimonial, and anecdotal.

Evidence and truth, then, are closely related. Strong evidence involves objective beliefs that have received public confirmation. Weak evidence is made up of subjective beliefs that have little or no public confirmation. Since truth is always partial, evidence is never perfectly strong. However, the more complete the truth of the beliefs that are represented in the evidence, the stronger it will be.

This section will discuss the three *components* of evidence. The components are characteristics of all evidence, no matter which type. The next section will examine the different types of evidence. Finally, we will discuss the evaluation of each type of evidence for strengths and weaknesses.

THE COMPONENTS OF EVIDENCE

In general, evidence is composed of three elements: statements that describe perceptions, statements that describe theories, and statements that express emotion. We are most familiar with the component of evidence that is based on perception: the "factual component," which will be discussed shortly. However, all evidence is also comprised, somewhat, of theoretical beliefs that cannot be directly observed or measured. Sometimes the theoretical component is an argument. Often, these theories provide a context or a background that is necessary for the factual component to be meaningful. This context is also a theoretical component. Evidence also has an emotional component. Of course, feelings are involved more in evidence that supports beliefs about values than in supporting scientific claims. Nevertheless, even scientific evidence has an emotional side, as we shall see. All evidence has these three components: descriptions of facts, reliance on theories, and appeals to feelings.

The Factual Component of Evidence. Of course, most people regard "facts" to be things or events that take place in the real world, whether we know about them or not. This idea is, of course, not wrong. Facts, we assume, do exist. There is a real world, and it is made up of facts. We are warranted in assuming that there is a world beyond our perception, one that is composed at least of sense-data, probably of objects. A fact is an event in the real world.

However, there is a difference between *facts* and *known facts*. It is one thing to claim that *there are facts* and another to claim that we *know the facts*. In the first claim, we are saying simply that there *are* facts, and that there is a real world made up of facts. As said before, this does not seem to be an unwarranted assumption. However, the second claim, that someone *"knows the facts,"* is much more controversial. A simple example: You fall down walking in the woods on a dark night and injure your knee. It is a fact that a real object lacerated it. However, you do not *know* which object did the damage. Thus, it *is* a fact that something lacerated your knee. Whatever it is, you can safely assume that it is real. However, you do not know what actually—really—scraped your knee. For that, you need to perceive what did it. We cannot know anything, facts included, unless we have a perception of them. Of course, facts that are not perceived by anyone are nevertheless facts in the real world. However, we cannot think about them, talk about them, or *use them as support for our beliefs* unless we *know* about them. In order to do that we have to first perceive them. However, we cannot be said to *know a fact* unless we know the *truth* about it. In addition, as we discussed in the previous section, we have a more complete truth about an idea when it has been publicly confirmed. A "known fact" is an idea based on a publicly confirmed perception. Subjective ideas about facts cannot be said to be "known facts," although we could call them "what some people think to be facts."

Think about it. What if the doctor who examines your injured knee believes a rare toxic root scraped it? Because of his diagnosis, he wants to amputate your leg! That a toxic root scraped your knee is "a fact the doctor believes." Wouldn't you rather that it be a *known fact* that a toxic root scraped your knee prior to having your leg amputated? Wouldn't you want to have more public confirmation of his idea about this "fact" before you underwent surgery? Wouldn't you want a "second opinion"? Of course you would; there is a world of difference between "what some people believe to be facts" and "known facts."

The factual component of evidence is stronger when it consists of known facts, and weaker when it consists of what some people believe to be facts. In other words, the factual component is stronger when public confirmation has carried the ideas about the facts beyond subjective to objective correspondence.

Public confirmation is not mere popular acceptance. For example, many people believe it to be a fact that the sun rises in the east. If questioned, they will point to the (rising) sun and say "Look, it is rising in the east, just like I said." Of course, the sun is not really rising at all. The earth is rotating around the sun, and the sun merely *appears* to be rising. It is a *known fact* that the earth is rotating around the sun, although it does not appear that way to our normal perception. How do we know that the sun is not rising? How do we know that the earth is rotating? If we relied on popular acceptance of ideas, we would probably still be claiming, as people did for centuries, that the sun revolves around the earth, and that it rises in the east and sets in the west. However, there is a great deal of difference between popular acceptance of an idea and its public confirmation. That difference, as has been mentioned several times, is critical thinking.

Standards of Measurement and Known Facts. The science of Astronomy has done a great deal of critical thinking over the centuries about the relation of the planets, stars, and other heavenly bodies. Astronomy has reviewed, evaluated, and revised its ideas many times since its beginnings about three thousand years ago in China. In order to accumulate "known facts" about the universe, Astronomy has done what every science must do; it has created *standards of measurement* by which it can engage in public confirmation to review, evaluate, and revise its ideas about the heavens.

In order to accumulate known facts, science needs to have *standards:* ideals, rules, or principles used to establish the degree of partiality or completeness of an idea. Scientific standards are usually established by the specific science itself. A standard of measurement is a rule or a principle used to rigorously and exactly describe perceptions. Astronomy, like every science and every social science, makes use of its own standards of measurement to evaluate its perceptions. For example, it uses "light years" to measure distance between heavenly bodies. Their chemical composition is studied with a spectroscope by measuring their heat by determining the color of the light they emit. These are conventional standards astronomers created in order to communicate with each other in seeking public confirmation of their ideas.

You don't have to be a scientist to use standards of measurement. We often use rulers, yardsticks, scales, and so on to measure perceptions in standard ways. For example, a watermelon may be weighed on a "standard scale" at fifteen pounds. Consumers agree to use the standard scale so that they can communicate with the grocer when it comes time to pay for the watermelon. Imagine what would happen if consumers brought along their own scales to the store. Some consumer scales would not measure the watermelon at fifteen pounds. What if they had no scales at all? Things would be very confusing. The store would not know how much to charge for the watermelon, and consumers would not know how much to pay.

Everyone having their own scale at the grocers is something like everyone having their own "facts they believe are true." Scientific standards of measurement are like having a standard scale at the grocers. The sciences seek objective, publicly confirmed truth by use of agreed upon standards of measurement. In fact, a great deal of scientific work consists of creating adequate standards by which to measure, understand, and communicate scientific observations. For example, the massive telescopes, the satellites, and the highly technical cameras used by Astronomy have greatly increased its store of known facts.

The use of agreed upon standards of measurement allows science to carry out the process of public confirmation in a rigorous, exact manner. Consequently, the factual component of scientific knowledge is the most objective, most complete knowledge of facts attainable.

Science is the investigation and explanation of facts; over the centuries science has developed methods of observing, standards of measurement, and ways of explaining its ideas that help it achieve far more objective truths about facts than any ordinary observations. Science, which is characterized by logical thinking, observes much more rigorously, adheres more rigidly to its standards, and measures far more exactly its perceptions than does any other way of seeking the truth.

THE FACTUAL COMPONENT OF EVIDENCE: KNOWN FACTS.   In the great majority of cases, facts that people believe on the basis of nonscientific perceptions are not objective enough to be used as evidence. Evidence is a support for a belief, and only known facts are capable of objective support. Of course, some beliefs (especially religious feelings and feelings about moral values) are unsupported by any known facts. However, sometimes nonscientific perceptions, "subjective ideas about facts," are claimed to support religious or moral beliefs. The *factual component* of evidence for the beliefs is very weak. However, that does not mean that the *evidence* for them is weak. Religious and moral beliefs do not rely on the factual component of evidence as much as they do on the theoretical and emotional components.

It is very common for people to make judgments about human nature on the basis of subjective ideas. However, the social sciences contain a large body of facts about human nature that should not be ignored. Psychology, the most reliable social science, has developed rigorous and exact methods of observing and explaining facts about human beings.

Psychological explanations for human behavior are much more likely to be objectively true than mere casual observations. For example, it is a commonly held subjective idea that alcohol consumption leads to aggressive, sometimes violent behavior. However, the Lang Study used psychological standards of measurement to test this idea and found no known facts to support the premise.[3]

The study used a cocktail of vodka and tonic; it was impossible to taste the vodka. The study used a standard of measurement known as the "double-blind" method of observation. The people measuring the results of the study did not know which of the subjects had been served the cocktail and which had been served tonic water alone. Of the subjects who received the cocktail, half were told they were being served only tonic water, and of those who were served tonic water alone, half were told they had vodka in their drink. Thus, the "double-blind" standard created a controlled observation; no one involved in the study could possibly influence the results consciously or unconsciously. The completed study disclosed that the subjects who were *told* that they had imbibed cocktails responded more aggressively to a provocation than those who had been *told* that they had drunk tonic water only. *The actual content of the drink had no effect whatsoever on the aggression displayed.*

Interestingly enough, the Lang Study may have shown that when people in our society *believe* they are drinking alcohol they feel that they have an excuse

---

3. Lang, A. R., et al. "Effects of Alcohol on Aggression in Male Social Drinkers." *Journal of Abnormal Psychology* 84 (1975): 508–518.

to be more aggressive. At any rate, the study did not confirm the common "subjective idea" that alcohol *causes* aggressive behavior. The known facts acquired by the exact methods of observation and the rigorous standards of measurement used by the science of Psychology disclosed that subjective ideas about the facts of alcohol and aggression are not objectively true.

The factual component of evidence is limited to the known facts accumulated in the sciences and social sciences. The factual component of evidence, however, is not the only component. Evidence has a theoretical component and emotional component as well.

THE THEORETICAL COMPONENT OF EVIDENCE.   As we have seen, a true idea is one that corresponds with perceptions. The factual component of evidence relates to this characteristic of truth. True ideas, however, are also coherent. They imply each other, and cohere in a reasonable way. The theoretical component of evidence is related to the coherence aspect of truth.

Truth is coherent in two ways: true statements that represent ideas cohere with each other, and expressions of emotion cohere with other emotional expressions, or feelings. The theoretical component of evidence is limited to the coherence of statements that represent ideas. Expressive statements and feelings make up the emotional component of evidence.

The theoretical component of evidence consists of *reasonable* support for an idea. The factual component of evidence consists of a *perceptual* support. The theoretical component can be present in two ways, as arguments or as background.

Arguments as the Theoretical Component.   Arguments are the most common examples of the theoretical component. The implication relationship between the premises and the conclusion theoretically supports the conclusion.

For an example of arguments as the theoretical component of evidence, let's take another look at the Lang study on the relationship of alcohol use and aggression. As we know, the study carefully measured its observations with the "double blind" method. No one, including the people passing out the drinks, knew which ones contained alcohol and which did not. Only the researchers, who had carefully set up the observation, knew who had the alcoholic drinks. Some subjects were told that their drinks had alcohol, but in reality, they had none. Other subjects were told they did not have alcohol, but they did. Some were told the truth about their drinks. All of the subjects were then subjected to a series of events that the researchers felt could elicit aggressive responses.

As we know, several known facts resulted from the researchers' observations. All of the subjects who had been told that they had alcohol, including those who actually did not have any, reacted more aggressively than the others. The subjects who had alcoholic drinks, but who had been told they did not, and those who had been told truthfully that they had no alcohol in their drinks equally acted with the same lack of aggression. The exact, rigorous scientific observations resulted in several representative statements of known facts.

However, what do these known facts *mean*? How are they to be interpreted? The conclusions of the Lang observations are (1) that alcohol does not play a significant role in aggression, and (2) that the social expectation that alcohol use causes aggression does play a significant role in aggression. These conclusions are not themselves known facts; they are theoretical inferences from known facts.

The theoretical component of the Lang study is as important to the study as the factual component. Known facts do not mean anything unless they are theoretically related to a conclusion. The theoretical component of the Lang study consists of at least five arguments. The first claims:

> The subjects did not know whether they were actually drinking alcohol. What a person does not know cannot influence his or her expectations. Therefore, the results of the study are not influenced by the subjects' own expectations based on their actual knowledge of their consumption or lack of consumption of alcohol.

The second argument claims:

> All of the subjects who believed that they had alcoholic drinks behaved aggressively; those who actually had no alcohol acted as aggressively as those who had alcohol. Therefore, believing that they had alcoholic drinks was the cause of their aggressive behavior, not the alcohol itself.

The third argument:

> The subjects who believed they had alcoholic drinks acted aggressively when they had no alcohol. Those who had alcoholic drinks but believed that they did not also acted aggressively. Therefore, the subjects' behavior could not possibly have resulted from a physiological cause.

The fourth argument:

> All behaviors have either a physiological or a psychological cause. The subjects' behavior did not result from a physiological cause. Therefore it resulted from a psychological cause.

The final argument:

> Aggressive behavior can be psychologically caused either by internal personal factors, or external social factors. The subjects had no knowledge, so internal factors could not have caused their aggression. The subjects share the same external social factors. Therefore, their aggressive behavior was psychological caused by external social factors.

The final conclusion of the Lang study is theoretically implied by the known facts gathered by scientific observations and by the conclusions of the other arguments. However, notice the first premise of the fourth argument:

> All behaviors have either a physiological or a psychological cause.

This premise is not a known fact, and it is not implied by the observations of the Lang study. It is a theoretical assumption. Most psychologists agree with it. They accept the theory that all human behaviors are the result of something in a person's physiology (the body) or psychology (the mind). They do not accept the theory that supernatural forces cause human behavior. For example, in the past, many people believed that the behavior of witches was not caused physiologically or psychologically, but by evil spirits. The science of psychology, after years of study, has rejected the supernatural theory. It is now believed that witches' behavior (as well as the behavior of those who labeled them as witches in the first place) was caused by psychological or physiological factors.

Science uses the theoretical component as much as it does the factual component. Science is much more interested in explaining known facts than in investigating them. In the very early days of science, factual knowledge was so important that it absorbed most scientific efforts. Of course, the search for known facts continues. However, science today is much more concerned with finding theoretical explanations for known facts than with simply accumulating "discoveries." The sciences possess a huge amount of known facts; understanding what they mean is the current scientific challenge.

The theoretical component is present in all evidence: that is, every support for a belief has an element of *reason* or *implication*. Evidence is not limited to known facts. Those facts must be clearly described and organized into arguments. Otherwise, no conclusions can be inferred from them. Scientific studies would be meaningless lists of known facts without the theoretical component.

Background as the Theoretical Component. The theoretical component of evidence is not limited to arguments and the explanation of known facts. It also provides "background," or direction to scientific study. For example, the results of the Lang study led many psychologists to question whether the amount of alcohol consumed is an important factor in aggression. The subjects in the Lang study had been given only the equivalent of one drink. Psychologists reasoned that if alcohol in small amounts is not a physiological cause of aggression, perhaps larger amounts are. Theoretically, it seemed reasonable to believe that a larger amount of alcohol would affect the physiology of the subjects more than a small amount, and, in turn, this would affect their behavior more. Psychologists devised a method of measuring the behavior of people after they had imbibed larger and larger amounts of alcohol. Of course, their study resulted in some known facts. Higher amounts of alcohol did not result in more aggression than lower amounts. Aggression did not occur at all unless the subject was provoked.[4] The Lang study provided a theoretical background for the new study. Part of the evidence for the new study's conclusions about aggression and alcohol is provided by the theoretical conclusions of the Lang study. Whenever conclusions from other studies are assumed they are referred to as "background assumptions." The theoretical component of evidence often consists of background assumptions.

New psychological research on the relationship between alcohol and aggression will be supported by the background theoretical component supplied

---

4. Taylor, S. P. and Sears, J. D. "The Effects of Alcohol and Persuasive Social Pressure on Human Physical Aggression," *Aggressive Behavior* 14 (1988).

by both studies. As science progresses, past studies become theoretical background evidence for new ones.

The theoretical component of evidence is not limited to science. Evidence for religious, moral, and political beliefs, as well as beliefs about art and other values, also has a theoretical component. Beliefs about values, however, are also supported by evidence that has a large emotional component.

THE EMOTIONAL COMPONENT OF EVIDENCE.   Values have a central role in our lives; moral, religious, political, and aesthetic values give us direction and meaning. Values are feelings about the importance of individuals, things, and events. Facts and theories do not primarily support values. They have a factual and theoretical aspect, but are mainly beliefs about feelings.

For example, let's assume that it is a known fact that Bill stole fifty dollars from the college bookstore. Theoretically, anyone who steals money is guilty of theft. Therefore, Bill is guilty of theft. The facts are known, and the theory is reasonable. Nevertheless, the question remains: Did Bill do something wrong?

Right and wrong are not facts, although the things people do that are right or wrong are facts. There is a factual component, then, to beliefs about values. If, for example, it was discovered that Bill really did not steal the money, then he didn't do anything wrong. However, even though he did steal the money, he *may* still not have done anything wrong. It depends on how we feel about what he did.

Right and wrong are not primarily theoretical beliefs, but the conclusions we come to about whether something is right or wrong are supported, in part, by a theoretical component. For example, if we believe stealing is wrong, and that Bill stole the money, then it stands to reason that what Bill did is wrong.

The belief that Bill did something wrong when he stole the fifty dollars requires evidence. Known facts and good reasoning are components of the evidence, but in the final analysis, once we have gathered the known facts and once we have a reasonable argument, the decision concerning the right or wrong of what he did is also supported by *feelings.*

For example, suppose Bill stole the money from the bookstore in order to purchase medicine for his sick mother. The facts are known: Bill stole fifty dollars from the college bookstore. The argument is reasonable: Anyone who steals is guilty of theft, consequently Bill is guilty of theft. But was his theft of fifty dollars from the bookstore *wrong*? Ted feels that it is wrong. He feels that "stealing is always wrong, whatever the motive." Anna feels that it isn't; "stealing in order to purchase medicine for his mother is theft, but it is not wrong."

Both Ted and Anna support their moral beliefs with evidence that has factual and theoretical components. They agree on the known facts. Their theories differ, but both are reasonable. The major difference between their moral beliefs is how they *feel* about what happened. Their feelings are the emotional component of the evidence they offer to support their beliefs. For example, Ted may feel that moral values are rigid laws, and that right and wrong are the same for everyone. He has evidence for this belief. He can refer to several known facts and he can present some reasonable arguments in its support. Anna, too, has factual and theoretical evidence for her belief that moral values are not rigid laws, but flexible rules. Nevertheless, they cannot agree on the moral value of Bill's theft.

The emotional component of evidence, such as the emotional component of truth, can be coherent in two ways, subjectively and objectively. A subjective coherence is present when there is a consistency of feeling. For example, if Anna feels that Bill's theft is not wrong, but that another person in exactly the same situation is wrong, then her feelings are not subjectively coherent. For example, Ted asks her, "What if Bill had stolen the money from you? Would you still believe that what he did was not wrong?" Anna replies that her belief would not change. This shows that the emotional component of her evidence is subjectively coherent.

If Ted points out to Anna that very few people feel the way she does, he is questioning whether her belief is objectively coherent. Let's assume that Ted's point is factually accurate; most people in their society do not feel the way Anna does. In this case, Anna's feelings are not objectively coherent. Her feelings are not shared.

Of course, this does not mean that Anna's moral feeling about Bill is "incorrect" or "improper." Her feelings are her own; they cannot be incorrect or improper. However, they are not publicly confirmed. As such, Anna has to recognize that the evidence for her belief about the moral value of Bill's theft does not have a *strong* emotional component.[5]

Anna can do several things about this lack of public confirmation of her feeling. She can explain the factual and theoretical components of her evidence more clearly. She can also communicate the emotional component more effectively. Of course, feelings are not communicated scientifically. The exact, rigid, and rigorous logical thinking of science is not an effective way to communicate how we feel. The character "Mr. Spock" on *Star Trek* tried to do that, and always failed. ("Well, Captain, my temperature is rising, and I believe I detect an increase in my heartbeat. Is that what you call an 'emotion?' ")

Emotions are best communicated in expressive language. Anna might give an impassioned speech or she might write a song or a poem that she can share with others. Perhaps she could produce a film, a video, or a play or she could write an essay or a letter to the editor of the paper that expressed her feelings. Of course, in all of these she would also include the factual and theoretical components of the evidence that supports her belief that Bill did nothing wrong. However, if she is to achieve public confirmation of her feelings, she needs to communicate them in expressive language.

Arguments, it will be recalled, often conclude with directive statements that instruct us to do something, think something, or to feel a particular way. Often an expressive statement will be offered in its support. As long as an empathetic understanding of the expressive statement shows it to be relevant, it is regarded as an emotional component of the evidence for the conclusion. Of course, if it is not relevant it is a fallacy of irrelevant emotion. Arguments about values always direct us to accept the values expressed in the argument. They also want us to change our feelings, and change our values.

---

5. Although Anna may personally feel "very strongly" about her belief, the lack of public confirmation of her feelings means that her belief's emotional component is not strong.

Sometimes we feel that anyone who wants to change our values is attempting to manipulate us. Most people think of values as "personal." They sometimes resist expressing them, and resent those who want to change them. Moral, religious, and political values are highly emotional, and it is very understandable that people feel very strongly about them. There is little doubt that most disputes, most fights, and even most wars are started over values. In some cultures, men are regarded as "good" only if they blindly accept the values of their fathers, and women are regarded as "good" only if they accept traditional female roles.

Traditional values are, for some people, a secure haven from the confusion that comes from living in a diverse world. They feel very strongly about them and have a great desire to "hang on" to those values. On the other hand, we need to recognize that traditional values, like all values, are primarily supported by feelings. For some, the feeling of security supports their trust in traditional values. For others, however, traditional values are not a source of security, but of being smothered, even crushed. There is nothing inherently right or wrong about traditional values. Whether one chooses to accept values for the security they can provide, or for the freedom they can allow, is often a matter of personal emotion and feeling. Disputes, fights, and wars do not solve the conflict between traditional and new values. All three simply increase the emotions of those who participate.

Rather than engage in heated disputes about values, we need to express them, empathetically attempt to understand them, and seek public confirmation for them. Critical thinking plays a very important role in this process. Our values can be reviewed, evaluated, and revised. We increase our knowledge of known facts by seeking public confirmation of our ideas. We become more reasonable by seeking public confirmation of our theoretical ideas. We can also develop our values by thinking critically about them.

Identifying the Components of Evidence. When attempting to identify the components of evidence in an argument or written piece, it is best to review the types of statements.

Representative statements describe the factual component. For example, "Seven people boarded the bus at five o'clock," is a statement that claims to represent a known fact.

The theoretical component can be in representative or expressive language. Statements that refer to conclusions from arguments often represent theoretical ideas: "The people on the bus must all work at Zip's restaurant, since they all are wearing the Zip uniform." Statements or expressions inferred by narratives, such as films, works of fiction, philosophical beliefs, or written pieces can also represent theoretical beliefs. "According to Plato, everyone seeks the truth individually, so the people on the bus are all searching for truth in their own ways."

The emotional component is always in expressive language: "I think Zip's is a good place to eat; I love the uniforms they wear there."

EXERCISES

▲ MOST INTRIGUING ISSUE

Write a one-paragraph description of the most interesting idea, topic, or process described in pages 229–239. Be prepared to explain what you find interesting in class discussion.

▲ THE MUDDIEST POINT

Write a sentence or, if possible, a paragraph that describes the idea, topic, expression, term, or process in pages 229–239 that you find most difficult to understand.

▲ CARTOONS AND DIAGRAMS

1. Provide a diagram that shows the relationship between strong and weak evidence with complete and partial truths.
2. Provide a cartoon that shows the relationship between facts, known facts, and public confirmation.
3. Provide a cartoon that illustrates the factual component of evidence.
4. Provide a cartoon that shows the theoretical component of evidence.
5. Provide a cartoon that illustrates the emotional component of evidence.
6. Provide a diagram that illustrates the relationship of each component of evidence to the type of language used to represent or express it.
7. Provide a diagram that clearly and specifically illustrates how large or small each component of evidence is in the Lang study.
8. Provide a diagram that clearly and specifically shows how large or small each component of evidence is in Anna's moral belief that Bill did nothing wrong.

▲ DEFINITIONS OF KEY TERMS

Provide a disciplinary definition for each of the following terms as they are used in this chapter. Most of the terms are not defined in the chapter, although their meanings are described by the context in which they appear. You need to review the material to create the definition yourself. Be sure to follow the guidelines for creating definitions on pages 78–81.

Truth	Evidence	Component of Evidence
Fact	Known Fact	Standard of Measurement
Factual Component	Theoretical Component	Emotional Component

▲ SHORT ESSAY QUESTIONS

Provide a written response of approximately 200 words for each topic. Your responses should be well organized, grammatically correct, and neatly produced.

1. Explain the relationship between publicly confirmed statements and strong evidence.
2. Explain: "A known fact, but not a fact, must be publicly confirmed."
3. Is it possible to know a fact without using a standard of measurement? Why or why not?
4. Explain why the "double-blind" used in the Lang study is a standard of measurement.
5. Explain why the theoretical component of evidence, while usually made up of arguments, is not limited to them.
6. Explain: "The factual component of evidence is made up only of known facts. A known fact is a publicly confirmed, objectively correspondent perception."
7. Identify the components of evidence in each of the following simple arguments. Consider hidden premises, too.
   a) It is always wrong to steal because stealing hurts people financially.
   b) The planet Mars, depending on the time of year, is approximately 35 to 53 million miles from earth. Therefore, it is much closer to us than the sun, which is about 93 million miles away.
   c) The same thing that causes most human misery caused the Great Depression: greed.
   d) Molasses is not a natural food; it is a residue left over from the heating and refining of sugar.
   e) Maple syrup is a natural food; it is obtained directly from the black maple tree.
   f) A fraud is a willful misrepresentation intended to deprive someone of a right. Jones, when he lied about his student status in purchasing a ticket, defrauded the theater.
   g) When Jones defrauded the theater, he did nothing wrong, since everybody lies sometimes.
   h) The film *Rashomon* is a classic; it has all the elements necessary. It has masterful editing, excellent lighting, magnificent acting, and Kurosawa's camera work is subtle, but direct.
   i) The popularity of a candidate is not a good indicator of whether or not the candidate is a good one. Therefore, although the great majority of people voted for Madeline Garrote, she may not be the best candidate for the position.
   j) Anyone who votes in the American presidential elections has the equivalent of two votes, because fewer than fifty percent of eligible voters go to the polls.
   k) More people should vote; in a country where less than fifty percent vote in presidential elections, fewer than twenty-five percent of the voters elect the president. That's a scandal.
   l) The results of the Lang study support my claim that the alcohol I imbibed last night had nothing to do with my aggressive behavior.
   m) Forty percent of the assaults in this country happen between the months of June and September. The hot weather must make people act in evil ways!
   n) Good and bad behavior is a choice people make in their own minds. It has nothing to do with the weather. Anyone who blames the weather for their bad behavior needs a lesson in ethics!

o) Since there is great security in the feeling that one is cared for, people who are in love are often exhilarated. It follows that the world seems to be a happy place to a person who's falling in love.

p) What a rare mood I'm in! I've got the world on a string; it's almost like being in love!

▲ QUESTIONS FOR DISCUSSION

Provide an essay of 300–500 words that responds to each of the following questions which ask for your opinion. You should respond by stating it, and by providing thoughts, examples, and insights that support it. You should be willing to revise your response; you may change your opinion during or after a class discussion.

1. The chapter claims that without a standard of measurement it is impossible to acquire a known fact. Review a science or social science course you are currently taking, or one you have taken, for some standards of measurement used in the discipline. How do these standards help with the definition and description of known facts?

2. The theoretical component of evidence is made up of arguments and background. The chapter discusses some of the Lang study's arguments, and goes on to describe how the Lang study has become background for other studies. However, the chapter does not discuss any background assumptions of the Lang study itself. What do you find to be some of the Lang study's background assumptions?

3. There is a great deal of discussion about political values in our democratic society. The chapter claims that there is a large emotional component in evidence for political values. But how about the factual and theoretical components? Shouldn't we expect political discussions to also include them?

4. Engage in a discussion with several of your colleagues in class on the question, "Does God exist?" Each person needs to respond "yes," "no," or "I don't know," and provide evidence that supports his or her response. Write down the support statements. What are the components of evidence raised in support of the beliefs that come up?

5. Engage in a discussion with several of your colleagues in class on the question, "Is capital punishment wrong?" Each person needs to respond "yes," "no," or "I don't know," and provide evidence that supports his or her response. Write down the support statements. What are the components of evidence raised in support of the beliefs that come up?

6. Engage in a discussion with several of your colleagues in class on the question, "Are grades important?" Each person needs to respond "yes," "no," or "I don't know," and provide evidence that supports his or her response. Write down the support statements. What are the components of evidence raised in support of the beliefs that come up?

7. Engage in a discussion with several of your colleagues in class on the question, "Is soccer more popular than football in America?" Each person needs to respond "yes," "no," or "I don't know," and provide evidence that supports his or her response. Write down the support statements. What are the components of evidence raised in support of the beliefs that come up?

8. Engage in a discussion with several of your colleagues in class on the question, "Are one-parent families harmful to children?" Each person needs to respond "yes," "no," or "I don't know," and provide evidence that supports his or her response.

Write down the support statements. What are the components of evidence raised in support of the beliefs that come up?

    9. Engage in a discussion with several of your colleagues in class on the question, "Should marijuana be legalized?" Each person needs to respond "yes," "no," or "I don't know," and provide evidence that supports his or her response. Write down the support statements. What are the components of evidence raised in support of the beliefs that come up?

    10. Engage in a discussion with several of your colleagues in class on the question, "Is racism a serious problem in America?" Each person needs to respond "yes," "no," or "I don't know," and provide evidence that supports his or her response. Write down the support statements. What are the components of evidence raised in support of the beliefs that come up?

▲ QUOTATION TO PONDER

"The heart has its reasons, of which reason knows nothing."
Blaise Pascal, *Thoughts,* 1670

▲ JOURNAL TOPIC

Review the discussion on UFOs you wrote about in the last section. What components of evidence does it offer?

THE TYPES OF EVIDENCE

There are four types of evidence: experimental, observational, testimonial, and anecdotal. Each type has factual, theoretical, and emotional components. Experimental evidence is almost exclusively factual and theoretical. Observational evidence is largely factual and theoretical, with very little emotion. Testimonial evidence has varying amounts of each component. Anecdotal evidence is largely emotional, with varying degrees of factual and theoretical components.

    The type of evidence is identified by the specific manner in which it is publicly confirmed. Public confirmation, as we have studied, involves objective correspondence and coherence. We will briefly examine each type of evidence and its manner of public confirmation.

EXPERIMENTAL EVIDENCE

Experimental evidence is the type of evidence found in natural science: Physics, Chemistry, Astronomy, Paleontology, Geology, Oceanography, Meteorology, Biology and Medicine. Each of these sciences has subdivisions. For example, Botany and Zoology are subdivisions of Biology. Sciences are also combined; for example Astrophysics is a combination of Astronomy and Physics. Geochemistry is a combination of Geology and Chemistry.

Experimental evidence is publicly confirmed in two ways. Objective and internal coherence is achieved by adhering to conventionally accepted standards of measurement and trustworthy arguments. Objective correspondence is achieved by *repeated confirmations.*

Natural science confirms that its ideas objectively correspond to perceptions by rigorously testing in the controlled environment of the laboratory. Other scientists test and retest these ideas in other laboratories under various conditions before they are accepted as objective truths. These repeated confirmations are the central feature of experimental evidence. Natural science constantly reviews, evaluates, and revises its ideas, eventually achieving virtually complete objective correspondence of its ideas with its carefully measured perceptions.

Each science achieves internal (subjective) and objective coherence by using clearly defined standards of measurement and pure logic.

The standards of measurement used to gather experimental evidence are more exact than those used by any other type of evidence. The arguments it uses are the most rigid of any type of evidence: In coming to its conclusions science makes use of mathematical calculations as well as pure logic. Each science demands that all of its new ideas cohere with what it already knows as well as with old and new ideas established by other sciences.

There is no more complete truth than that established by experimental evidence. The rigorous and repeated confirmations, exact standards of measurement, and adherence to the rigid methodology of pure logic and mathematics allow the factual and theoretical components of experimental evidence to be accepted as the strongest available. However, there is virtually no emotional component in experimental evidence. We will discuss this weakness.

OBSERVATIONAL EVIDENCE

Observational evidence is based on careful study of human behavior under *controlled conditions.* Observational evidence supports the ideas of the social sciences such as Anthropology, Economics, History, Political Science, Psychology, and Sociology.

Observational evidence is publicly confirmed in two ways. Repeated, controlled conditions of observation provide objective confirmation of the factual component. Observations by different researchers are repeated with different subjects. This is similar to the repeated testing used by the sciences.

The social sciences observe human behavior under the most rigorously controlled conditions possible. There are three levels of controlled observation: completely controlled, partially controlled, and noncontrolled. In a completely controlled observation something is purposefully provided to a limited group of subjects, but not to another group. Both groups are placed in identically controlled environments. Careful measurements are made of the differences in behavior between the two groups.[6] Complete control over observation, while always

---

6. The Lang study was a completely controlled observation.

desirable, is not always possible, due to impracticality or ethical restraints. Social scientists must often settle for partial and noncontrolled observations.

In a partially controlled observation, either the environment is not completely controlled, or there is only one observed group. In a noncontrolled observation, social scientists control nothing; they carefully measure and record behaviors of people in their own "natural" environment.

The theoretical component of observational evidence is publicly confirmed by the use of accepted standards of measurement. Observations are often quantified, that is, put into mathematical (usually statistical) terms. Each social science also has nonmathematical accepted standards of measurement. For example, historians have standards by which they distinguish reliable from unreliable documents.

There is an emotional component in observational evidence, but social scientists attempt to limit their personal involvement as much as possible. They do this by limiting their conclusions to what the theoretical and factual components of evidence allow.

ANECDOTAL EVIDENCE

Anecdotal evidence consists of an individual's personal accounts of his or her experience. This type of evidence is represented and expressed in fictional works, autobiographies, films, diaries, and in ordinary conversations about personal experiences. It may seem odd to think of a personal experience or a film as "evidence." However, when we want support for what we should believe in, feel, and do in our personal lives, we often turn to these sources.

Children's stories often provide evidence for beliefs about one's inner strength ("Cinderella"), in staying close to home ("Hansel and Gretel"), and in recognizing the beauty of nature ("Heidi"). Adults also tell stories; movies, short stories, plays, and novels often provide support for moral and social values. Anecdotes have factual and theoretical components but mostly consist of expressions of feeling.

The anecdotal evidence of the personal remembrance is of immense value in communicating the feelings and ideas of individual people. The stories told by African American slaves contain as much, if not more, evidence about the nature of American slave life than the social sciences. The personal account of the individual who *lived* the life of a slave can be more enlightening than the observations of historians who have had no intimate experience with slavery themselves.

Public confirmation of the factual component of anecdotal evidence can be achieved by objective correspondence with the perceptions of other individuals as well as with those of the natural and social sciences. The theoretical component is publicly confirmed by objective coherence with other individuals' beliefs and by the conclusions of the sciences.

An anecdote's emotional component is publicly confirmed as objective when people experience similar feelings about it. People rarely, if ever, have the same exact feelings about an anecdote. For that reason, objective correspondence or coherence of anecdotal evidence almost never takes place.

TESTIMONIAL EVIDENCE

Testimonial evidence should not be confused with anecdotal evidence. Testimonial evidence, in comparison with anecdotal evidence, is the evidence given by someone who is an appropriate *authority*. The credentials and experience of the authority publicly confirm testimonial evidence.

Authorities in the sciences and social sciences often offer experimental and observational conclusions without providing details of the evidence that support them. In a similar way, social critics and philosophers offer testimonial evidence in support of moral and political beliefs.

Credentials or experience objectively confirm an authority's expertise. Academic credentials from publicly accredited institutions, such as advanced degrees ("Masters of Science," "Masters of Arts," or "Doctoral" degrees) certify that the person has undergone periods of intensive study and research in the area in which the degree has been awarded. Professional institutions certify authorities who have passed examinations; optometrists, dentists, medical doctors, nurses, accountants, and attorneys have not only completed appropriate academic degrees but have also passed examinations that demonstrate their expertise.

Some authorities are not certified, but have enough experience in an area to be acknowledged experts. For example, a representative to the state legislature may have no certification in the area of environmental studies. Still, her years of experience in studying the ecological characteristics of her region, along with the dozens of environmental committees with which she has participated over the years, may very well qualify her as an "authority" in regional environmental issues.

Evaluating Evidence: Strengths and Weaknesses. Evidence is simply a statement or a belief that is offered in support of an idea or feeling. The strongest evidence is that which is publicly confirmed as objectively true. As we discussed earlier in this chapter, truths are always partial, and never complete. In the same way, evidence always comes in relative degrees of strength and weakness. The more objective, complete, and publicly confirmed the evidence, the stronger it is. Weak evidence is subjective, partial, and has little or no public confirmation. There is not a "black and white" difference between strong and weak evidence. *The strength or weakness of evidence is relative to its amount of public confirmation.* The more public confirmation, the stronger the evidence: the less public confirmation, the weaker the evidence. Let's look at a simple example:

> The sun rotates around the earth. The evidence for this is that my six-year-old sister told me it was true.

We know that there is no publicly confirmed experimental evidence in Astronomy that supports the example's conclusion. In fact, according to Astronomy, the conclusion is false. The six-year-old is not an authority on this subject. Thus, the example's evidence is extremely weak for two reasons. It is contradicted by publicly confirmed evidence from Astronomy, and its testimonial evidence does not come from an appropriate authority.

In order to simplify the task of evaluating evidence, we will examine the strengths and weaknesses of each type of evidence in relation to its components.

EXPERIMENTAL EVIDENCE: STRENGTHS AND WEAKNESSES. The factual and theoretical components of properly conducted experimental evidence are always extremely strong. Repeated experimentation and rigorous reasoning are required before the natural sciences give public confirmation to an idea. This means that experimental evidence provides the most complete truths available.

The emotional component of experimental evidence is very weak. We cannot rely on evidence from the natural sciences to support our feelings about values. There is no emotional public confirmation for scientific ideas; in fact, scientific ideas are virtually without emotion. The only emotional component in experimental evidence is the feeling of certitude that comes with it. Of course, scientists are often very emotionally involved in the subjects they study. Astronomers often love the heavens. Physicists enjoy the beautiful symmetry their subject matter exhibits. However, the great strength of the factual and theoretical components of scientific evidence comes at the price of ignoring personal feelings.

Thus, experimental evidence is strong when it supports ideas about facts and theories, but weak when it is used to support beliefs about values.

OBSERVATIONAL EVIDENCE: STRENGTHS AND WEAKNESSES. Human beings share many behaviors; there are many ways we are alike. Sociology, Economics, History, and especially Psychology strive to point out these similarities.

The factual component of observational evidence is very strong, due to the social science's methods of observation. However, even if a completely controlled observation results in a high degree of public confirmation of the factual component, this does not mean that theoretical conclusions inferred by it are equally strong. Human beings are unique; individuals who were not observed do not always behave the same as those who were. Studies are never repeated exactly because each study must observe different subjects. Some observations are impossible to carry out due to ethical considerations. Public confirmation in the social sciences is never as strong as in the natural sciences.

However, the social sciences have a great advantage over the natural sciences in one way; they obtain the strongest evidence we can possibly achieve about the *behavior of human beings.* Most of our practical concerns don't have anything to do with the objects and animals studied by natural science; they have to do with *people.*

Observational evidence from the social sciences provides much more objective support for ideas about human behavior than casual "people watching" or anecdotal evidence. Generally, the more public confirmation that the factual component of an observation has attained, the stronger are its theoretical conclusions. Thus, the strongest evidence we have about human beings comes from the social sciences.

ANECDOTAL EVIDENCE: STRENGTHS AND WEAKNESSES.   Anecdotal evidence is the support we provide for each other in achieving an understanding of what is most meaningful and valuable in our lives. Objectively confirmed anecdotal evidence is extremely strong in supporting personal decisions about values. It supports our beliefs about the worth of our ideals, our feelings, and our dreams. When we recognize that others share the values, feelings, goals, and dreams that mean so much to us, evidence for our beliefs becomes stronger. For example, organized religions provide anecdotal support for believers. So do political parties, activist organizations (The Sierra Club, People for the Ethical Treatment of Animals, Salvation Army) and "societies" that support artistic endeavors.

Anecdotal evidence supports our choice in many incidental ways. We choose not to smoke because we personally know a relative who is ill with emphysema. We don't use cocaine or alcohol because we have heard how adversely such drugs affected a professional athlete's career. We purchase a car because the people we work with all have a similar model and they tell us it's "a car to die for."

Of course, these decisions are even stronger when they are also supported by experimental and observational components from other types of evidence. For example, we may choose not to smoke cigarettes because of the strong experimental evidence that links smoking to an early death. We may decide to avoid use of recreational drugs because of the observational evidence that such drugs impair memory and ability to concentrate. Safety and performance records support our choice on the car purchase.

Anecdotal evidence that *only* has subjective emotional coherence is very weak. Even if there is no experimental or objective evidence for an objectively confirmed feeling—as is the case for many religious and moral beliefs—the anecdotal evidence still has a strong *emotional* component. Many people *feel* the *same way*. But the emotional component of an anecdote that is subjective is not *shared*; as a result, it is weak support for a belief.

Anecdotal evidence that is subjective, without any experimental or observational support, is very weak. The weakest anecdotal evidence is not only subjective but is also contradicted by evidence from the sciences. People sometimes base their values and their lifestyles on purely subjective feelings. No one, except a very small circle of confederates, shares their feelings, and scientific and observational evidence contradicts their beliefs. Drug addicts, people engaged in promiscuous sex lives, and others engaged in self-destructive ways of living usually support their values with subjective anecdotes of this type. They reassure each other in conversations and they refer to movies, music, and other anecdotes in seeking support for their beliefs. In a technical sense of the term, it could be said that the small group "objectively confirms" their beliefs. However, there is actually no critical thinking involved, and hence no public confirmation. No one who thinks critically shares their values, and there is also no support from experimental and observational components of other types of evidence.

Testimony. It is important to notice that authority is based on understanding. An authority is someone who *knows about* a subject. Thus the testimony of a theologian is stronger when it comes to support for beliefs about God than that of a meteorologist. A meteorologist has more authority when providing evidence about hurricanes than a theologian.

An authority is usually careful to point out any observational, experimental, or anecdotal evidence that supports his or her claims. It is rare for an appropriate authority to ask us to simply "take my word for it." Being an authority, the person recognizes the importance of providing the best available evidence for his or her beliefs.

The strongest testimonial evidence comes from authorities that are representing or expressing beliefs in their areas of expertise. It is sometimes very difficult to determine where these areas begin and where they stop. For example, Dr. Benjamin Spock, who was an acknowledged authority in Pediatrics, often made claims about moral and political beliefs that had nothing to do with his area of expertise. However, because of his understanding of human nature—he did know *a lot* about children and parents—some people accepted his authority in the areas of ethics and politics. Noam Chomsky, an authority in linguistics, has written several books and many short pieces about politics, especially political propaganda. Although he is not an appropriate authority in the area, many people take his political opinions very seriously. His understanding of language is related to his views on propaganda.

When authorities "wander" into an area in which they have no expertise at all, their beliefs do not provide any testimonial evidence. However, when there is a relation between their expertise and the area into which they have wandered, authorities provide some testimonial evidence. The closer the relation of the two areas, the stronger the testimony.

The strength of testimonial evidence (especially when it comes from a person who is an expert only in a related field) is always increased by experimental, observational, or anecdotal evidence from other sources. Of course, testimonial evidence from an expert in an area that is unrelated to the belief being supported is very weak. The weakest testimonial evidence comes from self-proclaimed "authorities" who literally do not know what they are talking or writing about.

The following diagram may be helpful in sorting out the degrees of strength and weakness in the different types of evidence.

Types of Evidence	Components of Each Type of Evidence	Degree of Strength When Publicly Confirmed
Experimental Evidence	Factual	
	Theoretical	
	Emotional	
Observational Evidence	Factual	
	Theoretical	
	Emotional	
Anecdotal Evidence	Factual	
	Theoretical	
	Emotional	
Testimonial Evidence	Factual	
	Theoretical	
	Emotional	

CONCLUSION

An objectively true belief has a high enough degree of objective correspondence and coherence to be accepted as publicly confirmed. Public confirmation is, as has been pointed out several times, not merely popular acceptance. Confirmation is actually a critical thinking process. The factual and theoretical components of experimental and observational evidence are objectively confirmed because of the rigorous reviews, evaluations, and revisions that the natural and social sciences demand.

For most people, the important questions in life are about values. The sciences provide the strongest theoretical and factual component in support of beliefs about values. However, both are very weak in terms of the emotional component. Only anecdotal evidence has a strong enough emotional component to support the heartfelt religious, moral, and political beliefs that provide direction and meaning to our lives.

However, emotional support cannot support beliefs about values all by itself. Feeling strongly about an issue is important support for one's opinion. Still, an opinion that is also supported by theoretical and factual considerations is much more objective than one that has emotional support alone. Even when the feelings supporting a belief are objectively confirmed, confirmation of the belief's factual and theoretical components is essential.

For example, a large number of racists have publicly confirmed their feelings about the inferiority of particular groups of people. The Ku Klux Klan, the

Aryan Nation, and other "white supremacist" groups refer to themselves as "religions." Their members meet regularly to objectively confirm that they all feel the same way about "inferiors." However, these "religions" have no objective confirmation of factual or theoretical components that support their beliefs. They only have emotional support. Consequently, it cannot be said that their *beliefs* are publicly confirmed. It is true that there is as much emotional support for these racist organizations as there is for many religious, moral, and political beliefs. However, support for these beliefs is not simply a matter of feeling. Facts and theories are required for support of beliefs about values.

We should think critically about values. Merely accepting them because we "feel good" about them is not enough. We need to go beyond our feelings and investigate the theoretical and factual components that support our beliefs. In order to do this, we need to be informed about the evidence provided to us by the sciences. For example, "white supremacy" has no support from natural or social science. On the contrary, Biology shows that a large, diverse "genetic pool" is much more capable of surviving and prospering in the world than a so-called "pure" pool limited to those with similar characteristics. History confirms that societies that attempted to isolate themselves from those who are "different" quickly become incapable of solving their own problems. Sociology and Psychology provide publicly confirmed evidence that racism is a learned behavior. Children have to be taught to hate people "who are different"; racism is not a "natural" reaction.

People have differences; our skin tones, our languages, our ethnicity, our genders, our abilities and personalities are individual characteristics. We share some of these characteristics with others. They are "like us" in these ways. Factual and theoretical evidence from the sciences supports pride in these characteristics. It makes sense that we would be interested in them. We may even form clubs and associations based on these shared characteristics.

On the other hand, some people have characteristics with which we are not familiar, and which we simply do not share. For example, a man with white skin who speaks Portuguese does not share the gender, skin tone, and language of a woman who has black skin and speaks Swahili. Does this mean that they cannot be interested in each other's ethnic heritage? Does it mean that they cannot appreciate each other's differences? Does it mean that they cannot accept, even love each other? Of course not. History, Sociology, and Psychology confirm that people, no matter their differences, often accept, appreciate, and love one another.

There is much more publicly confirmed evidence for belief in the values of acceptance, tolerance, and love of others than there is for racists' beliefs in segregation, bigotry, and hatred.

It is very popular to avoid criticism of values with which we disagree. We allow everyone to "do his or her own thing." How much of this popular attitude is based on a belief in tolerance, and how much is simply lethargy, fear, and ignorance? Most people are not aware that the factual and theoretical components of evidence are important support for beliefs about values. It is popularly assumed that however a person feels about them is all the support they can have.

It seems that critical thinkers have a responsibility to speak up. We need to engage in a public conversation about values and point out that all three components of evidence play roles in supporting them. We will investigate this responsibility of critical thinkers (as well as others) in Chapter 10.

Chapter 9 summarizes the main ideas we have covered in Chapters 2 through 8 and organizes them into a format that will allow a methodical review, evaluation, and revision of written pieces.

EXERCISES

▲ MOST INTRIGUING ISSUE

Write a one-paragraph description of the most interesting idea, topic, or process described in pages 243–252. Be prepared to explain what you find interesting in class discussion.

▲ THE MUDDIEST POINT

Write a sentence or, if possible, a paragraph that describes the idea, topic, expression, term, or process in pages 243–252 that you find most difficult to understand.

▲ CARTOONS AND DIAGRAMS

1. Provide a cartoon that illustrates the degrees of strength of experimental evidence.
2. Provide a cartoon that illustrates the degrees of strength of observational evidence.
3. Provide a cartoon that illustrates the degrees of strength of anecdotal evidence.
4. Provide a diagram that illustrates how the degree of strength of testimonial evidence is determined.
5. Provide a cartoon that shows how experimental evidence is publicly confirmed.
6. Provide a cartoon that shows how observational evidence is publicly confirmed.
7. Provide a cartoon that shows how anecdotal evidence is publicly confirmed.
8. Draw a cartoon that illustrates the difference in how experimental and observational evidence is gathered.
9. Draw a cartoon that illustrates three different ways anecdotal evidence is obtained.
10. Provide an illustration that shows the relationship of the fallacy of inappropriate authority to testimonial evidence.

▲ DEFINITIONS OF KEY TERMS

Provide a disciplinary definition for each of the following terms as they are used in this chapter. Most of the terms are not defined in the chapter, although their meanings are described by the context in which they appear. You need to review the material to create the definition yourself. Be sure to follow the guidelines for creating definitions on pages 78–81.

Observational Evidence   Anecdotal Evidence

Testimonial Evidence   Strong Evidence

▲ SHORT ESSAY QUESTIONS

Provide a written response of approximately 100 words to each topic. Your responses should be well organized, grammatically correct, and neatly produced.

1. Experimental evidence can be obtained from the natural sciences. Which of the natural sciences would be good sources for theoretical and factual components of evidence that support the belief that God does not exist? Be as specific as you can.
2. In addition to the emotional component of evidence that supports belief in the existence of God, in what type of evidence would you seek theoretical and factual support? Be as specific as possible.
3. Are there theoretical and emotional components of support for the belief that vegetarianism is a more moral way of living than eating meat? In what type of evidence would you seek them? Why?
4. Are there factual and theoretical components of support for the belief that vegetarianism is a morally wrong way of living? In what type of evidence would you seek them? Why?
5. What areas of expertise do you feel provide appropriate theoretical and factual components of testimonial support for the belief that abortion is not always immoral? Why?
6. What areas of expertise do you feel provide appropriate theoretical and factual components of testimonial support for the belief that abortion is always immoral? Why?
7. Describe which components of which types of evidence you feel support Thomas Jefferson's belief, "If a nation expects to be ignorant and free, in a state of civilization, it expects what never was and never will be."
8. Describe which components of which types of evidence you feel support Plato's belief, "The direction in which education starts you will determine your future life." (You should research Plato's degree of expertise on the subject in deciding whether or not his evidence is testimonial.)
9. Describe which components of which types of evidence you feel support Rachel Carson's belief, "The 'control of nature' is a phrase conceived in arrogance, born of the Neanderthal age of biology for the convenience of man." (You should research Rachel Carson's reputation among biologists, as well as her credentials.)
10. Describe which components of which types of evidence you feel support Pauline Kael's belief, "The words 'Kiss Kiss Bang Bang,' which I saw on an Italian movie poster, are perhaps the briefest statement imaginable of the basic appeal of movies." (You should research Pauline Kael's reputation and credentials in deciding whether or not her evidence is testimonial.)

▲ QUESTIONS FOR DISCUSSION

Provide an essay of 300–500 words that responds to each of the following questions which ask for your opinion. You should respond by stating it, and by providing thoughts, examples, and insights that support it. You should be willing to revise your response; you may change your opinion during or after a class discussion.

1. The chapter claims, "the strength or weakness of evidence is relative to its amount of public confirmation." Is this true for moral beliefs? Could a person be the only individual in the world that believed that something was morally wrong, and be right about it?

2. At times, it is very difficult to distinguish between testimonial and anecdotal evidence. For example, who would you describe as an appropriate authority on parenting? From whom would you expect strong anecdotal evidence? How would you determine which was which?

3. It is sometimes interesting to reflect on the anecdotal sources of evidence for our own values. For example, what are your feelings about capital punishment? Do you feel it is always wrong? Do you feel it should be limited to particular types of crimes, or limited further to extremely heinous crimes? What anecdotal evidence do you have for your belief? Be as specific as possible.

4. Scientific beliefs, according to the chapter, are supported by virtually no emotional component. Does this in itself mean that scientific beliefs about evolution are supported more strongly than religious beliefs about creation, which are primarily anecdotal?

5. The chapter claims that 'schools of thought' within sciences cohere internally but not objectively with one another. Explain how 'schools of thought' exist, even though each science agrees on its standards of measurement and its manner of public confirmation.

6. An occurrence of a fallacy of inappropriate authority is a good indication that testimonial evidence is weak. What fallacy, or fallacies, do you think are good indications that anecdotal evidence is weak? How about observational evidence?

7. Some organized religions claim that their beliefs have no support: that they are based on 'pure faith.' Are they correct? Is it possible to have a belief about values that has no support at all?

8. Law enforcement officials always examine the scene of a crime for "evidence." They often send objects they have found there to a laboratory for analysis. They then seek even more "evidence" from interviewing witnesses. Once they have apprehended a suspect, they provide "evidence" to the prosecutor. All of this "evidence" is gathered in order to support their belief that the suspect is guilty. Describe the types, as well as the components of each type, of evidence involved in a standard criminal investigation and trial.

9. Civil suits are noncriminal legal actions in which one person claims to have been damaged in some way by another. Imagine that you are the judge in a civil suit in which Deanna is suing Chicken Licken Take-Out. Deanna claims to have contracted salmonella poisoning from eating a chicken dinner purchased at Chicken Licken. Describe the types, as well as the components of each type, of evidence that you, as judge, expect to be presented by both sides in the trial.

10. You are about to purchase a used car from Bobby's Pre-Owned Beauties used car lot. Bobby himself shows you a car that he claims is an excellent buy; one that you will find completely satisfying. Describe the types, as well as the components of each type, of evidence that you will seek in making (or not making) the purchase.

▲ QUOTATION TO PONDER

"Talking the way a storyteller talks means being able to feel and live in the very heart of that culture, means having penetrated its essence, reached the marrow of its history and mythology, given body to its taboos, images, ancestral desires, and terrors."

Mario Vargas Llosa, *The Storyteller: A Novel,* 1989

▲ JOURNAL TOPIC

The chapter mentions that children's stories provide anecdotal evidence for particular values. Specifically, it says, "Children's stories often provide evidence for beliefs about one's inner strength (*Cinderella*), in staying close to home (*Hansel and Gretel*), and in recognizing the beauty of nature (*Heidi*)." Review at least two contemporary television cartoon shows meant for children. What anecdotal evidence is being presented for which values?

▲ PORTFOLIO PAPER

Write a 500-word paper, "The Importance of Evidence in Beliefs." In the paper, describe how truth is both coherent and correspondent with perception. Explain how coherence and correspondence is related to strength and weakness of evidence.

CHAPTER NINE

APPLICATION: THE FORMAT

CRITICAL THINKING IS A COMBINATION OF VERBAL AND LOGICAL THINKING

In order to carry out its task of improving thinking, critical thinking needs to review, evaluate, and revise thinking that has already taken place. We have previously discussed these activities. In this chapter we will combine these activities into a comprehensive organized format.

As we know, critical thinking is primarily verbal and logical. Thus, our format will be composed of the tools of critical thinking (Chapter 3), the elements and organization of arguments (Chapter 5), the types, components, and evaluation of evidence (Chapter 8), the standards of verbal thinking (Chapter 4), and the evaluation of logical thinking (Chapters 6 and 7). These components will be combined in the format, which will provide direction in the review, evaluation, and revision of written pieces.

AFTER STUDYING CHAPTER NINE

You should be able to critically evaluate written pieces by organizing the piece and describing its context. You should be able to apply the seven standards of good thinking by examining the piece for vague or ambiguous terms, and for fallacies. You should be able to examine the types and components of supporting evidence to the conclusion, and evaluate its strengths and weaknesses. You should be able to write a critical evaluation of a piece that clearly communicates your evaluation and suggestions for revision.

The Format will be explained in the next few sections. The chapter will also apply The Format to a relatively lengthy piece of writing. The last section of the chapter will explain how to apply The Format to your own writing process.

THE FORMAT

A format is an organizational pattern that is used to guide a process. Formats help organize complex tasks by setting out steps and guidelines. "The Format" is a specific organizational pattern to be used in applying critical thinking principles to written pieces. The following is the detailed version of the format, which itemizes each specific step. It is followed by "The Mini-Format."

The Format
Review, Evaluation, Revision of Written Pieces
Detailed Version

I. Review: Primary elements of the piece
  A. Identify the context and purpose of the piece
    1. Includes author, source, date, and other relevant circumstances
    2. Purpose is informative, sharing of opinion, or argumentative
  B. Identify and paraphrase (if necessary) the conclusion(s)
  C. Identify and paraphrase (if necessary) the stated support
  D. Identify and paraphrase (if necessary) the hidden support
  E. Identify and describe each statement as representative, expressive, or directive
II. Review: Organization
  A. Arrange the support and conclusion(s) clearly
  B. Identify and list important metaphors, allusions, word choices, and prejudicial expressions
III. Review: Evidence
  A. Identify and describe the types of evidence (stated and hidden)
  B. Identify and describe the components of each type
IV. Evaluation: Cognitive Critical thinking standards
  A. Clarity
    1. Identify and describe any vague or ambiguous terms
    2. Identify and describe any logical or verbal incoherence
    3. Identify and describe fallacies that interfere with clarity
      a) Fallacy of oversimplification
      b) Fallacy of shifting the burden of proof
      c) Fallacy of the straw man
  B. Accuracy
    1. Identify and describe strong evidence by type and component

    2. Identify and describe weak evidence by type and component

    3. Identify and describe any biased claims

    4. Identify and describe any fallacies of inappropriate authority

  C. Specificity

    1. Identify and describe any fallacies of overgeneralization

    2. Identify and describe any fallacies of unwarranted assumption

  D. Significance

    1. Identify and describe any irrelevant statements

    2. Identify any weakness in recognition of the complexity of the subject under discussion

    3. Review for any fallacies that weaken significance

      a) Identify and describe any fallacies of oversimplification

      b) Identify and describe any fallacies of irrelevant emotion

      c) Identify and describe any fallacies of mindless conformity

V. Evaluation: Attitudinal Critical Thinking Standards

  A. Sincerity

    1. Identify metaphors, allusions, word choice, and prejudicial expressions that indicate deliberate distortions of meaning and deliberate deceptions

    2. Identify and describe any deliberate attempts to misrepresent, minimize, or overlook publicly confirmed beliefs

  B. Respect for others

    1. Identify and describe any prejudicial expressions, metaphors, allusions, or choices of words that demean others

    2. Identify and describe any deliberate appeals to inappropriate authority that seem based on shared prejudices

    3. Identify and describe any deliberate attempts to ignore obviously appropriate authorities due to prejudice

    4. Identify and describe any deliberate fallacies of overgeneralization or unwarranted assumption that negatively or positively stereotype individuals

  C. Commitment to consensus

    1. Identify metaphors, allusions, word choice, and prejudicial expressions that indicate a willingness to resort to psychological and/or physical force to support a belief

    2. Identify and describe any deliberate attempts to select and reject testimonial evidence solely on the basis of subjective beliefs

    3. Identify and describe any fallacies of appeal to force based on persuasive definitions

VI. Judgment and critical evaluation

  A. Describe the context and purpose of the piece

  B. Summarize the evaluation in a critical evaluation essay

1. If the piece clearly meets the standards of good thinking, indicate its primary strengths and suggest any minor revisions
2. If the piece meets reasonable expectations, indicate its primary strengths and weaknesses, and suggest revisions
3. If the piece does not meet reasonable expectations, indicate its primary weaknesses, its strengths, and suggest revisions
4. If the piece clearly fails to meet reasonable expectations, indicate its primary weaknesses, any strengths, and suggest any revisions, if possible

THE FORMAT

REVIEW

Context
Author
Source   Date
Purpose

Organization
Conclusion
Support
Hidden Support

EVALUATE

Clarity
Any Vagueness or Ambiguity?

Sincerity
Any Fallacies of
Irrelevant Emotion
Mindless Conformity?

Accuracy
Weak or Strong Evidence?

Respect for Others
Any Fallacies of
Attacking the Person
Inappropriate Authority?
Any Demeaning Expressions?

Specificity
Any Fallacies of
Overgeneralization
Unwarranted Assumption?

Commitment to Consensus
Any Fallacies of
Appeal to Force?
Any Persuasive Definitions?

Significance
Any Fallacies of
Oversimplification
Straw Man
Shifting the Burden of Proof?

EVALUATION ESSAY

JUDGMENTS AND SUGGESTIONS FOR REVISION

The best way to apply the format to a written piece is to go step-by-step through the detailed version. Once you have done that with several pieces, the summary version will remind you of the proper procedure. Keep in mind that your purpose in going through the steps is to arrive at a judgment about the piece's overall quality. The results of the first four steps are summarized in the fifth step, an essay that recommends revisions in the piece.

Step I: Context.   The context of a piece consists of its author's cultural environment, writing style, and purpose. Every piece has at least one author, the person or persons who wrote it. It is important to know something about the author's cultural environment. Is he or she an acknowledged authority on the subject of the piece? Is he or she an authority in a related area? What other pieces on this subject—or on other subjects—has the author written? Does the author have political, moral, or religious convictions that are relevant to the piece?

It is important to know when the piece was written. A recent piece that discusses a timely issue should be read differently than an older piece that does not have the advantage of current information. The general cultural environment of older pieces should be identified. Juvenal's (an ancient Roman) written pieces on political corruption have a much different context than those written by Ellen Goodman (a contemporary American newspaper columnist).

We need to identify the source and style of the piece. Some sources are intended for a general audience, some for a more specialized audience. Newspapers, weekly newsmagazines, and monthly popular magazines are intended for general audiences. Journals limited to specialized professional or academic interests legitimately assume that the reader has a more extensive educational and experiential background than does a general audience. Journals often offer points of view that defend specialized interests. Identifying the source of the piece also provides information about the intended audience. The majority of persuasive or argumentative pieces are about topics that have already been the subject of discussion, especially among the intended audience. The piece may be responding to, or arguing against, a well-known point of view about a topic that has been broadly discussed. The author legitimately assumes that readers are familiar with it.

Written pieces have a purpose. In Chapter 4 we noticed that the five purposes of a written piece parallel the five functions of language: to represent, to direct, to commit, to express, and to perform. In addition, we noticed that each piece has a specific purpose. For example, a representative piece of writing may specifically describe an individual's opinion about pertinent facts in understanding a complex subject.

It is important to keep in mind that a written piece that shares opinions about the *factual or theoretical* components of evidence is representative, while one that shares opinions about moral, political, or religious values supported by the *expressive* component is expressive.

Our format is not meant to provide guidance for dealing with pieces with a purely representative or expressive purpose. It applies only to pieces with a directive purpose; specifically, those that attempt to persuade or those that attempt to convince. The difference between these two specific types of directive pieces lies in the way that the evidence supports its conclusions. Evidence in a persuasive piece is meant to "coax" the reader into an agreement with the conclusion. Coaxing involves sharing a point of view or opinion in order to solicit the reader's agreement. The persuasive piece's purpose is not to demonstrate or prove that the conclusion is the only reasonable conclusion. Rather, it attempts to plant a seed in the reader's mind in the hope that eventually the reader will agree, if only partially, with the conclusion.

Pieces whose purpose is to convince attempt to prove their conclusions by use of arguments. Such pieces are usually referred to as "argumentative pieces." They assert their claims about the truth of their conclusions much more forcefully than persuasive pieces. They claim to demonstrate an implication relationship between the premises and conclusion. They do not merely share an opinion and attempt to persuade us to eventually accept it; they attempt to prove that the conclusion is the only reasonable point of view on the topic. Argumentative pieces "convince" the audience; persuasive pieces "coax."

Argumentative pieces rarely leave room for any disagreement with the conclusion. Persuasive pieces usually contain more qualifying terms in presenting the conclusion than argumentative pieces. Persuasive pieces often make it clear that the conclusion is merely the author's point of view by providing some personal information about the writer in the piece. Argumentative pieces usually make no mention of the author at all.

Step II: Identifying and Organizing the Piece's Elements.   Support, both stated and hidden, should be identified and paraphrased if necessary. It is quite common to paraphrase the elements of written pieces in order to make them more straightforward and clear. Pieces often group two or three elements of support in a single sentence. Sometimes expressive and representative language is mixed together. The conclusion may even be unstated. The writing style of some pieces can make it difficult to clearly label a statement as "representative" or "expressive." Paraphrasing the support and conclusion is very helpful in these cases.

It is not necessary to identify *every* hidden assumption. Keep in mind that there is a difference between assumptions and hidden support. If there are important "gaps" between the conclusion and the stated support, they may be hidden support or merely assumptions. The detection of hidden support should be guided by empathy. If the "gaps" are generally accepted assumptions, there is no need to point them out. If they are not generally accepted, or if they are mistakenly generally accepted, they should be identified. The context and purpose of the piece is of great help in making the distinction between hidden support and assumptions. When in doubt, treat the "gap" as hidden support.

Organization is often time-consuming. However, the attention and time given to organization will help make the effort spent on evaluation more efficient.

We become quite familiar with the piece by identifying and organizing its elements. The identification and listing of metaphors, allusions, word choices, and prejudicial expressions will be helpful in evaluating the quality of evidence and reasoning in the piece. Weak evidence and fallacies are often detected in identifying and listing these terms.

The great majority of pieces in newspapers and magazines as well as television and radio scripts are persuasive. Argumentative pieces more often appear in professional and academic journals. Courtroom proceedings are also argumentative.

Step III: Evidence. The types of evidence, as well as the components of each type, should be identified and briefly described. Evidence is not always clearly one type. Sometimes experiments and observations are described in an anecdotal manner, or an authority will be quoted in regard to an observation or experiment. It can be difficult to decide whether an authority speaking outside his or her area of expertise is merely providing an anecdote or whether he or she is giving inappropriate testimony. If the authority's evidence gains its importance from his or her reputation as an expert in an "outside" area, then most likely inappropriate testimonial evidence is being provided. If the evidence is important in itself, and the authority is merely describing it as an interested person, the evidence is anecdotal. If the authority provides conclusions based on an experiment or observation within his or her area of expertise, the evidence is testimonial. It makes no difference if the authorities claims are true or false; what matters is whether the authority is speaking within his or her area of authority, and whether the evidence is based on the authority of the person providing it or on public confirmation.

Experimental evidence always provides details about the experiment and is rarely cited in pieces intended for a general audience. When a scientist's beliefs about facts or theories are described or quoted by a newspaper columnist, the evidence is testimonial, not experimental. When a columnist describes experimental or observational evidence, the evidence is anecdotal. The columnist did not carry out the scientific work, he or she is simply telling us about it. However, if the columnist describes the conditions of the observation, the evidence may be observational. It depends upon how much information is presented about the observation itself. When it is difficult to discern whether there is enough information about the observation, the support is probably anecdotal.

The components of each statement of evidence should be identified. The factual component describes ideas about observations and perceptions. It will be evaluated primarily in regard to their accuracy and specificity. Emotional components express feelings; they will be evaluated for significance. All seven standards are relevant to the theoretical component, which describes beliefs about the meaning of evidence. It is important not to confuse the factual with the theoretical; the former provides information, and the latter provides explanations of what the information means.

At the completion of the first three steps, we have completed the review of the piece. We now understand the piece.

EXERCISES

▲ Most Intriguing Issue

Write a one-paragraph description of the most interesting idea, topic, or process described in the chapter so far. Be prepared to explain what you find interesting in class discussion.

▲ The Muddiest Point

Write a sentence or, if possible, a paragraph that describes the idea, topic, expression, term, or process in the chapter so far that you find most difficult to understand.

▲ Cartoons and Diagrams

Cartoons are drawings that characterize or symbolize ideas, processes, or expressions in imaginative ways. Diagrams are drawings, charts, or tables that show how specific details of an idea, process, or expression are interrelated.

1. Draw a cartoon that illustrates "context" of written pieces.
2. Draw a cartoon that illustrates the three different purposes of written pieces.
3. Provide a cartoon that illustrates the difference between an informative and an argumentative piece.
4. Provide a cartoon that shows the difference between an informative and an opinion piece.
5. Provide a cartoon that shows the difference between an argumentative and an opinion piece.

▲ Definitions of Key Terms

Provide a disciplinary definition for each of the following terms as they are used in this chapter. Most of the terms are not defined in the chapter, although their meanings are described by the context in which they appear. You need to review the material to create the definition yourself. Be sure to follow the guidelines for creating definitions on pages 78–81.

Opinion Piece	Argumentative Piece	Informative Piece
Context of a Piece	Purpose of a Piece	Format

▲ Short Essay Questions

Provide a written response of approximately 200 words for each topic. Your responses should be well organized, grammatically correct, and neatly produced.

1. Explain the difference between an argumentative and an opinion piece.
2. Provide at least six different examples of sources of opinion pieces.
3. Provide at least six different examples of sources of argumentative pieces.

4. Can an opinion piece contain arguments? Does an argumentative piece contain opinions?

5. Explain and give an example of the differences in meaning between "convince" and "coax."

6. Explain why it is important to identify each supporting statement and the conclusion as representative, expressive, or directive.

7. Explain why each of the following is either testimonial, anecdotal, or observational evidence.

   a) As CEO of Big Giant Corporation, I want to inform you that Big Giant is not bankrupt, but in fine financial condition.

   b) As CEO of Big Giant Corporation, I want to inform you that statistics show that the American economy has taken a drastic downturn in the last three months.

   c) As President of Scott Bartine College, I want to inform you that the History department has hired a new faculty member.

   d) As President of Scott Bartine College, I want to inform you that historical studies show that Columbus was not the first European to discover America.

   e) As Chief Economist of Big Giant Corporation, I want to inform you that statistics show that the American economy has taken an incredible upswing in the last three months.

   f) As the Secretary of the Treasury of the United States Government, I want to inform you that despite the opinions of the CEO of Big Giant Corporation, the American economy has not taken a drastic downswing in the last three months.

   g) As the new History faculty member at Scott Bartine College, I want to inform you that Columbus was the first European to discover America.

   h) As Chief Economist of Big Giant Corporation, I want to inform you that Big Giant has increased profits by 6.8 percent this year. Please open your annual reports to page eighteen, where you will see the figures that support this information.

   i) As the Secretary of the Treasury of the United States Government, I would like to inform you that free speech does not include desecration of the American Flag.

   j) As CEO of the Big Giant Corporation, I want to inform you that the Secretary of the Treasury of the United States is an expert on free speech.

   k) As a member of the United States Supreme Court, I want to inform you that the Supreme Court does not believe that free speech includes desecration of the American flag.

   l) As a new faculty member in the History department, I would like to inform you that the Asch Study showed how easy it is for people to become victims of mindless conformity.

   m) As President of Scott Bartine College, I would like to inform you that our Psychology department recently confirmed the results of the Asch Study.

   n) As CEO of Big Giant Corporation, I would like to inform you that the results of the Asch Study on mindless conformity are of no interest to our corporation or to any American business.

   o) As Chief Economist of Big Giant Corporation, I would like to show you this chart and provide you with this report. Our Market Research Department completed both. They show that the Asch Study is no longer relevant to American business.

▲ QUESTIONS FOR DISCUSSION

Provide an essay of 300–500 words that responds to each of the following questions which ask for your opinion. You should respond by stating it, and by providing thoughts, examples, and insights that support it. You should be willing to revise your response; you may change your opinion during or after a class discussion.

1. The difference between an opinion piece and an argumentative piece can be subtle. Many opinion pieces contain arguments, and most argumentative pieces are intended to present a point of view. For example, in law, a judge's ruling on a case is referred to as an "opinion." In addition, the lawyers who present the evidence for each side in the case presented to the judge are said to "argue" the case. Is the legal establishment using the terms "argument" and "opinion" in the same way they are used in this chapter? Why or why not?

2. In your experience, what types of evidence do you encounter most often in written pieces such as newspaper editorials, opinion pieces in newsmagazines, and other "popular" publications? Do articles on recent scientific discoveries published in *Time* or *Newsweek* or *U. S. News and World Report* constitute experimental or observational evidence? On the other hand, are they testimonial evidence? Anecdotal? Do you feel comfortable citing such articles as evidence for your own personal opinions? Why or why not?

Step IV: The Cognitive Standards of Clarity, Accuracy, Specificity, and Significance. This is the first evaluation step. If the piece has been carefully reviewed, we already have some ideas about weaknesses and strengths. Nevertheless, it is important to follow each evaluative step. Each standard needs to be carefully applied to the piece.

Keep in mind that evaluation should be empathetic. The piece does not have to demonstrate that it adheres to the standards. It is enough that it does not violate any of them. Evaluation should always grant "the benefit of the doubt" to the piece. A violation of standards should be taken seriously only if it is clearly present.

Vague and ambiguous terms most likely surfaced during the review. Nevertheless, we need to carefully re-examine the original piece as well as our paraphrases. A vague term is one that has no apparent meaning. An ambiguous term is one that has several possible meanings.

Logical incoherence occurs when the conclusion of the piece seems to be completely nonrelated to the evidence. Verbal incoherence occurs when the piece's vague and/or ambiguous language prevents it from being meaningful. Before claiming a piece is logically or verbally incoherent, review it once more for hidden support. The piece is incoherent only if it is impossible to "fill in the gaps" with paraphrases of hidden support. The fallacies of oversimplification, shifting the burden of proof, and straw man often interfere with clarity. Always explain where and why a fallacy occurs.

Accuracy is evaluated by determining the level of public confirmation of the support. In general terms, strong evidence has, and weak evidence lacks, public confirmation. Keep in mind that each type of evidence is publicly confirmed in a different way. For example, do not demand that testimony explain how an experiment or observation was confirmed. If the evidence is testimonial, it is strong if the authority is an appropriate one.

When evaluating for specificity, determine if either the fallacy of overgeneralization or unwarranted assumption is present. Significance is evaluated by seeking fallacies of oversimplification, irrelevant emotion, and mindless conformity. These fallacies often ignore details or trivialize the subject matter. Irrelevant statements are improper if they are used to support the conclusion.

Step V: The Attitudinal Standards of Sincerity, Respect for Others, and Commitment to Consensus.   The metaphors, allusions, loaded words, and prejudicial expressions in written pieces can provide indications of attitudes. When the attitude is not obvious, we can examine them for indications of insincerity, lack of respect, and forceful attempts to persuade.

Persuasive definitions are often key to insincerity. Deliberate vagueness or ambiguity, oversimplifications or misrepresentations, and minimizations of evidence are also indications of a lack of sincerity. If the piece deliberately misrepresents or minimizes the value of evidence for an opposing point of view, a straw man fallacy may have been committed. Lack of respect is usually quite clear; prejudicial expressions, name-calling, demeaning word choices, insults, and so on always indicate disrespect. Fallacies in combination often indicate disrespect, for example, when a straw man fallacy trivializes someone's point of view in a demeaning way.

A piece that is not committed to consensus often resorts to excessive persuasion. This can take the form of the fallacy of appeal to force, use of persuasive definitions, or by the forceful presentation of narrow subjective beliefs.

Step VI: Judgment and Critical Evaluation Essay.   This step consists of an essay that summarizes all the previous critical thinking tools and expresses your view of the piece's worth. The essay should begin with a description of the context and purpose of the piece. If you have engaged in some specific instances of empathetic review or evaluation in which you gave the piece "the benefit of the doubt," you should describe them here.

The decision about the value of the entire piece can only be made after a thorough, detailed review and evaluation. Once you have gone through the process, you need to reflect on how many revisions the piece needs. Could it be made clearer if a few terms were defined? Are there so many unclear terms that the piece needs to be completely overhauled? Does the piece contain only a few insignificant fallacies? On the other hand, are there so many fallacies that it cannot be salvaged? Is the evidence strong enough to support the conclusion? Is it too weak? Is the piece well reasoned, but clearly prejudicial or insincere? Does it strive to persuade a little too forcefully? Is it a blatant threat? You, and only you, can respond to these questions and others like them. Of course, your essay should itself follow the standards of good thinking.

Clearly describe your judgment. Don't "waffle" or "sit on the fence." Make sure your comments are accurate; don't misrepresent anything in the piece. Explain any difficulty you had interpreting the piece. Your essay should be specific; if you find the piece reasonable, be specific about its strengths. Be specific about fallacies or weak evidence. However, your essay need not go into every single detail you described in the first four steps. The essay is a summary, and should describe what you feel are the most significant details of your review and evaluation. Keep in mind that your goal is to provide suggestions for revision. Your essay should conclude with your suggestions for revision. The more vague, unreasonable, and deceptive the piece, the more difficult it is to suggest specific revisions. Nevertheless, suggestions about definitions, evidence quality, removal of fallacies, and a change in attitude can be made. The essay should be empathetic; keep in mind that everyone, including the person who wrote the piece, has their own perception of the world. Your goal is to provide suggestions for revision in those perceptions; you need to make them sincerely, respectfully, and with an open-minded attitude.

This does not mean, however, that you need to avoid any appropriate recommendations for revision of the author's attitude. If the piece seems to be insincere, disrespectful, or overly forceful, it is quite appropriate for you to recommend a more empathetic approach on the author's part.

The following piece, "Television Violence Turns Kids into Killers," will be used to further explain the critical thinking format. Read the piece at least twice, reflect on how you would apply the format to it, and then follow along with the model.

Television Violence Turns Kids into Killers

¶1 We often wonder how we dare take tender eighteen-year-olds and throw them into a boot camp where they are turned into killers. Transforming peaceful young men and women into soldiers has one purpose: War. There aren't many good things about war, but if you find yourself in one, you need to try to win. So most of us accept boot camps along with other ugly military habits. It's evil, but necessary.

¶2 What about kids with automatic weapons cruising and killing each other on city streets? What about farm kids blasting away the teacher with Dad's hunting rifle? What about all the kids who laugh at the murders of teachers, parents, and public officials? Is that necessary? It certainly is evil.

¶3 Why do kids kill and laugh about it? No, its not because there are too many guns. It's not because of divorce. And forget the poverty problem. The reason kids kill? They are trained by television. Television turns out killer kids just like boot camp turns out soldiers.

¶4 The details are ugly. The military's first step in training killers is to humiliate, beat, traumatize, and brutalize the recruits. They are soon numbed to the point that they lose their identities and values. Television brutally numbs kids the same way. Very young children cannot tell the difference between fantasy and real life; they believe that television cartoon characters are real. They watch television, on the average, twenty-seven hours a week. That's twenty-seven hours of numbing brutality! Television violence is like a drug; it actually creates a hormonal and neurological response in the child's mind.

¶5 The second step in boot camp is brainwashing. Soldiers are encouraged to laugh and cheer at violence. They earn praise for going to violent extremes. Children cannot distinguish between programs and commercials; they associate television violence with their favorite candy, cereal, and soft drink. They soon become brainwashed barbarians who associate violence with pleasure.

¶6 Boot camp's third step in creating killers is to deprive them of the value of human life; they "shoot to kill" human silhouettes on the firing range. Eventually killing real people doesn't seem wrong. The same thing happens to kids who watch twenty-seven hours of robbery, rape, and murder every week. They've lost the value of human life.

¶7 The last step the military takes is to introduce killers as role models. Soldiers are taught to identify with their drill sergeant, the most brutal person they know. For kids, it means identification with the criminals they see on television. They imitate them. They kill their parents, their teachers, their classmates; they don't care who it is. They just want to be a killer.

¶8 America needs its killer soldiers; they are a necessary evil. America does not need killer kids. We need strict laws that ban all violence on television. Television executives won't stop this ugly terror until some of them are thrown in jail. Let's save our kids, and leave the killing to the soldiers.

Professor Erick Cod
Mathematics Department

EXERCISES

▲ Most Intriguing Issue

Write a one-paragraph description of the most interesting idea, topic, or process described in pages 256–268. Be prepared to explain what you find interesting in class discussion.

▲ The Muddiest Point

Write a sentence or, if possible, a paragraph that describes the idea, topic, expression, term, or process in pages 256–268 that you find most difficult to understand.

▲ Cartoons and Diagrams

1. Provide a cartoon that illustrates the primary characteristics of the ideal standard of clarity according to The Format.

2. Provide a cartoon that illustrates the primary characteristics of the ideal standard of accuracy according to The Format.

3. Provide a cartoon that illustrates the primary characteristics of the ideal standard of specificity according to The Format.

4. Provide a cartoon that illustrates the primary characteristics of the ideal standard of significance according to The Format.

5. Provide a cartoon that illustrates the primary characteristics of the ideal standard of sincerity according to The Format.

6. Provide a cartoon that illustrates the primary characteristics of the ideal standard of respect for others according to The Format.

7. Provide a cartoon that illustrates the primary characteristics of the ideal standard of commitment to consensus according to The Format.

▲ DEFINITIONS OF KEY TERMS

Provide a disciplinary definition for each of the following terms as they are used in this chapter. Most of the terms are not defined in the chapter, although their meanings are described by the context in which they appear. You need to review the material to create the definition yourself. Be sure to follow the guidelines for creating definitions on pages 78–81.

Logical Incoherence	Verbal Incoherence	Biased Claim
Irrelevant Statement	Persuasive Definition	Critical Essay

▲ SHORT ESSAY QUESTIONS

Responding to these questions will give you practice in applying The Format to the opinion piece on "television violence." You should answer them before reading the next section in which The Format is applied to the essay. You should then check your responses here with those in the "Model Evaluation."

1. What is the context and purpose of the piece?
2. The piece has two conclusions. What are they? Does one support the other? How?
3. List the main support, both stated and hidden, in the piece.
4. What are the types and components of evidence in the piece?
5. Do you notice any vague or ambiguous words or phrases in the piece?
6. What appears to be the strong and weak evidence in the piece?
7. Do you notice any fallacies of oversimplification, shifting the burden of proof, or straw man in the piece?
8. Do you notice any fallacies of inappropriate authority, overgeneralization, or unwarranted assumption in the piece?
9. Are there any irrelevant statements in the piece?
10. Do you notice any trivial expressions or weaknesses in recognition of the complexity of the subject matter in the piece?
11. Do you notice any fallacies of irrelevant emotion or mindless conformity in the piece?
12. Do you notice any persuasive definitions in the piece?
13. Are there any deliberate attempts to minimize or overlook the value of evidence that does not support the conclusions?

14. Are there any prejudicial expressions, metaphors, allusions, or word choices that demean others?
15. Do you notice any deliberate attempts to use vagueness and ambiguity to persuade psychologically or physically?
16. Do you notice any fallacies of appeal to force?

▲ Questions for Discussion

Respond to each question about the piece on television violence. You should review The Format often. When your responses are completed you should compare them with the "Model Evaluation" in the next section.

1. Describe the context and purpose of the piece.
2. Paraphrase or state the conclusions.
3. Paraphrase or state the stated support.
4. Paraphrase the hidden support.
5. Describe any metaphors, allusions, word choices, or prejudicial expressions that you notice in the piece.
6. Describe the types and components of evidence.
7. Evaluate the clarity of the piece.
8. Evaluate the accuracy of the piece.
9. Evaluate the specificity of the piece.
10. Evaluate the significance of the piece.
11. Evaluate the sincerity of the piece.
12. Evaluate the respect for others in the piece.
13. Evaluate the commitment to consensus in the piece.
14. Describe your judgment on the piece. Should it be revised? What specific suggestions for revisions do you have?
15. Combine these responses in a "first draft" critical essay.

MODEL EVALUATION OF "TELEVISION VIOLENCE TURNS KIDS INTO KILLERS"

Step I. Primary Elements of the Piece

Reading supplementary material helps identify the context and purpose of the piece. Let's imagine that the piece appears in Scott Bartine College's student newspaper, *Jabber*, on the "Faculty Opinions" page. According to the biography provided by the newspaper, Mr. Cod is a retired military officer with a masters degree in Mathematics. In a brief interview, Mr. Cod says that television executives are aware of the harm their programming does to children, although they won't admit it publicly.

The piece is an attempt to shed light on several cases in which children as young as twelve have murdered classmates, parents, and teachers. It also seems to address youth gang violence.

The fact that the piece appears in the college newspaper is an indication that it is a statement of Mr. Cod's opinion, not an argument. He is coaxing us to agree with him, not attempting to *prove* that his conclusion is reasonable and supported by strong evidence.

Opinion pieces often have two conclusions. The first conclusion usually identifies a cause or reason behind a problem, and the second directs us to do something about the problem. In this piece, the first conclusion can be found in ¶3. We can paraphrase it as follows:

Television training in violence is the only reason why kids kill (REPRESENTATIVE)

The second conclusion, found in ¶8, can be paraphrased:

Laws should be enacted that ban all television violence (DIRECTIVE)

The first conclusion is empathetically paraphrased. ¶3 explicitly denies that the availability of guns, the high incidence of divorce, and poverty have anything to do with the problem. The entire piece implies that televised "training" in violence is the *sole* reason why "kids kill." The words "kids kill" strikes us as an interesting choice of words. Their meaning is slightly vague, and certainly meant to inspire fear.

An empathetic reading of the piece leads us to believe that the second conclusion directs us to enact laws banning *all* television violence, not just violence in children's programming. In ¶6, it is claimed that "robbery, rape, and murder," are viewed by children. These subjects are not limited to children's shows. Although the conclusion would be stronger if it limited its directive to *children's* programming, the piece explicitly directs us to ban *all* television violence.

Once the conclusions are empathetically paraphrased, we have a good understanding of the piece's main point.

The stated support is empathetically paraphrased in nine statements.

1. Boot camp training is ugly, evil, and necessary. ¶1 (EXPRESSIVE)
2. The problem of kids who kill and laugh about murder is evil, but not necessary. ¶2 (EXPRESSIVE)
3. Availability of guns, family breakdowns, and poverty have no influence on kids who kill. ¶3 (REPRESENTATIVE)
4. Television brutalizes and numbs kids just like the military traumatizes recruits. ¶4 (REPRESENTATIVE)
5. Just like the military brainwash recruits, television brainwashes kids into associating violence with pleasure. ¶5 (REPRESENTATIVE)
6. Twenty-seven hours of television viewing every week deprives kids of the value of human life, just like time on the firing range does to recruits. ¶6 (REPRESENTATIVE)
7. Kids identify with criminals and killers on television just like recruits identify with drill instructors. ¶7 (REPRESENTATIVE)

8. American needs killer soldiers, but does not need killer kids. ¶8 (EXPRESSIVE)

9. Television executives won't stop the ugly terror of television violence unless some of them are thrown in jail. ¶8 (EXPRESSIVE)

The hidden support:

1. Military training effectively numbs and brainwashes recruits to associate violence with pleasure and identify with brutal role models. (REPRESENTATIVE)

2. Television violence's psychological effect on kids is as deep and pervasive as that of military training on recruits. (REPRESENTATIVE)

3. It is not enough to limit or restrict television viewing by kids; all television violence must be eliminated. (EXPRESSIVE)

4. The only way to eliminate television violence is to legally ban it. (expressive)

5. Once television violence is eliminated kids will not kill anyone. (REPRESENTATIVE)

Discussion of the Primary Elements of the Piece.   Four of the statements of support are expressions of feeling, and five are representations of perceptions. It is common for half the support to be expressive in opinion pieces about moral and political issues. The first two expressive statements (#1, #2) express moral feelings. Number eight is a political and moral expression because it uses the word "needs" in the context of "necessary evil" in the first two support statements. The term "needs" could appear to be ambiguous; however, an empathetic review should accept that it is not used in the sense of "required for national security." There is nothing in the piece that suggests that meaning of the term. The ninth statement of support expresses the feeling that television executives have a low moral character. We know from the author's interview that he believes the executives know about the harm that their programming causes, but won't admit it publicly. Number nine, then, should not be regarded as a representative statement. It is not predicting behavior. The expressive language ("ugly terror," "thrown in jail") reveals that it is expressing disdain for the executives' lack of concern.

The first representative statement (#3) makes a claim about society in general. The other four claim that, for children, viewing violence on television is "just like" military training. These are representative statements because they describe a perception. Presumably, if others observe military training and children's behavior, their perceptions will correspond with those of the piece.

The hidden support is quite clear. The assumption that military training numbs, brainwashes, and so on (#1) supports the first conclusion. So does the claim that television violence has as deep an effect as military training (#2).

Number three supports the second conclusion. It is an expressive, not a directive statement instructing us to eliminate television violence. It may appear to be doing so because the word "must" is often used in giving instructions. The second conclusion in the piece directs us to use legal prohibition to eliminate violence. This hidden premise expresses a feeling ("not enough" . . . . "must") about the moral and political seriousness of the issue, and *supports* the conclusion.

The piece clearly feels that the *only* way to eliminate television violence is by legal prohibition (#4). This statement could be regarded as representative of a theoretical belief, namely that legal prohibition could reasonably be shown to be the only possible way to eliminate television violence. On the other hand, number four may be an expression of moral indignation and political resolve: "Television executives are unwilling to cease violent programming. Thus, we are left with no alternative; the law must force them to stop." Once more, the interview with the author is the deciding factor. Number four is an expression of feeling rather than a theoretical representation because the author has already expressed his disdain for television executives.

The fifth hidden support is representative because it *predicts a future perception;* once television violence is eliminated, we will no longer perceive any kids killing anyone. The difference between a "future perception" and the expression of a moral or political feeling is sometimes difficult to discern. However, in this piece, all the stated support implies that television violence is the *only* factor in the problem of kids killing people (Hidden Support #4). An empathetic review, then, should not regard this statement as an expression of a moral and political feeling about the problem, but as a prediction of the successful resolution of the problem.

Of course, the piece assumes that killing is morally bad, and that it is socially undesirable for children to kill people. These are objectively confirmed moral positions. They are not controversial, and thus do not need to be identified as hidden support.

STEP II. ORGANIZATION OF THE PIECE

The piece has two conclusions, so both should be included. The conclusion about the problem "supports" the conclusion that something should be done about the problem. As mentioned earlier, many opinion pieces contain at least two arguments. Organizing them is not complex. We simply organize the first argument, and then list its conclusion as the first stated support for the second argument.

Conclusion #1

Television training in violence is the only reason why kids kill. ¶3 (REPRESENTATIVE)

Stated Support

Boot camp training is ugly, evil, and necessary. ¶1 (EXPRESSIVE)

The problem of kids who kill and laugh about murder is evil, but not necessary. ¶2 (EXPRESSIVE)

Availability of guns, family breakdowns, and poverty have no influence on kids who kill. ¶3 (REPRESENTATIVE)

Television brutalizes and numbs kids just like the military traumatizes recruits. ¶4 (REPRESENTATIVE)

Just like the military brainwash recruits, television brainwashes kids into associating violence with pleasure. ¶5 (REPRESENTATIVE)

Twenty-seven hours of television viewing every week deprives kids of the value of human life, just like time on the firing range does to recruits. ¶6 (REPRESENTATIVE)

Kids identify with criminals and killers on television just like recruits identify with drill instructors. ¶7 (REPRESENTATIVE)

American needs killer soldiers, but does not need killer kids. ¶8 (EXPRESSIVE)

Hidden Support

Military training effectively numbs and brainwashes recruits to associate violence with pleasure and identify with brutal role models. (REPRESENTATIVE)

Television violence's psychological effect on kids is as deep and pervasive as that of military training on recruits. (REPRESENTATIVE)

Conclusion #2

Laws should be enacted that ban all television violence. ¶8 (DIRECTIVE)

Stated Support

Television training in violence is the only reason why kids kill. ¶3 (Conclusion #1) (REPRESENTATIVE)

Television executives won't stop the ugly terror of television violence unless some of them are thrown in jail. ¶8 (EXPRESSIVE)

Hidden Support

It is not enough to limit or restrict television viewing by kids; all television violence must be eliminated. (expressive)

Once television violence is eliminated kids will not kill anyone. (REPRESENTATIVE)

The only way to eliminate television violence is to legally ban it. (EXPRESSIVE)

Important Metaphors, Allusions, Word Choices, and Prejudicial Expressions. Once the support is organized, we review the entire piece for indications of bias and prejudice. Chapter 4 discusses metaphors, allusions, word choice, and prejudicial expressions in detail. A metaphor describes something unfamiliar by comparing it to something more familiar. An allusion is an idea or feeling that is suggested or insinuated. We examine word choice for "loaded words" that express bias or prejudice. Prejudicial expressions are a clear indication of an attitude that lacks respect for a targeted group.

METAPHORS.   There are four metaphors in the piece.

Tender eighteen-year-olds ¶1

Ugly military habits ¶1

Television violence is like a drug ¶4

Brainwashed barbarians ¶5

The first two, both in the opening paragraph, describe the military in a contrasting manner. The recruits are described as "tender," and the whole military as an "ugly habit." The contrast between the innocent recruits and the "ugly military habits" that turn them into killers is clear. The metaphors imply that television, too, takes innocent children and turns them into killers. What are television's "ugly habits"? No doubt, television has a "habit" of brutalizing and brainwashing children, just like the military. The word "habit" also has connotations of drug use in our society. The third metaphor expands on the image of drug use, and implicitly compares television to drug pushers, one of the most despised groups of criminals in this society. The fourth metaphor refers to the innocent children's condition after prolonged exposure to television violence. They are transformed into "brainwashed barbarians." Our familiarity with the term "barbarians" is limited, but we know that we don't like them. The metaphors all imply that television violence is an ugly programming of innocent children into killer kids.

ALLUSIONS.   The piece makes at least three allusions, all of them of questionable accuracy. The moral depravity of television executives is alluded to in paragraph eight. They won't stop their ugly brainwashing unless we "throw them in jail." The allusion to their lack of moral principle and self-restraint is clear. Television executives are not publicly confirmed as morally deprived. In fact, most people are aware of at least some efforts that they have made to reduce television violence.

Virtually every paragraph alludes to the barbarity of the military. The allusion seems to be without public confirmation; many people in our society criticize the military, but not for barbarity. It is regarded as inefficient, unprepared, and overly technological by some. Nevertheless, the "barbaric" label is not common.

Finally, the whole piece alludes to the belief that people, or at least children, are susceptible to a robot-like "programming." Children are "turned into" killers by watching twenty-seven hours of television each week. Few share this belief, so it must be recognized as controversial.

WORD CHOICE.   Negative expressions are found in at least six instances.

Killer Kids ¶3	Killer Soldiers ¶8
Numbing Brutality ¶4	Ugly Terror ¶8
Brainwashing ¶5	Thrown in Jail ¶8

Instead of these loaded terms, others could have been used:

Troubled Children	Professional Military Personnel
Uninteresting and Gross Behavior	Current Programming
Attitudinal Indoctrination	Incarcerated

The piece reveals a biased attitude toward the military and television executives by choosing negatively loaded words to describe them and their activities. If the piece had replaced them with less negative terms, such as the ones suggested above, it would have displayed a more appropriate attitude, as we shall see now.

PREJUDICIAL EXPRESSIONS.   The piece seems to be prejudicially biased against three groups: television executives, the military, and the children who have become "killer kids." It is easy to stereotype these children in a negative way. They have killed their parents, teachers, and classmates. We are puzzled and frightened at their behavior. However, all of the metaphors, word choices, and allusions to them in the piece are negative stereotypes. Nowhere does the piece mention that any child driven to murder must have individual psychological difficulties that go far deeper than "just wanting to be a killer." The "killer kids" are the target of several prejudicial expressions that stereotype them as "brainwashed barbarians" who are numbed by the drug-like violence they watch on television.

STEP III. EVIDENCE IN THE PIECE

Since the author is a Mathematics professor, he has no expertise in the subject of television's influence on children. However, it is clear from the context that he is a retired military officer. His credentials and experience do not diminish the importance of the fact that he uses negative metaphors, allusions, and loaded terms in describing the military. Nevertheless, his testimonial evidence about the military is appropriate. He is an authority on the minor factual and theoretical claims he makes about the military.

The piece contains no reference to any studies on the relation of television viewing and violent behavior in children. In fact, the social sciences have publicly confirmed the conclusions of several studies that television violence has an effect on violent behavior. However, no studies have confirmed that such behavior is only the consequence of watching television violence. Biological and environmental factors, as well as social factors having nothing to do with television, are also confirmed to be involved with violent behavior in children.

The piece ignores standards of measurement accepted by the social sciences. Studies, as was mentioned above, are ignored. Consequently, there are no descriptions of the types of observations that support the claims about television, violence, or the moral depravity of television executives. The claims are very general; the results are not described statistically. For example, the piece cannot possibly mean to imply that every child who has been exposed to television violence is a "kid killer." The absence of any studies or statistics means that the evidence about television, violence, and television executives is not observational, but anecdotal.

The testimonial evidence about the military is mostly factual. Although it is common knowledge that recruits go through basic training in boot camps, the piece claims that basic training is made up of four primary elements: Brutalizing and loss of identity; Brainwashing; Deprivation of the value of human life; Killers as role models. Obviously, the loaded words used to describe these four elements are emotional.

The anecdotal evidence is primarily theoretical. The claim that there is a direct relation between television violence and killing is the primary support in the piece. The anecdotal evidence has an equally strong factual component. Assertions about the amount of time children spend watching television, the inability of children to determine that cartoon characters are imaginary, and so on, are based on personal observations of the author. Factual claims about the moral depravity of television executives are also anecdotal.

EXERCISES

▲ QUESTIONS FOR DISCUSSION

Review your responses to Short Essay 1–6 and Questions for Discussion 1–4 in the last set of exercises. Identify differences between your responses and those of the "Model Evaluation." Do not assume that your responses are "wrong" if they disagree with the Model. Discuss the differences and come to a consensus with members of the class and your instructor.

STEP IV. EVALUATION OF CLARITY, ACCURACY, SPECIFICITY, SIGNIFICANCE

The process of review provides many opportunities to note failings in reaching the ideal standards of good thinking. Of course, the piece is not required to demonstrate that it meets the standards. Rather, it is our responsibility to point out where it has not met them. The "burden of proof" is on us.

As usual, we need to exercise empathy. We always give the piece "the benefit of the doubt" during the evaluation process.

Clarity. The piece contains several vague terms that seriously interfere with its clarity. The term "violence" is both vague and ambiguous. Throughout the piece, it is used ambiguously to refer to military violence, which is physical, and violence on television, which is visual. The two are not the same, but the piece uses the same term for both, confusing the issue considerably. In addition, "violence on television" is not defined. In paragraph six, an allusion is made to the crimes "robbery, rape, and murder." However, in paragraph four, an allusion is made to "cartoon characters," who are rarely depicted as engaging in those crimes. Both conclusions require support from claims about the seriousness of televised violence. The first directs us to "ban" all violence from television. Consequently, the piece needs a definition of the term.

In the first paragraph, "Other ugly military habits" is vague. So is "evil, but necessary." These vague terms are not clear descriptions of any facts about the military; nor are they clear expressions of feelings. What are the "habits"? Why are they "ugly"? What does "evil but necessary" mean in this context? It is impossible to publicly confirm these beliefs because they are simply too vague to be understood.

The anecdotal reference to television being "like a drug," and that "it actually creates a hormonal and neurological response in the child's mind" is vague. The piece vaguely claims that the responses to watching television include a "numbing brutality." It does not provide a clear description of the hormonal and neurological responses, and it does not describe what it means by "numbing brutality."

In the fifth paragraph, children are said to be "brainwashed" to "associate violence with pleasure" because they see commercials for candy and other treats during the violent programming. "Brainwashing" is a vague term.

It is also not clear what "associating" means in this context, due to its ambiguity. Does "associate" mean a normal mingling of the two experiences in the child's mind for a moment or two? Or does it mean that the child will correlate violence with pleasure for a long time? Does the term mean that the "association" of violence and pleasure ends when the commercial is over? Does it mean that these children *seriously and permanently* relate violence and pleasure the way that most people relate love and pleasure? The piece appears to imply the latter. At any rate, the term "associate" is far too ambiguous to be clearly understood. The fallacy of oversimplification is committed in this and in the fifth paragraph.

To claim that children are "brainwashed" and that they "associate violence with pleasure" is to trivialize the complexities involved with the influences of television on children. Both terms vaguely refer to complex psychological processes that are not fully understood by expert observers. The fallacy consists of presenting the complicated processes as if they were simple operations that could be described in trite phrases.

Paragraph six claims that the children (and the soldiers) have "lost the value of human life," another vague term. If the meaning of the phrase is "no concern for human life" the claim is very serious. Should we take it to mean that the children have a *complete* disregard for all human life?

In the last paragraph, the second conclusion wants "strict laws" that ban "all violence" on television. Both terms are vague. How "strict" should the laws be? Does the word refer to "strict" enforcement? "Strict" punishments? What is the definition of either one? Does a strict punishment mean five days in jail? Twenty years? What does the piece have in mind?

In conclusion, the piece seriously suffers from a lack of clarity. The key term "violence" is not defined, and is used ambiguously. The fallacy of oversimplification trivializes complex psychological processes. The lack of clarity makes it very difficult to understand what the piece is attempting to say.

Accuracy.   The piece lacks any strong evidence for either conclusion. The emotional component of the testimonial evidence makes use of loaded words that express strong negative feelings about the military. While there are many people who would morally criticize the American military, few would confirm the feeling that recruits just out of basic training are "brainwashed killers" who have "lost the value of human life."

Factual and theoretical components in the piece are limited to anecdotal evidence. In addition, they do not describe facts and theories derived from the personal experience of the author, but are based on (we assume) his personal observations and conjectures. The factual and theoretical components of anecdotal evidence can be relatively strong *if* they are descriptions of personal experiences. The facts and theories in the piece should be supported by observational or testimonial evidence. If the piece referred to some publicly confirmed observations, or to an authority in the field, the evidence would be much stronger. As it is, the accuracy of the piece must be regarded as very limited.

Specificity. Ideally, a piece will contain detailed, precise definitions, descriptions, and explanations. Fallacies of overgeneralization and unwarranted assumption should be avoided.

There are several fallacies of overgeneralization in the piece. Paragraph six overstates the effect of shooting at human silhouettes on the firing range when it claims that it deprives soldiers of "the value of human life." Clearly, there is no public confirmation of this belief. Some people feel that this training makes soldiers *insensitive* to human life, but few would go to the extreme of claiming it *deprives* them of the value of human life. The paragraph commits the fallacy a second time when it overstates the evidence for the claim that children, too, have "lost the value of human life." Perhaps violence on television leads to a diminished sensitivity to human suffering. However, the evidence does not go so far to support the more general belief.

The fallacy of unwarranted assumption occurs whenever the conclusion is primarily supported by a controversial or false hidden premise. This fallacy occurs at several times in the piece. Paragraph four claims that children watch twenty-seven hours of television every week. This is not controversial. Most surveys agree that, on the average, children watch television about four hours a day. However, in paragraph six the assertion that they view twenty-seven hours of violence, specifically "robbery, rape, and murder" is an unwarranted assumption. A hidden premise is assumed:

The television viewing of children is limited to violence.

The assumption that children see twenty-seven hours of "robbery, rape, and murder" is unwarranted. Children watch comedy, nature, and educational programs that are not violent and certainly contain no scenes of robbery, rape, or murder.

In paragraph eight, the expressive statement, "Television executives won't stop this ugly terror until some of them are thrown in jail" is an unwarranted assumption. The statement expresses a judgment about the moral character of television executives as a group. Moral judgments need more than subjective emotional confirmation if they are to be taken seriously. They need a factual and theoretical component and at least a small amount of public confirmation. This judgment has some of the latter. A few informed people—a small minority—share the belief that television executives are morally depraved. However, the judgment in paragraph eight does not provide any factual or theoretical components. Furthermore, it assumes that the executives share an *extremely* low moral character; they won't stop their "ugly terror" until some of them are punished. This is clearly an unwarranted assumption. Television executives may be a depraved group, but there is no reason to assume that they won't change their ways unless they are sent off to jail!

Of course, the hidden supports in every piece are assumptions since they are not stated. However, there is a difference between an assumption and an unwarranted assumption. In this piece, every hidden support is unwarranted.

The hidden support:

> **1.** Military training effectively numbs and brainwashes recruits to associate violence with pleasure and identify with brutal role models. (REPRESENTATIVE)

This assumption about military training is unwarranted because it is false. Perhaps American military training could be more civil. Nevertheless, to claim that it numbs and brainwashes recruits into sadistic brutes is simply untrue.

> **2.** Television violence's psychological effect on kids is as deep and pervasive as that of military training on recruits. (REPRESENTATIVE)

This assumption is very controversial. Military training is a twenty-four hour, seven day a week ritual. Even if children are watching television twenty-seven hours each week, at least two-thirds of the week is spent in other activities. It does not seem possible that television programs could have the deep, pervasive psychological effects of military training.

> **3.** It is not enough to limit or restrict television viewing by kids; all television violence must be eliminated. (EXPRESSIVE)

The assumption is that parents and other caretakers cannot control television viewing by children, and that there are no technological ways (for example, the "V Chip") to ensure that children do not see violence on television. Both of these possibilities have been discussed publicly; it is difficult to imagine that the author is not aware of them. The assumption is clearly controversial, perhaps even false. In either case, it is an unwarranted assumption.

> **4.** The only way to eliminate television violence is to legally ban it. (EXPRESSIVE)

This expressive assumption is related to the piece's claims about the moral depravity of television executives as well as the interview with Mr. Cod, in which he says that television executives are aware of, but unwilling to publicly admit, the harm television violence causes.

This hidden support contains an interesting allusion, also found in the immediately preceding hidden support and in the unwarranted assumption in paragraph eight that the executives won't clean up the violence until some are "thrown in jail." Without legal prohibition, the executives cannot be jailed. Is there an underlying assumption that television executives currently have a legal right (freedom of speech) to decide how much or how little violence their programming contains? Is the legal prohibition needed in order to remove this right? Is there a negative attitudinal assumption concerning freedom of speech underlying the piece?

> **5.** Once television violence is eliminated kids will not kill anyone. (REPRESENTATIVE)

The unwarranted assumption here is obvious; the claim is not true. The claim is also an overgeneralization. Of course, it may be the case that an elimination of television violence would *reduce* the number of tragic killings.

The piece has far too many unwarranted assumptions, two of which are very controversial: (1) children are viewing a large (twenty-seven hours a week) amount of violence, and (2) parents and other caregivers cannot monitor children's viewing in person or by technological means. The piece's conclusion directs us to enact legislation that will "ban all television violence." However, until these controversial unwarranted assumptions are investigated, the conclusion lacks reasonable support.

Significance.   The piece fails to recognize the complexity of the relationship between television violence and the tragedy of children murdering their teachers, parents, and schoolmates. If television violence is the *only* reason these crimes are committed, they should be happening more often. The killings do not occur with enough regularity to be caused by television violence. Millions of children are exposed to the supposedly immense amount of violence on television, yet only a handful have killed anyone. Television violence may *contribute* to the tragedies, but the reasons for them are far more complex than any single factor.

The piece oversimplifies the significance of the issue in two ways. In the first place, "killer kids" is a trite description that trivializes the complexity involved in the psychological disposition of children driven to murder. The second paragraph dramatizes their situation in a way that makes it appear that most children in urban and rural environments are engaged in violence and murder. *If* that were true, and if it were true that television violence clearly causes the violent behavior, then the conclusion may be worth taking seriously. However, neither belief has any public confirmation. The piece oversimplifies the complex factors that lead a child to kill someone.

Second, the term "brainwashing" indicates that the piece oversimplifies the complex psychological and sociological influences of television on children. Of course, that there are such influences is commonly accepted. However, "brainwashing" is a far too simplistic and vague description of them.

Not only does the piece treat these two complex issues in a trite, simplistic manner but it also trivializes the complexities of children's television. It simply alludes to the moral depravity of television executives as the *only* factor involved with violence on television. However, there are many others. Our society enjoys violent entertainment. We watch hockey, football, boxing, professional wrestling, and other violent athletic events. We flock to violent movies, read violent novels, and extol violence in much of our popular music. We also watch violent television programs. The point is that violence is on television for a complex interplay of many reasons. Television executives are responding to them. To claim that they provide violence because they are morally depraved is trite.

The piece oversimplifies the issue in too many ways. It has little, if any, significance.

Step V. Evaluation of Sincerity, Respect for Others, Commitment to Consensus

Sincerity. At this point in our detailed evaluation, it is appropriate to evaluate the author's attitude. We have already noted his questionable assessment of the moral character of television executives and his exaggerated claims about sadism in American military training. We have questioned his views on freedom of speech, a commonly held moral and political value.

Evaluations of sincerity, respect for others, and commitment to consensus require an identification of *deliberate* attempts to misrepresent ideas, demean people, or force acceptance of beliefs. In order to evaluate whether these are deliberate, rather than innocent mistakes, we need to have an idea about the author's motives. Chapter 4 pointed out the difficulty in knowing our own motives, and emphasized that it is much more difficult to understand those of other people. This is especially true when we are evaluating a written piece because the person is not available for a conversation. However, we can examine the piece's metaphors, allusions, loaded words, and prejudicial expressions. These often give indications of insincerity, lack of respect, and overly forceful persuasion.

In the piece, there are two indications of insincerity. The first is in the metaphor, "television violence is like a drug" in paragraph four. The deception involved in this metaphor is that children somehow become "addicted" to television violence. It may be true that they form a habit of watching violent programs. Nevertheless, it is not true that their habitual viewing has the physical or psychological force of a drug addiction. This unwarranted assumption does not appear to be an honest mistake. It fits in too well with the second deception, found in the following paragraph.

The metaphor, "brainwashed barbarians" claims that the "killer kids" are not responsible for their actions, since they have been caught in the evil web of television executives. The executives, like drug pushers, are characterized as transforming innocent and easily swayed children into robotic social renegades.

Both of these metaphors indicate that the author is being less than sincere with us. Is he attempting to help us find the truth about the tragedy of children caught up in murder? That does not appear to be the case. He is more interested, it seems, in exploiting them in order to convince us that television executives deliberately use the techniques of military indoctrination to turn children into criminals.

Respect for Others. The allusions to television executives' lack of moral principles are found in paragraphs eight and three. As we have already seen, the piece deliberately stereotypes them as morally bankrupt individuals who won't stop brainwashing children unless a few of them are thrown in jail.

Allusions to the military characterize their training methods as sadistic brainwashing.

The term "killer kids" belittles the children caught up in these violent tragedies. Written pieces claiming to shed light on their situation should not denigrate them. Name-calling indicates an attitude of disrespect. The criminal actions of the children should not be used as an excuse to disrespect their point of view. How are we ever to understand their motivations and beliefs if we don't take them seriously? Respect for others acknowledges that their perceptions are worth understanding. Certainly, we are repulsed by the murders committed by these children. Their moral character, in some cases, repulses us.

However, respect for others does not imply acceptance of their values. It simply means that every person, no matter their values, should be granted the opportunity to communicate their beliefs and opinions. What do these children think about the motivations for their crimes? What do they feel about television violence? These questions cannot be answered unless we respect them enough to at least give them a hearing. Name-calling closes off that possibility.

The piece shows lack of respect for the military, the children, and the television executives; in other words, for everyone connected to the issue.

Commitment to Consensus. An attitude that is committed to consensus views truth as the outcome of public consensus, which in turn is established by engaging in dialogue. Any physical or psychological attempt to force beliefs on people indicates unwillingness to seek consensus. One way this is done is by dismissing or ignoring any evidence or authorities with which the piece disagrees.

The third paragraph dismisses three important sources of evidence by a subtle use of the fallacy of shifting the burden of proof. We are told that two commonly cited reasons for children's psychological problems—family breakdown and poverty—and the wide availability of guns has nothing to do with the problem. No reason is given why we should ignore these three factors, although each one of them is commonly believed to be relevant to the issue.

It is the author's responsibility to tell us *why* these factors can be so abruptly dismissed. His contention that they have nothing to do with the issue is controversial. The contention of those who claim that family breakdowns, poverty, and easy access to weapons are factors in the issue is not controversial. However, the author cleverly leaves it to someone else to explain why the three factors *should be* considered.

Once the author has abruptly dismissed these three factors, he conveniently points his finger at television violence as the *only* factor. This, in turn, allows him to demonize the television executives as "violence pushers" solely responsible for the "brainwashed killer kids."

The fallacy dismisses three factors that would benefit anyone's understanding of the issue. By deliberately rejecting them so quickly, the author reveals that he is much more interested in persuading us that television violence is the only factor than he is in contributing to a public dialogue on the issue.

STEP VI: JUDGMENT AND CRITICAL EVALUATION ESSAY

The last step in the detailed format is a summary of the preceding review and evaluations. It begins with a brief description of the context and purpose of the piece, then discusses the evaluation. It concludes with suggestions for revision. The essay should adhere as closely as possible to the seven standards of good thinking.

CRITICAL EVALUATION OF "TELEVISION VIOLENCE TURNS KIDS INTO KILLERS"

"Television Violence Turns Kids into Killers," is an opinion piece written by Mathematics professor Erick Cod in the October 13 issue of Scott Bartine College's weekly student newspaper, *Jabber*.

The piece does not provide a definition or even a general description of television violence. Its claim that children are brainwashed into associating violence with pleasure is vague and ambiguous. The piece ambiguously suggests that children acquire sadistic tendencies for life from watching television, a very controversial claim.

All of the evidence is anecdotal. However, no personal experiences with the children or television executives are discussed. The author's biography indicates that he is a retired military officer, but his discussion of military training suffers from oversimplifications. There are no references to any controlled observations of the effects of television violence on children, although dozens of such studies have taken place in the last twenty years.

The unwarranted assumption that children watch twenty-seven hours of violent programming a week is clearly false. Children may watch that much television, but not all of it is violent. The assumption that all television executives are morally depraved is unwarranted. The assumption that parents, caregivers, and technological devices cannot control the amount of violence children see on television is also unwarranted; there is a large amount of anecdotal evidence to the contrary.

The piece oversimplifies the complex psychological, biological, and environmental factors that lead a child to commit murder. It attempts to deliberately deceive us about the tragedy and turmoil in these children's lives by demeaning them as "killer kids." The term stereotypes them as robotic zombies in the control of morally bankrupt television executives. Finally, the piece tries to psychologically force us to accept its bizarre conclusions by abruptly dismissing three factors—dysfunctional family life, poverty, and easy access to guns—which most likely have something do with the children's motivations.

The piece needs to be completely revised. A definition of television violence and evidence taken from controlled observations on the effects television violence has on children are essential. The exaggerated allusions to military training should be eliminated. Name-calling should be eliminated. The three dismissed claims must be investigated. The revised piece may be able to show more clearly and with more detail that television violence is one of several factors in the lives of children who choose violence as a way of dealing with their lives.

EXERCISES

▲ QUESTIONS FOR DISCUSSION

1. Review your responses to Short Essay 5–16 and Questions for Discussion 7–14 in the set of exercises before the last set. Identify differences between your responses and those of the "Model Evaluation." Do not assume that your responses are "wrong" if they disagree with the Model. Discuss the differences and come to a consensus with members of the class and your instructor.

2. Evaluate Question for Discussion #15 (your first draft critical essay). Use The Format in the evaluation, just as if you were evaluating an opinion piece by someone else. Alternatively, exchange and evaluate first drafts with another student. Use The Format.

3. Evaluate one of the essays in the appendix. Use The Format.

THE MINI-FORMAT

Not every evaluation needs the specificity of the detailed format. Shorter pieces can be evaluated with The Mini-Format, which is a summary of the longer version. Long pieces can also be evaluated this way. However, it should be remembered that The Mini-Format is a summary. It does not give details on the primary elements or organization of the piece. The detailed format provides a checklist by which every standard can be thoroughly applied. The Mini-Format does not provide the fallacies and other details useful in applying each standard. When you use The Mini-Format, consult the detailed format often. That way you will be less likely to overlook specific elements in the organization and evaluation of the piece.

Using The Mini-Format.   Oversimplification and a lack of detailed analysis are major roadblocks to an adequate use of The Mini-Format. You should have a thorough understanding of all of the elements of review and evaluation before you use The Mini-Format. The best way to earn that understanding is to use the detailed format on at least one or two of the opinion pieces in the appendix. The experience will give you a good review of the material in the course, as well as practice in applying it to written pieces.

The Mini-Format: Review.   The author, date, source, and purpose are identified. The conclusion and support (stated and hidden) are identified. Only the major support statements, the ones that directly support the conclusion, need be listed. The conclusion and major support statements are listed in appropriate order.

Statements are not labeled as representative, expressive, or directive. Important metaphors, allusions, word choices, and prejudicial expressions are identified, but not listed. Types and components of evidence in major support statements are described.

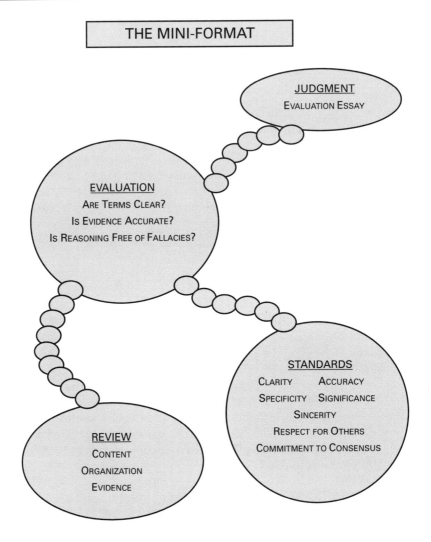

THE MINI-FORMAT

JUDGMENT
EVALUATION ESSAY

EVALUATION
ARE TERMS CLEAR?
IS EVIDENCE ACCURATE?
IS REASONING FREE OF FALLACIES?

STANDARDS
CLARITY   ACCURACY
SPECIFICITY   SIGNIFICANCE
SINCERITY
RESPECT FOR OTHERS
COMMITMENT TO CONSENSUS

REVIEW
CONTENT
ORGANIZATION
EVIDENCE

The Mini-Format: Evaluation.   The piece is evaluated according to the seven standards, but not in as much detail. Vague and ambiguous terms are identified, but are listed only if they have a serious impact on the conclusion. The strength and weakness of the evidence is reviewed, but only evidence that is particularly strong or weak is described. The piece is reviewed for fallacies, but only those fallacies that seriously weaken the piece's reasoning need be listed. Attitude is evaluated by a review of fallacies and identification of any persuasive definitions and demeaning expressions.

The Mini-Format: Judgment and Critical Essay.   The decision about the quality of the piece is based on the review and evaluation. This decision should be empathetic, reasonable, and motivated by a sincere desire to achieve a consensus. The essay should summarize the findings of the review and evaluation of the piece, much like the essay that concludes the detailed format.

The Mini-Format: A Model. The Mini-Format evaluates the essay, "Television Violence Turns Kids into Killers" with the same empathy, rigor, and purpose as that of the detailed format. It is simply less detailed.

Review. "Television Violence Turns Kids into Killers" is an opinion piece written by Mathematics professor Erick Cod in the October 13 issue of *Jabber,* Scott Bartine College weekly student newspaper. The piece is an attempt to shed light on several cases in which children as young as twelve have murdered classmates, parents, and teachers. It also seems to address youth gang violence. The piece has two conclusions. The first is "Television turns out killer kids just like boot camp turns out soldiers." ¶3) The main conclusion is "We need strict laws that ban all violence on television." The primary support for the first conclusion is hidden, but can be paraphrased as "The military effectively brainwashes recruits to enjoy killing other human beings." The support for the main conclusion is also hidden: Television violence's psychological effect on children is as deep and pervasive as that of military training on recruits." The main conclusion is also supported by the hidden premise "the only way to eliminate television violence is to legally ban it." Two stated supports are especially important. The piece denies that family breakdowns, poverty, and easy access to guns have any bearing on children killing anyone. Second, the piece claims that television executives won't stop television violence until some are thrown into jail.

The piece uses two loaded terms, one for the children who have killed others, "Killer Kids," and "Killer Soldiers" for trained recruits. Children undergo "brainwashing" in violence when they watch television violence, which is called an "Ugly Terror."

The evidence is anecdotal. There are no cited studies and no authorities are quoted.

Evaluation. The lack of a definition of "television violence" is the most serious difficulty the piece has with clarity. The anecdotal evidence does not refer to any of the studies (there are several) done on aggression and television violence. The evidence is limited to Mr. Cod's personal views of the similarity between military training and the television viewing habits of children. The piece commits the fallacy of oversimplification several times, but most seriously when it ignores the complexity of the psychological, biological, and environmental factors involved in a child who murders anyone. The unwarranted assumption that parents and caregivers cannot control children's television viewing also weakens the piece. Television executives are assumed (unwarranted) to be so morally depraved that they will not improve programming unless some are given time in jail. The piece attempts to persuade us that legislation that would "ban all television violence" is the *only* solution to the problem. When it tells us to ignore family breakdowns, poverty, and easy access to guns as possible factors in the problem, the piece reveals a lack of commitment to consensus as well as a lack of a sincere desire to discover the truth.

Judgment and Critical Essay.   The Mini-Format requires a less specific critical essay than the more detailed format. For example, notice the differences between the longer critical essay in the previous section and this one.

Critical Essay

(Mini-Format)

"Television Violence Turns Kids into Killers"

The piece does not meet reasonable expectations for an informal statement of opinion. Is the author discussing a cartoon in which a character is pushed off a cliff? Is he talking about a "true crime" drama that glorifies "robbery, rape, and murder?" The lack of a definition of "television violence" makes the whole piece unclear.

The piece's claim that military recruits are brainwashed to the point where they "lose respect for human life" is an oversimplification. Since the author has military experience, and can be assumed to know something about the training recruits receive, it appears that he is not being sincere in this claim. He also seems to be more concerned with convincing us of his position than with reaching a consensus on the truth. He tells us to ignore factors that many authorities believe to be important: family breakdowns, poverty, and easy access to guns.

The piece does not refer to any observational evidence from any of the many studies on television violence and children's aggression. The problem is far more complex than the piece would lead us to believe. When the piece ignores the complex interplay of biological, environmental, and psychological factors involved with childhood violence and claims that only one factor (television violence) is important, it commits the fallacy of oversimplification. The piece commits the fallacy of unwarranted assumption when it ignores the role of parents and primary caretakers in controlling children's television viewing. It commits the same fallacy when it claims that a few television executives must be "thrown in jail" in order for the industry to cease its "brainwashing" of children.

The piece should be completely revised. "Television violence" should be defined. References to military training should be more truthful. Studies of children's levels of aggression and television violence should be summarized, or reference to authorities on them should be made. Oversimplification of the complexities of a child's motives in killing should be avoided. The piece could help us come to a consensus on the importance of television violence in these tragic killings, but only if it defines its terms, presents reliable observational or testimonial evidence, and avoids fallacies.

CONCLUSION

A great deal of thinking about important issues takes place in writing. Worldwide issues, as well as local problems, are often defined and discussed in the press, in academic studies, government policy statements, and other pieces of writing. Unfortunately, the written pieces that deal with the issues and problems often do not consider their complexity. Key terms are left undefined, important evidence is overlooked or deliberately ignored, and fallacies are substituted for good reasoning. Authors, instead of contributing to a consensus on the essential elements of the piece, often write with the intention of advancing their career or of persuading others to adopt their political agenda. Consequently, their pieces do not clarify the issues or encourage honest discussion; they do the opposite. They mystify the issues and encourage quarrelsome disputes.

World issues and local problems are complex, but they do not have to be mysteries. There are always going to be different opinions about issues and problems; people have different perspectives, different values, and different needs. The more we quarrel, the more mysterious our world becomes to us, and the further we move from respectful discussion and sincere consensus about our common issues and problems.

We are not doomed to quarrels, disputes, and wars. There are ways to work together in seeking understanding and solutions. One of the ways to do this is critical thinking. We can clarify issues and find evidence that makes them more intelligible. We can engage in specific, significant discussions about problems. We can approach complex issues with the goal of achieving a consensus. It is not written in stone that we must mystify and confuse ourselves. We are not forced to advance our personal careers and political agendas at the expense of a better world. Critical thinking works; it really does improve the way we perceive the world, its issues, and its problems.

However, critical thinking requires information, organization, and effort. We need to be informed; that is, we need to know the relevant information that the sciences and social sciences have to offer us. We need to listen to the philosophers, poets, musicians, and artists of our time and culture, as well as those from other times and cultures. Critical thinkers need to be good students. That doesn't mean that good grades are required; *learning* is required.

Critical thinkers need to be organized. The Format provides a pattern that contributes to the organization of an evaluation of written pieces. It is lengthy and quite intense. However, the effort expended in following it will result in a rigorous and well-organized approach to the evaluation of written pieces. The process becomes habitual. Experienced critical thinkers habitually approach written pieces with The Format in mind. Once you have mastered the material in this course and are thoroughly familiar with definitions, summarizing, paraphrasing, the seven standards of good thinking, logical thinking, the types, components, strengths, and weaknesses of evidence, you are ready to use the Mini-Format. If you organize your evaluations according to either format, you will be applying everything you have learned in this course.

Critical thinkers are committed to a search for understanding and solutions, not to "winning" debates, achieving power, or gaining wealth. We live in a society that encourages us to "compete" with others and "defeat" them in debates, political life, and in economic achievement. Competition is a wonderful element of games. Competing with others athletically and intellectually often motivates us to a higher quality performance than we thought possible.

Worldwide issues and local problems are not games. It is one thing to win a debate competition in school. It is quite another to "defeat" a person in need of help who is not quite articulate enough to state his or her case. Political power and wealth can be great forces in understanding and developing solutions to problems. However, when politics and economic realities are treated as if they were games, they are regarded as "prizes" to be won. Consequently, power and wealth are not used as tools to make the world a better place for all human beings, but to adorn the egos of a few self-seeking individuals.

So far, this course has studied the tools and methods of critical thinking. By using them, we can improve thinking, and by doing so, improve our world. We have yet to study the personal characteristics of critical thinkers. The next (and last) chapter investigates the values and leadership characteristics of critical thinkers.

EXERCISES

▲ MOST INTRIGUING ISSUE

Write a one-paragraph description of the most interesting idea, topic, or process described in the chapter. Be prepared to explain what you find interesting in class discussion.

▲ THE MUDDIEST POINT

Write a sentence or, if possible, a paragraph that describes the idea, topic, expression, term, or process in the chapter that you find most difficult to understand.

▲ SHORT ESSAY QUESTIONS

Provide a written response of approximately 200 words to each topic. Your responses should be well organized, grammatically correct, and neatly produced.

1. Describe five things in The Format that are not included in the Mini-Format.
2. Provide three examples in which The Format would be more appropriate than The Mini-Format. Also provide three examples in which The Mini-Format would be more important.
3. Review the "Conclusion" section. Describe the personal characteristics you believe are essential to a critical thinker.

▲ QUESTIONS FOR DISCUSSION

Choose one or more of the written pieces from the appendix. Evaluate it using The Mini-Format.

▲ PORTFOLIO PAPER

Review your paper, "The Importance of Evidence in Beliefs," which you wrote after completing your study of Chapter 8. Thoroughly evaluate your own paper using The Format, and revise it appropriately.

CHAPTER 10

CRITICAL THINKING IN THE HOME, AT WORK, AND IN THE COMMUNITY

THE PURPOSE OF CRITICAL THINKING

The goal of critical thinking is to improve thinking. As we have seen, reaching this goal involves us in a great deal of detailed, rigorous, and empathetic work. Thinking, while it is a natural human act, is not done well without *standards, organization, empathy,* and *effort.* That last word should not surprise us. Except for the occasional "lucky break," anything that is worthwhile comes to us only when we make an effort. Certainly, efforts expended in improving thinking have tremendously improved our human condition.

Reflect for a moment on the vast improvements in life provided by the natural sciences. Our understanding of medicine has grown from superstitious beliefs in magic potions, spells, and chanting shamans to scientific recognition of the interrelationship of the body with its physical-chemical environment. As our thinking about medicine improved, so has our health. In the fourteenth century, over three-fourths of the population of Europe died from plague in less than

AFTER STUDYING CHAPTER TEN

You should be able to describe the importance of creativity and intuition to critical thinking, and describe the goals, rules, and guidelines involved with brainstorming, and to take an active role in brainstorming. You should be able to explain and apply the five step problem-solving method. Finally, you should be able to describe the three characteristics of critical thinkers and use them in evaluating your own strengths and weaknesses as a critical thinker.

twenty years. In the seventeenth century, a plague nearly destroyed the population of London. Ninety percent of those who contracted the disease died. Today, the bacteria that cause the plague are still with us. They didn't just "go away." However, medicine offers drugs and preventive vaccines that can keep us free from the disease. The science of medicine banished them from our lives.

Of course, the scientific approach differs from superstition in many ways. However, the primary difference between the two is in their divergent attitudes toward tradition. Superstition regards tradition as "sacred." The rituals, spells, and potions of the past are habitually and persistently repeated. Science, on the other hand, thinks critically about tradition; it revises traditional practices and theories whenever they are evaluated as inadequate.

A very good example of science's revision of tradition is the development of technology. The automobile, airplane, telephone, radio, television, and computer have changed every aspect of human life tremendously in the last one hundred years. In fact, we have gone through more changes in the past one hundred years than in the past thousand! Ordinary people now travel and communicate more rapidly and more efficiently than in the dreams of the wealthiest kings and queens of the past. It took Columbus almost three months to sail across the Atlantic in 1492. Perhaps one amazing contrast is the fact that the Wright brothers' first wobbly flights at Kitty Hawk, North Carolina took place in late 1903. Today, more than ninety years later, the Concord makes the flight from New York City to Paris in less than four hours! The pioneers' trek from St. Louis to the American West took months of hardship and toil. Thousands of children died on these journeys. Today we drive efficient automobiles along paved highways lined with convenience stores, restaurants, and motels.

All of the progress in travel and communication in the last one hundred years is the result of critical thinking. Not being satisfied with the status quo, engineers, scientists, and other critical thinkers continually review, evaluate, and revise technology.

Communication technology has progressed rapidly in the last twenty-five years. The hardware used in telephones, video technology, and computers has gone through massive developments. This has vastly improved communication, data storage and retrieval, and education technology.

At one time, "wizards" and other "wise men" guarded information more closely than diamonds and gold. Those who had information had a possession more precious than mere wealth. Without knowledge, wealth was useless. Ancient kings would gladly give the clever sages whatever they desired in exchange for their "secrets." Information remained a "private possession" for centuries. As little as fifty years ago, information was still the prized possession of a few "learned" aristocrats hidden away in prestigious universities and government offices.

However, the Internet, the "information superhighway," which is an international electronic library and communication network, provides everyone in the world access to information and the ability to communicate. Not only can anyone with access to it use the Internet to find information, anyone can also add to it. One no longer needs to have the official approval of those holding political and social power to communicate a point of view. The Internet is the most significant leap in information and communication technology in the history of civilization.

Like those in medicine and travel, the developments in communication and information technology are the results of critical thinking.

The social sciences have also vastly improved our lives. For example, mental illness was regarded as "demon possession" up until the very beginnings of the nineteenth century. "Civilized" people responded with superstition and ignorance when they encountered abnormal behavior. They were terrified by it. However, controlled observation of abnormal behaviors revealed them to be symptoms of illness, not "spiritual punishments." Today we recognize that mental illness is truly an *illness,* not a mysterious condition that defies explanation. We no longer fear the mentally ill, but have compassion for them, and seek to alleviate their pain.

The social sciences have also helped us overcome our fears of those who are "different" in other ways. Observation has shown us that skin tone, ethnicity, gender, sexual preference, religious beliefs, and all the other things that used to separate people into "superior" and "inferior" groups are simply differences, not pecking orders.

Self-understanding has progressed along with our understanding of others. We know that inherited characteristics and environment shape our personalities. We understand more about perception, language, and the brain than at any time in history.

All of this progress in understanding others and ourselves is due to critical thinking. Our technological, information-based culture didn't "just happen." Of course, there have been a few "lucky breaks," but progress has been primarily the result of effort expended in review, evaluation, and *improvement* of our world.

It is important to realize that critical thinking—not science, technology, or information—is the *essential* factor in progress. It is common knowledge that science and technology have also been agents of barbarism. Natural science has given us germ warfare, nuclear weapons, and other horrible weapons that have only one purpose: to kill human beings. The social sciences have spawned scores of stratagems used to manipulate, deceive, and demean. "Psychological warfare," "brainwashing," and "behavior modification" are schemes one might expect of a primitive shaman.

Indeed, some social critics believe that an unbiased assessment of the role of technology and science in our lives must conclude that both have done more harm than good. For every disease that has been eliminated, pollution or toxic wastes have caused another. We can provide food to anyone who needs it, but we choose to use it as a weapon of war. We are able to travel faster than sound; but we aim missiles with nuclear warheads at every city in the world. At present, although we know that racism is a result of ignorance and fear, we continue to institutionalize race as a primary means of personal identity. In the United States, bigotry and racial fear are still rampant. The poor in our country are overwhelmingly people of color. The primary cause of death of African-American young men is homicide. Twenty-five percent of African-American young men are incarcerated in jails and prisons.

We cannot be proud of the fact that over one million human beings are imprisoned in the United States, a rate six to ten times higher than most industrialized nations. Nor can we be proud of our use of technology to spy on people, pry into their private lives, and expose their secrets on television, and gossip about them on the Internet.

The social critics have a very good point. Science, social science, and technology offer no guarantee of progress. Primitive life, while it was not as comfortable as ours, may have been more peaceful, less shallow, and much less anxiety-ridden. However, the only way to decide whether science and technology are doing more harm than good is to review, evaluate, and revise their place in our world. Critical thinking has moved us from superstition to science and technology, and critical thinking can move us from our current problems with science and technology to new solutions.

Critical thinking *criticizes*. We have a tendency to regard criticism as a negative activity. The problem with criticism is that it too often merely points out the "bad" without making any suggestions for improvement. This lack of positive direction is what makes a negative attitude so distasteful. Most people like to have a "positive attitude," and shy away from any sort of negative criticism whenever possible. "What good does it do to be negative?" is a common question. It is a very good question.

 A positive attitude is one that tries to see the good in things. Unlike a negative approach, a positive attitude does not seek to "tear down," but to "build up." Critical thinking is not a negative activity. True, it does not mindlessly accept the status quo; it criticizes it. However, to go along with whatever society currently believes does not reveal a positive attitude. It reveals personal lethargy and lack of responsibility. Those who mindlessly conform are not motivated by a positive attitude; they are motivated by fear of change or by immaturity. A positive attitude sees the good in change; it recognizes that change is inevitable, and seeks to make changes that improve our world.

The world can be improved. It can be made a better place for everyone. This belief has carried us from superstition, ignorance, and fear to the world in which we live at present. Our world has problems, the great majority of which are due to the way we think. Critical thinking seeks to make the world a better place—to solve problems—by improving the way we think about the world. Of course, much of that thinking takes place in written pieces, and so far, we have focused on reviewing, evaluating, and revising them. No doubt, the more clear, accurate, specific, and significant our writing, the better our thinking will be. The more sincerity, respect, and commitment to consensus we achieve, the more effectively we will communicate with each other. With the growth of communication technology, especially the Internet, writing has become extremely important. Critical thinking, as we have seen, provides the best way to improve thinking, writing, and communication.

However, critical thinking is not limited to written pieces. It is also involved with solving problems. A problem is a specific disturbance in life. A car that won't start, a word processing program that refuses to print anything, or a cut that won't heal; each is a "problem." On a grander scale, the entire world shares problems such as illiteracy, malnutrition, sexually transmitted diseases, and prejudice. These problems must be addressed and eventually solved if we are to continue to improve our ways of living. They will not solve themselves; nevertheless, those of us who think critically about them will solve them.

PROBLEM SOLVING: INTUITION AND CREATIVITY

Written pieces are often very important aspects in problem solving. The information we have about problems and their possible solutions is usually recorded in writing. We communicate with others, whether it is via the Internet or in reports, opinion pieces, newspapers, journals, magazines, and so on, in writing. Everything we have studied so far about verbal and logical thinking is an essential element of problem solving.

However, for problem solving oral discussion is as important as writing. Those who are affected by them usually discuss problems. When the car won't start, we need to talk with the mechanic, explain what occurs when we turn the key, what doesn't occur, and so on. When the printer won't print, we talk about the problem with other people, especially with those who have had the same experience. For example, on a grander scale, there are daily international discussions on the problem of illiteracy taking place at the United Nations. Experts discuss ways to overcome malnutrition and sexually transmitted diseases during conferences sponsored by the World Health Organization, the Red Cross, and others. The people involved in these discussions are seeking new ideas about ways to solve problems. They are very much aware that creative proposals have a better chance of success in solving these massive problems than old ideas and traditional remedies. Of course, old ideas are not inherently poor ideas. Nevertheless, if the old ideas and traditional remedies are already in place and the problems remain, obviously, new, useful ideas that supplement or replace old ideas are very welcome.

Conferences bring people together so that they can share their views "face to face," without the interference of the written word. When we talk with each other in person, we are able to communicate with the full range of expressive and representative meaning that language offers. An oral discussion often "gets us to the point" much more efficiently than writing because we are able to "connect" with others in a way that writing rarely affords. For example, we can understand subtle allusions with the help of gestures. When we don't completely understand what the other person is saying, we can interrupt and ask for clarification. We can "feel" a moral or political "common ground" with another person when we talk with them; or we can "sense" that we have different basic values. When we are "face-to-face" with another person, we are able to request the degree of clarity, accuracy, specificity, and significance that we feel is necessary for understanding and communication. We are able to "feel" the degree of the other's sincerity, respect, and commitment to consensus much more accurately in a face-to-face encounter than we can with the written piece.

Oral discussion is greatly supplemented by these "feelings" we have of other's meanings and attitudes. These "intuitions" about other people are much more common in discussion than in reading written pieces.

Intuition is not limited to insights about other people. We also have intuitions about ideas and beliefs.

Intuition. Intuition is a sudden recognition that an organizational pattern possesses or lacks particular characteristics. An "organizational pattern" is a characteristic of any perception. A person's face has an "organizational pattern." A painting or a map has an "organizational pattern." A discussion, in which patterns are heard, rather than seen, also has an "organizational pattern." As we are using the term, an organizational pattern is simply the organizational component of a perception. Intuition is a type of thinking that is different from verbal and logical thinking. Verbal thinking is based on language; intuition is based on non-verbal perceptions. Logical thinking is based on inference, while intuition is based on immediate comparisons and contrasts. However, intuition understands, processes, and communicates; it is a type of *thinking*.

For example, psychologists have studied the facial expressions of people who are lying and contrasted them with those of people telling the truth. Their observations tell us that most people sometimes are able to separate liars from truth-tellers by observing facial expressions. Agents for the Secret Service (the federal agency responsible for the safety of the President of the United States) who have been trained to examine facial expressions closely are much better at it than anyone else. The agents' intuitive thinking has been improved by training.

Psychological observations have also revealed that people of cultures as different as the United States and New Guinea (who had no experience with television or movies) agreed upon the meanings of different facial expressions. The psychologists asked subjects from Europe, Asia, and South America to indicate what emotion they noticed in photographs of Americans posing with the emotions of anger, fear, happiness, disgust, sadness, and surprise. All of the groups, including the Fore, an isolated group of people in New Guinea who had absolutely no previous contact with Western culture, correctly identified the emotions being portrayed. Several years after the observations, the psychologists videotaped the facial expressions of the Fore, asking them to mimic designated emotions. When American college students were shown the videos, they easily identified the emotions being displayed. These observations are evidence that intuition of the emotions behind facial expressions is usually accurate.

Intuition appears to be intimately associated with the selective and interpretive functions of perception. We can select particular aspects of a person's facial expressions and correctly interpret them as indicating a particular emotion. For example, we all have had the intuition that a child is unhappy. One look at the protruding lower lip, the weepy eyes, and lowered head is all we need to recognize that the child is sad. We may even have been successful in recognizing that someone is lying; the smile is not quite "genuine," and the eyes "shift." Intuition selects aspects of facial "patterns" and interprets them (sometimes correctly, sometimes incorrectly) as displaying particular characteristics. Intuition is not limited to facial features.

For example, you may have noticed that there wasn't enough space in a room for the number of people invited to a discussion there. You didn't have to measure the space; you simply looked at the room and suddenly recognized that it was too small.

Imagine that you are sitting in your favorite chair, absorbed in a great novel. Unexpectedly, you "feel" that something isn't quite right. You listen to what appears to be a strange sound. Then, all at once, you realize that it is the sound of the bathtub overflowing! You leap from the chair and race to the bathroom and discover your six-year-old has decided to bathe the family dog. You did not have to infer that the sound was that of the overflowing tub; you immediately knew what it was. Intuition directly interpreted what you heard.

One more example of intuition is the feeling we sometimes have about moral or religious beliefs. A person may say, "I don't have any rational basis for my belief that God exists; I just feel that it is true." This person is claiming to have an intuition about the truth of his or her religious belief. The "organizational pattern" of the world and his or her feelings about it reveals the existence of God. Some philosophers believe that our moral values are based solely on intuition. For example, they claim that we "sense" that lying is morally wrong when we do it to defraud someone out of their life savings, but morally right when we lie in order to save someone's life. These philosophers argue that we make moral decisions of this kind very quickly: too quickly to involve logical or verbal thinking. We simply "recognize" what is right and wrong in the organizational pattern of human relationships.

Intuition, then, is the type of thinking that immediately recognizes particular characteristics. Of course, like every other sort of thinking, it does not always result in publicly confirmed beliefs. In fact, a major difficulty with intuition is the lack of any standards by which we can distinguish "good intuitive thinking" from "poor intuitive thinking." For that reason, intuition alone cannot be relied upon for any serious beliefs. Anything we intuitively know must be evaluated by the standards of verbal and logical thinking.

EVALUATING INTUITION.   Intuitions are similar to "hunches"; they are immediate mental connections of perceptions to meanings. Imagine that you are at a racetrack with some friends betting on the horses. Each of you puts a dollar in the pot. The group comes to a consensus on which horse should come in first and then bets the accumulated funds on it at the pari-mutuel window. You have a "hunch" that horse number seven will win the next race. You do not have any reasons for your hunch; it is simply an intuition. When you tell your friends that you think number seven will win, they ask you to support your belief with some reasoning and some evidence. They are asking you to evaluate your intuition.

Our natural tendency is to evaluate the quality of the intuition on the basis of how strongly it is felt. That is, you could say to your friends, "I know that number seven will win because I have a very strong feeling about this horse." Unfortunately, your friends are not impressed. They realize that intuitions are often wrong even when they are strongly felt. Indeed, if strong intuitions were all we needed to gain the truth, clairvoyants and fortune-tellers would be in very high demand! The sad fact is that our "strong" hunches are wrong as often as our "weak" feelings are right; and neither is right very often. If intuition could be evaluated on its own terms, many more people would win at horse races, lotteries, and the stock market.

In the absence of any way to evaluate intuition on its own, we can only resort to the standards of verbal and logical thinking. Clarity and accuracy seem to be especially appropriate standards for intuitions, which are often rather vague. Of course, intuitions can be biased as easily as verbal or logical thought. Thus, they should be evaluated for sincerity, respect, and commitment to consensus. Are the intuitions specific? Are they significant? These questions must also be asked of our intuitive thinking.

In addition, some evidence is necessary before intuitions can be accepted as even subjectively true. For example, although there is little factual or theoretical evidence for religious or moral beliefs, it is always appropriate to ask that they cohere emotionally. Thus, the intuition that it is wrong to lie in order to gain money but right to lie in order to save someone's life should have some sort of "glue" that emotionally holds the logically separate beliefs together. The emotional feeling that "lies that help people do no harm, while lies that gain money hurt the people it is taken from" supports the intuition emotionally. The support may be sufficient for an individual person to adopt the intuitive belief as part of their moral code. Of course, it they want others to share that code, they will have to provide more evidence. Public confirmation of moral beliefs requires a degree of theoretical and factual components.

INTUITION IN ORAL DISCUSSION.   In oral discussions, therefore, intuitions work in two ways. First, we have intuitions about the characteristics of other people in the discussion. We "intuit" that they are being sincere, deceptive, respectful, overly persuasive, and so on. We may even have feelings about their level of expertise; for example, we may feel that they are appropriate authorities. Second, we have intuitions about the subject matter under discussion. Sometimes these intuitions "come from left field" or "out of the blue." We have no idea "where they came from," but we feel quite strongly that they are worth discussion. As we shall see, this characteristic of intuition—its ability to come up with an original, unexpected idea or feeling—is an important element of problem solving.

Creativity.   Creativity is the ability to generate new and useful ideas. (An idea that is new but useless is not regarded as a creative idea; it is simply a new one.) New ideas cannot be generated out of nothing; they come from perceptions, ideas, and feelings stored in the memory. We cannot know what we have not experienced; even a new idea has a background as a selected, organized, and interpreted sensation. However, memories can be taken apart, combined, and changed by mental activity. Thus, we have a memory of a horse we have seen, of a bird, and of silver shining in the sun. We can take the ideas apart and combine them into a winged horse with a silver mane and tail, flying through the blue sky. Creativity is the mental activity of changing individual memories into new and useful ideas. Of course, it is a very complicated activity. Cognitive psychologists point out that creativity occurs in every type of thinking; a gymnast who comes up with a new routine is thinking spatially in a creative way. A scientist, for example Copernicus, who created the idea of the heliocentric solar system, thinks logically, mathematically, and verbally in a creative way. Artists who astound us with their visions on canvas, in bronze, in words, or in film are the most obvious examples of creative thinking.

You were thinking creatively when you put together cartoons that illustrate concepts in critical thinking. For example, you could have illustrated the difference between an opinion piece and an argumentative essay as an exercise in Chapter 9. Your cartoon could have pictured two stick people, one standing at a podium coaxing an audience to agree with his feelings about the meaning of a poem, the other an attorney in a courtroom attempting to prove to a jury that a suspect was "guilty as charged." In creating the cartoon, you relied on memories as the "raw materials" out of which you fashioned your "finished product," the cartoon. Perhaps you have used stick people in cartoons before, so you simply adapted them to the ideas assigned. However, you also had to remember the distinctions between opinions and arguments or your cartoon would not have been very useful. You were not able to simply "slap together" some memories or ideas and come up with a creative cartoon. You had to think about the assignment first. You had to recall some specific information about opinions and arguments from the course, then you proceeded to take those ideas apart and put them together in a new, useful way.

CREATIVITY, VISUALIZATION, AND FREE ASSOCIATION.   Creative thought often involves what cognitive psychologists call "visualization." Literally, this means to have pictures in our heads. For example, imagine two clocks (not digital clocks; these two have hour hands and minute hands). Clock "A" reads 7:30. Clock "B," 3:25. Which clock's hands are closer together? In order to answer this question, most people mentally *visualize* two clocks. They mentally "see" the distance between the hands. Creative thought also involves "mental seeing." Ideas are remembered as images and are then taken apart and combined. Thus, a city engineer may visualize a section of the downtown traffic grid freed of any congestion. She does this by combining her memories about the grid as it is (congested) with her ideas about a new monorail system. She generates a new, useful picture by synthesizing the two ideas. Of course, the actual process is much more complex than this example. The main point is that visualization seems to be a large part of creative thinking.

Cognitive psychologists believe that most of our memories have a visualization component. That is, we usually have a mental image when we remember an idea. Some ideas, especially abstractions such as "love" or "truth," are remembered as words and sentences. However, there is a consensus that the relationship between memory and creativity, especially the creativity involved in problem solving, is very strong.

Images are easily manipulated. They can be taken apart, put together with other images, and so on, at will. For example, the silver-winged horse and the downtown traffic grid free of congestion are rather easy to picture. Creative ideas can also be generated by attention to words and sentences. Memories are stored in verbal form as well as in pictures. "Word-memories" can be useful to creative thought in two primary ways. The first is the obvious remembrance and combination of words in new and useful ways. Thus, the mayor's speechwriter can come up with a creative way to describe how the new monorail will decrease or even eliminate congestion in the downtown area. Instead of merely writing, "the monorail will greatly reduce traffic congestion," he can recall appropriate metaphors and make word choices that will result in a more creative speech. "The monorail" becomes "the sleek silver sky train" and instead of "reducing congestion," it "sails above a serene and comfortable city completely free of smog and clamor."

Words also stimulate creative thought in a more subtle way, known as "free association," a term for gaining access to combinations of words hidden deeply within the memory or, according to some psychologists, the "unconscious." Thus, a person merely says anything that comes to mind, not censoring or editing them in any way. Psychotherapists use free association to encourage clients to retrieve unconscious memories that are at the root of their personal difficulties. However, free association is also used to stimulate creative thinking. For example, when you are prompted with the word "rat," you may think of the word "cat." The next word you think of may be "dog," and then "pet." Suddenly, the word "get" comes to mind. Obviously, it has little to do with the meaning of "pet." It simply rhymes with it. According to the technique of free association, you say it anyway. The next word may be "money," and the next could be "bunny." It makes no difference how or why you come up with the words you do. The creative process is stimulated by free association because it allows us to "free" ourselves from normal, noncreative associations in a playful way. Think about it: How else could you move from the idea of a rat to a bunny in a few seconds?

EVALUATION OF CREATIVE IDEAS. New ideas are much easier to come up with than creative ideas. Creative ideas are not only new; they are also useful for a specific purpose. Thus, the first evaluation of any creative idea questions its usefulness for a specific purpose. Any assumptions about its practical application need to be investigated. Are they warranted assumptions? New ideas are often far too general or "too idealistic" to be of any practical value. We need to ask whether the idea is an overgeneralization. Many ideas that are proposed as creative are exposed as simply new ideas once they are evaluated for achieving a specific purpose. Creative thought can be very disheartening; creativity is not an easy type of thinking. Like all thinking, it requires great effort. The process of creative thinking is one in which a single creative idea is generated out of a very large number of new ideas. The greatest barrier to successful creative thought is lack of persistence.

Creative ideas must be clear; any vagueness hinders their usefulness. The standard of clarity for creative ideas is no different than for any type of thinking. Creative ideas must *communicate*; they must be understandable. This does not mean that everyone must be able to understand them immediately. Creative ideas, like many other ideas, require study and patience before they can be grasped completely. We should not confuse an idea's clarity with simplicity. An idea can be extremely complex and profound, yet clear for those who take the time and effort to understand it. An unclear idea is one that is so vague that it defies understanding even by those who persistently investigate it. For example, some people find classical music terribly vague. It doesn't communicate with them. However, if they give some time and effort to the study of Music Appreciation they find that classical music begins to make more sense. This is a common experience in Music Appreciation courses. Creative ideas, whether in music, painting, sculpture, or literature, are often puzzling at first glance. Their complexity can be confusing. Persistence and familiarity usually alleviate confusion.

When evaluating creative ideas, the primary concern is with specificity and clarity. An idea, no matter how new, cannot be of any use if it is overly general or vague. Like intuitive thinking, creativity can be of immense value in solving problems. After all, if the old, "tried and true" ideas could solve the problem, the problem wouldn't exist! It would already have been solved in the old "tried and true" ways. By definition, problem solving requires intuitive and creative thought. In the next section we will investigate brainstorming, a problem-solving technique that stimulates intuition and creativity.

EXERCISES

▲ MOST INTRIGUING ISSUE

Write a one-paragraph description of the most interesting idea, topic, or process described in the chapter so far. Be prepared to explain what you find interesting in class discussion.

▲ THE MUDDIEST POINT

Write a sentence or, if possible, a paragraph that describes the idea, topic, expression, term, or process in the chapter so far that you find most difficult to understand.

▲ CARTOONS AND DIAGRAMS

Cartoons are drawings that characterize or symbolize ideas, processes, or expressions in imaginative ways. Diagrams are drawings, charts, or tables that show how specific details of an idea, process, or expression are interrelated.

1. Provide a creative cartoon that illustrates the importance of problem solving.
2. Provide a creative cartoon that shows how scientific progress has benefited and yet encumbered our lives.
3. Draw a creative cartoon that illustrates the difference between a positive and a negative attitude in relation to critical thinking.
4. Draw a creative cartoon that provides a good illustration of intuition.
5. Provide a creative cartoon that shows three faces, one of which is angry, another happy, and a third sad. Show your classmates the cartoon, and see if they intuitively identify the emotions.
6. Provide a creative cartoon that shows the difference between creativity and intuition.
7. Draw a creative cartoon that shows a good example of a creative thinker at work.
8. Draw a creative cartoon that shows the difference between a creative idea and a merely new idea.
9. Draw a creative cartoon that illustrates the importance of visualization for creative thinking.
10. Draw a creative cartoon that shows the importance of free association for creative thinking.

▲ Definitions of Key Terms

Provide a disciplinary definition for each of the following terms as they are used in this chapter. Most of the terms are not defined in the chapter, although their meanings are described by the context in which they appear. You need to review the material to create the definition yourself. Be sure to follow the guidelines for creating definitions on pages 78–81.

Problem	Intuition	Creativity
Organizational Pattern	Visualization	Free Association

▲ Short Essay Questions

Provide a written response of approximately 200 words for each topic. Your responses should be well organized, grammatically correct, and neatly produced.

1. Paraphrase and explain the meaning of this statement in a way that makes its meaning clear to a person who has not taken this course: "Critical thinking seeks to make the world a better place—to solve problems—by improving the way we think about the world."
2. Explain why oral discussion is especially appropriate for problem solving.
3. Paraphrase and explain the meaning of this statement in a way that clarifies it for a person unfamiliar with this course: "If old ideas and traditional remedies are already in place and the problems remain, obviously, new, useful ideas that supplement or replace old ideas are very welcome."
4. Explain how an "organizational pattern" is involved with the intuition that there is "something wrong" in the chapter's example of the six-year-old bathing the family dog.

5. The chapter points out that Secret Service Agents have been trained to intuitively recognize organized facial patterns involved with lying. Can you tell when people are lying? What facial organizational patterns do you notice?
6. Provide examples and thoroughly explain how intuitive ideas are evaluated.
7. Provide examples and thoroughly explain the relationship between visualization and creativity.
8. Provide examples and thoroughly explain how free association is related to creativity.
9. Provide examples and thoroughly explain how a creative idea or production, such as an artwork, film, or literary work, can appear to be vague to a casual observer, and yet actually be clear.
10. Provide examples and thoroughly explain how creative ideas are evaluated.

▲ QUESTIONS FOR DISCUSSION

Provide an essay of 300–500 words that responds to each of the following questions which ask for your opinion. You should respond by stating it, and by providing thoughts, examples, and insights that support it. You should be willing to revise your response; you may change your opinion during or after a class discussion.

1. The chapter points out that "some social critics believe that an unbiased assessment of the role of technology and science in our lives must conclude that both have done more harm than good." Review the chapter and explain why you agree or disagree with these social critics.
2. The chapter claims that "with the growth of communication technology, especially the Internet, writing has become extremely important." Do you agree with this statement? Why or why not?
3. Do you feel that the Internet offers more opportunities for solving problems than it does in creating problems? Provide specific details about the Internet and explain your response. (You may need to discuss the Internet with a librarian or other authority on the subject.)
4. Are you an intuitive thinker? If so, describe an example of your intuition and explain it in relation to "organizational patterns."
5. Have you ever had an intuitive idea during a discussion? Was it a good idea? Explain the process you went through, especially the organizational patterns involved.
6. Do you think that successful investors have intuitions about the stock market? If you do, explain what organizational patterns are involved. If you do not, explain what sort of thinking you believe achieves successful investment. (You may need to discuss stock market investment with a Business professor or another authority on the subject.)
7. We often think of artists, writers, and musicians as being creative. However, businesspeople, scientists, and athletes also prize creativity. Explain how one or more of these groups thinks creatively.
8. Creativity is described as thinking that generates new and useful ideas. Do you think that being familiar with the Internet offers opportunities for creative thinking? Why or why not?

▲ QUOTATION TO PONDER

> *"Research has documented how social factors can influence creativity. For example, creativity may be reduced when someone is watching you while you are working, when you must compete for prizes, and when someone restricts your choices about how you can express your creativity. In some cases—but not all—creativity may be reduced when you are offered a reward for being creative."*
>
> Margaret W. Matlin, *Cognition* (1998)

▲ JOURNAL TOPIC

Reflect on your experiences in using The Format or The Mini-Format in Chapter 9. Do you recall using intuitive or creative thought while reviewing, evaluating, and making suggestions for revision? Describe any instances in which you did. Even if you did not, explain how you feel about the proper role of creative and intuitive thought in using The Format.

▲ PORTFOLIO PAPER

Almost every movie is a story about people dealing with serious problems. What was a good movie you saw in which the characters used intuition and creativity in helping to solve a problem? Provide details and examples of intuition and creativity from the film in your 500-word essay.

BRAINSTORMING: GENERATING INTUITIVE AND CREATIVE THOUGHT

"Brainstorming" is a term that was first coined in 1938 by a group of American advertising executives led by Alex F. Osborn. They made up the word in order to have a name for an aggressive problem-solving strategy: "to take a problem by storm." Osborn provided the definition of brainstorming in his book, *Applied Imagination,* in 1963: "Brainstorming is a conference technique by which a group attempts to find a solution for a specific problem by amassing all the ideas spontaneously contributed by its members." Osborn developed brainstorming as a way of stimulating creative ideas. His concern was primarily in business and advertising, but he devoted considerable attention to encouraging the development of creativity and resourcefulness in education, government, and personal relationships. Osborn assumed an influential, national leadership role in the area of creative problem solving. Consequently, he traveled the country, giving workshops for educators, consulting with business executives, and addressing popular audiences.

CREATIVITY AND "INHIBITION"

Osborn was convinced that everyone is capable of creative thinking, but that most people are too "inhibited" to develop their imaginations. To be "inhibited" is to be afraid to explore beyond what we perceive to be socially acceptable behavior. Frank Smith, a contemporary linguist and critical thinking theoretician, agrees with Osborn's theory of inhibition. He believes that we are inhibited in relation to creativity because we feel that everything we do should be somehow socially acceptable and useful. Children, who do not have that feeling, exhibit creativity in singing, dancing, and making pictures. It seems almost natural for them to "color outside the lines." However, as adults, says Smith, we have adapted to a society that is concerned only with the *results* of our activities. We cease to enjoy them for what they are in themselves. Consequently, adults do not paint because they feel they have no "message" to get across. They will not sing or dance out of fear of being ridiculed for doing something "useless" or "acting like a child."

Recent research by cognitive psychologists supports Osborn and Smith. Their observations reveal that we tend to be less creative when other people watch us work, when they restrict our choices, and when they offer prizes. When we feel that our creative work should *result in something valuable*, such as winning a prize or receiving a monetary reward, our level of creativity goes down. As adults, we are aware that everything we do is evaluated by its outcome. The "reward" for our work—our pay and social status—is directly related to the accomplishments we achieve in working. Consequently, we find ourselves in a very difficult situation in regard to creativity. We are afraid to be creative because we are afraid that the results of our efforts will not be useful. This is a legitimate fear. As we have already seen, genuine creative ideas are not simply "new and different." They are also *useful*. Thus, we have a tendency to avoid any creative activity because we are afraid our creative efforts will not result in a creative outcome, but only in something unimportant, trivial, and unappreciated. Therefore, most of us are hesitant to act in new or creative ways, or even to entertain new or creative thoughts. We take the "safe route," and act and think in conventional, "tried and true" ways. We leave creativity to children and to professional entertainers.

Osborn was fully aware of the inhibitions surrounding creativity in our society and developed techniques that help us to overcome our fears of creativity and incorporated them into the brainstorming process. We will now look into these techniques more closely.

CREATIVITY AND AUTHORITY

An individual who has success in solving problems in the past tends to rely on the same solutions when encountering problems in the present. He or she develops a "favored solution." When the present problems are similar to those of the past, the favored solution usually results in success. For example, a student who has done well on examinations in the past by memorizing course material has a tendency to use memorization in preparing for exams in her new courses. Memorization is her "favored solution." If the courses are of the same type, for example History courses that contain a large amount of names, places, and dates to be remembered, she continues to succeed. However, she will not be successful in her Critical Thinking course if she uses her "favored solution" because Critical Thinking is a course in which the development of the process of thinking is more important than the material content of the course. For example, she may memorize every step on The Format in Chapter 9. However, her success in the course will not be determined by how well she remembers it. She needs to apply it well in order to succeed. Her "favored solution" is not appropriate for her new course.

Successful methods of problem solving and consistent application of favored solutions can place individuals in roles of high social and personal esteem. For example they are promoted to increasingly more responsible positions in the workplace. A business executive who succeeds in problem solving acquires a reputation for being capable and knowledgeable. Consequently, he begins to identify success, prestige, and rewards with the specialized method and favored solutions of the past. The executive's self-image is of a capable, knowledgeable, successful authority. His personal identity and self-esteem are directly related to the way he feels others perceive him: an expert problem solver. As long as the problems he encounters are similar to past problems, his methods and solutions succeed and his self-image remains intact. He has a storehouse of solutions and methods that have proved workable in the past.

However, when a new type of problem emerges, the executive tends to limit his thinking to the methods and solutions that he has successfully used. The new problem, though, is a *different* type of problem. He finds that his old ideas are not relevant in this new situation. Of course, his self-image and self-esteem are threatened. He feels that he cannot use his "tried and true" ways of thinking, and yet recognizes that he is too inhibited to leave them behind.

When the executive meets with his subordinates in order to solve the new problem his creativity suffers. He feels threatened; his self-image and self-esteem are "on the line." He recognizes that his position as an authority is in jeopardy. The subordinates, on the other hand, are also inhibited, not only because of their own reluctance to think creatively, but also because they feel threatened by the executive's inhibitions.

This very difficult situation can lead to "groupthink," in which the executive and subordinates become more interested in protecting the self-image and authority of the executive than in actually solving the problem. Consequently, the group fails to explore any alternatives to the executive's favored solutions. Whatever he suggests is automatically accepted. The subordinates rationalize that "the boss knows what he's doing," although they suspect that the problem will remain unsolved. In addition, the group does not look into the risks involved in accepting the executive's solutions. The members focus on past successes and the reputation of the executive, not on possible outcomes of their decisions.

Success in problem solving, and the reputation and authority that come with it, can actually hinder the creation of new ideas in solving new problems.

Lack of previous success in problem solving may be one reason why children are more creative than most adults. One illustration of this is the story about a large tractor-trailer that was stuck under an overpass. The driver and the police were baffled as to how to remove the trailer, since it was wedged firmly between the base of the overpass and the street. The city engineer was eventually called in, who proclaimed that the truck would have to be destroyed. The truck driver responded angrily that the low level of the overpass had not been adequately marked, and that if anything, the overpass would have to be dismantled. The police were anticipating a violent episode. A ten-year-old girl approached the confused group of professionals and asked, "Why not just let the air out of the tires?" Of course this was a solution that none of the adults had considered. According to Osborn, they had too much success in past problem solving, and their self-esteem was in jeopardy. The child, unencumbered by past successes, came up with a new idea.

Authority figures inhibit creativity in several ways. Their own successes establish their favored solutions, which in turn provide them with a self-image they are usually reluctant to shun. They tend to inhibit the creativity of others simply by observing and judging their own creative work. As we have seen, when people feel that they are being observed, especially by someone in a position to reward them for their work, they tend to be less creative. In addition, if the others sense the vulnerability of the authority, they may find themselves protecting him by engaging in groupthink.

Authority figures and inhibitions are the two major stumbling blocks to creative thinking. Osborn's brainstorming techniques are attempts to break down both stumbling blocks by removing the "work" of problem solving and replacing it with "play." In other words, brainstorming is a problem-solving process that seeks to rediscover the playful, uninhibited attitudes of childhood.

Brainstorming: The Goals and the Process

The key to the success of the brainstorming process is the removal of inhibitions that impede creative thinking. This is accomplished by setting goals that remove participants as far as possible from the two major causes that inhibit creativity. The first cause is the normal association of "usefulness" with creative thinking. The second is the threat to creativity caused by authority.

The Goals.   There are two goals in brainstorming, each of which are meant to enhance creativity. The first is a large quantity of new ideas that represent the imagination and intuition of everyone in the group. The second goal is a review, evaluation, and revision of those ideas into a limited number of promising, *useful* ideas. It is very important that the first goal—to generate a large quantity of original ideas—be taken literally. There should be no concern with actually solving a problem in seeking the first goal. Inhibitions are caused, in large part, by a need to provide something useful. The first goal dispenses with that need. The participants in the brainstorming process simply attempt to come up with a large number of *new* ideas. The appropriateness of the ideas as useful solutions is not considered at all in terms of the first goal.

The second goal is concerned with the usefulness of the ideas generated in relation to the first goal. The two goals are separated during the process. Usually, a different group than the one that met the first goal achieves the second goal. This ensures that the first goal will be met without any inhibition.

It is normal for a brainstorming group to come up with from fifty to one hundred ideas in a thirty-minute session. If the group achieves a number of ideas within this range, it has met the first goal. The second goal is met when about five percent of the generated ideas are selected for further review, evaluation, and revision. In meeting the second goal, the ideas are specifically evaluated and revised for clarity and usefulness.

The Process: Roles and Preliminary Notification of the Topic. The influence of authority and inhibition are consciously sidestepped in brainstorming by encouraging a playful, relaxed attitude.

The brainstorming process consists of a group of from five to nine people. Larger groups are acceptable, but no group should have more than twelve members. It is best to have an odd number of participants, since this discourages "pairing off" from the group. Some members have assigned roles. One is the "overseer," who makes sure that everyone in the group participates fully in the process. Authority figures should not be assigned to this role, since it could provide a position from which they dominate the discussion. Another person takes the role of "recorder." This person keeps a list of ideas as they are mentioned. Since every idea must be recorded, this person should be able to take good notes and yet participate with the group. The "timekeeper" watches the clock, since brainstorming sessions are usually limited to thirty-minute intervals. A "reporter" is assigned to present the results of the session to those responsible for meeting the second goal.

The roles are not leadership positions, but simply assigned tasks. Once the overseer has started the session, he or she steps out of the role of overseer unless the group gets bogged down and needs to be stimulated to continue to pursue ideas. The timekeeper has a very limited task. He or she merely needs to announce to the group when there are fifteen, ten, and five minutes left in the session. Of course, the reporter does nothing special until the session is completed. The recorder takes notes; he or she will confer with the reporter at the conclusion of the session to work out any difficulties in reading handwriting, and so on.

In some situations, the recorder may choose to not participate in the group discussion. Such a decision should be made with care. Part of the value of brainstorming is the solicitation of ideas from people not normally asked to submit ideas to the organization. That is, if possible, people with low levels of authority are asked to take part in the sessions because their ideas will be fresher and less inhibited than those of the authority figures. This is especially true when the topic of brainstorming has to do with generating ideas about better ways to operate the organization itself. For example, a small business that seeks to improve its production and sales should include every employee, even those not involved directly with those two areas. In an educational setting, students and clerical staff (not only faculty and administrators) should be invited to sessions seeking creative ideas in regard to improving the quality of education.

Under the best conditions, a brainstorming group will have been presented with the topic of discussion twelve to fifteen hours before the session takes place. They are asked to think about the problem if they choose. However, they should not bring any notes with them to the actual session. The purpose of the twelve to fifteen hour advance notice is to allow participants to feel comfortable with the topic when they begin the session. This saves participants the time and energy involved in "getting used to" the topic.

In addition, participants are asked to wear clothing not normally associated with their work. Business executives may be asked to come to the session in whatever clothing they wore over the weekend. Students, clerical staff, and faculty may be asked to wear "theme" clothing: for example "clothing worn on the farm," or "clothing worn to the beach." This advance notice about clothing helps the participants understand the playful nature of the session.

Food is always a good idea at a brainstorming session. Authority roles tend to become less formal when food is shared, and participants feel more playful when they can munch on a potato chip. Food also supplies energy; and while brainstorming is fun, it is also hard work.

The Process: Beginning the Session.   Before the discussion begins, participants are encouraged to "mingle" for a few minutes, sharing food, engaging in conversation, and settling on the assigned roles. The roles can be assigned by lottery, or people can volunteer for them. Of course, under no conditions, should authority figures assign roles.

Brainstorming sessions often begin with "icebreaker" games. For example, a box of index cards with names of animals (cows, dogs, horses, and so on) can be presented; each person takes one. Once everyone has settled into their seats, the overseer announces, "Everyone give their animal sound!" The participants then "moo," "bark," or "whinny," depending upon which card they picked. Of course, many other games can be played so long as they ease tension and promote a playful attitude.

Another interesting way to begin a session is to provide each participant with a "new identity." Cards are passed out to each participant. The cards list a peculiar occupation or unusual hobby, and a clever nickname. Throughout the session, participants are referred to by the nickname. This technique is valuable for breaking down inhibitions due to authority. On the other hand, some sessions simply ask participants to draw a small cartoon character that illustrates a hobby or an interest they have outside the work environment. They take turns describing their cartoons to everyone else.

The mingling, assignment of roles, food, and "ice-breaker" games are fun; but they are very important. The beginning of the session sets the scene for the creative work that follows.

The Process: Establishing the "Three Rules." If possible, participants select their own chairs at a round table. At each chair, a piece of paper is found that briefly and directly establishes the three rules governing the session. These rules are meant to inform everyone of the nature of brainstorming without departing from the playfulness established during the beginning of the process. These rules are usually phrased in a very informal way that encourages lightheartedness. For example:

Rules for Brainstorming

1. Self-doubt and fear of making a mistake or of feeling like a fool are not allowed.
2. Dignity, personal sensitivity, and outright stuffiness are to be abandoned.
3. Concern for the dignity, sensitivity, and stuffiness of others is absolutely forbidden.

These "rules" establish the informality and playful atmosphere of the brainstorming session for the participants. The session begins with a wide-open atmosphere. At times, people become almost rowdy. Of course, all of this is desirable since the goal is to overcome inhibitions. Once the participants have fully digested the "rules," they are ready for the guidelines.

The Process: Guidelines. In order to bring the participants into a manageable group the overseer passes out the list of guidelines to each one. These may be listed in a humorous way, but it is essential that the participants take them seriously. The overseer should briefly explain each guideline, and inform the participants that he or she will remind them during the session if any of the guidelines are not followed.

The guidelines are helpful in establishing the practical functioning of the process. Each one has a distinct purpose.

1. **Criticism Is Ruled Out**

   The attitudes of the participants should be flexible, encouraging, receptive, and playful. If someone proposes an idea that one of the participants does not like, he or she should ignore the idea. Participants should never criticize any idea, since this causes the participants to "censor" what they say or to be inhibited in some other way.

2. **Quantity Is Sought**

   The greater the number of ideas, the more the likelihood of discovering useful ideas in the second session. This is not only a statistical fact; it is a psychological insight. Once ideas begin to flow, new ideas become more numerous and original. Participant should strive for a large number of ideas; leave the decision on how good or bad they are to the second session. Only five percent of the ideas generated in the first brainstorming session will prove to be useful. The more ideas, the better.

3. Intuition and Creativity Are Welcome

Wild, crazy ideas are needed. Whatever comes into the participants' minds should be spoken out loud. Participants should take "wild stabs" at ideas with an attitude of abandon. Try to build upon ideas, by combining ideas and playing with words.

4. Play with Ideas

In addition to contributing ideas of their own, participants combine and improve the ideas of others by combining and extending the ideas generated. Free associations, word games, role-playing, puns, and metaphor making are encouraged.

The Process: Generation of Ideas. Brainstorming is a group effort. When participants share ideas they "feed off" one another and come up with new ideas they would not have thought up on their own. By working—playing—together, they modify, substitute, rearrange, combine, and have fun with each other's ideas.

The session begins with the overseer providing a very brief description of the topic. Participants are assured that they need not stay with the topic during the session. It is merely a place to begin. The whole point of the brainstorming sessions is to generate ideas; it is up to the post-conference to decide whether they are "on topic."

It is very important that participants *ignore* the *quality* of ideas while brainstorming. The overseer may have to remind them to make no judgments concerning how "worthwhile" any of the ideas may be. They should strive to generate as many ideas as they possibly can.

The fourth guideline encourages participants to use free association, to role-play, engage in word games, and to make puns and metaphors. Role-playing involves participants in pretending to be someone else—perhaps they adopt an identity based on their new "nickname." One example of a word game is the "alphabet game" in which participants follow one another in supplying a word or idea that begins with successive letters of the alphabet. The first person mentions an idea that begins with the letter "a," the next participant with "b," and so on. This game usually falters at the letters "q," "u," "x," and "z." The overseer should suggest that they be skipped. The goal is to generate as many ideas as possible.

Free association is a great way to generate ideas in a group. A participant says a word, then the person sitting next to him or her immediately follows with another word. As the group engages in the process, more and more ideas come out more and more rapidly. As the participants become quicker in saying their words or ideas, they become less inhibited. The ideas quickly build.

There should be no moments of silence during a brainstorming session. When the thirty minutes of idea generation have been completed, participants should be exhausted. Usually, they take a twenty-minute break, mingle, and compare notes. As individuals become more familiar with brainstorming, they come to recognize that although it is a fun activity, its goal is quite serious. The generation of new ideas is a very important aspect of problem solving.

The Post-Brainstorming Conference: The Second Goal. When the brainstorming session is completed, the new ideas are reviewed, evaluated, and revised. As we will discuss later in this chapter, there are two specific places in problem-solving methodology where brainstorming is appropriate. It is very useful in describing and defining problems, and also helpful in coming up with possible solutions to problems.

The post-brainstorming conference can involve the same groups that participated in the brainstorming or it can be limited to the authority figures in the organization. Ideas should be selected, not rejected, during the conference. That is, criticism is still "ruled out" during the post-brainstorming conference. A positive selection of ideas encourages those involved to revise ideas rather than reject them. Many a good brainstorming session has been spoiled by a post-conference in which all potentially creative ideas were thoughtlessly discarded!

Only about five percent of the ideas are going to be worth considering, and of those, the great majority needs to be revised. This may seem to be a very small number of ideas; however, if the brainstorming session resulted in eighty ideas, we can expect four or five of them to be worth serious consideration. Many businesses and organizations are very happy to have one or two genuinely creative ideas—new and useful ones—when it comes to solving their problems.

Sometimes, the entire brainstorming group is invited to review and evaluate, and discuss the ideas selected in the post-conference. Organizations that gain consensual acceptance of new ideas in this way often find that participants are happy to accept and "take ownership" of them. When an organization or business makes use of creative ideas to solve its problems, changes occur in the way people live and work. They are usually much more willing to accept those changes when they have had a hand in creating them.

EXERCISES

▲ MOST INTRIGUING ISSUE

> Write a one-paragraph description of the most interesting idea, topic, or process described in the pages 305–313. Be prepared to explain what you find interesting in class discussion.

▲ THE MUDDIEST POINT

> Write a sentence or, if possible, a paragraph that describes the idea, topic, expression, term, or process in pages 305–313 that you find most difficult to understand.

▲ CARTOONS AND DIAGRAMS

> Draw a cartoon that illustrates the three conditions that cognitive psychologists believe inhibit creativity.

1. Draw a cartoon that shows how authority figures become inhibited in solving problems.
2. Provide a cartoon that illustrates at least two characteristics of groupthink.
3. Provide a cartoon that illustrates the two major causes that inhibit creativity.
4. Draw a cartoon that shows how the two goals of brainstorming are achieved.
5. Draw a cartoon that shows the four roles in a brainstorming session.
6. Provide a cartoon that illustrates the three rules of brainstorming.
7. Draw a cartoon that shows the four guidelines for brainstorming.

▲ DEFINITIONS OF KEY TERMS

Provide a disciplinary definition for each of the following terms as they are used in this chapter. Most of the terms are not defined in the chapter, although their meanings are described by the context in which they appear. You need to review the material to create the definition yourself. Be sure to follow the guidelines for creating definitions on pages 78–81.

Inhibition	Authority Figure	Brainstorming
Self Image	Overseer	Ice-Breaker

▲ SHORT ESSAY QUESTIONS

Provide a written response of approximately 200 words for each topic. Your responses should be well organized, grammatically correct, and neatly produced.

1. Why do you suppose people tend to be inhibited from creative work when they are being watched?
2. Why do you suppose people tend to be inhibited from creative work when they are competing for a prize or when they are offered a reward?
3. Do you agree that the more authority you have, the less creative you are apt to be? Why or why not?
4. Alex Osborn once said that all inhibitions to creative work come down to one thing: "Fear of making an ass of oneself." Do you agree? Why or why not?
5. Clearly paraphrase the three rules for brainstorming in order to explain them to someone unfamiliar with this course.
6. Explain how each of the four roles in a brainstorming session contributes to a lowering of inhibitions.
7. Why do you suppose that some brainstorming sessions ask participants to wear special clothing?
8. Do you feel that your own creative work would be enhanced if you knew the topic of discussion fifteen hours before the session started? On the other hand, would you be more creative if you found out at the very beginning of the session? Why?
9. Can a brainstorming session be valuable if the participants get "off topic" immediately? Why or why not?
10. Do you have any examples of "ice-breaker" games appropriate for beginning a brainstorming session? If so, describe one or more of them.

▲ QUESTIONS FOR DISCUSSION

In your brainstorming group, decide upon an overseer, a recorder, a timekeeper, and a reporter. Spend thirty minutes coming up with as many ideas as you can in regard to the following topics.

If practical, you may want to wear "theme clothing" for the session, engage in some "ice-breaker" games, or adopt nicknames.

Once you have finished the session, your reporter may be asked to share your ideas with another group, who will then act as your post-conference group. Your group, in turn, may take on that role for that or another group.

1. The college cafeteria has been saving used teabags for several decades. Teabags, of course, are small bags made of thin paper attached to a small, heavier paper tab by a string and tiny paperclip. All the bags are full of dry, used tea. There are literally thousands of these bags in the cafeteria basement. What are some creative ways these bags can be used that will benefit the college?

2. Your college has requested your group to come up with a new name for the school, along with a new mascot. The college would like the name and mascot to reflect the ideals as well as the realities on your campus. What are some creative suggestions for a name and mascot?

3. A local television station has volunteered thirty minutes a week air time to your college if you can come up with a creative way to fill it. The station wants faculty and students to be involved with the program. What are some creative suggestions your group can come up with for the show?

4. After twenty years of playing intercollegiate football, your college has decided to abandon the sport. The football stadium, practice field, and athletic center (formally used to house equipment, provide locker space, showers, and so on) are now available for other uses. What suggestions can your group provide to the college for using the stadium, practice field, and athletic center?

5. Your college has recently acquired seventeen million dollars from a wealthy former student's estate. The problem is that the estate requires that all the money be spent on "academic benefits" within a five-year period. None of the money can be left over after that time, or the college loses the entire seventeen million. What suggestions can your group provide to the college in spending the money?

6. The student government at your college has decided to prohibit alcohol and tobacco at all future functions. They have asked your group to come up with some creative ideas to discourage students from using alcohol and tobacco not only at college functions, but also in all other activities. What suggestions can your group provide the college to promote student abstinence from tobacco and alcohol?

7. A student has approached your group for help in selecting a theme for her campaign for student body president. She wants to emphasize free speech, ethnic and racial tolerance, and increased participation by students in the student government in her campaign. What suggestions can your group offer her?

8. Three students at your college were recently arrested for vandalism of a business near campus. The owner is irate. Other business people who serve college students are also angry. They have formed an association that plans to meet with the college's president in the near future. In the meantime, the president has asked your group to offer her some suggestions that would help "calm the waters" between the business people and the students. What suggestions can your group offer the president?

9. The bus drivers in your college community have gone on a strike that most people believe will last for several months, leaving hundreds of students without transportation to their classes. Some of these students live hours away from the campus. The bus drivers' union is aware of the hardship their strike is causing the students and has volunteered to help in any way; any way that is, that does not involve driving the buses or transporting the students in any way. They are willing to spend up to three thousand dollars in helping the students get to class. What suggestions does your group have for the union?

10. The author of your critical thinking textbook has asked your group to provide five creative ideas that could improve the text. What suggestions does your group have for him?

▲ QUOTATION TO PONDER

"It is now a known fact that nearly all of us can become more creative, if we will. And this very fact may well be the hope of the world. By becoming more creative we can lead brighter lives, and can live better with each other. By becoming more creative we can provide better goods and services to each other, with the result of a higher and higher standard of living. By becoming more creative we may even find a way to bring permanent peace to all the world."
Alex F. Osborn, *Applied Imagination*, 1963

▲ JOURNAL TOPIC

Reflect on the value of brainstorming in our society. What aspect of it—the military, government, entertainment, business, or education—do you think uses brainstorming most often? Why do you feel this way? Which aspect do you think could benefit most by brainstorming more often? Why? Write down your thoughts in a 300–500 word essay.

PROBLEMS

Problems and puzzles are not the same. The later are artificial challenges such as those encountered in a mathematics course. For example, Cynthia has been asked to calculate how many hours it takes to get from Philadelphia to St. Louis if she is driving at an average speed of fifty-five miles per hour. Of course, she is not personally involved in the trip. The "math problem" is actually only an artificial challenge—a puzzle. Problems, on the other hand, are always personal. They are specific difficulties that interfere with or keep us from achieving a "desired outcome," something we actually need or want. Imagine that Cynthia, at home in Philadelphia, received a telephone call from a potential employer in St. Louis. She has been selected to interview for a "dream job," but has to be there in only a few days. Getting to St. Louis from Philadelphia is not a puzzle. It is a *problem;* she is challenged by the difficulties involved in covering the long distance in a short time. She cannot afford to fly. She doesn't own a car. The trains running between the two cities make too many stops. How can she get to the interview on time? Take a bus? Impossible!

Our lives are full of problems. Obstacles and difficulties stand between what we have and what we need or want in every aspect of life. We all have problems in our personal and family lives, in the workplace, and in our social and political communities. It is common for problems to overlap, to "compound," and to "get all mixed up" in many ways. Political problems are often intermingled with problems in the workplace, or even in the family, for example.

Problems are always specific; a problem that one person has is not necessarily shared by anyone else, even by those in similar situations. For example, Cynthia may feel that the solution to her problem is to borrow the money for an airplane ticket to St. Louis. She feels that her problem is solved. She arranges to leave Philadelphia on Monday. However, her group report in American Literature class is due on Tuesday morning. Other students in her group are counting on her to do her part in the report. They do not share her problem in getting to St. Louis. Her absence is a problem for them. The professor will excuse Cynthia from class that day, but he still expects the group to report.

Now the group has a problem: how to give the report without Cynthia's contribution? Her solution to her problem has caused a problem for the group. They must find a way to include her contribution in the report, even though she will not be present.

Of course, solutions to problems are always satisfying. A problem solved is an obstacle overcome. However, life is not simple. Every solved problem causes other problems. A solved problem causes a change in the situation, and change always brings new problems. Cynthia, who solved her problem by borrowing money, now has a new one—how to pay it back. The members of her group have a problem they didn't have before—how to give a good report without her. Even the professor now has new problems. What should he do about the grade for the group's report? What about Cynthia's grade?

There is no such thing as absolute progress; every time a problem is solved, new problems emerge. Our personal and family lives may seem to be "full of problems" at times. However, more often than not, these problems emerge due to our solutions of previous problems. Successful communication, organization, and production in the workplace depend upon effective problem solving. Nevertheless, no matter how well we communicate, organize, and produce, new problems will always emerge.

It is not difficult to realize that our personal and workplace lives are constantly involved with problems. The more mature we are, the more we expect to encounter emergent problems. However, it can be difficult for even the most well-adjusted, mature person to recognize that social and political solutions can never be absolute. Many people have a longing for social-political "utopias": perfect societies in which no one has a problem. The word "utopia" (coined by Thomas Moore in his book *Utopia*, published in 1516) actually means "nowhere." A utopia is an ideal model of a perfect social-political world. Of course, we can imagine a utopia in which every person is always treated with love and justice, and use that image as a standard model by which we can criticize real societies and governments. Ideal standards, however, are never completely realized. Political and social radicalism mistakenly seeks to establish utopian visions in the real world. The "worker's paradise," "world-wide democracy," and other "pure and perfect" societies sought by political radicals may make sense as ideal models. History, however, is full of tragic experiments in making the ideal model a reality. Millions of innocent people have been imprisoned, tortured, and murdered in the process of establishing a "perfect" world. As members of society, we need to keep in mind that while we can always solve specific problems, we will never be without them. Every solution is temporary; a new problem will always eventually emerge.

Every solution, whether it is social-political, personal, or a workplace solution contains within it an "emergent problem"; a new problem that results from the solution of a previous problem. We can classify emergent problems in four ways. They are anticipated or unanticipated, affiliated or nonaffiliated.

EMERGENT PROBLEMS

An emergent problem is one that results from a previous solution. Of course, every problem is "emergent" but we use the term in order to emphasize that solutions *always* result in new problems. It is usually desirable, although not always possible, to control the solution so that its emergent problems are less complicated and less serious than the previous problem we have just solved. The classic "killing a fly with a shotgun" solution results in a much more serious emergent problem (a kitchen ceiling that now needs extensive repair) than the original problem—a fly buzzing over the sink.

An *anticipated emergent problem* is one that is obviously involved with the solution. The use of a shotgun to kill a fly buzzing over the kitchen sink *obviously* involves an emergent problem. Regrettably, *anticipated* emergent problems are not always *literally* anticipated. The emergent problem is obvious, but unrecognized. This is what happens when we act on a solution without thinking critically. Anticipated emergent problems can be avoided by taking a planned approach to problem solving. For example, Cynthia can anticipate an obvious emergent problem in regard to her group report in American Literature. Without her contribution, the whole group will be penalized. She can avoid this problem by providing her thoughts in writing to others in the group and by explaining her absence to the professor before she leaves Philadelphia. By planning her solution, Cynthia avoids the anticipated problem. If she had not planned a solution, and had simply left for the interview in St. Louis without notifying anyone, the anticipated emergent problem would have remained behind, waiting for her when she returned.

No matter how well we plan, *unanticipated* problems always result from solutions. No one can anticipate all of the changes a solution makes in a situation. Even well-planned solutions that anticipate emergent problems result in unanticipated problems.

Cynthia did not realize for several months that her flight to the interview was only the beginning of a series of distractions from her studies. The American

Literature group report was only a small problem compared to those that came up in *all* of her courses upon her return. She was so distracted by the prospect of the "dream job" that she couldn't concentrate on anything else. She checks the mailbox and waits by the telephone, hoping to hear from the employer. Her studies and her grades suffer. She did not anticipate this problem; it was not obvious.

A problem, either anticipated or unanticipated, that emerges for the person or group who solved the previous problem is called an *affiliated problem.* The problems associated with Cynthia's studies are affiliated emergent problems because they are problems *for her.* One that emerges for those not involved with the previous solution is a *nonaffiliated* problem. Cynthia's flight to St. Louis for the interview may have resulted in either anticipated or unanticipated problems for other people. She borrowed the money for the airline ticket from her roommate Ramona, who thought that she had enough money for next semester's tuition. However, Ramona's textbooks cost much more than she thought they would; she cannot afford to pay for both the books and tuition. Ramona's problem is nonaffiliated because she did not directly participate in Cynthia's solution. Cynthia anticipated that Ramona might be short of funds, but borrowed the money from her anyway. The emergent problem is *anticipated and nonaffiliated.*

Unanticipated, nonaffiliated emergent problems are those that no one could possibly imagine. For example, Cynthia's interview had wonderful results—for Cynthia. She got the job. Of course, the four other interviewees were not hired. They must continue to seek employment. They have, as far as Cynthia is concerned, *unanticipated, nonaffiliated* emergent problems. Cynthia's solution (getting the job) is their problem. Like most job applicants, Cynthia did not consider the plight of her competition. Their emergent problems result from her success, but are not problems for Cynthia.

In general, the fewer anticipated problems a particular solution generates, the better. The least desirable solution to a problem is the one that results in anticipated affiliated problems. For example, if Cynthia had *stolen* the money for the airline ticket, the anticipated affiliated problem would have been much more serious than the problem she solved. It is remarkable how often people solve personal problems in a way that generates anticipated affiliated problems. For example, Bob has a health problem that is caused by smoking cigarettes. He solves the problem by taking up chewing tobacco! The anticipated affiliated problem is obvious; his health will continue to suffer even more.

A solution that anticipates some nonaffiliated problems is usually more desirable than one that anticipates affiliated ones. Cynthia's competitors have to continue to seek employment because she got the job they were seeking. Her solution results in nonaffiliated problems. Since no solution can possibly avoid *all* emergent problems, it is better that her solution results in problems for other people than for her.

Of course, there are situations in which it is more appropriate to seek solutions that avoid nonaffiliated problems, even at the expense of affiliated problems. Parents often choose to sacrifice their own interests for the benefits of their children. For example, they borrow money to pay a child's college tuition. Their solution results in an affiliated problem—they place themselves in debt. The parents could have required their child to take on the burden of tuition, a step that would have avoided the affiliated problem. However, their parental love and perhaps a feeling of moral obligation intervened.

At times we are able to come up with solutions that anticipate no emergent problems. All this means is that we don't know what they will be. We don't know if our solution will result in affiliated or nonaffiliated problems. We only know that they will be unanticipated. Part of solving problems well is to discuss possible solutions with others. In this way, anticipated emergent problems become clearer.

DISCUSSION AND PROBLEM SOLVING

The more we discuss problems, the better the chances that we will anticipate emergent problems. Oral discussion is usually more practical in personal and family life than written discussion. Some families even have brainstorming sessions. In the workplace, people often share their ideas about problems orally. Brainstorming is quite common. Written memos and email are often used to discuss problems at work. In some types of work, for example in government agencies, written discussions are much more common than oral conferences. Social and political problems are discussed in magazines, newspapers, and other written sources as well as in oral discussions on television.

Discussions should be evaluated by the standards of verbal and logical thinking. Part of the practical task of critical thinking is to ask others to be as clear, accurate, specific, and significant as possible when discussing problems. People should be sincere, respectful, and seek consensus.

Individuals often feel that their needs and problems are unique, especially when they are personal. However, even personal problems can be defined and approached much more effectively through discussion. We should not underestimate the value of a discussion with a good friend, a family member, or a professional counselor.

As a rule, discussions about problems should include as many involved people as possible. A family problem should be discussed with everyone in the family. A problem at work should involve everyone affiliated with it. Two of the major benefits of a democratic society are free speech and free press; they allow anyone to openly and candidly express their views about social and political problems.

At some point, the discussion must focus on *which* solution will be implemented, and on *who* will implement it, on *how* it will be implemented, and on *when* it will be implemented. Discussion alone, however, cannot solve problems; *action* is required. Only actually *doing something* can change the situation for the better. Problem-solving action is always taken with a degree of uncertainty.[1] If we wait until we are completely sure that we are implementing the very best solution, the problem will overwhelm us. Postponing action until we are certain about it is no way to solve problems! On the other hand, action should

---

1. Leadership in solving problems always involves guiding others in taking action during a time of *uncertainty*. Critical thinkers have a responsibility to take on this leadership role. More on this topic is discussed in the "Interview," which concludes this chapter.

be planned, evaluated, and revised. The "balancing act" between giving proper discussion to a solution and implementing the solution in a timely manner is difficult. Experience in problem solving usually helps us find the proper point where discussion abates and action begins.

THE FIVE-STAGE PROBLEM-SOLVING METHOD

Many problems are solved rather quickly. We recognize them, discuss possible solutions, and put a solution into practice rather quickly. For example, Cynthia did not need to engage in a formal problem-solving method in deciding how to get to her job interview. The main task we have in regard to problems is to solve them. When we can do so in an informal, quick manner, we should.

Serious problems, especially those that involve a large number of people, are usually too complex for informal, quick solutions. In addition to the possible solutions, we need to consider emergent nonaffiliated problems. We need to include as many people as possible in the discussion. We may need to evaluate our skills, resources, and other factors. Problems encountered in the workplace and in social-political life are usually best approached with the five-stage method.

Stage One: Facing the Problem.   Denial is a common reaction to problems. Problems can be psychologically difficult to accept. This is not only true on the personal level; whole societies sometimes refuse to face their problems. For example, nearly twenty-five percent of all children under the age of six in the United States—about six million—live in poverty. This is a serious problem; the nutritional, educational, and social needs of one-fourth of the nation's children are not being met. The number of them joining the ranks of the impoverished is rapidly increasing. In the past twenty years it has gone up by twelve percent. What will be the future problems for individuals, families, and for society at large if this trend continues to grow? Yet, how many Americans are willing to face this problem?[2] Americans as a group seem much more willing to deny these and affiliated problems children experience in our country. A problem cannot be addressed, let alone solved, unless it is recognized. At times, facing the problem and leading others to face the problem can be a major task: a problem in itself.

Once the problem is faced, it must be discussed. This leads us to the second stage.

Stage Two: Describing the Problem.   The problem must be understood; that is, we need to define or describe it in a way that allows for an eventual solution. It is not enough to simply face the problem. It must be described well. Critical thinking tools and standards are used to review, evaluate, and revise the description until we have reached a consensus on the nature of the problem. For example, the problem of child poverty needs to be described clearly

2. You may want to check on these tragic statistics. They come from The National Center for Children in Poverty at Columbia University's School of Public Health. They issued their most recent study in 1998.

and accurately. We need specific descriptions. The full significance of the problem needs to be addressed.

Brainstorming is an effective way to describe a problem, for two reasons. First, the brainstorming process results in a clear and accurate description. A large quantity of relevant descriptions from people aware of the problem is created. The list is evaluated by people who have expertise in the area, all of whom should be sincere, respectful, and committed to a consensus about a clear, accurate, specific, significant description. Serious social problems such as child poverty can only be described in lengthy written reports. These are shared with everyone involved: politicians, business leaders, educators, health care professionals, and so on.

The second reason brainstorming is an appropriate way to describe a problem is because it provides a unified perspective on the problem. The more people who are involved with the problem's description, the less likely it will ignore important aspects of it. Consequently, the eventual solution should result in few, if any, *affiliated* emergent problems. People *who* are affiliated with the problem will point out different aspects of it in which they are involved only if they are included in the brainstorming sessions. When their points of view are included in the description, they are less likely to be the source of emergent problems later.

Social problems—even those involving children—have a tendency to polarize people. Some individuals have political and social agendas that do not allow them to embrace (or even face) issues of poverty and health care. Others find such problems to be personally energizing. Brainstorming sessions have a tendency to bring polarized people together. The process of "playing with ideas" involved with the problem reveals common interests and allows for mutual understanding. While it is not practical to have every single person involved with complex problems such as child poverty engaged in a brainstorming session on the topic, those who are able to participate should be able to find common themes.

Once a consensus on the problem's description is achieved, the third stage is put in effect.

Stage Three: Creating Imaginative and Practical Hypotheses. A *hypothesis* (plural, *hypotheses*) is a suggestion of a possible solution to a problem. It is a "what if" statement: "what if we did such and such. . . ." Brainstorming sessions suggest a large quantity of imaginative hypotheses. Of course, intuition and imagination are involved. Brainstorming sessions often result in "draft proposals," which are lengthy descriptions of hypotheses. These are made available to experts who evaluate their practicality. A truly creative hypothesis—one that is new and useful—comes out of this process. Creative hypotheses that reflect the feelings and ideas of everyone involved with the problem are very difficult to produce. Practically, it is virtually impossible to satisfy everyone. However, the description of the problem in Stage Two and the creation of the hypotheses in Stage Three involve people from as many points of view as possible. This means that everyone involved has an "ownership" of the process.

One of the greatest stumbling blocks to effective problem solving is the unwillingness to *include* as many affiliated people in the process as possible. Unanticipated emergent problems will increase in number and in seriousness in direct proportion with the lower number of affiliated people consulted in the problem-solving process.

Stage Three concludes with the post-brainstorming conference's selection of the most promising hypothesis. This hypothesis can be very complex; certainly, for example, if we had a hypothesis concerning the problem of child poverty in America, it would be quite involved.

Stage Four: Testing the Selected Hypothesis.   The fourth stage is an action stage; the time for discussion and brainstorming gradually ends, and actual activity begins. A controlled observation in which the hypothesis can be tested is created. Experts are consulted to provide advice on how to control the testing environment. Standards of evidence must be determined; what will constitute a successful test? What will constitute a failure?

This stage is often met with resistance from those not involved with the problem-solving process. If the previous stages were not inclusive, it is quite possible that resistance to the testing stage will be successful. For example, if child-care providers had not been included in the second and third stages of the process of solving the problem of child poverty, they would most likely resist any testing of the proposed hypothesis. They would have every right to do so, since their expert advice was not included in the process. Not only would the hypothesis lack their insights, but they would have no ownership of the testing process.

Others, too, often step in and attempt to halt testing of hypotheses. Traditionalists—people who value the stability of reliance upon past practices—tend to oppose any creative solutions on the grounds that innovation upsets the "tried and true" ways of doing things. Sometimes people will have political, moral, or religious objections to testing hypotheses.

Since objections to testing are inevitable, the fourth stage requires communication as well as resolve. When objections are met with rational discussion the chances of nonaffiliated emergent problems are reduced. That is, the more discussion problem solvers engage in with traditionalists, political, moral, and religious objectors, the more likely their objections will be either taken into account or abandoned. In no way should discussion with objectors be seen as persuasive "public relations" attempts. Sincerity, respect, and a commitment to consensus should guide them. Discussion with objectors should be seen as part of the testing stage, along with continual review, evaluation, and revision of the hypothesis itself. Testing involves thorough reviews, evaluations, and revisions of the hypothesis. Eventually it is revised to the point where a proposed solution can be anticipated.

Stage Five: Implementation of the Solution.   It is remarkable how often people will go through the first four stages of problem solving, only to fail to fully implement the solution. For example, there have been several studies of child poverty in America. Several proposals have been tested with good results: employer day care, paternal leave policies, and increases in the availability of preschool education and bilingual education. Political solutions including drug rehabilitation and part-time employment or educational opportunities for parents have been tested and judged successful.

For whatever reasons, the problem has not been solved; it is getting worse. Perhaps the hypothetical solutions were generated without enough participation from those who now object to them. Perhaps there are serious unanticipated affiliated and nonaffiliated emergent problems with solutions proposed so far. It is difficult to imagine any problem more serious than that of childhood poverty, but obviously something is standing in the way of its solution.

Of course, once a solution to a problem is successfully implemented, it begins to change the situation. Soon emergent problems begin to surface and a new cycle of problem solving begins.

The problem-solving method consists of five stages.

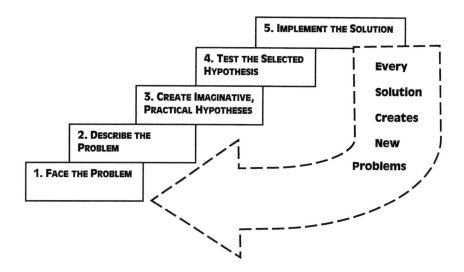

Of course actually solving problems is much more complicated than the simple diagram. Everything we have discussed in this course in critical thinking is involved in solving problems. We need to think verbally and logically, and evaluate our own ideas and the ideas of others according to the appropriate standards. We need to be able to brainstorm, define terms, summarize, and paraphrase. All of our judgments need to be empathetic. In addition to all of this, we need to be informed and have a thorough understanding of the strengths and weaknesses of evidence.

In a way, critical thinking *is* problem solving. After all, when we review, evaluate, and revise something, we are improving it, or solving its problems. When we are improving our own writing, or making suggestions directed toward improving another person's writing, we are solving the written pieces' problems.

We join in a brainstorming session in order to help solve problems at home, at work, or in the community. A critical thinker acknowledges that problems must be faced, thought about, and acted upon in order to improve our personal and family lives, to make our workplaces more efficient and caring, and to contribute to the improvement of social and political life. Critical thinkers not only have verbal and logical techniques at their command. They share a commitment toward making the world a better place. We can gain a deeper appreciation of the personal characteristics of critical thinkers by examining them in more detail. The following section, "An Interview with a Critical Thinker," provides some concluding thoughts on those personal characteristics.

Conclusion: Interview with a Critical Thinker

You gave a previous interview in which you claimed that critical thinking is the opposite of war. Would you expand on that remark?

We should all be thankful that young Americans have little experience with war. Your parents' generation, on the other hand, lived with war all through their lives. Many of them were born just after or during the Second World War, went through childhood during the Korean War, and grew out of adolescence during the Vietnam War. For most of them, and for me, war is the one thing in life that is an unmitigated evil. When I say that the opposite of critical thinking is war I mean that war is an agreement by different nations to *avoid* reviewing, evaluating, and revising. They are going to "fight it out" and kill each other's children. It is incredible that grown adults would abandon reason and empathy to that point. That they would send their children, whom they should nurture, to the slaughter; this is absolute evil.

War is an abandonment of critical thinking. Of course, that does not mean people stop their perceptive and cognitive processes. They do plenty of that in war: plot, plan, deceive, create strategies and tactics, and do a lot of other kinds of thinking. Some even write poems, novels, and historical studies about war. People make a living off of it. They manufacture guns, missiles, bullets, and caskets. Some people think and think about war. Nevertheless, no one does much critical thinking during a war.

That's what happened to Socrates, you know. He sat in the marketplace in ancient Athens, thinking critically about every subject under the sun. He was especially driven to revise Athenian beliefs about justice and love. He did not hide his evaluations from the power figures. He spoke openly, fully intending to be heard. He found most Athenian values to be nonempathetic, irrational, and vague. They loved pleasure, power, and fame. Socrates suggested that they revise their beliefs. He felt that they should love truth, justice, and personal integrity. In order to catch their attention, he often claimed that Sparta, the archrival of Athens, was a better place to live. During one of the wars between Sparta and Athens, a group of power brokers declared that Socrates was a traitor. They had a trial, found him guilty, and executed him. Socrates tried to think critically during a war, and became a fatality.

That's another reason why critical thinking and war are oppositions. They have an antisymbiotic relationship. In a symbiotic relationship two organisms foster and ecologically maintain one another's lives. Neither can survive without the other. Nature is full of symbiotic relationships. War and critical thinking are antisymbiotic; they kill each other. War weakens and can destroy critical thinking, and critical thinking does the same to war. So now it might be clearer what I mean when I say that critical thinking and war are opposites.

You seem to take critical thinking so seriously! Do you believe that we should think critically all the time?

Goodness sakes, no! Critical thinking is a specific type, not the best type, of thinking. It's true that human beings think *in one way or another* most of the time. Professor Gardner describes seven or eight types of thinking. Critical thinking, though, is a particular type of thinking. It is used to evaluate thinking when there is a problem with it. We couldn't possibly think critically all of the time; we wouldn't have anything to think critically about if we did that!

I wish that people would stop using the term as a synonym for "good thinking." Critical thinking is highly verbal and logical. There is much more to life and to thinking than words and inferences! The most important part of my life is the time spent with my family and friends. Usually we talk, laugh, and share each other's worlds. I love to hike in the mountains, swim in clear lakes. I love to be entertained by Hollywood, by silly television programs, and by popular fiction. My relationships with cats, dogs, and other animals are valuable to me. The point is that life is made up of innumerable different activities, each of which calls for various types of thinking. So, no, I don't think critically all of the time and I don't think you should, either. Critical thinking is a very important part of life, but it shouldn't be confused with life itself.

Yet you have said "critical thinkers have an attitude about life that sets them apart." What do you mean by that?

A critical thinker is a person who accepts his or her responsibility to nurture thought. For example, a woman who is also a mother is not *only* a mother. She may have a job, a career, a husband, a sister, friends, and a multitude of interests that are only peripheral to being a mother. Still, she is a mother, and nurturing her children is central in her life. A critical thinker is a person for whom the nurturing of thought has a central role.

I have often said that a critical thinker has three attitudinal characteristics. He or she is *perceptually and intellectually alert, motivated by the principle of "constructive discontent," and is imaginative and open to others.* Let me briefly discuss each characteristic. To be physically alert is to maintain one's general health. I think that a balanced diet and exercise help us clearly perceive the world. We listen and read better when our health is good. Being intellectually alert means to be attentive to new ideas, to make an effort to understand them. Critical thinkers resist the physical and intellectual lethargy that our culture encourages us to adopt.

The principle of "constructive discontent" is an apparent paradox; to be "constructive" is to build up, and to be "discontent" is to be dissatisfied. However, we cannot build up something—be positive—unless we are initially dissatisfied—negative—about it. I cannot improve my own thinking unless I am dissatisfied with it. I cannot build up my society unless I am negative about it. A critical thinker is motivated by the belief that everything has something wrong with it, and that what is wrong can be made better. It's like problem solving; every solution brings out new problems.

Being imaginative and open to others means that critical thinkers consciously seek to create innovative solutions and try to free themselves from bias. These two things are very closely associated. Being open to others means to be empathetic, to be able to accept their perspective as if it were one's own. Looking at things through another's eyes is the first step in opening ourselves to new, imaginative ways of thinking. Continued dialogue with others, especially those we feel are "strange" or "different," nurtures imagination. It also combats lethargy.

Critical thinkers don't think critically all the time. However, they have an energetic, open approach to problem solving. Critical thinkers engage in conversations in order to empower and nurture thinking in others. Critical thinkers want to make the world a better place. You could say that they are leaders and nurturers at the same time.

Expand on that last remark, please. What is a "leader and nurturer"?

Let me put it this way; not all leaders are generals. Not all leaders order people around. We need to recognize the difference between leaders and dictators. A leader is someone who nurtures others, who empowers them. A leader shows other people how to improve their situation. A leader shows them ways to achieve their dreams for a better life. Leaders gain trust by earning respect. Martin Luther King, Jr. was a leader. Dictators steal other people's power; they destroy their hopes and dreams. Dictators inspire fear and self-doubt; they weaken others and then manipulate them. Hitler was a dictator.

Critical thinkers are leaders. They are sincere, respectful, and seek consensus. They nurture improvements in their own and in others thinking.

Is there any advice you could give aspiring critical thinkers in closing our interview?

I would say that the most important thing to remember from a course in critical thinking is the philosophical puzzle known as "the two-world assumption." Think about it often. Keep in mind that the world you know and take for granted is your own perceptual world. Others do not perceive or think in the same way that you do. Each of us carries a whole universe of meaning within. The only way we can share a world is by communication.

Second, don't forget the standards of verbal and logical thinking. The more clear, accurate, specific, and significant our thought, the better we understand, process, and communicate. The more we sincerely seek truth, and the more respect we have for others, and the more we seek consensus, the better our communication. Stay open to others, listen to them, and empathize.

The last thing I want to leave you with is something you don't learn in school. It is a simple piece of advice that has been passed along from generation to generation since the beginning of civilization: Abandon despair, cynicism, and lethargy. Dare to hope and to dream. "Keep your eyes on the prize"; a better world for each and every human being.

EXERCISES

▲ Most Intriguing Issue

Write a one-paragraph description of the most interesting idea, topic, or process described in pages 316–327. Be prepared to explain what you find interesting in class discussion.

▲ The Muddiest Point

Write a sentence or, if possible, a paragraph that describes the idea, topic, expression, term, or process in pages 316–327 that you find most difficult to understand.

▲ Cartoons and Diagrams

1. Provide a cartoon that shows the difference between problems and puzzles.
2. Provide a cartoon that shows the differences between affiliated and nonaffiliated emergent problems.
3. Draw a cartoon that illustrates the differences between anticipated and unanticipated emergent problems.
4. Provide a diagram that clarifies important details in the Five-Stage Problem-Solving Method.
5. Draw a cartoon that illustrates the first and second stage of the Five-Stage Problem-Solving Method.
6. Draw a cartoon that illustrates the third stage of the Five-Stage Problem-Solving Method.
7. Draw a cartoon that illustrates the fourth and fifth stage of the Five-Stage Problem-Solving Method.
8. Provide a cartoon that illustrates the belief that "critical thinking nurtures thought."
9. Provide a cartoon that contrasts leadership and dictatorship.
10. Draw a cartoon that illustrates the three characteristics of a critical thinker.

▲ Definitions of Key Terms

Provide a disciplinary definition for each of the following terms as they are used in this chapter. Most of the terms are not defined in the chapter, although their meanings are described by the context in which they appear. You need to review the material to create the definition yourself. Be sure to follow the guidelines for creating definitions on pages 78–81.

Problem	Emergent Problem	Hypothesis
Lethargy	Symbiotic Relationship	Constructive Discontent

▲ SHORT ESSAY QUESTIONS

Provide a written response of approximately 200 words for each topic. Your responses should be well organized, grammatically correct, and neatly produced.

1. Explain why "every problem is an emergent problem."
2. Why is empathy important at each stage of problem solving?
3. Explain why brainstorming is an effective way to describe a problem.
4. The chapter claims that critical thinking is problem solving. What does that mean?
5. Explain the Five-Stage Problem-Solving Method for a person who has not taken this course.
6. The interview claims that war and critical thinking are "antisymbiotic." What other things strike you as antisymbiotic with critical thinking?
7. The interview claims that war and critical thinking are "*anti*symbiotic." Provide three examples of things you believe *are* symbiotic with critical thinking.
8. Describe two specific ways in which our society encourages us to be lethargic about critical thinking.
9. Explain the way critical thinking "nurtures thought" for someone who has not taken this course.
10. Explain each of the three characteristics of critical thinkers for someone who has not taken this course.

▲ QUESTIONS FOR DISCUSSION

Provide an essay of 300–500 words that responds to each of the following questions which ask for your opinion. You should respond by stating it, and by providing thoughts, examples, and insights that support it. You should be willing to revise your response; you may change your opinion during or after a class discussion.

1. The interview claims that critical thinking and war are opposites, and that war is an "unmitigated evil." Do you agree with these beliefs? Why or why not?
2. The interview claims that critical thinking is not the same as "good thinking" and that we shouldn't think critically all the time. At the same time, it claims that critical thinkers are "leaders who nurture thought." Are these claims clear? Do you agree with them? Why or why not?
3. Take a good look at yourself. Are you a critical thinker according to the interview's three characteristics of critical thinkers? What are your strengths as a critical thinker? What are your weaknesses?
4. Summarize the interview's claims about leaders and dictators. Do you agree with them? Why or why not?
5. Select a specific serious personal problem you imagine hinders someone from achieving his or her educational goals. Describe how you and your group

apply the Five-Step Problem-Solving Method in solving it. Be sure to minimize the emergent problems as much as possible.

6. Select a specific serious family problem you imagine hinders a family from achieving their communication goals. Describe how you and your group apply the Five-Step Problem-Solving Method in solving it. Be sure to minimize the emergent problems as much as possible.

7. Select a specific serious problem in the workplace you imagine hinders a business from achieving its financial goals. Describe how you and your group apply the Five-Step Problem Solving-Method in solving it. Be sure to minimize the emergent problems as much as possible.

8. Select a specific serious problem in the workplace you imagine hinders a college from achieving its goals in serving students' needs. Describe how you and your group apply the Five-Step Problem-Solving Method in solving it. Be sure to minimize the emergent problems as much as possible.

9. Select a specific serious social or political problem you imagine hinders our society from achieving it goals for its citizens. Describe how you and your group apply the Five-Step Problem-Solving Method in solving it. Be sure to minimize the emergent problems as much as possible.

10. Select a specific serious social or political problem you imagine hinders the world from achieving its goals in regard to international peace. Describe how you and your group apply the Five-Step Problem-Solving Method in solving it. Be sure to minimize the emergent problems as much as possible.

▲ QUOTATION TO PONDER

"A leader has to engage people in facing the challenge, adjusting their values, changing perspectives, and developing new habits of behavior. One may lead perhaps with no more than a question in hand."
Ronald A. Heifetz, *Leadership without Easy Answers,* 1994

▲ JOURNAL TOPIC

Review all of your journal entries. In your final entry, describe several specific ways in which you have developed your critical thinking ability while taking this course.

▲ PORTFOLIO PAPER

Review your recent portfolio paper on the movie in which you noticed intuition and creativity being used to solve a problem. Reflect further on the film. Select a serious personal, family, workplace, or social or political problem experienced by characters in the film. Describe how it was solved in the movie. Imagine that you are in the movie, and that the characters seek your advice in solving the problem. From your perspective as a critical thinker, what would you advise? How would your advice have affected their lives for the better? (If the film you chose for the previous portfolio assignment is not appropriate for this exercise, select a different one.)

APPENDIX

OPINION PIECES

CONTEXT AND PURPOSE

Imagine that this piece appears in *Good Parents,* a monthly magazine many people buy in the checkout lane at the supermarket. The author, Jane Swegell, a fourth-grade teacher who has taught at the same private elementary school for twelve years has written several articles for the magazine in the past, all on raising children. She is single, and has no children of her own.[1]

READING AND SUCCESS

by Jane Swegell

When we were children, my younger sister spent hours by herself. At first my parents were worried about her lack of friends. It wasn't "normal" in our suburban neighborhood for a pretty middle-school girl to hide away in her bedroom all by herself. What was she doing in there? "I'm reading," she would say. "Leave me alone."

I read books, too, but not the same ones. While I was casually flipping pages in a Stephen King novel my sister was absorbed in the classics. I loved *The*

This appendix consists of five opinion pieces on topics of current interest. Pieces on parenting, science and religion, criminal justice, privacy, and legalized gambling are provided for your critical evaluation using The Format or The Mini-Format.

---

1. The magazine, as well as the people and sources "quoted" in the article are not real, and no resemblance to any real persons, publications, or events is intended.

Shining. It was a real treat to see the movie on video years later. She hated King. He was too popular for her tastes. *Pride and Prejudice, Emma,* and *Wuthering Heights* were her favorites. She didn't care to see the films.

Both of us went through a lot of pages. We had little choice, come to think of it. My mother and father read the newspaper every day, read the newsweeklies, and both had novels on the bedstead. We also had social lives. We read, but we did other things, too. My mother was worried. "What's to become of her?" she would say, sadly looking at her youngest tucked away with another Jane Austin classic.

As it turned out, she became an optometrist—a *married* optometrist! She and her husband have two children. She even has a social life, and, naturally, she still reads a lot of novels. We live in different places now. I teach fourth grade in a small private school on the West Coast, and she is back in the same Midwest suburb in which we grew up.

Reading was good for her, and for me. We read for pleasure as children, and the hours we spend tucked away by ourselves led to accomplishments in school and eventual success in our personal careers.

John Heisey, professor of early childhood development at Berry College, author of *Read to Your Child,* cautions parents on selecting "good books" for their children, even those they read to toddlers. "Kids don't plead with you to read instructions on how to get into the best college or professional school," he writes. "If they want you to read a comic book to them, don't hesitate." When a child learns to associate reading with pleasure early in life, they will develop into independent readers later and that college you want them to attend will beg them to enroll! Heisey says that once a child establishes reading as an entertainment, he or she will select books as a leisure activity. The time spent in reading for pleasure is the most important predictor of a child's reading ability in elementary school. According to Heisey, the more pages a child reads, the better her comprehension, vocabulary, and reading speed.

Reading helps children establish "reading thinking," the sort of mental activity involved with comprehension. A child who reads for pleasure automatically encounters punctuation, writing styles, and literary conventions that become part of her approach to reading school assignments. Vocabulary and reading speed increase as she hurries toward the final chapter of an exciting novel. Children learn to think by reading; their brains are exercised as they follow literary patterns of organization and thought. They also learn a lot from pleasure reading. Their world is broadened by excursions to places and times far beyond the worlds of their nonreading peers.

Nonreaders struggle with reading assignments. According to Dr. Leona Farthade, reading specialist at Williams Community College, children who don't read on their own time usually spend most of their time trying to "get through" reading assignments. The child who picks up a book only when it is demanded of her will become an adult who reads with difficulty. For example, complex reading assignments in college will be seen as challenges in themselves. The course material becomes secondary to just "plowing through" the pages.

"It's ironic," says Farthade, "that parents will cheer their children on in athletic endeavors, believing that he or she will get a 'full-ride' scholarship someday. They would do much better to encourage the child to read." Farthade points out that there are a lot more scholarships for good academic students than there are for athletes, and that the academic scholarships are easier to get. "Look at it this way," she writes, "your child can spend three hours a day shooting basketballs, while my child spends none. Your child will obviously be a better player than mine will be. But if my child spends those three hours a day reading something she enjoys, I firmly believe she will end up going to a much better college than your child does." Farthade makes good sense; the ACT and SAT don't ask for any baskets; they want a demonstration of good reading comprehension, vocabulary, and thinking skills.

Of course, schools teach reading but there is not nearly enough time allotted for the type of success we want for our children. In my fourth-grade classroom, we are able to spend only about fifteen minutes a day on independent reading. I spend most of that time helping poor readers decode stories they should have been able to read in the second grade. I firmly believe that if a child is to achieve any academic success, she should constantly be reading for pleasure at home. I recommend that my fourth graders complete reading a 200-page book every two weeks.

So what's a parent to do? Throw away the television and the computer and lock Sammy and Sarah away in the closet with a flashlight and a book? Not really; take the positive approach instead. You can start by reading to your child every day, even after they learn how to read on their own. Here's a few other tips:

When you send them to bed, don't object if they want to stay up and read for a few minutes. If they continue reading for several hours, don't complain.

Take them to the library and be patient while they select books.

Give them books and magazine subscriptions for birthday and holiday presents. There are some great publications out there.

Don't forget that your child will be encouraged to read by watching you read. So, find yourself a good book and settle down on the couch in full view.

Good reading is the easiest path to success in life. And good reading is easy to encourage. It begins with reading for pleasure.

CONTEXT AND PURPOSE

The following imaginary piece addresses an issue that has been discussed by philosophers, scientists, and educators for many years. You may need to do some research in the library if you are not familiar with the debate. The article appears in a large urban newspaper in the "Science and Technology" section. The author is a professional journalist who specializes in popular culture.

SCIENCE AND RELIGION SHOULD NOT BE MIXED

by David Harleson

You would have thought that by now the debate between science and religion would be over. The religious people should have given up years ago in trying to explain the workings of the universe. They should leave it to the scientists, who know what they are talking about. The scientists, you would think, would have left it to religion to yammer on about the earliest beginnings of things as well as the ultimate end, not to mention the entire moral faultfinding in between. The ensuing struggle may destroy science in this country, along with the reasonable approach to life that comes with it.

Science and religion, if they had any sense, would avoid each other like the two schoolyard bullies who agreed to a truce in order to exploit their own victims. Surely there is enough grant money available to the scientist without jumping into the never-never land of religious beliefs. And the preachers must have enough in the collection plate without wandering into the laboratories of scientific knowledge. But greed is the great common denominator in our world.

The scientists started the whole thing. They just can't seem to leave the religious believers alone. For example, biologists first got into the faces of the faithful by explaining away their deepest convictions as nothing more than evolutionary survival skills. As if it were not bullying enough to wield the "evolution" club—a concept that every righteous religionist hates passionately—they have to link it with religious values, adding insult to injury. Why do so many people believe in God? According to the biologists, it's because theism gives them and their evolutionary ancestors the necessary psychological motivation to fight hard against enemies, and thus survive the evolutionary struggle. Why believe in religious moral values? Well, say the scientists, these beliefs provide unity to social groups, which then act together in raising children, establishing agriculture, and—you guessed it—progressing up the evolutionary ladder.

The religious side met the challenge with a vengeance. Why is the world plagued with sexually transmitted diseases, starvation, and terrorism? They smirk and respond, because God is angry with us. It doesn't end there. What's the cause of global warming? Why is it possible a meteor could come flying out of the sky and blast us to smithereens? They give the same answer; God's not happy with us.

It's been over a century since Darwin's *Origin of Species.* The scientists seemed to have won the day back then, at least in the law courts. The Scopes trial was in 1925 but still gets as much attention as the latest sensationalistic ax murder. The religionists want public schools to teach something they call "creationism" as if it were a science. No, that's not fair. What they are really saying is that science is actually a *religion* As such, evolution is a *scientific-religious belief,* just like creationism. So let's be open-minded about it all and teach them both!

I guess the dodo bird, that famous victim of evolutionary extinction, must have died out because it did something really upsetting to the Divine Plan.

You would think that the scientists would rant and rail about religion's in-roads on their turf. Sorry to disappoint you, but the fact of the matter is that they have joined up. In an effort to secure even bigger grants and more social approval, scientists are now pretending that some of the religious "theories" are worth taking seriously. There are now "scientific studies" such as "Biblical Archeology," being taught in colleges around the country. "Can God Be Found in the Cosmos?" was recently the subject of a lecture—billed as scientific—at a prestigious university in this city. Courses in sociobiology are being taught in taxpayer-supported universities, as if moral and religious questions are worth scientific scrutiny.

Repeatedly, the religious bullies come at the scientists with the war cry, "You don't know anything for sure! All of your 'knowledge' is only a theory. You're always changing your mind!" They fail to understand that science is self-correcting and based on facts. The religious folks seem to have confused physics with psychic hot lines, astronomy with astrology, and chemistry with chimeras. Scientific findings, according to these religious "scholars" are nothing but opinions. But not so for their own religious truisms; oh no. These have the support of the "unshakable faith" of the true followers, who prove their theorems by writing checks and dropping greenbacks in the religious coffers.

Their little scheme is clear; the religious bully has decided to take on the science bully by claiming "separate but equal." By clever use of grant money, use of the media, and pseudoscientific ranting, they have lowered science to the level of religion in the scientifically naïve public's mind. Once the masses swallow that spoonful of pablum, the next tactic will be to let them in on "the real truth." It won't be long until we have the spectacle of grad school science professors joining with empty-headed New Agers waving their arms and howling mumbo-jumbo at the moon. Science will be a memory, another victim of the love of the dollar.

CONTEXT AND PURPOSE

Imagine that this piece appears as a "letter to the editor" of your daily newspaper. The paper recently carried a story that described the event in the letter. Two high school students were convicted of manslaughter in the death of their infant daughter. Robert James, the father, threw the newborn infant into the river that rushed behind the local motel in which it was born. The body was never found. Karen Mohan, the mother, became ill at home that evening. Robert cooperated with authorities, but Karen refused to testify or offer any statements to the authorities about what happened. The couple plans to marry once they have completed the penalties provided by the judge. We do not know the person who wrote the letter.*

---

*All of the "information" presented here is purely imaginary and is not intended to refer to any person.

TO THE *UNION DAILY* EDITOR,

Am I the only person in this town who is shocked and horrified at Judge Buthade's decision in the Baby Murder Case? Am I the only one who has been following the grisly story since it first appeared in the *Union Daily*? I must be, because no one else has raised one word of outrage. Or is it that you don't print their letters? Well, you better print this one! I'll sue if you don't.

Let's get it straight about what happened. This kid Robby got his girlfriend pregnant. He begged her to have an abortion because he wanted to "be free" and go to college. She refused, mainly because she was afraid to tell her mother. At least that's what Robby says. The girl—the mother—won't say anything. Somehow, she fooled everybody and carried the baby to term, giving birth at the Green Shamrock Motel on March 4th. As soon as she was born, "Baby Girl," (the only name this poor child ever had) was taken by her father, stuffed in a plastic bag provided by the motel for dry cleaning, and thrown into the raging Cottle River, never to be seen again. They would have gotten away with this murder if Karen weren't so ignorant. She went home without delivering the afterbirth and soon began to hemorrhage. Mom and dad took her to the emergency room. That's where Karen's mom was told her daughter had given birth. A few days later, Robby James admitted to her and to Karen's dad that they had tossed their granddaughter into the Cottle.

Enter Judge Buthade, who heard everything about the case during two weeks of testimony. He saw Karen's diary, where she wrote that she couldn't wait to "get rid of this thing inside me." He read her letters to Robby, in which she said, "I want to make fun-fun again, honey, but right now I can't. Oh, darling, I want to have you again, soon!" As for Robby, he told Judge Buthade that he tried to convince Karen to get an abortion "almost every time we talked," but that she wouldn't go through with it. "She was really scared of her mom," said Robby.

So what was the judge's decision? He sent Robby to prison for two years. And Karen? The girl who was so afraid of her mother's wrath that she killed her newborn infant? Twelve years! How can this be just? I know justice is supposed to be blind, but this is ridiculous!

What's the difference between what Karen did and what thousands of high school girls do every day? I mean, what's the difference between throwing away a newborn and killing a baby before it's born by having an abortion? There is no difference! Abortions are legal in this state. Karen could have gone to any number of physicians and obtained one. There is no requirement that she notify her parents in our state. She could have had the abortion, been properly cared for, and gone on her way. An ugly chapter in her life would have been completely avoided.

Why didn't Judge Buthade criticize Karen's mother for being such a fool? Why didn't he send her to prison instead of her vulnerable daughter? I am outraged! If this girl had had an abortion no one would have known. But now, because of her foolish mother, she is going to prison for twelve years!

Robby, of course, being a male, gets away with only two years. He's the one who threw baby in the river! Judge Buthade's decision is absolutely wrong. Robby should be in prison for the rest of his life. Karen did nothing wrong. Her mother should be ashamed.

Sincerely,
Stephanie Larsdale

CONTEXT AND PURPOSE

This imaginary piece, written by a political activist who has campaigned for public office, addresses the use of technology to monitor people in a free society. He lost the last election for governor by several million votes to a popular politician, the current governor.*

KISS YOUR PRIVATE LIFE GOODBYE

by Fred Ungersol

Our country is full of wackos who think they were kidnapped by aliens, met Elvis on Mars, and have had dinner with Bigfoot. I don't like these people any more than you do, but I believe their opinions are their own business. In other words, I don't agree with the governor about his proposed identification cards. According to the governor, who has decided to fancy herself as a technological wizard, it would be a great idea for every citizen of the state to be issued a card that included a magnetized strip or even a microchip (does she really know what a microchip is? I doubt it) that would contain "essential information." Such as? Well, she wants your name, height, weight, and color of eyes, hair, and skin. She wants to know your fingerprints, voiceprint, and she wants to scan your retina while she's probing you for everything else. Her brilliant idea is to hook everyone up to a "big computer" so that the bureaucrats can get to know every man, woman, and child intimately. Every year, each one of us would have to renew the card.

So why does she want to intrude on our privacy in this way? Well, she says that health care records, tax reports, and employment data would be much improved. If you fall over in the street, the governor can flip you over, take out your wallet, and find out if you are allergic to aspirin. Great idea! Of course, she could also find out if you paid your taxes and if you are on welfare, too. Maybe she'd withhold the aspirin if you're past due and on the dole.

---

*Everything in the piece is purely imaginary.

Why stop with the health, tax, and employment stuff? Let's track ex-convicts, deadbeat dads, and other social pariahs. How about gun owners, drug addicts, and members of religious cults? Shouldn't the governor know about your religious and political affiliations, too? What's to keep her from including a record of the books you read, the videos you rent, and the movies you attend? Anyone who would oppose her technological dictatorship would be identified as a radical, you can be sure. Fall down in the street with that on your card, and they won't even give you a drink of water.

Her assurances to the contrary, there's no way the governor can satisfy our fears that she is attempting a privacy coup in this state.

All of the greatest political leaders in our country's history have warned us to beware of those who would rob us of our privacy. Of course, there's the occasional weirdo who just beamed back from sharing biscuits and gravy with The King on the Red Planet, and there's a few more fog-heads who think the governor really needs to know everything about our private lives. There's a lot more of us, though, who think with a sober, clear mind. We know who we are, and soon the governor will know who we are too. Let's get rid of her—can you say "impeachment?"—before it's too late!

CONTEXT AND PURPOSE

Imagine that this piece appears in *The Lockers,* a monthly magazine favored by college sports fans. The author is Diggs Benedict, an acknowledged authority on college athletics. Assume that the information in the article is taken from reputable sources. However, you may want to do some research in the library or on the Internet to check on its accuracy.*

GAMBLING: THE NEXT PLAGUE

by Diggs Benedict

Listening to Jalwan Anderson, you tend to forget he was once a promising student-athlete, believed by some to be the next great defensive end for the Winsap College Warrior football team. He's still going to school, and he says the classes are fine. However, they don't have a team at the school where Jalwan now spends his time. Moreover, when he graduates with his two-year junior college degree, it won't be in business, his major as a Warrior. He won't be leaving the campus, either. The only major offered is in custodial work—that's being a

---

*All of the "information" presented here is purely imaginary and is not intended to refer to any person.

janitor—and the State Prison doesn't let you go home just because you got all A's in sweeping the floors and polishing the bars on the windows.

Jalwan's in jail. He'll be there with all the rapists, robbers, and murderers for another five years unless the parole board goes soft with him.

It all started as "fun."

"It was easy," says Jalwan. "I started out just checking the Internet for the point spreads, picked my teams, and gave this company called SportsBet my credit card number. They automatically deposited everything I won in my bank account."

He started his Internet gambling on basketball games from his dorm room. Jalwan's mom and dad gave him the computer as a high school graduation gift, hoping it would help him earn the high grades necessary to keep the combination athletic-academic scholarship prestigious Winsap offered him.

"We were so proud of him," says Sophia Anderson, Jalwan's mother. "He is a very talented young man, and he worked so hard."

He worked hard on the football field, too. As a freshman, Anderson rolled up more quarterback sacks than any player in Winsap history. His impressive size, speed, and obvious intelligence are indications of a potential star. That first season was a thrilling one.

"I guess once the season ended, I felt like I needed something to keep me on the edge, you know?" he says with a downcast look. "I really enjoyed all the attention from playing football, and I thought maybe I could keep it coming if I got the reputation of a big time gambler. Lots of guys were doing it."

Jalwan's not alone, that's for sure. Americans will bet more than six hundred million dollars in cyberspace this year on more than fifty online sports gambling sites. Most of them are licensed in foreign countries, such as Antigua, where sports gambling is legal. Due to legal technicalities, the United States is helpless in banning the sites, although several bills are before Congress that would reduce Internet gambling considerably.

So what's wrong with a college kid placing a few bucks on a basketball game? Nothing, so long as it's only a few bucks. But it doesn't stop there. College kids already know about drug and alcohol addiction; they've heard about it all their lives. About how drugs can steal your soul and alcohol can ruin your life. The schools, their parents, and the government have teamed up to warn them about the dangers.

Of course, the same three groups—schools, parents, and the government—have also been quite enthusiastic about the lottery. It's the greatest thing since after school candy bar sales to raise funds for extracurricular activities, such as sports programs. As taxpayers have gotten more and more reluctant to fund after school activities, the lottery has stepped in to take up the slack. Schools love the extra funding, parents bring home tickets hoping to scratch off a winner, and the government is happy to have finally found a tax that everyone likes.

Trouble is, some like it too much. Gambling is being called the silent addiction. You can't smell it, you can't see it in a kid's eyes. But the widespread advertising for lotteries and the wide-open availability for innocent-appearing opportunities, such as sports betting, have turned more kids into gambling addicts than ever before.

Every state except Hawaii and Utah has some form of legal gambling. The hype that surrounds it lures kids into believing that gambling is a thrill they can't do without. Gambling has become an "in thing." It doesn't take long for many kids to become addicted. Many social scientists that have studied the facts agree that gambling addiction is a bigger problem than drug addiction, including tobacco. The instant access to betting sites on the Internet allows college kids to bet and lose large amounts of money without leaving their dorm rooms. Pretty soon it's a lot more fun to click on the betting parlor than do your homework in calculus. Of course, when you win things are great.

"I'll never forget my first big win," says Jalwan, "it was five hundred and seventeen dollars. I won it on a college basketball game between two teams I'd hardly heard of. It was pure luck."

He says he couldn't believe his good fortune, but when he checked his bank account the following morning, there it was; as much money as his parents were able to send him for personal expenses once a month.

"I spent it all on my friends, that same day. We had a steak dinner at a fancy restaurant. I paid the tab. It was so easy. That night I found another game and put down fifty bucks. I lost. I bet another, and lost that one, too. I don't remember the next time I won, but it didn't take long until I was hoping to win so I could cover my losses. It got really bad in a few months time."

So bad that Jalwan ran up six thousand dollars on his charge card, the limit. That's when he got his big idea and took his first plunge into full addiction.

"I thought, all I need is one more night. The NCAA tournament was starting, and there were lots of games I needed to bet on. All I had to do was get another charge card. You know, somebody else's."

He took his girlfriend's card when she wasn't looking that night, convinced that he could win a bundle and get it back in her purse without her knowledge. It didn't work. He'd run up around two thousand dollars and feared returning the card until he'd won enough to cover the losses.

"It became a nightmare," says Jalwan. "The more I bet, the more I lost. I couldn't get a winner if my life depended on it. I quit studying, quit going to class. The only stuff I read was about the games."

Three nights into the NCAA tournament and the girlfriend's card was maxed out, too. He destroyed it, hoping that she would think a stranger had stolen it. He left his dorm room around midnight, looking, as he puts it, "for something, *anything* that would get me back in the mix. I was really wired, very tight."

How tightly he was wired became clear to Claudine Jefferson that night. She testified that she was resting at the bus stop after three hours study in the Winsap library. Jalwan Anderson—all six foot five, two hundred seventy pounds of him—demanded her purse. Claudine tried to talk him out of it. "He was sweating and acting so nervous. But he looked like such a normal guy, I thought maybe he was playing a game with me. I thought I'd talk to him a little, see what was going on. I said, 'c'mon, you don't want to rob me, do you?' I think

I even smiled at him. He said something about 'don't mess with me,' and hit me in the face. Then he hit me again. It was awful."

How awful? Awful enough for five years in the slammer. Claudine's recovered now. It took about three months for her injuries to heal. She's not bitter. She says she's taken psychology courses and understands the way addictions work. People change, and don't act as they normally would. "I don't blame him personally," she says, "it was the gambling addiction that did it. Lots of people have it. I can forgive him." Jalwan's girlfriend doesn't share those generous beliefs. She refused to be interviewed, saying only that she thinks his sentence was too lenient.

This incident makes one thing clear to me, and if you have a brain in your head, you'll agree. It's time to stop the foolishness before it gets worse. Every state should get rid of its lotteries. Today. The Congress should outlaw gambling on the Internet. Now. The longer we wait, the more kids will get addicted.

You might get a kick out of buying a lottery ticket. You might like to click on a sport-betting site on the Internet and slap a cyberspace twenty down on your favorite team. Its fun, you might think. That's what Jalwan thought, too. Before the nightmare.

Suggested Reading

"Joseph McCarthy." *New Columbia Encyclopedia.* 1975.

Abramson, Jill, and Jane Mayer. *Strange Justice: The Selling of Clarence Thomas.* Houghton Mifflin, 1994.

Arendt, Hannah. *The Life of the Mind.* Harcourt, Brace, Jovanovich, 1978.

Asch, S. E. "Opinions and Social Pressure." *Scientific American* 193 (1955): 31–35.

Beyer, Barry, K. "Critical Thinking: What Is It?" *Social Educatio.* (April, 1985): 270–276.

Bloom, Benjamin S., et. al. eds. *Taxonomy of Educational Objectives: Handbook I: Cognitive Domain.* David McKay Company, 1956.

———, eds. *Taxonomy of Educational Objectives: Handbook II: Affective Domain.* David McKay Company, 1964.

Bruner, Jerome S. *On Knowing: Essays for the Left Hand.* Harvard University Press, 1966.

Caine, Renate Nummela and Geoffrey Caine. *Making Connections: Teaching and the Human Brain.* ASCD Publications, 1991.

Chomsky, Noam. *Language and Mind.* Harcourt, Brace, World, 1968.

Clinchy, Blythe McVicker. "On Critical Thinking and Connected Knowing." *Re-Thinking Reason: New Perspectives in Critical Thinking.* Ed. Kerry Walters. State University of New York Press, 1994.

Copi, Irving M., and Carl Cohen. *Introduction to Logic.* MacMillan, 1990.

Davidson, Donald. *Inquiries into Truth and Interpretation.* Oxford University Press, 1984.

Dewey, John. "Renascent Liberalism" (1935). Reprinted in *The Philosophy of John Dewey,* 643–665. University of Chicago Press, 1981.

———. *Experience and Nature.* (1929). Dover Publications, 1958.

———. *Freedom and Culture.* (1939). Capricorn Books, 1963.

———. *Logic, The Theory of Inquiry.* Henry Holt and Company, 1938.

———. *Reconstruction in Philosophy.* (1920). Beacon Press, 1957.

———. "Does Human Nature Change?" (1938). Reprinted in *Philosophy of Education,* 184–192. Littlefield, Adams, and Company, 1958.

Ekman, Paul, et. al. "Universals and Cultural Differences in the Judgments of Facial Expressions of Emotion." *The Journal of Personality and Social Psychology* 5, (1987).

Ennis, Robert H. "A Concept of Critical Thinking." *Harvard Educational Review* (Winter, 1962): 81–111.

Facione, Peter A. *Critical Thinking: A Statement of Expert Consensus for Purposes of Educational Assessment and Instruction.* California Academic Press, 1990.

Ferguson, Andrew. "Pardon Me if I (Still) Smoke." *Time* (30 June 1997): 32.

Ferguson, Charles A. *Talking to Children.* Cambridge University Press, 1977.

Fogelin, Robert. *Wittgenstein.* Routledge and Kegan Paul, 1976.

Gallo, Delores. "Educating for Empathy, Reason, and Imagination." *Re-Thinking Reason: New Perspectives in Critical Thinking.* Ed. Kerry Walters. State University of New York Press, 1994.

Gardner, Howard. *Multiple Intelligences.* Basic Books, 1993.

Gendlin, Eugene T. "Subverbal Communication and Therapist Expressivity: Trends in Client-Centered Therapy with Schizophrenics." *Person to Person.* Eds. Carl Rogers and Barry Stevens. Pocket Books, 1973.

Greenspan, Patricia. *Emotions and Reasons: An Inquiry into Emotional Justification.* Routledge, 1988.

Habermas, Jurgen. *Moral Consciousness and Communicative Action.* Trans. Christian Lenhardt and Shierry Weber Nicholsen. MIT Press, 1993.

Heifetz, Ronald. *Leadership without Easy Answers.* Harvard University Press, 1994.

Hempel, Carl G. "Studies in the Logic of Confirmation." *The Concept of Evidence.* Ed. Peter Achinstein. Oxford University Press, 1983.

Hostetler, Karl. "Community and Neutrality in Critical Thought." *Re-Thinking Reason: New Perspectives in Critical Thinking.* Ed. Kerry Walters. State University of New York Press, 1994.

Jason, Gary. "Fallacies Are Common." *Informal Logic* (Spring, 1989): 101–106.

King, Alison. "Inquiry as a Tool in Critical Thinking." *Changing College Classrooms.* Ed. Diane Halpern. Jossey-Bass Publishers, 1994.

Kuhn, Thomas. *The Structure of Scientific Revolutions.* University of Chicago Press, 1962.

Lang, A. R., et. al. "Effects of Alcohol on Aggression in Male Social Drinkers." *Journal of Abnormal Psychology* 84 (1975): 508–518.

Matlin, Margaret W. *Cognition.* Harcourt Brace College Publishers, 1998.

McPeck, John E. *Teaching Critical Thinking.* Routledge, 1990.

Meier, Deborah. "Supposing That. . ." *Phi Delta Kappan* (December 1996).

Morris, Charles, ed. *Mind, Self, and Society from the Standpoint of a Social Behaviorist.* University of Chicago Press, 1934.

Osborn, Alex F. *Applied Imagination.* Charles Scribner's Sons, 1963.

Paul, Richard. *Critical Thinking: What Every Person Needs to Survive in a Rapidly Changing World.* Center for Critical Thinking and Moral Critique, 1990.

Perry, Marvin, et. al. *Western Civilization: Ideas, Politics, and Society.* Houghto, Mifflin, 1996.

Rawls, John. *A Theory of Justice.* Harvard University Press, 1971.

Rogers, Carl R. *On Becoming a Person: A Therapist's View of Psychotherapy.* Houghton Mifflin, 1961.

Rogers, Carl. *A Way of Being.* Houghton Mifflin, 1980.

———. *On Becoming a Person.* Houghton Mifflin, 1961.

Rorty, Richard. *Achieving Our Country.* Harvard University Press, 1998.

Siegel, Harvey. *Educating Reason.* Routledge, 1988.

Smith, Frank. *To Think.* Teachers College Press, 1990.

Sternberg, Robert J. *In Search of the Human Mind.* Harcourt Brace College Publishers, 1998.

Tannen, Deborah. *The Argument Culture.* Random House, 1998.

Walters, Kerry. "Introduction."*Re-Thinking Reason: New Perspectives in Critical Thinking* Ed. Kerry Walters. State University of New York Press, 1994.

Weston, Anthony. *A Rulebook for Arguments.* Hackett Publishing Company, 1987.

Whitehead, Barbara Dafoe. "What They Want to Teach Your Child About Sex." *Reader's Digest* (February 1995): 155–160.

Wittgenstein, Ludwig. *Philosophical Investigations.* Trans. G.E.M. Anscombe. MacMillan Publishing Company, 1973.

INDEX

ABOUT THE AUTHOR

Jon Stratton earned his Ph.D. in Philosophy from Southern Illinois University at Carbondale in 1972, where he concentrated on philosophy of language. His philosophical interests continue to center on the relationships of meanings, signs, and symbols. He has taught Philosophy, including critical thinking, informal logic, and symbolic logic at Walla Walla Community College in Washington State for over twenty-five years. His main interest in life is his family: Marleen, Melissa, and Cami.